In Their Own Write

States, People, and the History of Social Change

Series editors Rosalind Crone and Heather Shore

The States, People, and the History of Social Change series brings together cutting-edge books written by academic historians on criminal justice, welfare, education, health, and other areas of social change and social policy. The ways in which states, governments, and local communities have responded to "social problems" can be seen across many different temporal and geographical contexts. From the early modern period to contemporary times, states have attempted to shape the lives of their inhabitants in important ways. Books in this series explore how groups and individuals have negotiated the use of state power and policy to regulate, change, control, or improve people's lives and the consequences of these processes. The series welcomes international scholars whose research explores social policy (and its earlier equivalents) as well as other responses to social need, in historical perspective.

1 Writing the Lives of the English Poor, 1750s–1830s
Steven King

2 The People's Health
Health Intervention and Delivery in Mao's China, 1949–1983
Zhou Xun

3 Young Subjects
Children, State-Building, and Social Reform in the Eighteenth-Century French World
Julia M. Gossard

4 Indentured Servitude
Unfree Labour and Citizenship in the British Colonies
Anna Suranyi

5 Penal Servitude
Convicts and Long-Term Imprisonment, 1853–1948
Helen Johnston, Barry Godfrey, and David J. Cox

6 In Their Own Write
Contesting the New Poor Law, 1834–1900
Steven King, Paul Carter, Natalie Carter, Peter Jones, and Carol Beardmore

In Their Own Write

Contesting the New Poor Law 1834–1900

STEVEN KING, PAUL CARTER,
NATALIE CARTER, PETER JONES,
AND CAROL BEARDMORE

McGILL-QUEEN'S UNIVERSITY PRESS
Montreal & Kingston · London · Chicago

ISBN 978-0-2280-1432-4 (cloth)
ISBN 978-0-2280-1433-1 (paper)
ISBN 978-0-2280-1535-2 (ePDF)
ISBN 978-0-2280-1536-9 (ePUB)

Legal deposit fourth quarter 2022
Bibliothèque nationale du Québec

Printed in Canada on acid-free paper that is 100% ancient forest free (100% post-consumer recycled), processed chlorine free

Library and Archives Canada Cataloguing in Publication

Title: In their own write : contesting the new poor law, 1834-1900 / Steven King, Paul Carter, Natalie Carter, Peter Jones, and Carol Beardmore.
Names: King, Steven, 1966- author. | Carter, Paul, active 2003, author. | Carter, Natalie (Researcher), author. | Jones, Peter (Historian), author. | Beardmore, Carol (Carol Anne), author.
Series: States, people, and the history of social change ; 6.
Description: Series statement: States, people, and the history of social change ; 6 | Includes bibliographical references and index.
Identifiers: Canadiana (print) 20220389438 | Canadiana (ebook) 20220390037 | ISBN 9780228014324 (hardcover) | ISBN 9780228014331 (softcover) | ISBN 9780228015352 (PDF) | ISBN 9780228015369 (EPUB)
Subjects: LCSH: Poor—Great Britain—History—19th century. | LCSH: Poor—Great Britain—Social conditions—19th century. | LCSH: Poor laws—Great Britain—History—19th century. | LCSH: Public welfare—Great Britain—History—19th century.
Classification: LCC HV245 .K56 2022 | DDC 362.50942/09034—dc23

Contents

PART TWO
Pauper Agency

PART THREE
Contestation

Tables and Figures

TABLES

FIGURES

All images are used by kind permission of The National Archives.

Preface

The roots of this project lie in tea and biscuits during a break at the Writing the Lives of the Poor conference hosted by the German Historical Institute London in November 2013. This conference had developed out of an Anglo-German research project examining pauper letters from Germany and Great Britain under the leadership of professors Andreas Gestrich and Steven King. Paul Carter had given a paper on pauper letters contained within The National Archives Poor Law Union correspondence collection (MH12), and the break became a detailed meeting between Carter and King on the probable numbers of letters the archives might hold, the varied content of the letters, and some estimate of their geographical coverage. Subsequently we continued our discussions on what opening up these letters from across the whole of England and Wales would mean for an understanding of nineteenth-century poverty and welfare from the perspective of the poor themselves. We later conducted a pilot exercise before planning the larger funded project for which the present book is the major output.

It was readily apparent in this planning process that we would have to sample MH12, given the number of poor law unions in England and Wales, our long time-frame, and the sheer volume of correspondence. Our first decision was that the only sensible course of action was to identify and collect data for a broadly "representative" subset of poor law unions. From there many approaches could have been taken. Each had strengths and weaknesses. It would for instance have been possible, by fusing together centrally collected union level statistics and local finance records, to tension the rate base and nominal measures of demand, allowing us to compare and contrast policies and pauper experiences in broadly conceived "richer" and "poorer" unions. This approach to sampling might have yielded coverage of fewer unions than was eventually achieved, but we could notionally have tested whether more "generous" unions generated less pauper correspondence than harsher ones, given that there may have been less to complain about. On the other hand we knew that most poor law unions co-located very different sorts of parishes, often with very different poverty problems and certainly with very different rate-raising capacity. Measures such as per-capita relief, proportions of indoor paupers and so forth were thus a complex amalgam of local attitudes and practices. Even after the advent of union chargeability in the 1860s, these local disparities continued to influence policy, practice, and experience. In our pilot exercise we sought to test whether unions that were obviously "richer" (in terms of the rate base) or more "generous" (in terms of per-capita relief) generated fewer letters of all sorts than more parsimonious places. Subsequently, and encouraged by an anonymous referee for this book, we returned to the question for the whole corpus and found that there are no systematic or sustained differences in the scale, form, or intensity of writing between notionally rich and poor places. This should not be surprising. King has argued persistently in regard to the Old Poor Law that what mattered to the "generosity" of relief was primarily region and community type, and there is little reason to think that this pattern could or would have changed rapidly post-1834.[1]

Other approaches to sampling were also discussed, tested, and rejected. Thus, we considered looking at a larger number of unions but only at times of organisational and policy change in the New Poor Law, acute periods of national economic distress, or moments in the sentimental architecture of welfare, including for instance the crusade against outdoor relief or the advent of local democracy in local elections for poor law guardians in the 1890s. The team decided that developments in the practice and rhetoric of agency were better captured by a continuous chronological sample of a slightly smaller number of unions. Consideration was also given to a more spatially concentrated dataset focusing on all the unions in a selected number of counties, an idea that eventually fell by the wayside because we expected to find a rich canvas of words, experiences, and agencies at the national level and because we wanted to do justice to a Welsh-English comparison, given the comparative lack of research on Wales.

Finally, the team did some initial work on whether the sample should be driven by a categorisation structure that focused on population turnover in different unions using proxies such as inter-censal changes in population size. As one of the referees for this book subsequently reminded us, the progressive ending of minimum residence requirements for relief up to the 1860s or the sheer need of highly mobile or transient populations could put financial pressure on certain types of unions and might lead to disproportionate numbers of letters, scandals, and causes of complaint. In fact our pilot work identified places such as Basford (Nottinghamshire) which had prodigious numbers of letters and witness statements despite muted growth and migratory turnover, and other places with extraordinarily high migration levels (such as Wolstanton and Burslem, Staffordshire) with more limited material. In our final sample, it is certainly true that some urban unions with higher migratory activity generate significant numbers of letters from poor writers and advocates, but so do some largely or wholly rural unions that were rather more "sleepy." In the end we decided to sample primarily on the basis of socioeconomic community type and secondarily on region/spatial coverage, collecting data for 102 unions spread across most English and Welsh counties. Appendix 1 deals with this sampling process at greater length.

Using this exceptional dataset we set out to conduct a study of Victorian pauper lives from below. The conceptual basis of this approach and its roots in the experiences and outlooks of ordinary people, specifically the voices of those who were historically marginalised, is now well understood and does not need rehearsing here.[2] Against this backdrop, it is in many ways puzzling that it has taken so long to examine the Victorian poor law (with all its associated symbolism) through the history-from-below lens. In our new account we find that in letters, petitions, and statements the Victorian poor were able to articulate their concerns, fears, and ideas of welfare justice. In doing so they drew, at least in part, on a new and different blueprint for what they believed *should* have constituted a welfare process. Our writers and their advocates pointed to administrative inconsistencies and the failures of poor law officials who fell short of delivering on their own rules, and railed against the injustices of the local and central authorities together for impinging upon what the poor considered their natural rights to welfare with dignity and respect. They sought to exercise, and did exercise, agency in a system that notionally afforded none.

Of course, a New Poor Law history from below privileges the voices of paupers, the wider poor, and their advocates. Very early on in our data collection process it became obvious that the stories of these people – and even those of the officials with whom they dealt – carried over from the Old Poor Law to the New. This was true of the initial overlap period as unions were formed but also had extended chronological reach into the 1840s and even 1850s. It is inconceivable that these writers and (later) their children, neighbours, and successors were somehow suddenly cut off from the linguistic registers, expectations, agencies, and rhetorical modes of the Old Poor Law in 1834.[3] For this reason, many of our chapters have discussion of the linkage between the two systems. Readers will also note that Part One contains significant discussion of the central systems of the New Poor Law and the particular role of advocates in fostering the agency of the poor. Neither focus is incompatible with a history-from-below approach but some explanation is nonetheless required. Thus, the MH12 archive remains sparsely used in welfare histories – a reflection of its scale, complexity, and *apparent* randomness – and some discussion of the means by which it can be *and was meant to be* interrogated provides a vital backdrop to the book. Moreover, it became clear in the first weeks of this project that the attitudes, words, and processes of the Central Authority had a profound impact on who wrote, how often, with what language, and with what impact. This is not to say that poor people wrote what officials wanted to hear or that the discouragements we encounter in chapter 4 crushed agency and contestation. It *is* to observe that the poor acquired an intimate sense of the principles, limitations, and organisational framing of the Central Authority and employed this knowledge in their local engagement with welfare. A New Poor Law history from below cannot be separated from the operation and presence of the local and national State. It is for this reason that chapter 1 starts with the voice not of a pauper, as one might expect, but of an official. It might equally have started with that of an advocate, since it also became clear early on that such people were an important conduit for the experiences and sentiments of the poor, a source of language and knowledge for poor writers, and a powerful force for encouraging agency on the part of the poor and their communities, much as had been the case under the Old Poor Law.

Whatever voices take precedence in our chapters, there are potential problems in reading, interpreting, and weighting them, over and above the sheer diversity of writing abilities that we encounter. These are shared with all studies based upon epistolary sources and are also common to their Old Poor Law counterparts. Did those who signed pauper or applicant letters really write them or did they use scribes who intertwined their own voices with that of the signatory? Did the poor write according to particular published or particularly well-known templates? How representative were those who wrote? Whose voices do we miss in this suite of evidence? And does mediated testimony (for instance in witness statements) have the same explanatory power as that which comes first hand? We address these issues throughout the book, but an initial close reading of the sources is reassuring. Thus, while there is evidence in the occupational structure of workhouse populations that institutions were full of potential scribes, and that communities themselves contained ever more literate people as the nineteenth century progressed, there is no persuasive evidence for the systematic or substantial use of scribes in any of our material. Indeed, almost all scribes seem to have identified themselves in letters where they had a hand, and it is certainly the case that mediated letters of this sort are less common than under the Old Poor Law. Nor is there any evidence that free-form texts (that is, things other than petitions or witness statements) used standard formats or templates, even for parts such as opening and closing addresses. In terms of representativeness, we find the same broad spectrum of writing and grammatical qualities as under the Old Poor Law and it is notable that many of the serial letter writers in our sample went out of their way to tell the Centre that they were representative of and speaking/writing for other workhouse inmates, applicants, and recipients of outdoor relief. As chapter 2 shows, our corpus contains plenty of mediated testimonies in the form of witness statements or advocate letters, and ultimately we follow the growing acknowledgement in historical socio-linguistics, welfare, and criminal history that mediation does not snuff out or diminish the voices of the less powerful.[4]

Three further issues to do with readings of the sources inflected our discussion both of how to frame the research project and of the writing of this book. First, by focusing on the central archive of the New Poor Law we inevitably concentrated on complaints of mistreatment ranging from having to abide by petty rules to allegations of abuse, rape, tyranny, and cruelty. People who had no complaints or indeed had positive experiences of relief and interactions with the New Poor Law rarely wrote letters to the Centre or, as far as we can see, to local guardians.[5] Moreover, while some of our writers turned to the Centre as a first resort, most set out efforts – sometimes sustained efforts – to deal with their issues in person or writing at the local level. They understood the Central Authority as a court of last resort. In this sense not only do we privilege complaints but we do so for a particularly determined subset of the poor. These broad focus issues are a motif of most national studies with similar reach and ambition, but in our case their potential impact is substantially blunted by more positive aspects of the data. Thus, much of the material is of such richness and depth that it is possible to move beyond the act and fact of complaint and to discover an impressive array of rhetorical and practical agency. Even if our corpus is orientated toward the determined and single-minded writer, the texts they sent are often not confined to their own experiences or to the parameters of the matters that provide the central framing for approaching the Centre. The people we encounter are spread across the occupational spectrum of Victorian Britain, and we even pick up the sentiments and experiences of the wholly illiterate, as for instance in examples of paupers asking others to write for them while they dictated the text.

A second discussion at the start of the project was how to "read" the texts to be collected, given that contestation and the continual disputing of one version of events over another would be at the conceptual heart of our analysis. We decided at the outset to move away from simple dichotomies of truth versus lies or fact versus fiction. In the tri-partite epistolary world that we consider – poor writers/advocates, officials, the Centre – all parties can sometimes be detected telling lies, magnifying failings into crises, or sensationalising their stories so as to advance their case or defend themselves from further action. Yet, blatant lies on the part of the poor were a blunt and untrustworthy tool to secure a hearing and remedy, given that their complaints would be copied and laid before the very people they criticised and all stories could be checked. Hence many paupers protested innocence if guardians or union staff alleged their complaints were false, supplying additional verifiable evidence of character to undermine such accusations in their later letters, or calling on advocates who might include in their letters evidence of investigations and what they had observed prior to writing. A system that rewarded narrative consistency was not easy to "game," given a complex matrix of checks and balances. Officials likewise might find their lies and narrative inconsistencies exposed in inquiries, by advocates, and in the press, sometimes turning to attempts at undermining the character of the poor writer in order to negate or reduce the impact of the truths that they told. For these reasons we chose to consider *all* our material as to some degree fictive; that is, containing embellishments, clumsy expression, partial pictures of the circumstances and processes described, imperfect recollections, and flourishes that were a reflection of the individual or the moment in which they wrote. Such an approach puts the onus on us to read for silences alongside words, motives alongside motivations, and to look for that which is widespread or systematic alongside that which is systemic, and our approach from the outset has been to explore these issues with a combination of corpus-level work and detailed case studies.

Terms such as "systemic" and "systematic" are of course slippery, and our book is underpinned by a tri-partite conceptualisation of the undoubted failings of poor law process. At the level of the Centre many of the basic rules and regulations that were initiated to shape local practice sought to discourage or ban abuse, tyranny, peculation, and the unconstrained power of guardians and their staff. More than this, the Centre established clear mechanisms through which pauper complaints about such practices should be made and then investigated. In this sense the stories told by the poor, their advocates, newspapers, and sometimes even officials cannot be said to reflect the systemic failings of the New Poor Law itself. Yet the Centre also chose where to focus its regulatory and supervisory activity, and from the very beginning this was on matters of finance and numbers relieved rather than the experiences of poor writers, paupers, and poor communities. It is telling that our team had to wade through tens of thousands of audit reports in order to find interspersing letters by or about the poor. This bias in the structural focus of the Centre had ripples in a second level of administration, where individual unions could seek to bury complaints in administrative process, deny failings because officers followed the rules and spirit of the law, and try to undermine the character of those who complained. Not all unions acted in this way and there was much that was particular to a constellation of staff and paupers or moments in the history of a place. Even so, and as the Centre sometimes acknowledged, there could be long-run systematic and sometimes even systemic failings at union level. At a third conceptual level, however, agency depends upon the space in which it might be exercised as well as the determination of those to wield it. We see repeatedly in the collective corpus how indoor and outdoor paupers, the wider poor, and advocates sought out the space created by the gap between the rules of the Centre and the practical operation of its oversight function, and sought to increase its size where possible.

The final issue arises out of the first two and might broadly be understood as our "philosophical approach" to the material. We encounter some breathtaking allegations of cruelty: rape and sexual grooming; starvation; callous disregard for the aged and sick; severe child punishment; paupers as the victims of administrative incompetence; and the punishment of paupers who dared to complain. On the other hand we find startling examples of pauper or advocate agency and a persistent and often subtle determination to challenge even minor breaches of rules or sleights by officials and staff. A system that was in some ways designed to publicise harsh treatment but hide its extremes was more malleable than its architects intended or envisaged. Similarly, our material reveals both scandalous and admirable behaviour by poor law staff and other officials, sometimes juxtaposed in a single case. In short we can easily find evidence that the New Poor Law represented "perhaps the most sustained attempt to impose an ideological dogma, in defiance of the evidence of human need, in English history."[6] There is also fractured evidence to support the view that the Centre was "not so very harsh. In their rules for medical care, diets, schooling, discipline, health, and in their flexible application of the workhouse test, they showed a benevolent concern for the welfare of the paupers."[7] Navigating these nominally very different perspectives is complicated by the fact that as a team we bring our own (complementary and competing) values to the evidence, a function of different personal histories, political standpoints, and views on the current state and future of the welfare system. We all choose an ethical standpoint when we decide what we will write about and how we will write about it. Many of our paupers, poor people, and advocates arguably made exactly the same choices. Against this backdrop, we do not seek to rehabilitate the workhouse or gloss over abuse. We do, however, focus on the agency of the poor and their advocates and argue that the power of the central and local state could be and was systematically challenged, constrained, and contested. In a New Poor Law history from below, the right to write and be heard is the core experience.

One further aspect of our work – absences – also requires discussion in this preface. When considering which groups of the poor to focus on we discounted two in particular: children and the broadly conceived "mad poor." The former are well represented in the corpus through local inquiries, either as victims or in presenting evidence. Their presence in the letter sample is rather more fleeting and only rarely do we capture children in their own words. This is not to say that they had no agency. Indeed, we have written on this very subject elsewhere.[8] It is to argue that children were more often used as tool and reason for the agency of others. The "mad" have a rather more determined, if somewhat fluid, presence in our material, and once again we have written about them in other places.[9] At the core of their experience of the New Poor Law, however, was the process of circulation: between asylums and workhouses, homes and workhouses, boarding-out facilities and homes, for instance. To engage fully with this group would have meant a very different exercise to that intended here and would (as again we have argued elsewhere) require a different conception and linguistic register of agency.

There are also further absences. We effectively end our analysis in 1900, for instance, both because much of the central archive post-1900 was destroyed in Second World War bombing and also because the coming of poor law democracy and the later Liberal Welfare Reforms generate a very different welfare system. The chapters are organised largely on the basis of the type of poor writer, rather than the reasons for which they wrote. This is unavoidable, given that the vast majority of our letters (and even supplementary material such as related newspaper articles) combine multiple "causes" of complaint. We see this most clearly in the long texts of serial writers, but even shorter pieces might combine for instance hunger, ill-treatment of children, and peculation on the part of officials. Single central motifs as a means of classification are thus rare. Finally, though we sometimes go to great lengths to trace the "backstory" of writers (advocates, officials, and the poor), others are observed in their moment. In part this reflects the sheer scale of record linkage that would be required to systematically recount the history of all writers, something presently better suited to individual union studies. On the other hand, in our pilot project it became obvious that there was no consistent relationship between a particular history and the frequency, content, and motivation of letters. Those falling down the social scale seem to have been more inclined or more able to write longer letters than others, but even here we find very short communications from those who had once held office or prominent jobs. Length of residence, relief history, disability status, or family size seem not to have been systematic influences on who wrote or what they wrote, such that we adopted more familiar categorisations that included gender, age, and health.

Stephen Reynolds in his reflections as a middle-class man living in the poor fishing community of Sidmouth (Devon) in the early 1900s noted that the poor man "knows vaguely … that only by a succession of miracles, a long series of hair's-breadth escapes and lucky chances, does he stand at any moment where he is."[10] Most of "our" writers directly or indirectly express a similar sentiment. But the fact is that for the vast majority of them an engagement with the New Poor Law was not lifelong. They had been "somebody" before entering the workhouse or accepting outdoor relief and would go back to those lives, however defined, as circumstances changed. Such people had stocks of knowledge, attitudes, belief systems, and expectations built up often over many years, and these were brought to bear on the way that they constructed their poor law experience. A sense that they could, should, and would have agency is in one way unsurprising, but as an issue it has figured remarkably lightly in the historiography, to which we now turn in our opening chapter.

Acknowledgements

This book is underpinned by a dataset of prodigious proportions, comprising some four million words of writing by, for, or about the dependent poor between 1834 and around 1900. None of this would have been possible without the award of the Arts and Humanities Research Council project grant "In their own write" (AH/R002770/1; PI King and CI Paul Carter), which started in 2018 and ended in July 2021. We are profoundly grateful to the AHRC. While the core team (all of whom are authors on this book) transcribed some of this material, most of the discovery and transcription work was done by the volunteers in our Pauper Letters Research Group. They have collectively given some thirty-four thousand hours of their time to the project, organised and given talks, taken part in our regular seminar series, and published some of their own research. The group (based at The National Archives, and across Worcestershire, Nottinghamshire, and Cambridgeshire) have worked tirelessly and imaginatively on the project. Our volunteer conference in June 2021 generated a number of ideas for further collaborative work. Without you, this book would never have left the starting blocks. We also thank Dr Sue Hawkins, who joined the project and ensured the smooth running of the volunteer groups, data transcription, and volunteer seminars and conferences, as well as authoring many of the blogs for our ongoing website: https://intheirownwriteblog.com/about/. We also thank Gerard Ahearn in The National Archives Collection Care Department for his conservation work on the core project documents and Rosie

Morris in Education and Outreach for her work on producing the archive survey map. Finally, many thanks to The National Archives staff across the board from the press office, education department, research team and document services department. We have taken up acres of shelf space in the staff reading room and made a whole series of public engagement and press interventions, going well beyond anything promised to the AHRC. Our story continues with an AHRC Follow-on Funding Grant (AH/V010565/1; PI Paul Carter; CI King) that will provide an interactive educational resource and associated lesson plans for schools.

In terms of individuals, Steven King would like to thank Professor Elizabeth Hurren for her continuing guidance in the art of good storytelling. Natalie and Paul Carter would like to thank their son, John Stephen, for his patience and forbearance while his parents frantically juggled lockdown, home schooling, working from home, and researching and writing for this book.

Members of the Pauper Letters Research Group:

Sarah Bradley, Carol Bricknell, David Cooper-Smith, Isobel Dams, David Finlow, Celine Fernandez, Simon French, Ann George, Linda Hanson, Margaret Hathaway, Catherine Hill, David and Gill Howden, Imelda Johnson, Lucy Johnson, Pam Jones, Anna Kingsley-Curry, Natalie Lane, Judy Lester, Matthew Malone, Jean Moore, Jill Moore, Ann Morton, Ian and Sally Naylor, Maureen Newton, Felix O'Kelly, Anthea Poppleston, Sue Rick, Joanna Robinson, Amy Scott, Julie Smeaton, Liz Smith, Jane Somervell, Ann Taylor, Jenny Tudbury, Evan Upole, and Derek Wileman.

Conventions

- All emphasis in quoted primary material is original unless otherwise stated.
- All (mis)spelling, grammar, punctuation (or lack of it), textual features, and capitalisation in quoted primary material is faithful to the original.
- From 1834 to 1847 the Central Authority was styled the Poor Law Commission (PLC); between 1848 and August 1871, the Poor Law Board (PLB); and from 1871 to 1919, the Poor Law Department within the Local Government Board (LGB). For clarity we use "Central Authority" or "Centre" unless it is essential to refer to a specific body.
- Square-bracketed text in quoted material signals words or letters that were unclear in the originals; the enclosed text is thus our closest reading.
- "Indoor relief" was welfare provided to paupers in the workhouse; "outdoor relief" refers to cash or in-kind payments made to non-workhouse residents.

In Their Own Write

I

Thinking about the New Poor Law

INTRODUCTION

On 31 May 1835 Thomas Stevens, clerk to the Bradfield Poor Law Union (PLU) in Berkshire, wrote to Samuel Lucas, who had previously been the parish overseer for Tilehurst and was now the relieving officer[1] for Tilehurst. The letter attempted to ensure uniformity of response to the claims of the poor across the different districts of the union. It said:

> The Relieving Officers are requested to pay particular attention to the following points – In the report, on cases of application for relief to the Board the ages of the applicant & his children should always be stated, his last employment & the cause of his present necessity as nearly as can be ascertained, & the date of the application and all other particulars relative to the case. Rule 27 of the Union. 2nd Directs in cases of sudden & urgent necessity to give such temporary relief as each case may require either by taking the Pauper into the Workhouse or else affording relief out of the House in articles of absolute necessity but not in money.[2]

Reading such text, it is not hard to see why many contemporaries regarded the New Poor Law of 1834 (positively or negatively) as a fundamental break from the more intimate and largely parochial administration of welfare under the Old Poor Law.[3] The 1834 act established a new Central Authority (at first called the Poor Law Commission: PLC) charged with organising the New Poor Law, bringing more uniformity to practice, and monitoring local activity much more heavily and regularly than could ever have been done by the magistrates who notionally oversaw the Old Poor Law. Parishes were now to be grouped into unions with variable but substantial populations, and the link between local poverty and its local relief, a cornerstone of the Old Poor Law, was partly swept away.[4] At the heart of the new system was to be the workhouse, a place where families were split up, a monotonous diet imposed, and work tasks allocated to the able-bodied and those deemed work-shy, who many public commentators had come to assume were inflating relief bills in the early 1830s. Outdoor relief in monetary form was, as we can see in the Bradfield circular above, to be discouraged except in the most exceptional circumstances.[5] Unions were to be directed by Boards of Guardians, elected male (and later in the century female) ratepayers from each parish who, it was assumed by the architects of the New Poor Law, would seek parsimony over profligacy. Under them sat a new professional administration of relieving officers (dealing with initial applications for relief), medical officers, clerks, accountants, and layers of workhouse staff led by a workhouse master and matron.[6] In the mid-1830s and for some years beyond, many of these lower levels of staffing were peopled by those who, like Lucas, had earlier held office under the Old Poor Law, in asylums, or in the army, and had little idea about how the New Poor Law was intended to be run. The Bradfield circular is a clear indication of this lack of clarity, which was found across England and Wales.[7]

Read as a whole canvas, the 1834 poor law reforms can be understood as a fundamental intrusion of the national state into local affairs, part of a wider attempt to construct an information state.[8] Certainly many public commentators, local and regional landowners, and ratepayers also imagined the New Poor Law in this way. This expropriation of local power sat alongside the creation of a considerable national and local bureaucracy in which those making day-to-day decisions about welfare were sometimes spectacularly ill-equipped to do so and frequently misinterpreted rules. Such issues, intertwined with conceptual developments such as less eligibility, the passing of the Anatomy Act of 1832 (meaning that the friendless pauper was likely in death to end up on the anatomy table), and the sense that the ability of the poor to negotiate relief as they had done prior to 1834 was being crushed, ensured that the earliest histories of the 1834 legislation focused on resistance and violence.[9]

Press reaction was in some quarters notably hostile. Throughout the nineteenth century *The Times* and other newspapers, magazines, and journals such as the *Lancet* and the *British Medical Journal* ran episodic and vitriolic campaigns against workhouses and other aspects of the poor law. There is little doubt that these attacks gained traction with middle-class readers and also chimed with the criticisms by the labouring classes and the dependent poor themselves.[10] Unsurprisingly against this backdrop, contemporaries and subsequent historians both came to understand the character and function of the New Poor Law and the everyday experiences of those who spent time under its authority, through the lens of scandal. Indeed, highly publicised scandals were sometimes so potent that they are understood to have changed the structures of central governance, the remit of the poor law and the purpose of relief.[11]

We revisit many of these themes in the rest of this chapter and the wider book, but there were also other changes to policy and process that had enabling consequences for the poor. Thus, as the Brackley (Northamptonshire) guardians reached the end of their process of union formation in September 1835, they passed a resolution that:

> the Relieving Officers do provide a proper place in each Parish for Payment of the Paupers and Distribution of bread and provisions (the same in no Case to be a Public House Beer Shop or any other Shop) and give Notice to the Churchwardens and Overseers of the several Parishes of the day, time and place they intend to pay the Paupers in their respective Districts.[12]

This decision – an example of a purely administrative ruling repeated across England and Wales – had fundamental implications post-1834. Under the Old Poor Law, the claims of the poor were entirely dependent in terms of reception and action on the times and timing of the overseer. Now the poor had a definitive and timed locus to press their claims and, as Steven King has demonstrated, they used such new administrative certainties to limit and then roll back the impact of the New Poor Law on their everyday lives.[13] This is not, of course, to dismiss scandal and suffering. Indeed, such adverse experiences are at the centre of thousands of complaints made by the Victorian poor and their advocates in the letters, multi-signature petitions, and witness statements made during official investigations which appear in this book. Rather, we suggest that such complaints and the rationales behind them speak to the need for more nuanced considerations of the historiography, a matter to which we now turn.

CONSTRUCTING THE NEW POOR LAW

Early studies of the New Poor Law, often conducted from the top down and with a focus on summative central records and broad policy directions, were largely negative in their rendering of the new welfare regime. Successive Central Authorities were weaker than they ought to have been, outdoor relief remained the modal form of welfare in most places and at most times, initial success in containing and reducing costs was whittled away over time, staffing was professionalised and optimised in terms of numbers at a much slower pace than was originally envisaged, and scandals sapped political and public support for the poor law and its institutions.[14] By the 1880s, as the last serious attempt to (re)institute the principles of the 1834 act in the form of the crusade against outdoor relief failed, national and international conversations about pensions, the causes of poverty, child welfare, and sickness insurance had begun to undermine the very rationale of the deterrent New Poor Law and to remove certain groups from the workhouse environment.[15] The traction of this broad picture is in part a reflection of the fact that over the last three decades, research on the Old Poor Law has very significantly outpaced that on the New in both quantity and depth. Indeed, it remains the case that in empirical terms our understanding of the detailed working of the post-1834 landscape at the local level is based upon perspectives from a remarkably small (and heavily London-focused) collection of union studies.[16]

This is not to claim that the literature has been static. Welfare historians have begun to debate the purpose of the New Poor Law, a question central to an understanding of its successes and failures. Thus, if we see it as an attempt to curtail outdoor relief and to prevent the able-bodied claiming welfare by placing compulsory residence in the workhouse front and centre, the New Poor Law was a striking failure. At times of trade-cycle downturn in the manufacturing regions, workhouses could get nowhere near coping with the numbers of under- and unemployed workers. Even in "normal" times, the vast majority of the dependent poor had a relatively low chance of ending up in the workhouse. Similarly, if we understand the New Poor Law as an attempt to create a national standard of welfare and the mechanisms (surveillance of accounts; central direction on staffing; orders; inspections) by which relative uniformity of practice in England and Wales could be created, maintained and extended, the record is a patchy one. We now understand that Welsh guardians were remarkably adept at wrong-footing the Central Authorities and their inspectors, thereby retaining an effective autonomy in welfare matters in a system that was supposed to afford little.[17] Moreover, the increasing volume of work on a wider spatial canvas *within* the English context suggests that one of the most striking features of the New Poor Law from 1834 until at least the early 1900s was variability of practice, sentiment and, consequently, of pauper experiences. Some ratepayers in urban-industrial communities cautiously welcomed the prospect of unionisation, as did their southern rural counterparts.[18] Once formed, even adjacent unions could operate in very different ways in relation to religious observance amongst workhouse inmates, responsiveness to workhouse visiting committees, and attitudes towards the aged. In this context, it is possible to read the power of the Centre, often communicated in orders and circulars through delegated powers, as strictly limited.[19] The failure of most places to adopt the principles of the crusade against outdoor relief in the later nineteenth century, even though it had been officially enabled (though not strictly officially mandated), is a case in point.[20] It is thus unsurprising to see Gregory Clark concluding from his recent econometric comparison of the economic and social costs and benefits of the Old and New Poor Laws that the 1834 act "had no measurable social benefits."[21]

Yet, alternative readings are also possible. As Karel Williams suggests, if the central purpose of the New Poor Law was to reduce levels of relief spending in southern agricultural areas and rejuvenate poor law administrations in the same areas, then the record of achievement is perhaps more sustained.[22] Moreover, if we understand a major intent of the 1834 legislation as being to undermine a growing sense of rights to welfare on the part of applicants, then the fear and loathing often attributed by contemporaries and subsequent historians to relief in the workhouse might signal the New Poor Law as "successful." Indeed, the fact (revisited below) that workhouses rapidly came to be filled with people who were not able-bodied could easily be understood as a measure of the success of administrators in curbing the appetite of the able-bodied for welfare.[23]

These numerous and competing readings extend to a second strand of the historiography, that dealing with what might broadly be understood as the phasing of the New Poor Law. Early writers constructed chronological staging posts or transition points, with such chronologies broadly patterned onto the changing law, central organisation, or tone of central guidance. While welfare historians have not agreed on the exact phasing of these staging posts, their powerful conceptual hold on our understanding of the New Poor Law can be seen in the contents pages of core surveys of the period from 1834 to 1930.[24] Such approaches have informed a tendency for some historians to focus their research largely on discrete moments or time periods rather than ask longer-term questions about issues like continuity and change in pauper experiences or public attitudes to the workhouse.[25] More recent empirical research, however, coalesces around the sense of local poor law policy as both more variable and more organic than attempts at broad periodisation allow.

Nowhere is this change of focus clearer than in attitudes towards, and experiences of, medical care. The legislation of 1834 had almost nothing to say on this matter save allowing outdoor relief and other forms of welfare outside the workhouse where someone was in medical need. For Anne Digby and Anne Crowther, the permissive nature of such legislation meant that in the initial decades of the New Poor Law, the sick poor would have witnessed a marked deterioration in the scale and quality of health care in comparison to their experiences under the Old.[26] Subsequently King has shown that during the 1820s and 1830s parochial relief came increasingly to be associated with the provision of medical welfare. Guardians in the post-1834 period thus inherited a pattern of need and spending for which they were completely unprepared.[27] Once this initial "shock" had passed, however, we can find evidence of a poor law seeking to expand and codify its medical presence.[28] It seems clear from the work of Felix Driver and others that the building of workhouse spaces devoted to medical care proceeded rapidly and gathered pace after 1850. Graham Mooney is thus able to argue that workhouses (by which he means workhouses in London; the issue has still to be tested more widely) became receptacles for the sickest of the sick poor, in effect taking those most likely to spread disease out of their communities and reducing death rates below what they might otherwise have been in the wider population.[29] Death rates do not always bear out this view, but the sense that after 1850 the spaces of the workhouse and New Poor Law became increasingly medicalized is clear from the wider historiographical literature. As we see in the work of Kim Price, workhouse scandals were often medical scandals, and the fact that the role of medical officer became so politicised – often a bone of contention between Centre and locality – points firmly to ever greater poor law engagement with medicine, medical people, and medical processes.[30] Even by the 1890s, achievements were patchy, as is confirmed by a wide-ranging *British Medical Journal* report from 1894,[31] but on the eve of the democratisation of voting in poor law elections it is nonetheless clear that organic and incremental change had become a leitmotif in this area. Such observations are significant for some of the core themes of this volume because organic change – that which originated with unions and that forced upon them by inquiry and scandal – would have signalled to poor people the essential malleability of the rules and philosophies of the poor law itself.

At the heart of questions of continuity and change in welfare practice and policy stand individuals, and a third strand of the historiography (though one as yet inadequately codified) has developed with an increasing sense of the New Poor Law as not only a legal entity but necessarily as a network of people. Thus, Samantha Shave shows persuasively that "policy process" was dependent on the attitudes and experiences of individuals who had the power to shape national regulations.[32] While sustained and systematic study of the poor law inspectors who were crucial to the formation of poor law unions and their subsequent relations with the Centre is still lacking, patchy evidence points clearly to their personalities and political views as important variables in the complexion of local welfare policies.[33] At that local level, Douglas Brown's work on how contracts (for equipment, food, and so on) came to be formulated under the New Poor Law, allied with Kim Price's research on the nature of medical contracting, speaks keenly to the sense that the economics of welfare was linked with local patronage. Both authors trace subtle regional nuances in the nature and value of contracts and the mechanisms for awarding them, observations that demand greater testing through micro-studies but also point to the acute importance of individual relationships in the poor law that would have been visible to paupers and the prospective poor.[34]

Guardians and their backgrounds were crucial to such practices, and there has in recent historiography been a move away from talking about the "Board" as a collective and towards the need to understand individual actors. The laws, orders and circulars of the New Poor Law embodied a potentially powerful framework for the prevention of tyranny and limitations on local power. As Geoff Hooker and Karen Rothery have suggested in the Welsh and English contexts respectively, however, the individual personality of guardians mattered. From the very outset in 1834 and right through to the democratisation of Boards of Guardians, powerful personalities retained the ability to fundamentally shape local policy for better or worse.[35] The same broad conclusions also apply to officials – matrons, workhouse masters, relieving officers, nurses, schoolteachers, and porters – who staffed the day-to-day administration and delivery mechanisms of the New Poor Law.[36] The path to professionalisation and adequate vetting of these officers and employees was rocky and uncertain, as the literature on workhouse scandals has often demonstrated and as we have argued earlier. Even in the 1890s, it was possible to find the recycling between unions of staff with a record of cruel and harsh behaviour towards the poor, sometimes notwithstanding criminal convictions.[37] Similarly, some unions had an ingrained track record of employing and then dismissing unsuitable staff and running their institutions at considerably below the optimum or even basic staff-to-pauper ratios.[38] On the other hand, some places witnessed early professionalisation and long periods of relatively harmonious relationships. While the personal character of staff was only one factor colouring local welfare practice, we have come to see that it was much more important than has been allowed by earlier top-down accounts of the New Poor Law.

This observation might be extended to the importance of the personalities of those who stood outside the New Poor Law and sought to hold it to account. Voluntary workhouse visiting committees had a patchy existence in the 1860s, 1870s, and 1880s, but where they did exist came to exercise considerable leavening power over the quality of workhouse practice and staffing behaviour.[39] In this endeavour the personalities of the visitors, who often had to confront guardians with uncomfortable truths, made a difference. Similarly, journalists, writers, social investigators, religious figures, and editors – those seeking to compromise the poor law but also some trying to support or improve it – often succeeded through force of personality rather than by virtue of the strength and timeliness of their writing.[40] Just as important for the character of local poor law regimes were the personalities of individual paupers or applicants, and their sponsors and families. However we characterise them – rabble-rousers, grumblers, agitators, or legitimate protestors and champions of popular notions of justice – very many felt that they could and should contest welfare decisions and often literally reshaped local practice. In all these senses, then, the New Poor Law needs to be understood both as an artefact of law and as a meeting point of individuals and individual attitudes and sentiments.

For many of these individuals – and a fourth core strand of the historiography – the workhouse was the central, even totemic, focus of their activity and experience. In this respect, Crowther's foundational survey of the English workhouse in 1981 intended to set a research agenda for the future.[41] This aim has only partly been realised. The long-recognised conclusion that for most people, most of the time, and in most places, outdoor relief continued to be the mainstay of contact with the welfare system is given substance both in the work of those who look at census material and in our own analysis, where a desire for outdoor allowances was routinely sought and strongly rhetoricised. Nevertheless, census studies also show that workhouses became a refuge (or containment area) for variable constellations of the insane, aged, orphaned or abandoned children, mothers of bastards, the sick and (episodically) the unemployed and unemployable, with a constant stream of transient vagrants passing over these core groups.[42] Changes to national regulations or guidance (for instance, guidance on cottage homes from 1884 or the Old Age Pensions Act of 1908) took certain groups out of the workhouse context, but the fact that the institutional fabric of the New Poor Law consistently had to be orientated to deal with the problems of life-cycle groups for which it was never intended is striking.

Against this backdrop, a focus on the modest and grudging spending patterns of recalcitrant unions highlighted in earlier literature has only gradually given way to a focus which incorporates the massive changes to the physical fabric of the New Poor Law.[43] Drawing on Driver's periodisation for investment cycles, we now understand that workhouse buildings were in a constant state of actual or planned physical flux.[44] Guardians or their agents talked about, researched, planned, and called for information on a huge range of fabric changes across a spectrum from expensive rebuilding through extension, to minor adjustment. Much of this talking, planning, tendering, information-gathering, and correspondence with government and financiers came to nothing, but the very fact of the discussions reveals an organic poor law struggling almost from the outset to repurpose itself towards the needs of the sick, children, the aged, and those with mental and physical disabilities. More than this, workhouses were part of a burgeoning institutional network for the poor and vulnerable of nineteenth-century England and Wales, including voluntary and subscription hospitals, lunatic asylums, orphanages and adoption centres, and specialist institutions for the blind, deaf, and disabled. The poor sometimes – perhaps often – traversed numerous institutional contexts, as did the staff who encountered them. Such experiences, as we shall see in later chapters, could inform attitudes and expectations on the part of those who settled, however briefly, in the workhouse context.

This said, however, a further compelling feature of the post-1981 welfare literature has been how little we still know about the experiences and the material, emotional, and social lives of workhouse inmates, and the often contradictory nature of such knowledge as we have. Thus, Peter Gurney and Carl Griffin (focusing on widely reported scandals) have both argued that the workhouse – by design, neglect, or fraud – came to be centrally yoked to experiences of starvation, hunger, and poor diet.[45] In our own material we find evidence that workhouse inmates regularly contested the quality and quantity of food and often referred to hunger and starvation in their letters and statements. We also find accusations that relieving officers allowed outdoor paupers and claimants to starve to death. On the other hand we see conflicting narratives of pauper experiences. For example, workhouse clothing has come to be understood as a "uniform" with all the associated symbolism of regimentation and submission, as well as drab, ill-fitting, and (as paupers themselves sometimes asserted) insufficient.[46] Yet, to judge by the number of times paupers were prosecuted for leaving the workhouse with their issued clothing, workhouse clothes might have been of sufficiently high quality to generate value in the second-hand or pawnbroking market. As part of our wider project we have found evidence that both the Centre and many localities could go out of their way to avoid workhouse clothing being construed as a uniform either by those who wore it or those who saw it.[47]

Contradictory perspectives can also be discerned in relation to workhouse punishment. There were central rules on what infractions could be punished and on the nature, duration, and severity of such punishments.[48] While over time the Centre sought to restrict child punishments, we now know from the evidence of punishment books, and from paupers' and advocates' allegations of illegitimate and informal punishments, that the poor could be subjected to various degrees of physical and emotional tyranny.[49] Yet formal punishments (that is to say recorded punishments for the infringement of set workhouse rules) were not inflicted on *all* disruptive paupers as a matter of routine. Rather, workhouse staff chose who and what infraction to formally punish, and often did so in the context of trying to understand which aspects and incidents of bad behaviour posed the greatest threat to the stability of the workhouse regime, policed as it almost always was by inadequate staffing numbers.[50]

These historiographical complexities have tangled roots. Despite central direction, supposedly standard rules, record-keeping, accounting, and spending methods, local situations and decision-making outweighed standardisation throughout the New Poor Law period. The small cadre of staff and some of the legal restrictions placed upon the Centre made for limited progress. Issues of variability (across space) and volatility (across time) colour our understanding of the workhouse in particular. Richard Talbot, for instance, has shown conclusively that the two unions serving Stoke-on-Trent had completely different attitudes towards workhouse residence – and thus very different complexions of workhouse populations – notwithstanding a shared economy, social structure, and locational architecture, with workhouses only three miles apart.[51] Unpicking the modal experiences of inmate paupers is challenging work and requires large-scale and systematic study. A further problem is that while we usually know the rules, regulations, and broad policy thrusts that shaped workhouse regimes from the central records and from local or national newspaper coverage, the question of how the poor actually experienced institutional regimes is partly locked into complex and voluminous union archives in county record offices. Such records have often not proven as illuminating as welfare historians hoped, with the minutes of Boards of Guardians, for instance, frequently neglecting to record detailed local investigations or riots, even though we know from newspapers that such things were happening. Meanwhile, core records are often absent, with long runs of admission and discharge books (for instance) frequently missing. By contrast the central archives are voluminous and there has been very little work on the history of nineteenth-century welfare systematically linking local and national record sets.[52]

Above all, however, our lack of a unified historiographical picture on how inmates collectively, and life-cycle groups such as the aged, sick, and single mothers in particular, experienced the workhouse is explained by the fact that the institution already has a clear cultural and historiographical moniker. Driven by a methodological and philosophical focus on scandals, we have come to understand the workhouse as a dark place, a site of confinement and harsh treatment. Viewed from the perspective of national newspapers or the minutes of evidence to commissions of inquiry, a litany of abuse makes disturbing but compelling reading. This remains so even if we now understand that some contemporary claims of inhumane conduct by poor law officials were manufactured as part of the local politics of the New Poor Law or blown out of proportion by its opponents at local and national levels. In our own records, complaints of children being whipped with stinging nettles, masters parading with pistols and cudgels, sexual abuse, and aged inmates being given to lunatics as playthings provide evidence of tyranny even where (as was *normally* the case) such experiences did not magnify into national or local scandals in the sense of official investigation and condemnation or press coverage. In such contexts, the poor are inevitably construed as being subject to the power of the state (central and local) and institutional staff, emerging as victims or powerless onlookers when called to give evidence at inquiries, and sometimes as rioters prosecuted when institutional tensions boiled over.[53] Against this backdrop, residents are seen first and foremost as inmates rather than as individuals who spent some or much of their life-cycles outside such institutions and, when resident in institutions, retained and defended regular contacts with their communities outside.[54] Autobiographical accounts by former workhouse inmates suggest that we can trace a human capital penalty to such sojourns, and many individuals *did* reflect bitterly on their personal experiences, as seen also in regular reports in the press from the 1860s.[55] How representative these retrospective accounts of the "workhouse experience" are can be debated, but they may lead us to underplay the capacity for individual and collective agency and deter the search for evidence of more positive and accepting attitudes towards workhouses such as a willingness to embed them in an identifiable makeshift economy much as their counterparts under the Old Poor Law had done.[56]

It is this ingrained notion of powerlessness that we want to challenge. Our own project reveals that reports of ostensibly scandalous treatments and punishments were occasionally made up by paupers in ultimate acts of agency so as to strategically leverage power in an institutional environment that attempted to deny them any. Most allegations, however, seem to have had some basis in reality, and our intent here is not to reinvent workhouses as caring institutions. Rather, for both indoor and outdoor paupers and for applicants we argue that the lens of overt, deadly, and highly publicised scandal gives a very lopsided view of the character and role of the New Poor Law and its institutions. The sense of individual paupers continuously bereft of agency and unable to find mechanisms through which they could resist and successfully challenge authority recedes when we look carefully at their own writing.

AGENCY, NEGOTIATION, AND NAVIGATION

Work on themes such as the agency of the poor, relief as a negotiated outcome, the workhouse as a space of contestation, and the navigation mechanisms used by paupers and poor applicants to traverse the welfare system, has been slim. These are now familiar themes for the Old Poor Law, but addressing them in the post-1834 context fuses together both generic obstacles – "agency," for instance, is often casual shorthand for a variety of everyday normative practices – and specific ones.[57] In terms of the latter, while it is comparatively easy to find out what the function of a particular workhouse room or space was, it is much more difficult to discern what "went on" there – workhouse gardens, as an example, provided food for inmates but were also sites of sexual encounters, peculation, and the punishment of children. Within the workhouse itself, a focus on plans and on the surviving physical fabric in heritage workhouse sites such as Southwell and Gressenhall encourages us to see their interior spaces as discrete, rather than as connected wholes in which the poor interacted in myriad small and fleeting ways that encouraged gossip, frustration, sex, confusion, enmity, and the accumulation or dissolving of tensions with staff.[58] Some of this connectivity is revealed in the national scandals or local inquiries that, as we note above, have become the dominant lens. But in such instances (and through the public reporting of them), perspectives on agency, negotiation, and navigation are often garnered only through the mediated and directed voices of the poor and their interlocutors.[59]

It is in this context that the historiography has come to focus particularly on the experiences of the poor as revealed in moments of extreme tension, or by iconic groups of paupers. The rewards have been rich. Our own research, for instance, strongly supports David Green's sense that teenage girls and young women were reported as a troublesome group for guardians and their staff to manage.[60] Vagrants were even more problematic. It is now clear that their numbers rose considerably during the nineteenth century and that the so-called casual wards of workhouses were places where ill-treatment, harsh conditions, resistance, and contempt melded together in a potent and toxic mix. The increasingly vocal critics of the deterrent workhouse focused disproportionately on vagrants and their attitudes and experiences. Indeed, one of the most iconic exposés of the chronic overcrowding, poor conditions, and abusive behaviour sometimes found in large urban workhouses was facilitated by someone pretending to be a vagrant and spending a night in a casual ward.[61] Yet, at the same time, reporting of this story suggests a powerful subtext, in which vagrants and their advocates contested the decisions of workhouse staff, conditions in casual wards, and the breaking of rules by guardians.[62] More than this, the literature on vagrants gives a clear sense that this group actively used workhouses to foster their lifestyle and that, notwithstanding the moral outrage of New Poor Law staff at local level, unions found it impossible to effectively deal with these assertions of agency.[63] Of course, vagrants spent only short periods of time in workhouses, though they often made repeated visits over long periods. Even for this group, then, we as historians can easily miss the micro-experiences of contestation, action, inaction, gossip, sullenness, sloth, symbolic acts such as damaging poor law fabrics, and negotiation that James Scott characterises as the weapons of the weak and which are classically deployed in sequestered places like workhouse rooms and corridors.[64] Such everyday acts of resistance shaped the way the New Poor Law was constructed in the minds of paupers, applicants, and the communities from which they were drawn and influenced the part it played – or was seen as being able to play – in life-cycles of dependence and independence.

For one other group of the recipient population – the sick poor – the historiography affords us a rather better angle. Through the work of Kim Price, Elizabeth Hurren, and Sambuhda Sen, we now know that the sick and dying poor could be subject to breathtaking neglect and contempt causing acute suffering.[65] The Central Authority was particularly attuned to the threat that such neglect posed to public and political support for its existence and could be quick to act with local inquiries, the censure of local boards, and forced resignations of staff. Yet we also know that the sick and their relatives were neither voiceless nor powerless. They obtained the support of advocates, publicised cases in the press, wrote (see chapter 11) to the Central Authority in considerable numbers, and actively contested all aspects of their care from diet and medicine, to clothing and attendance. It is clear that the sick poor could think and act strategically. They had an often deep knowledge of the law and rules of the New Poor Law, and were remarkably eloquent in their sense that certain basic standards of care must be offered both inside and outside the workhouse. Supported by a public opinion that was informed ever more clearly by a recognition that sickness and its consequences were and ought to be remediable, the persistent augmentation of the medical fabric of the workhouse is evidence of the force of these demands "from the inside."

These perspectives are important, but they also point to an important gap in our understanding of the New Poor Law. Apart from a small handful of autobiographical or memorial narratives, there are currently, as we noted above, few first-hand accounts of the thoughts, emotions, and everyday experiences of paupers and poor applicants themselves.[66] Consequently, we have too often assumed by default that those applying for or receiving welfare under the New Poor Law were voiceless, both absolutely and in comparison to their counterparts under the Old Poor Law. There has in turn been surprisingly little take-up of David Englander's posthumous call for historians to search out the letters written by paupers and claimants to the Centre seeking information or intervention, or contesting care and allowances given or withheld in localities.[67] Our failure to access such material means that we have casually assumed that those in workhouses or on outdoor relief were at best minimally literate, ill-informed, disorganised, or isolated, and thus unable to consistently contest their treatment, shape policy, or employ languages of rights, expectation and obligation.[68] Moreover, we have missed much of the nuance about how those groups – children, the aged, "bastard" bearers, and the sick who were not at the forefront of the collective unrest that sometimes punctured workhouse regimes – experienced and navigated workhouse residence or union decision-making processes.

At so many levels, then, the words of the poor mattered. This book is all about finding and understanding such words; about a New Poor Law history from below in which the binary distinctions that have shaped writing on the post-1834 period – centre-locality; punished-punisher; pauper/applicant-staff/guardians; rules-resistance; success-failure; control-chaos; power-powerlessness; and dependence-independence – simply dissolve. Here, *inter alia*: workhouse regimes may not always have been as controlling and isolating as we think; the Central Authority was not as insulated from paupers and their advocates as early commentators such as Crowther thought; developing literacy opened up new rhetorical and strategic possibilities for poor people to contest the welfare offer; the poor and their advocates had a deep and powerful knowledge of the law and practice of welfare and of the tenor and reach of public opinion; the capacity for collective action through working-class organisations was strong; cultural and administrative power could not be used by local guardians and staff with the discretion and force usually assumed; ways of understanding and navigating the everyday contours of the workhouse differed according to age, gender, cause of poverty and also region; the poor and their advocates elaborated and developed a wider set of narrative strategies linking into cultural norms of the period – dignity, Christian philanthropy, camaraderie, solidarity, natural rights, exogeneity, and humanity – as Victorian Britain came to maturity; and the rules of state welfare were, and were meant to be, malleable, such that most aspects of local policy were contestable and *were* contested. Without re-evaluating the New Poor Law and its aims as a broadly positive scheme of welfare, it is nonetheless the case that many paupers were able to find space within the system to challenge, resist, and define their own notions of what "welfare" should look like. We might, in other words, understand the poor as having (and knowing that they had) agency in a system that notionally afforded them none. In turn, such an approach offers us the chance to relocate the very poorest into wider debates about a whole range of nineteenth-century issues, including the nature of working-class agency and the desirability of working-class solidarity, sexual cultures and cultures of sexual abuse, literacy, old age, the rise of a putative healthcare system, the development of the press and public opinion, the nature and meaning of community, and the changing and diverse contours of citizenship.

SCAFFOLDING

At the core of much of our research lies the concept of agency. As Megan Webber and others have pointed out, defining this term is not unproblematic in cases where we try and fuse together simultaneously an understanding of intent, mechanism, reception, and outcome.[69] For this book, however, we understand agency as resting on the twin pillars of intent and belief rather than simply on outcome. Thus, the letters of paupers and poor applicants both embodied and were a vehicle for a sense that their authors had the right to express concerns and contest decisions. Through writing, action, the giving of evidence, and the accumulation of small everyday acts of insubordination, workhouse inmates and the outdoor poor intended to shape the day-to-day regimes to which they were notionally subject. Their voices seeped into popular and political discourse, and of course popular and political discourse seeped into their voices, sometimes with the support of overtly political organisations. Some letters may have been unanswered, the poor (particularly the workhouse poor) punished for writing, improvements in the administration of welfare short-lived – and the strength of the pauper voice may have dwindled or magnified depending on who was in the workhouse or on the applicant list – but agency does not, in our sense of it, necessitate success or obvious quantifiable outcome. Indeed, because poor writers and welfare recipients believed that they could and should have agency, even the smallest gains at local level or with the Centre nourished an *intention* to really have agency. As we shall see in chapters 2 to 4, the poor and their advocates kept on writing in very substantial numbers even as central and local authorities did their best to reduce a sense of entitlement to do so, because (as some writers directly acknowledge) every word of each response, every instruction for local guardians to inquire, every newspaper article or shift in public opinion, and every investigation of a central inspector sustained a deep-seated belief in the potential rewards of exercising agency.

We do not, of course, claim that agency was untrammelled, chronologically or spatially consistent, or always substantial and unchallenged. Throughout our book we encounter situations where administrative, punitive, organisational, and personal power could be used effectively against poor claimants, paupers, and witnesses both inside and outside the workhouse. Organised silence, exemplar punishments, claims of administrative oversight, cronyism, intimidation, and outright violence could be and were used to mask abuse of power in the union context. Some guardians and union staff were just evil. On the other hand, the poor and their advocates also had, found, and manufactured powerful weapons to confront abuse.

Some of these – gossip, surliness, symbolic acts and, occasionally, bigger organised moments of rebellion – are familiar from the work of James Scott. Others – backward-looking appeals to custom and Christian paternalism or the re-invention of rhetorical and actual notions of citizenship so as to appropriate the intellectual ground of the powerful – resonate with the work of Edward Thompson. And above all, the New Poor Law inherited a set of paupers and advocates deeply familiar with rhetoric of right, law, obligation, and duty whom welfare administrators persistently struggled to control and, at times, actively colluded with. In the chapters that follow, then, we shall see all the actors on the New Poor Law canvas contained in, boxed by, and traversing complex (perhaps increasingly complex) matrices of power or constraint. Here the smallest action and word had significance. Everyone knew it.

We explore this broad framework using correspondence by or about the poor in 102 of the more than six hundred poor law unions that were gradually formed after 1834. Alongside this material we consider a deep and vibrant set of supplementary records, the whole amounting to four million words of transcribed material. Such resources are amenable to numerous methodological approaches. Most of the substantive chapters are framed and informed by corpus and historical sociolinguistic analysis. At its simplest, we count words and phrases (and their grammatical and rhetorical equivalents, given sometimes fleeting orthographic ability) using the corpus package *WordSmith*. We also code and classify smaller subsets of the data and analyse trends in language and rhetoric over time, letter series, or space, using the corpus package *Sketch Engine*. This broad framing exercise is supplemented by simple categorisation of material, as for instance when we look at the number of advocates and the occupational and social composition of the advocate base both in its own right and in relation to the same issues under the Old Poor Law. These approaches drive our qualitative analysis, which focuses around case studies of places, people, regions, administrative process, and life-cycle groups. Such stories are sometimes laid bare in the sources. More often they require a degree (and often a substantial amount) of record linkage to make them intelligible.

The resulting book has three parts. In part 1 we engage with the process of finding and hearing voices: those of paupers and applicants but also of advocates, officials, and people who gave evidence. Chapter 2 reviews the historical foundation of the key archival collection used in this study, the correspondence which flowed between local unions and the London-based Central Authority, and investigates the intricacies of the sources themselves. It also examines in a quantitative sense the nature of the pauper voice emerging from the central archive. Chapter 3 switches the focus from the poor to those who advocated for them, analysing the different types of letter-writing advocate, and the scope and substance of their letters. Finally in this section, chapter 4 investigates the response of the Central Authority to advocate and pauper letters, looking in particular at how far officials at the Centre felt compelled to reply, the extent to which they intervened on behalf of the poor and the likely impact of their replies on the claimed and articulated agency of the poor.

Part 2 focuses on the broad question of agency, looking at how poor writers and their advocates sought to influence and contest the welfare decisions they encountered. Chapter 5 takes a corpus-level view, highlighting broad continuity and change in the referential tropes and linguistic registers employed by poor writers. While we can see a striking new rhetorical infrastructure developing over the course of the New Poor Law, we ultimately suggest that there was a well-understood architecture to the writing of the poor and those who took up their cause. Chapter 6 further examines one of the most compelling changes observed at corpus level: the extent to which the poor "knew" (and were prepared to use) the law, processes, and soft regulations of the New Poor Law and understood the nature and remit of the Central Authority with which they engaged. In looking at this interaction between the users and administrators of welfare, the chapter examines how the poor sought to engage with welfare authorities through the mechanism of their own rules and regulations in order to extend and enhance what they articulated to be their rights to welfare citizenship. Chapters 7 to 9 explore questions of power, agency, control, navigation and experience under the New Poor Law through case studies of three "classic" dependent groups. Thus, chapter 7 considers the rhetoric, strategy, and agency specific to the different groups of women who engaged with the Central Authority. Although the 1834 report and legislation were often silent on the female pauper, women were not silent in regard to their welfare concerns, and the resulting pauper letter archive contains numerous texts from single, married, and widowed women. Through this material we look at the propensity of women to deploy registers linked to backward-looking conceptions of the proper place of a woman (dependence, deference, respectability, and their role as mothers and wives) versus those linked to "current" notions of authority, power, and rights. Chapter 8 switches attention to one of the most combative segments of the poor – the aged. This group complained of being compelled to go into the workhouse against their will, often insisting on a right to be relieved out of doors; and many of those who did find themselves inmates protested about harsh work regimes, inadequate diets, separation from life partners, and poor medical treatment. Crucially, they did so mostly on the basis of rights that they claimed specifically on the basis of their elderly status, and this chapter will investigate just how far the strategies that were resorted to by the elderly and their advocates, including the continued application of older notions of "entitlement," influenced the formulation of policy. Finally, chapter 9 focuses on the most totemic of poor law welfare recipients – the able-bodied. The orthodox narrative about the treatment of the able-bodied under the New Poor Law is an intensely pessimistic one, and there is no doubt that the main restrictions and reforms of the new regime were aimed at deterring such paupers. On the other hand, and as we shall see, the able-bodied poor writing from inside and outside workhouses deployed a sophisticated rhetorical toolbox to establish and maintain a crucial veneer of deservingness.

Finally, part 3 addresses the issue of how, how far, and how successfully the New Poor Law and its stakeholders could deter, contain, or weaken the agency of poor writers. Chapter 10 explores the consequences of the fact that poor writers and those who gave evidence were routinely identified to the relevant local authority when they were asked to respond to issues raised. This process of official investigation left the pauper complainant open to retributive action in the form of petty but incremental punishments designed to make life in the workhouse or on outdoor relief less palatable and the institution harder to navigate. Even here, however, we shall see that the threat of punishment was partly balanced by the prospect of central surveillance and that the poor showed a remarkable propensity to carry on complaining. Chapter 11 is a case study of the sick poor and the notional limits of agency. We shall see that these writers very often felt themselves to have been badly served by the new structures of the post-1834 welfare world. They complained about the refusal of union medical officers to attend them in the first place, about the inadequacies of the medical attention that they did receive, and about the limits that were placed on their medical care, including its premature and peremptory withdrawal. Detailed investigation suggests that while such failings were not systematic, the abuse of the sick was frequent and sometimes routine. We ultimately conclude, however, that the sick poor garnered more agency over the period as a whole. Finally, chapter 12 takes an overarching view of the changing ways and contexts in which the poor exercised agency, and we argue that writing a New Poor Law history from below suggests that contestation and negotiation were, at most times and in most places, normative.

PART ONE

Finding and Hearing "Voices"

2

Navigating and Measuring

INTRODUCTION

In March 1841 Mary Herbert was recorded in the outdoor relief lists for the York Poor Law Union (PLU) in Yorkshire as having received one shilling per week for thirteen weeks.[1] She was still recorded in the same lists in 1845, 1846, and 1847, at the latter date aged seventy, a widow (corrected to say "single"), and in regular receipt of two shilling per week.[2] In January 1848 Herbert herself wrote to what was by then the Poor Law Board (PLB) claiming that she was unable to do anything to earn her livelihood[3] and consequently had applied to the York guardians, informing them that she belonged to the Pickering PLU (Yorkshire) but that since the "new Settlement Act [she] had been thrown upon the Parish of St Maurice in York," moving later to York St John.[4] They had initially allowed her two shillings weekly, then stopped relief and said she was to go back to Pickering. In ordering her to leave, one of the guardians had threatened, she wrote, "to throw my things into the Street." She now asked whether "Mr Hansfield has all the law in his own hands, and if he can throw my things in the Streets as he has threatened, and if they can force me to go into the Workhouse at my Age."[5]

Herbert's answer from the PLB stated that they were unable to intervene in individual cases but that a copy of her letter would be sent to the York guardians for their consideration.[6] The guardians in turn responded that Herbert's relief had been stopped because she had refused to give evidence of settlement to the relieving officer.[7] This letter from York was heavily annotated by William Golden Lumley, PLB assistant secretary, and a reply critical of the guardians was dispatched. It stated that discontinuing Herbert's relief on these grounds "was not justifiable," and that, "By so doing the Gns would appear to have used means to extract evidence in a matter where they had no jurisdiction." Furthermore, the Centre deemed that "it is not to be expected that paupers will in all cases be ready to give evidence as to their settlement voluntarily" and reminded the guardians that they could not refuse relief to those who were truly destitute.[8] Returning to the local records, we learn that Herbert reappeared in September 1848, then receiving 1s 6d.[9] Indeed, she was still in receipt of outdoor relief in 1851 when, according to the census, she was a "Pauper Housekeeper," seventy-six years old, disabled, and living alone.[10] Mary Herbert's case illustrates the value of utilising local and national records, which usually supplement and complement rather than replicate each other. More than this, it points directly to the intent and exercise of agency. Her letter to the Centre had the desired effect of forcing the union not only to reinstate relief but to continue it for years. In the process the guardians were admonished, something which must have provoked anger in their ranks but also raised hope for other paupers minded to write.

The emergence of this picture of agency, negotiation, and contestation is crucially dependent on the retention and preservation of records created and/or collected by, or at the request of the Central Authority, and it is thus remarkable that so little has been written on their archive. Paul Carter's annotated transcription of the early Bradford (Yorkshire) PLU correspondence remains the only one of its type. In it, he touched on how this material was created and collated, the administrative practices shaping the correspondence, and the variety of subjects covered.[11] Carter and Natalie Whistance subsequently provided an overarching account of the "union correspondence archive" to 1871. Additionally, Carter and King have delved deeper into the technicalities that governed correspondence, focusing particularly on how the Centre developed a more complex/refined level of organisation over time.[12] Our still-limited understanding of the nature, scale, and scope of the central poor law archive is reflected in the lack of engagement with central records in many studies of individual unions. Remedying this imbalance is one aim for a book looking at how the poor themselves experienced, contested, and navigated the New Poor Law. The chapter will therefore begin by analysing the administrative systems that required, generated, received, and retained records like those relating to Mary Herbert between 1834 and 1900. Furthermore, we will put these core sources into the wider context of some of the associated records to which they directly link and through which the wider archive can be interrogated in greater depth. The chapter moves on to consider the sources that underpin our book and the crucial question of how we can and should "measure" the pauper voice. Initially, however, it is important to understand the post-1834 archive in the context of its Old Poor Law equivalent.

THE LAST DECADES OF THE OLD POOR LAW

As chapter 1 has suggested, between 1601 and 1834 parishes constituted the administrative heart of the Old Poor Law, although townships (divisions of parishes), towns, and early incorporations (collections of parishes) were also periodically responsible for the management of the poor. Its officers and representative bodies (chiefly overseers and vestries) generated a complex archive which at its most complete might include parish rate books, overseers' accounts, correspondence, vestry minutes, settlement examinations/certificates, and removal orders. There are, however, three things we should note about the records of the Old Poor Law. First, they were created within a welfare regime that had local discretion at its core. Differences in poor relief practices across the more than fifteen thousand nineteenth-century parishes of England and Wales ensured that the scale and scope of recorded data differed substantially both according to parish and over time. Second, even where parishes followed ostensibly similar practices, there was no consistency at all in the nature and depth of the information recorded.[13] Central government data collection from the 1770s gave some impetus to the use of standardised data forms, but the lack of any inspectorate, or even a centrally mandated structure, made gains patchy and fragile.[14] Finally, of course, the survival of poor law material is immensely variable across the country, and any ideal or typical archive is correspondingly rare.

One feature that is consistent among the majority of Old Poor Law archives is records relating to settlement and belonging.[15] The Settlement

Act of 1662 had established the terms under which all English and Welsh people obtained a place of settlement, or legal belonging, for welfare purposes: birth, marriage, paying of local rates, renting property to the value of at least £10 per annum, or the serving of an apprenticeship.[16] While the mechanisms for getting and changing settlement developed over time, the principle remained that only an applicant's parish of settlement was liable for payment of their relief. The question of where someone was settled thus became central to matters of welfare, and this question (increasingly complex as more people moved more frequently) carried over into the New Poor Law, as we saw with Mary Herbert above. For those leaving their place of settlement, a certificate signed by local officers and countersigned by local magistrates could be obtained. This represented a pledge for that parish to pay the future welfare bills of the persons named.[17] How frequently such certificates were issued is unclear – the fact that some parishes maintained specific lists of "certificate men" as part of the parochial record suggests more often than is usually allowed – but it is clear that their use was in sharp decline by the 1780s.[18] For those without certificates (and even some who did have them), dependence or the threat of it might trigger a settlement examination to trace the personal history of an individual and thus the relative liabilities of parishes.[19] In turn, the non-settled poor might find themselves forcibly removed to a parish of settlement or "encouraged" to leave a host parish with threats, orders, or bribes.[20] The treatment of Mary Herbert by the York PLU signals the continuation of these practices and considerations under the New Poor Law.

That said, it is clear that the majority of those who *could* have been removed from any place were not in fact forced to go. Removal was expensive and contested, and the poor showed an extraordinary propensity to simply return; and so from the 1780s a series of inter-parish agreements developed and coalesced to form the out-parish or non-resident relief system. Such agreements meant that settlement parishes paid relief to the poor in host communities, often for decades. The character and rationale for this system are now well known and do not require elaboration here, but its practical operation has important consequences for the rest of this book.[21] While those who lived at a distance sometimes travelled back to their settlement parishes when in need, most negotiated relief via epistolary exchanges.[22]

They might write in their own hand or enlist the writing, words, and support of a respectable advocate who would have acted as "a persuasive indicator of truthfulness, need and deservingness."[23] The earliest commentators disagreed on the extent of survival of these sources.[24] More recent work has clarified this matter. Thomas Sokoll, in his comprehensive study of Essex pauper letters, acknowledged the "erratic pattern of record survival" which the letters shared with other loose parish documents as opposed to bound books such as overseers' accounts.[25] He described his 758 pauper letters not "as a physical archive of its own," assigning it to the category of "an artificial collection" which was geographically uneven across the county.[26] Nonetheless, his work brought new possibilities to welfare historians, who could for the first time systematically analyse the words, thoughts, and strategies of poor people. The issue of pauper letter survival rates was taken up more fully by King in his *Writing the Lives of the English Poor*. He suggested that many more letters were written than have survived and that some of the substantial collections – of more than a thousand letters per parish – standing at the heart of his study were once the modal archive form. Letters are not always easy to track down but the available corpus of published and unpublished sources (largely covering the period from 1780 to 1834) now stands at some 25,000 items. Through these documents, King argues, we can understand that the relief offered by the Old Poor Law was essentially negotiated. The rules of the system were, and were meant to be, malleable, and officials expected to both receive and reply to pauper and advocate letters. While the poor – settled or otherwise – had no right to relief, they had a right to write and did so using a linguistic register and set of strategic tropes not so very different from those of parish officers themselves.[27] These observations are important for any study of the New Poor Law. As our Preface has suggested, the post-1834 administration inherited deeply ingrained traditions of epistolary negotiation and contestation of relief.

THE NEW POOR LAW ARCHIVE

The 1834 New Poor Law created a new set of central-local relations which were underpinned by a sense that only a central body would have the necessary sources of information and resources to oversee broader aspects of pauper management. Thus only a rule-making Central Authority could be vested with the discretionary powers to carry the New Poor Law into effect.[28] One of the early tasks of the newly created Poor Law Commission (PLC) was to group parishes into unions. By 1835 there were 111; by 1838 that number had grown to 594. Parishes that operated under pre-1834 local acts or which were already part of existing incorporations were initially excluded from the unionisation process, but their autonomy was reduced over time until by the 1860s the number of unions had reached 646.[29] This figure remained pretty constant during the lifetime of the Central Authority, though further unions were created, others were augmented, and over time parishes were occasionally moved from one union to another.[30] While historians disagree (as we saw in chapter 1) on the extent to which regional and local practice varied between places and diverged from central rules, in discussions concerning the rise of the information state, the bureaucratic revolution of the New Poor Law is often cited as a prime example of the more effective centralisation of government.[31] And it is undeniable that 1834 *did* represent a dramatic shift in the way in which information on, about, and from the poor concerning welfare was gathered, recorded, and utilised.

In this sense, information *management* became a key function of the Central Authority because it reached dramatically into the daily business of the newly created unions.[32] As Edward Higgs reminds us, central government extended its geographical reach by re-fitting local government into a tool for carrying out central policies.[33] One of the essential aspects of this "re-fitting" was the production of detailed forms and books for local use.[34] New sets of records were created, including: Board of Guardians' minute books, outgoing letter books, workhouse committee books, and admission and discharge registers, out-relief books, non-settled poor registers, pauper punishment books, and application and report books.[35] In 1835 the PLC appointed Charles Knight & Co. of Ludgate Street as publisher "by authority," and many poor law researchers will be familiar with the imprimatur of this company on paper-based union records.[36] Knight was not, however, provided with a monopoly. John Shaw & Sons of Fetter Lane and James Truscott of Blackfriars Road competed for union contracts. Outside London, smaller provincial print businesses were sometimes used, so that unions could spend their rates within the local economy.[37] From the Centre's perspective the important thing was not whose stationery was used, but whether it met their data collection standards.[38] An unsurprising corollary was that the Centre filled their circulars and annual reports with instructions to officers on what data to collect and how it should be presented.[39] Indeed, even before unions were first formed, the Centre was active; the initial annual report of the PLC contained copies of official documents or circulars setting out what parish officers in the pre-declaration period were to do.[40]

As with union stationery, publications conveying instructions, advice, and guidance were also subject to market economics. A large number of regular and *ad hoc* published guides were printed, including Charles Knight's *The Union's and Parish Officers' Year Book*, George Dudgeon's *The Duties of Overseers of the Poor and Assistant Overseers*, and William Cunningham Glen's *The General Consolidated Orders Issued by the Poor Law Commission*.[41] Such volumes were monitored, if only informally, by the Central Authority's staff. John Graves, one of the assistant poor law commissioners, complained that *Shaw's Union Officers' Manual* of 1847 had included "an error so important that it deserves to be corrected by cancelling the page where it occurs in the unsold copies, or by inserting a slip with notice of erratum." The offending section advised that as a general rule "no pauper is chargeable to the parish in which, being destitute, he applies for and obtains relief." Graves made the case to the commission that "much good would be done, and much ignorance and error obviated, by a more general gratuitous circulation of your General orders, or, at least, of the more important of them."[42] He also complained that in the Abergavenny PLU (Monmouthshire), as with other unions for which he was responsible, he had "met with books, (sometimes printed in provincial towns) which vary, occasionally in important particulars, from the proscribed forms."[43]

Such determined advice, along with regulations and rules, meant that legal compliance was centrally channeled. The requirements of the Centre, however, went beyond mere legal compliance. A key staple of its annual reports was data on relief expenditure, such that local recording methodologies had to share a strictly uniform approach to facilitate such comparison.[44] Officials were thus presented with detailed formats for parish rate books, rate receipt books, and quarterly balance sheets.[45] As the New Poor Law developed, clarifications to existing formats were made. In addition, unions were regularly instructed to collect new data, resulting in new records and thus (for the later research community) additional archives. For example a new information requirement was imposed in 1841, when the PLC re-emphasised and updated the rules and regulations concerning pauper punishment. This updating, they claimed, followed reports of recent "excessive or improper punishments" suffered by some pauper inmates at the hands of staff.[46] It included a new form that defined the critical information to be collected in all instances of pauper punishment across England and Wales. The form (figure 2.1) was printed in a January 1841 circular letter to all Boards of Guardians and reprinted in the *Annual Report* of the same year.[47]

For the first time, in this form (the importance of which becomes apparent in chapter 10) the offences and punishments that took place in the workhouse were recorded in a systematised way. This allowed the Central Authority to compare and contrast union practices as required.[48] Moreover, such record-keeping meant that individual officers could be held to account in two distinct ways: first, by guardians through local union visiting committees or at weekly guardians' meetings where punishment books were to be inspected; and second, the books were to be part of the Central Inspectorate's investigations into any claims of unfair and disproportionate punishment. This provision was made clear by the Central Authority, which informed Boards of Guardians that any omission or inaccurate data would lead to a presumption of concealment. In practice the low survival of punishment books may point either to uneven engagement with these requirements or subsequent archival losses.[49] Nonetheless, via examples such as this we can see that the formatting of the myriad blank books, ledgers, and registers into which almost all poor law business was entered by union officers was an immense undertaking, one through which the Central Authority used its administrative power to shape the activities of local government and hold it to account.

The newly formed unions also dealt with a plethora of incoming and outgoing correspondence. Much of this circulated between individual unions and the Central Authority, but there was also abundant correspondence with their own individual officers, parishes (usually overseers), local

FORM.

No. of Case.	Name.	Offence.	Date of Offence.	Punishment inflicted by Master or other Officer.	Opinion of Guardians thereon.	Punishment ordered by Board of Guardians.	Date of Punishment.	Initials of Clerk.	Observations.

Given under our hands, and seal of office, &c.

2.1 Form for recording data on pauper punishments
Source: *Seventh Annual Report of the Poor Law Commissioners, 1841*, 118.

tradespeople, magistrates (individually or via petty or quarter sessions), ratepayers and, of course, paupers and their advocates. Incoming correspondence at union level (being loose papers) rarely survives.[50] Larger collections of local outgoing copy letter books can, however, be used to track the recorded responses. These include the date and addressee along with the verbatim text itself. For example, John Carling wrote in early 1853 to the Ripon PLU (Yorkshire) asking for relief. Carling's letter is lost but it generated a response from the Ripon clerk, who advised that he should apply to the relieving officer in his district (Carlton) and that the officers there would then write formally to Ripon.[51] We thus get a sense of the initial letter and the likely complexity of a notionally complete union archive. In the latter context it is no surprise to find that local union staff sometimes developed subject and name indexes to keep track of their records and increase their effectiveness in data management.[52]

Of course, the desire for administrative control and comprehensive data gathering shaped how the Central Authority collected and preserved its own incoming correspondence, registers, indexes, and (for the PLC period only) minutes. Significant parts of the central spaces were given over to administrative and record-related business. In 1836 the "Office" occupied six floors: the first two levels had three record rooms; the first level also had an occasional copying and dispatch room; the third level (ground floor) had a messengers' room which doubled as a dispatch room as well as another defined dispatch room; the fifth level had a large "register room," with the sixth level (attic) having both a copying room and reference room.[53] This dedicated space was required in order to deal with the enormous quantity of paperwork that now comprises the Central Authority's poor law archive within various Ministry of Health series at The National Archives (TNA), including: correspondence between the Centre and other government departments, assistant commissioners and inspectors, unions, and "miscellaneous correspondence and papers"; Central Authorities' orders and circular letters; registers of paid union officers; and subject indexes for correspondence. The largest single part of the entire collection is the vast correspondence that makes up series MH12.[54]

As well as creating rules and orders, the Centre had a responsibility to take note of and respond to *all* correspondence. Even at an early stage this was a huge task. By 1845 the PLC had received some 300,000 letters, giving it a deep insight into regional particularities of welfare management.[55] In turn, when union officials wrote to the Central Authority querying a local issue or pauper case, the central response often formed the basis of a precedent on which more general rules and regulations were then based. These were formalised in circulars and orders which were distributed to unions, individually or collectively, in a kind of virtuous circle. The Centre was thus keen to ensure the retention of all correspondence, as it was answerable to Parliament for its work. Yet, the contemporary archival phraseology "union correspondence" is potentially misleading. MH12 *is* primarily an archive comprising the correspondence between two levels of bureaucracy, the Central Authority and clerks to the various unions. However, others in official and non-official roles also wrote and, most significantly for our current purpose, MH12 includes, *inter alia*: letters from workhouse inmates, those in receipt of outdoor relief and people who were poor but not currently receiving relief (usually complaining that their applications had been refused); letters from advocates; multi-signature petitions (which might include a mix of all of these groups); witness statements (recorded during local or central investigations); and newspaper cuttings.[56] These are the core documents on which the following chapters rely and which, above all others, give us an unprecedented insight into the thoughts, feelings, and experiences of the poor themselves. We return to the documents as sources later in the chapter.

Officials recognised that the success or failure of the PLC rested largely on union correspondence and the ability to mine and manage the "big data" which could be gleaned from it. The assistant commissioner, Charles Mott, perfectly articulated the aspirations of the new Central Authority, expressing the assurance that:

> when the means of obtaining information, by correspondence with the different boards of guardians, shall have been established, and local information on all subjects can be procured in a short space of time, with facilities hitherto unattainable; when, in short, the new system, in all its branches, is fully and properly developed, it cannot fail to produce results which will procure for it the support, and for its originators the gratitude, of the country.[57]

One of the major problems facing the newly formed commission, however, was ensuring the survival of the correspondence itself. The potential for day-to-day loss as individual items circulated is illustrated in a complaint by one of its own employees, John Johnston, who noted that:

> on removing the Old Papers of 1834–5 and 6 into the passage to make room for those of 1837 and the then current year of 1838 it was found that the passage would not contain more than about half consequently the remainder of the Papers have been on the floor ever since and Subjected to be tossed about every time the Room has to be Swept out – thus rendering it very difficult to find former papers when wanted.[58]

Lost letters in turn reduced the efficiency, and undermined the reputation of the Centre. Thus, in 1836 Charles Pinson wrote from the Liverpool Vestry (Lancashire) referring to a letter from Thomas William Coke of Holkham Hall (Norfolk) and an enclosed recommendation for employment. The text was annotated by a PLC clerk, who stated that an insufficient reference had been given and the papers could not be found. A further annotation noted that the papers had been found but that it was by then too late to send them on.[59] In July 1840 a series of internal notes was exchanged concerning missing correspondence, including one from the PLC to Edward Senior, an assistant commissioner, referring to a set of missing papers which had "still" not been found.[60] Perhaps unsurprisingly, when it was resolved in the 1840s to index the correspondence, a decision was taken that these loose letters and papers would be brought together by union, in date order, and bound into volumes. This decision was pivotal. Binding the correspondence not only made indexing and tracking paperwork easier but it physically protected the correspondence itself, not least from being weeded out by future custodians and archivists.[61] The fact that material from the 1840s onwards (and retrospectively for earlier material) was bound in this way means that we can be confident that, as long as the volume for a particular year survives, it will contain almost all the letters received or sent.[62]

Besides binding the material, other administrative actions taken by the Central Authority aided its ability to record and then retrieve material. Each piece of received correspondence was given a number (and sometimes a letter) followed by a year. These "paper numbers" were physically written onto the correspondence in the central top section of the page, along with the union number in the top right hand corner.[63] The paper numbers were entered with other information into various Central Authority registers (a theme to which we return below) and provided a key means of reference. The development and scope of this administrative process and archive is important in and of itself as an example of administrative power. A second form of administrative intervention, however, generates sources that can tell us something about how the poor might have understood and navigated the New Poor Law. Thus, MH12 also contains the draft responses from the Centre (confirming that at the broadest level poor writers were engaged in correspondence with officials)[64] and annotations that fed into those drafts. Some 90 per cent of incoming correspondence was annotated in this way, giving us a unique glimpse into the thought processes of those through whose hands it passed. As King has suggested for the Old Poor Law, the fact that letters were written tells us little about their reception, just as a decision made on a case reveals little about the thoughts, deliberations, emotions, and agonies of the person making that decision. It is only when we find contemporaneous annotations to the text that we get some insight into how a letter was understood.

This is not to say that every annotation gives us the sort of detail we would wish. As with the Old Poor Law there was a spectrum of responses.[65] At its most basic we may find a note to "Put by," indicating that a response was not required or should be held off unless further papers were received. More frequently there are detailed though still short annotations, often using stock phrases suggesting that a standard response should be given. Even these short annotations can give us an insight into how the Centre viewed the letter. They show what material was considered important and reveal the limits of the Centre's ability to respond. Chapter 4 takes this matter further, arguing that stock responses were often created as a result of the legal parameters within which the Centre had to operate. At the other end of the spectrum, however, are detailed and complex discussions involving more than one person, each evaluating particular aspects of a case and deciding how best to respond. Usually, each annotation was initialled and dated by the person who had written it. Collectively, these additions reveal a dynamic union correspondence process resulting in deep and complex layering of data.

Moreover, such letters were not just passed between staff within the central office. There are many examples where the advice and opinion of the relevant member of the poor law inspectorate was sought before deciding how best to respond. These officials spent little time in London, travelling around their designated counties carrying out the business of the Central Authority.[66] Therefore, in order to solicit views the letter would have been sent out to them. We can often see this recorded on the correspondence itself. Whenever a letter was received at the Centre it was ink-stamped with the date. On some correspondence we see two or more stamps with different dates, indicating that the letter, once initially received, was sent on elsewhere and then sent back a few days later, being stamped a second time on its return. An emblematic example is that of a letter sent in 1867 by William Clarke, who lived at Bulwell (Nottinghamshire). Clarke complained that the bread he had been receiving as relief had been under-weight and that he had confronted the baker, who managed to get Clarke's relief stopped.

He now found himself in the Basford workhouse.[67] The letter was dated 30 August 1867 and first date-stamped on 2 September 1867. It was written on a small piece of paper and so (routine with many letters of this size) was glued by one of the clerks onto a backing sheet (figure 2.2). This backing sheet provided a space where annotations could be made when, as here, the initial text took up all of the space on the letter itself.[68] The first annotation was simply "H.B. Farnall," suggesting that the letter be directed to Harry Burrard Farnall, the inspector responsible for the Midlands district. This first annotation (dated 3 September 1867) was initialled "FF," probably Francis Fletcher, assistant secretary to the PLB. The second annotation (dated 5 September 1867) was signed by Farnall himself, directing that in the first instance a copy of Clarke's letter should be sent to the Basford guardians for their observations. The letter was then returned to the PLB and received a second date stamp when it re-entered the office on 6 September 1867. Once back with the Centre a further annotation (dated 7 September 1867) was initialled by Fletcher, directing that the letter be acknowledged and attention promised with a copy to be sent to the guardians for their observations.

A second example, from the aged inmates of Barnsley workhouse (Yorkshire), complained that old people were not getting their food rations. Unusually, this letter (dated 2 November 1854) was addressed to Farnall himself and annotated by him on 3 November 1854. Farnall stated that he had received the letter and suggested that, with the PLB's agreement, he would "make the necessary enquiry." When received by the Board the first time, the letter was date-stamped 4 November 1854 and attached to a backing sheet on which subsequent annotations were written. The first was to annex the prescribed weekly diet sheet, and the second (6 November 1854) was to "Return to Mr Farnall To make the suggd Enquiry."[69] The letter with its annotated backing sheet was thus sent out again to Farnall, generating a second date stamp of 18 November 1854. The correspondence following this letter in the volume was the report of the inquiry conducted by Farnall. This report was dated 17 November and also date-stamped 18 November, indicating that on this date the initial letter was returned to the PLB along with the report. Thus, while MH12 is now an archive fixed in time and space, its records were – and were meant to be – an organic, dynamic, and fluid tool, part of the developing information state. Correspondence travelled

SEP 2
1867.

[Willi]am Clarke a parish[ioner] of Bulwell in Basford Union Notts aged 66, Coal miner and harvest man Has for several years suffered in consequence [of] apoplectic attacks, on this acc[ount] he has been obliged to become chargeable but has been able to follow the business of repairing rush bottomed chairs at Clay Cro[ss] in the Union of Chesterfield. Cla[y] Cross is more populous and a busier place than Bulwell offering greater facilities of employment. Also he has a daugh[ter] living there who is kind and considerate towards him making Clay Cross a much preferable pla[ce] of residence than Bulwell or its vicinity. He has receive[d] weekly

In the first instance a Copy of this should go to the Guardns of the Basford Union for their observations.
A. D. Farnall
5th Sept /67

2.2 Letter of William Clarke of Bulwell (Nottinghamshire), 1867
Source: TNA: MH12/9252/175, 34335/1867, ff. 239–40, William Clarke to the PLB, 2 September 1867.

across the country from writer to central administrator, possibly on to assistant commissioners, and back again, prompting new correspondence at every turn. This was happening at a considerable pace, often only a day passing between each layer of activity. In turn, information circulation on this scale necessarily required a complex registry and indexing system to ensure that material was filed where it was supposed to be, and resulted in numerous footprints relating to individual paupers, cases, and unions in the different archives of the New Poor Law outside MH12.

Unfortunately, the main register of incoming union correspondence and most original indexes were destroyed during the Second World War. However, we know that the Centre almost immediately after 1834 established a registry system which ran through its nineteenth- and twentieth-century paperwork. All material received was recorded in registers noting the writer, the writer's location, date of writing/receipt, summative details of the content, and details of the response, including summary contents.[70] The "paper number" of each piece of correspondence was also recorded in the respective registers, so that administrators wanting to return to earlier material or cross-reference to other record sets could use the registry system to track the original piece of correspondence. Thus, for instance, registers of paid staff in local unions were referenced via paper numbers back to the union correspondence.[71] This is important because some allegations of illegally reduced diets, ill-treatment, or neglect by paid staff within our sources resulted in local investigations by guardians or the assistant commissioners or inspectors. Where wrongdoing was uncovered and resulted in censure or staff dismissal, these details were recorded against the officer's name in the paid staff registers. Thus, George Saunders, the workhouse master at Southwell (Nottinghamshire), was reprimanded in 1898 over the death of Joseph Bramley and this reprimand was marked against him in the staff register.[72] Bramley had been brought into the workhouse against his will by the local guardian and relieving officer. The investigation initially focused on the activity of these two individuals, but it was later discovered that Saunders had been absent from the workhouse without leave and had attempted to cover this up. Tracking back from the original paper number in the paid staff register, we find a multitude of relevant records (letters, newspaper cuttings, telegrams) in the union correspondence.[73]

The registry system is important for other series that contextualize case studies found within MH12, including the correspondence between the Central Authority and its inspectorate.[74] The same would be true of indexes, but although we know that several indexes were created to reference the nineteenth-century correspondence, only one key set survives. The "Subject Indexes of Correspondence" was created from the mid- to late 1840s (but backdated to 1836), at which time the Commissioners decreed that indexes were required for both the minutes of the PLC and its own correspondence.[75] This series – essentially a thematically organised summary and reference system for correspondence that might set precedent[76] – utilised the registry system and referred back mainly to union correspondence, although there are also references to the assistant commissioners' correspondence and to the miscellaneous correspondence series. Using the paper and union number and the date of the register (which corresponds to the year of the MH12 volume), we can match the summarised correspondence to its relevant union volume and find the original letter.[77] Thus, in the register for 1856–59 under the heading "Officers: Generally: Complaints – Suspension – Resignation – Dismissal etc," we find a reference to a "Conviction of Schoolmaster for inflicting undue punishment of pauper boy." Next to this description there is a string of paper numbers written above the number 333.[78] This bottom number (333) is the union number for Tynemouth (Northumberland). If we then find the MH12 volume for Tynemouth which covers 1856 and search until we encounter the first paper number in the list (28893), then we discover a draft letter from the Centre to the clerk at Tynemouth PLU transmitting an enclosed extract of "The North & South Shield Gazette" dated 3 July 1856 regarding George Reavley, schoolmaster at the workhouse, who was convicted of assault on a boy named Michael Cain. The PLB asked for the guardians' observations on the matter. There follows in the records the newspaper cutting summarizing the case.[79]

UNDERSTANDING AND MEASURING THE SOURCES

The voices we are concerned with, then, are enmeshed in a rich structure of source strands that amplify and codify their meaning. As under the Old Poor Law, they have a *particular* place rather than a random one. In this context, we set out to identify and collect a number of core categories of data, starting with the thousands of letters written by paupers and the non-pauper poor. This distinction is an important one for our purposes. A poor person would be legally defined as a pauper only when they were in receipt of relief.[80] If we are interested in capturing *only* pauper voices then this definition seems clear enough. Yet, a core feature of our corpus is the rapidity with which the status and resultant categorisation of the poor for our purposes changed. An example of a pauper letter would be that of Thomas Oscroft, a fifty-three-year-old labourer who wrote from Arnold (Nottinghamshire) in January 1850. He explained that he had two ruptures, a tumour upon his liver, and an abscess in his neck. In addition his wife was "Trubled with the Rhumatick fever at this time." Oscroft noted that he had been in receipt of outdoor relief amounting to 2s 6d and a bread allowance per week, but that some six weeks previously his cash payment had been reduced to only 1s 6d. Having "Been at the [local] Board several times all of no use,"[81] he felt compelled to write. Much as paupers under the Old Poor Law approached prominent local figures when in desperation, so Oscroft wrote to the PLB. Margaret Wallace, by contrast, was a poor woman trying to acquire some out-relief but was not yet technically a pauper. She wrote from Durham (figure 2.3) complaining that the relieving officer had refused to pass on a letter to the local guardians and also prevented her from appearing before them to plead her case. Wallace later managed to attend a guardians' meeting "but they refuse to aid and assist me to gain an honest livelihood for my young family and self, until my husband's release from Durham Prison," which would have been some ten months later. Wallace's main objection was that the guardians refused her out-relief and "wished us to become inside *paupers*."[82]

In some cases the question of the status of the writer becomes very complex indeed. Thus, Ann McKaan wrote from Manchester (Lancashire) in late 1864 explaining that as a poor widow with a small child she had applied to the Manchester relieving officer but was only given the option of the

2.3 *Opposite* Letter of Margaret Wallace, Durham Poor Law Union, to the Poor Law Board, 7 May 1870

Source: TNA: MH12/3025, 21218/1870, Margaret Wallace, Durham, to the Poor Law Board, 7 May 1870.

21,218

111/11

97 Framwellgate Durham 7th May 1870

Gentlemen,

In my present distressed state, I feel bound to appeal to you for your kind advice and assistance, and also beg to lay before you the accompanied copy letter, copy of which I gave to Mr Thomas Gowland, relieving officer of this parish whom promised to lay the same before the "Durham Board of Guardians" and he did not only refuse to do so, but likewise prevented my appearing before them on the same day in question, after having detained me 3 hours waiting the above Guardians meeting, and after same gave me 1/- he had previous given me 6d –

I have been allowed to appear before the Board on two different occasions, but they refuse to aid and assist me to gain an honest livelihood for my young family and self until my Husbands release from Durham Prison the latter part of February next – but wished us to become inside paupers –

I have to pay 1s/10d per week for rent together with all rates –

I go out to work when I can and am earning on an average 4s/or 5s/ per week and I only pray that I may be allowed a little per week to assist us, and prevent us from hunger and starvation, I have done my utmost to exist, but have been obliged to sell and dispose of part of my husbands goods, in addition have had to pawn our Clothes –

My husband was convicted (for the first time in his life) on the 1st of March last and received 12 months sentence, and you Gentlemen will perceive the contents of the accompanied copy, an answer at your convenience will oblige

Yours very humble & Obedt

Margaret Wallace

The Poor Law Board

Whitehall (or elsewhere)

London

workhouse. When she refused, a small temporary allowance had been provided but this was later stopped and she was again given the option of the workhouse. Her letter on this occasion was an appeal for outdoor relief. So McKaan had applied as a poor person, then became a pauper on receipt of her temporary allowance, and then stopped being a pauper when that allowance was discontinued. She was latterly in a position where she remained poor but had the option of becoming a pauper.[83] These intricacies shape the way we should read, and count, the voices of poor people.

Our second type of core document is the advocate letter. Here a supporter would take up and argue the case of an individual, a specific group of poor people/paupers, or sometimes a more generic, less personal grouping such as "the poor." Advocates might be employers, landowners, politicians, officials, landlords, professional men and women, working-class organisations, neighbours, more affluent family members, or indeed paupers themselves. Thus, within the correspondence from the Bradford-on-Avon PLU (Wiltshire) we find an advocate letter written by James Butterworth on behalf of his former servant Selina Bainton. Her husband had gone to America in the previous year in the hope of "bettering his condition" and intending to send for his wife and family. He had not succeeded, however, and Selina had been forced to apply for relief for her four children. This relief had at first been granted but was now refused, with the guardians wanting instead to take her children into the workhouse. Butterworth (figure 2.4) gave an account of the woman's good character and asked if it would not be better for the guardians to continue with the outdoor relief.[84] While this particular letter is clearly summative and in the voice of Butterworth himself, other advocate letters suggest a more active involvement of paupers and poor applicants in the text and rhetoric employed, giving them a status between mediated texts and first-person letters.

The partially or fully mediated voice is continued in our third set of core documents: thousands of pauper witness statements.[85] Some were little more than brief notes collected by the local authorities or a local inhabitant and then passed to the Centre for reference or inserted into a local union document such as a minute book. Others were more formal and resulted from investigations by local officials into cases of mismanagement, mistreatment, or neglect. Copies of these locally produced witness statements

Bradford, Wilts
Sepr. 7th 1866.

To the Right Honourable
The Poor Law Commissioners.

As a parishoner and Rate payer in the parish of Bradford on Avon, Wilts, I beg to submit the following case for your consideration, on the part of Selina Bainton, formerly a Servant in our family, and who has always borne a most excellent character for honesty and industry.—

Some twelve months ago her Husband left her, in the hope of bettering his condition in America, but since being there, has been unfortunate, and has not been able to send for his Wife and family as he intended and desired.— Under the circumstances she was compelled to apply for parish allowance, and up to last week, has been receiving 1/6 a week each for her 4 Children – all under

2.4 Letter of James Butterworth to the Poor Law Board, 7 September 1866
Source: TNA: MH12/13675, 36284/1866, James Butterworth, Bradford-on-Avon, to the Poor Law Board, 7 September 1866.

were often sent to the Centre by union officials with guardians' observations on their enquiries. Even more formal statements, often sworn, were taken as part of official enquiries run by assistant commissioners and poor law inspectors, who authored reports on troubling cases, with witness examinations and a set of recommendations.[86] Figure 2.5 shows the evidence of Charlotte Guest, a Kidderminster workhouse inmate (Worcestershire) who found the young boy John Perks tied in a bag which was hung from a pair of steelyards: "I asked him who put him there – he said the Porter – with that he began to cry." Thomas Saunders, the Kidderminster PLU clerk, stated that Perks had been tied in the sack by John Stokes as "punishment for making water in his bed – The boy having a complaint over which he has no control."[87] Nor should we forget that advocates and social investigators also took sworn and unsworn statements from paupers and poor applicants and were not averse to either publishing such statements or sending them to the Centre with a demand for action.[88]

These different contexts are likely to have shaped who was willing to talk, about what and with what degree of specificity, such that one witness statement cannot be regarded as inevitably akin to another. While it is clear that acts of mediation do not nullify original voices, given that some statements were products of an official process driven by specific lines of questioning, we might expect that the poor and union staff would withhold or strip back aspects of their testimony. Others might take the fact of an inquiry as the opportunity to deal in impressions, gossip, embellishment, lies, and score-settling. The wildly different testimonies of paupers, staff, and poor writers who had been in the same place at the same time and witnessed the same event provide an important caution in this respect. These were in the end strategic documents, and writers often voiced a desire to be interviewed under oath, thus demonstrating a keen understanding both of official systems of investigation and of the value of a willingness to account for their complaints and accusations. For example, in the very first line of Mary White's complaint that her clothes were infested with vermin in the

2.5 *Opposite* Witness statement of Charlotte Guest, Kidderminster workhouse (Worcestershire), 12 September 1840
Source: TNA: MH12/14017/116, 10586/B/1840, extract from the evidence of Charlotte Guest, 7 September 1840.

1058 [illegible] Copy (148)

Borough of Kidderminster }
County of Worcester }

7th September 1840

At a Petty Sessions at the Guildhall
Present The Mayor
William Boycot Esquire

Mr Saunders Clerk to the Board of Guardians complains of John Stokes the Porter of the Union with having tied James Perks a poor Boy an Inmate of the Workhouse up in a Bag by way of punishment for making water in his bed the Boy having a complaint over which he has no control

Charlotte Guest wife of John Guest an Inmate of the Workhouse says in consequence of what I heard in the Workhouse on Friday morning about ½ past seven o'Clock I went into a room called the Tool house which adjoins the Entrance Hall of the Workhouse the Door was open I went in I saw a Bag apparently with some thing in it hanging up on a pair of Steelyards the bottom of the bag being about a yard from the ground - I said "Perks" and the little boy answered - I asked him who put him there he said the Porter - with that he began to cry - I observed that the bag was tied up at its mouth close down upon his head it was a dirty Potatoe Bag and it was tied so low that there was not room for the Boy to stand upright I went to Mr Stevens he was in the Kitchen I told him about it. I said do you know where the Boy Perks is - and I told him where he was and the Governor went towards the place - the Porter was in his Lodge near the Hall -

Wandsworth and Clapham (Surrey) workhouse, we learn that: "[T]he writer of this letter is willing to come forward *to swear* to the disgusting conditions [of] the clothing in the Wandsworth and Clapham Union."[89] Timothy Peirce's letter of varied complaints about the Clutton PLU porter also stated that the offences he enumerated "can be sworn to, if required."[90] J. Moses, who wrote from the Newport workhouse (Monmouthshire) concerning the bullying tendencies of Mr Flint, one of the union officers who had oppressed the elderly inmates for many years, asked for a formal inquiry as "they [the inmates] will be afraid to tell the truth unless they be sworn."[91] The poor knew very well that an inquiry was a place for strategic agency beyond the letters they sent to the Centre. This complex backdrop to all witness statements (staff, paupers, and advocates) means that we must use the source with care.

In these contexts, at least, giving evidence was an individual action. Sometimes, however, we are also able to hear the collective voice, and our fourth core document set in MH12 comprises multi-signature petitions. These include texts from advocates, paupers, and other poor people, and of course collections of all these different categories. Some multi-signature documents have large numbers of names. For example, about 150 people petitioned from Kirkby Malzeard in 1851 against the establishment of the Ripon PLU.[92] Others were signed by fewer people. Figure 2.6, for instance, is a petition from Thomas Hartley, William Thornhill, James Hardiman, and Samuel Smith, all inmates of the Kidderminster workhouse and all in their seventies. They set out a series of grievances concerning the state or availability of food, beer, and tobacco, and also complained that the chaplain neglected his duty and many of the sick died without seeing a minister.[93] The latter accusation (especially when set against the punitive provisions of the 1832 Anatomy Act) would have had controversial resonance, a fact the petitioners would have been aware of.[94] In such circumstances some withheld their names. Thus, in July 1869 workhouse inmates at Poplar (Middlesex) wrote to complain about a new dietary. It was claimed that the stew was "almost literally ... potato broth," the potatoes themselves were "so bad that 1/3rd of them are useless," and that the whole dietary was "insufficient both in quality and quantity." The complaint was anonymously signed: "The Voice of The Inmates of Poplar Union Workhouse."[95] Such petitions should not surprise us. In the wider communities from which paupers and poor applicants were drawn, petitioning culture grew exponentially in the nineteenth century, both as a form of process and as a mechanism for impelling government action. The wording, structure, purpose, and rhetoric of petitionary culture should have been a portable currency, and we return to this matter in chapter 5.[96]

The final set of core documents is newspaper cuttings, which appear interleaved with the correspondence for several reasons. Sometimes they were enclosed by union clerks (or another administrator such as a magistrate's clerk or coroner) as a way of reducing verbatim transcript or summary. This could be the proceedings of a guardians' meeting as written out in full by a reporter, or it might be the proceedings of an investigation, in which case we sometimes find witness statements written up in the newspaper report itself. Less common but still present in the archive are occasions when a pauper, advocate, or poor applicant chose to share their grievance directly with a newspaper in order to reach maximum audience. We see all these aspects in the case of a newspaper clipping sent in from the Cardiff union (Glamorgan; figure 2.7). In June 1847 Richard Lewis Reece, coroner, wrote to the PLB concerning the death of William Smith. Rather than write out the whole case Reece sent in a piece reported in the *Cardiff and Merthyr Guardian*, entitled "DEATH ACCELERATED BY ILL-USAGE." The author of the article was himself writing as an advocate for the poor man, seeking a full inquiry into the conduct of union officers. It is a lengthy piece giving much background to Smith's working life. Also reproduced in the newspaper were numerous detailed witness statements which concentrated on the alleged failure to provide appropriate poor relief and medical attention resulting in the untimely death of Smith.[97] Social investigators also wrote to newspapers and then sent in clippings with accompanying letters to contest local practice directly with the Centre.[98] In their turn, poor applicants, paupers, and witnesses sometimes quoted newspaper reportage in their own

2.6 *Following pages* Letter of Thomas Hartley, William Thornhill, James Hardiman, and Samuel Smith, to the Poor Law Board, 27 December 1864
Source: TNA: MH12/14023/221, 49842/1864, ff. 305–6, Thomas Hartley, William Thornhill, James Hardiman, and Samuel Smith, to the Poor Law Board, 27 December 1864.

To Her Majestys Poor Law Commissioners

Kidderminster Union Decr 27th 1864

530
9
49842
63

Whee they Undermentioned men belong=ing to the above mentioned Union wish our complaints and grivevances to be Redressd, which is as follows

Thomas Hartley	age 77 years		the Marks of the above mentioned
William Thornhill	75		+ + + +
James Hardiman	78		
Samuel Smith	73		

1st The Cheese some time ago was found fau[lt] with, the gardians were said to have tasted it and said it was very good now was it of the same quallity as wee receiv'd wee kow not, However it was Skim milk Cheese wee receivd. wee do not expect to have the best Cheese, but wee expect to have the 2d best as that was nothing but skim milk Cheese, and as our chief support is bread something is requird norishing with that bread, 2d Case. Itbeing a law that all men in Union upwar[ds] of 60 years of age should receive the following indulgences, Half a Pint [of beer] pe[r] day. half an ounce of Tobbacco per Wee[k] five ounces of butter per Week, Now Not half the people as are intitled to this get it. this causes Disputes among the inmates to Whitings such parshallity, in other Unions they get their rights without any trouble –

3d – Claws. To wee complain against our Chaplain of not doing his Duty in this Union, as many sick persons come in this place never see a minnester from the time the come in untill the time they are carried out dead, and some of the sick appartments he has scarcely ever or never enterd, Now the roman Chatholick priests visset their sick with care and great attention but the church of England is Neglected Now to make it more plain, when he first came here he preached twice on a Sunday once on a Thursday in the Week, and attend the sick regular, on his Salu=ary being reducd, He reduced his Spiritual dutys except Christmass days and good fridays, now he comes once on Sundays only about one Hour a Half. the governor does more duty than he does, he reading prayers Night and morning, he preaches the gospel when he does come, and lays down good precepts, Never the less examples are before precepts

THE CARDIFF AND MERTHYR GUARDIAN.

D[illegible]H ACCELERATED BY ILL-USAGE.

On S[illegible] forenoon an inquest was held at the Railway Hotel, [illegible] before R. L. Reece, Esq., coroner, on view of the remains of a poor Englishman named William Smith, who died suddenly the day previous under circumstances calculated to induce an opinion that his death had been accelerated by the harsh and cruel conduct of certain parties at Newbridge. As the case has excited considerable interest, we give a full report of the evidence taken.

Barbara Smith (wife of deceased) sworn:—My husband was about 42 years of age—was a collier by trade, but had lost the use of his arms by an explosion in a coal-pit. I have been married to him about twelve years: he had met with the accident before I married him. I am a Scotchwoman. Ever since we married we have got our living by going from one county to another selling things—such as stay laces and other trifling things. We never had a single half-penny of parish relief till this year. We have been in Glamorganshire about two months. We went down as far as Llanelly, in Carmarthenshire, and then returned through Swansea, Neath, Aberdare, and from Aberdare to Newbridge. We arrived at Newbridge a fortnight last Thursday [i.e., May 20th]. We were there a week before I applied to any one, and then I applied to Superintendent Thomas for advice: he told me to get a doctor directly, and if he would not come, he (Mr. Thomas) would give me a paper. My husband had been ill, and had got worse. He was formerly a very healthy man—strong constitution—and could eat any sort of food. He complained of a pain in the kidneys. About two days before he arrived at Newbridge he had weakness in his legs; previous to which time he was a very strong, healthy man.

Jones, overseer of the parish, who would go with m[e] Davies [so we understood witness]; but he (the over[seer]) not go with me—he gave me a note. I gave the no[te] Davies, and he then gave me an order directly to tak[e] relieving-officer.

At this stage of the proceedings Mr. Evan Davies, [illegible] John, relieving-officer of Cardiff, entered the room, [illegible] followed soon afterwards by Mr. Paine, surgeon.

Witness proceeded: I took that note to the relieving [illegible] having to walk eight miles there and eight miles back. [illegible] him at home this time when I got there.

The Coroner: "This time." What do you mean b[y] time?" Had you ever been there before?

[illegible]: I had been there before without an order [illegible] Davies; and his wife told me it was of no use to [illegible] without an order from the surgeon. [illegible] think this was [illegible] week, because it was on Monday last I went the second [illegible]

The Coroner: Why did you not tell us of this before [illegible] you have been giving a detailed account of the whole [illegible] and have omitted a most important circumstance. You [illegible] more careful.

Witness: Excuse me Sir, I am in such trouble.

The Coroner: Yes: but do try and recollect yourse[lf] [illegible] is a most important enquiry. It is very strange that [illegible] not tell us before that you had made a fruitless journ[ey] [illegible] relieving-officer's residence.

Witness proceeded: I found the relieving-officer a[illegible] It was an open note I had with the surgeon. I read th[illegible] part of it, but could not read the writing. I gave the r[elieving] officer the note. It was at Llantrissent I saw him.

2.7 Newspaper cutting enclosed in letter from Richard Lewis Reece, Coroner, Cardiff, to the Poor Law Commission, 12 June 1847

Source: TNA: MH12/16248/43 and 44, 12614/B/1847, ff. 53–5, newspaper cutting from the *Cardiff and Merthyr Guardian* concerning the death of William Smith, 12 June 1847.

words or otherwise intimated that they were aware of the public circulation of such information. While the so-called democratisation of literacy makes this sort of engagement more plausible, such material points to something further: the poor and their advocates were well aware of the power of public opinion and were actively engaged in trying to use and shape it, a strategy that we take up in our fifth chapter.[99]

We have discussed the nominal problems with using this suite of material in the Preface. One key question still remains for the current chapter: how should we "measure" the scale, complexity, and depth of the pauper voice as it appeared in the corridors and offices of the Central Authority and other fora such as guardians' meeting rooms? This is no simple task and raises three issues: the scale and depth of our sample; how that sample maps onto the wider archive; and consideration of the ways in which the voices of poor

Table 2.1
Core document set

Paupers	Letters and petitions	1,409
	Witness statements	1,443
Poor Persons	Letters and petitions	628
	Witness statements	925
Advocates	Letters and petitions	1,699
Total	All	6,104

Source: MH12. Local Government Board and Predecessors: Correspondence with Poor Law Unions and Other Local Authorities, The National Archives.

people and their advocates might have been amplified beyond the text on the page. Initially, then, table 2.1 outlines the dataset which emerges from the collection exercise outlined above. The whole core corpus consists of just over six thousand items, to which we have then added for specific purposes replies from the Central or local authorities to poor writers, and other documents or document copies contained within the correspondence that did not fall neatly into any of our core categories. These include: settlement documents, pamphlets, interview memoranda, declarations, and copies of guardians' minutes.

Table 2.2 shows the gender distribution of authorship in the core sample. We could conclusively determine gender for 3,521 letters and petitions, including thirty-seven co-authored by male *and* female writers, mostly elderly couples seeking out-relief and wanting to avoid the workhouse. Some 2,953 (84%) were sent by men and only 531 (15%) by women, almost certainly a reflection of the convention that men wrote for families throughout our period.[100] When we turn to the 2,368 witness statements from paupers and the wider poor, this stark imbalance is somewhat reversed. Removing three statements jointly produced by men and women and two cases where we were unable to assign gender, we find that some 1,481 (62.7%) were produced by women. This pattern is important and potentially signals that men and women negotiated and confronted power and authority under the poor law in very different ways. In chapter 7 we return to this theme.

Table 2.2
Gender distribution of authorship in the core sample

	Female and male	Female	Male	Unidentified	Total
Advocate letter	4	84	1,450	131	1,669
Advocate petition	2	0	28	0	30
Pauper letter	17	288	1,002	64	1,371
Pauper petition	3	3	27	5	38
Poor person's letter	9	144	439	14	606
Poor person's petition	2	12	7	1	22
(Letters and petitions subtotal)	37	531	2,953	215	3,736
Witness statement (pauper)	1	845	596	1	1,443
Witness statement (poor person)	2	636	286	1	925
(Witness statements subtotal)					2,368
Grand total	40	2,012	3,835	217	6,104

Source: MH12. Local Government Board and Predecessors: Correspondence with Poor Law Unions and Other Local Authorities, The National Archives.

Other features of the core dataset are also important for subsequent chapters. Figure 2.8 is based upon the dates at which letters or statements were sent to the Centre. It takes our total sample, removes the 103 pieces for which no month was recorded, and apportions the documents evenly across all twelve months, generating an expected distribution on the assumption that there is no seasonal bias in the sample. This is then converted to a base index figure of 100, and the line "monthly index" calculates how much above or below (in percentage terms) the actual monthly distribution of texts stands. We can see that with the exception of a blip in May, a disproportionate number of our texts were sent in the harshest winter months, clearly pointing to compromised family economies, illness or death, and increased winter workhouse residence as tipping points for our writers. King has

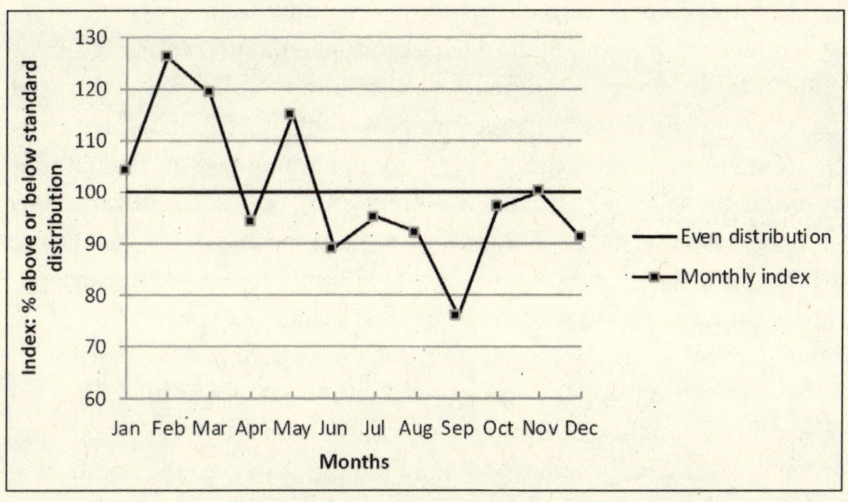

2.8 Seasonality in the core sources
Source: MH12. Local Government Board and Predecessors: Correspondence with Poor Law Unions and Other Local Authorities, The National Archives.

traced a very similar seasonal patterning to Old Poor Law letters.[101] Broadly the same seasonal distribution can be found amongst advocate letters, as we might have expected, given the likely inter-correlation of pauper and advocate writing. Less obviously, there was also a winter focus to the subsample of witness statements, suggesting that seasonal stress influenced the entire operation of the poor law in the nineteenth century. While determining whether someone was an indoor or outdoor pauper or writer is sometimes difficult, some 36 per cent of our core letters and petitions (excluding advocate letters) were written from inside the workhouse.

Understanding the significance of these bare figures is not a simple matter. On one level, we can contrast them to the number of paupers actually relieved under the Victorian Poor Law.[102] Yet the kinds of local records best suited to this purpose survive patchily. In turn, the collection of data by the Centre was relatively limited, given its national scope and remit, with pauper numbers only routinely gathered for 1 January and 1 July of each year.[103] Yet, the Centre required a mass of supplementary data, such that by the 1840s local authorities were required to collate and tabulate regular (as well as more *ad hoc*) returns. These were then published as part of the Centre's annual reports, and figure 2.9 uses this material to give a broad sense of the numbers in receipt of relief as a backdrop to our measurement of the voices of the poor.[104] Pauperism peaked during the 1840s, regularly reaching above 1.5 million people per annum. The numbers fell dramatically from the late 1840s, although this decrease may have been influenced by changes in data collection. Other peaks came in the mid-1860s and the late 1860s to early 1870s. These figures do not, of course, represent initial applications for relief and we should be clear that a significant proportion of the letters, petitions, and statements from and by the poor and their advocates in our corpus were appeals against relief refusals as well as offers of relief rejected by the applicant. In other words, the underbelly of dependency was probably significantly higher and more intense than even the numbers in figure 2.9 allow.

Set against this backdrop, our millions of words of evidence constitute a small subset of potential poor voices. On the other hand, a casual mapping of table 2.1 onto figure 2.9 is highly misleading. King, in his national survey of Old Poor Law letters, remarks that although the poor wrote in large numbers we cannot know in any real sense the number of letters originally sent, and thus cannot ascertain the representativeness of what survives.[105] As we saw above, however, for the post-1834 period, correspondence by, about, or for the poor and sent to the Centre was treated on a par with official letters and ultimately bound into the relevant union volumes. This means that we *can* logically jump from our data to a rough estimate of the overall presence of our core document types in the *whole* archive, assuming that the yield patterns and dimensions for our sample unions are replicated across all unions for which records survive. Figure 2.10 conducts this exercise for the period 1834 to 1896, with the latter cut-off date reflecting the onset of substantial losses to the MH12 series as a whole. Figure 2.11 amalgamates our different categories. These two graphs offer a tantalising window into the pauper voice. The inter-correlation of advocate and poor voices is more or less seamless until the 1890s, whereas witness statements (and thus the underlying inquiries) have a distinctive chronology of their own, with notable peaks in the first decades of the New Poor Law and then again as the crusade against outdoor relief was in full swing.

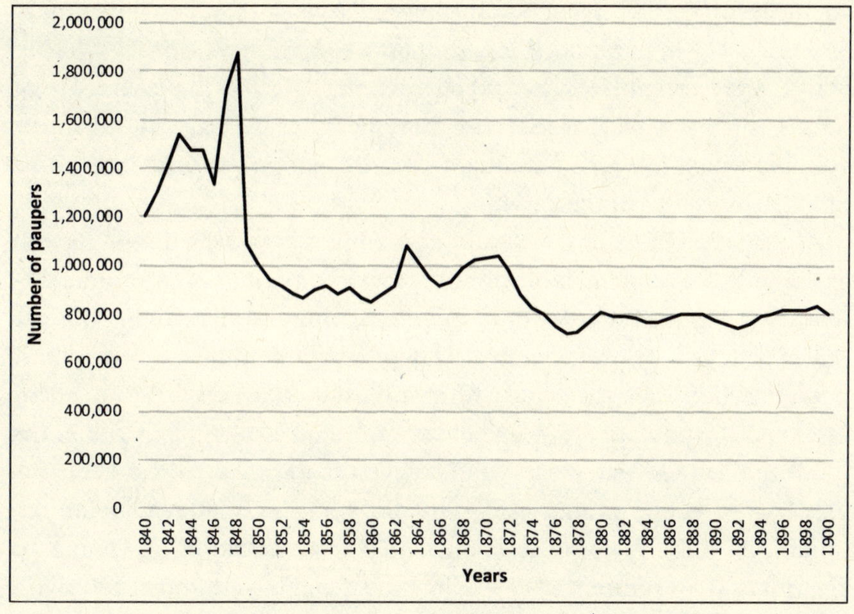

2.9 Relief numbers in England and Wales, 1840–1900

Figure 2.11 to some extent masks as much as it reveals in terms of the amalgamation of different chronologies. In particular it encourages us to see a link between "writing" broadly defined and the economic circumstances of the hungry forties, when in fact the spike of inquiries and witness statements at this time seems to represent the initial crystallisation of long-term opposition to the deterrent workhouse principle.[106] Nonetheless, the graph is revealing. Thus, the causative links between writing and broad exogenous events that we expected to find are sometimes absent, superficial, or contradictory. Moments of Chartist activity in the early part of figure 2.11 feed neither into the writing of the poor in a quantitative sense nor (as we shall see in chapter 5) into the linguistic registers employed. On the other hand, the upsurge in writing in the 1890s certainly reflects an intensification of overt political and trade union advocacy (to which we return in chapter 3). The cotton famine generated regional spikes in writing (most obviously about the denial of outdoor relief) but it had a minimal effect on the national sample.[107] By contrast, depression in the 1880s does seem to have had an impact on the writing of poor people and advocates and on the number of witness statements, albeit less so than we might have expected. There may to some extent have been a counteracting effect in the emergence of policies such as the Cottage Home movement or new waves of infirmary building which removed potential writers (children; the sick) from some of the prior causes of their writing.

As with the Old Poor Law, peaks and troughs in writing do not map in any seamless or inevitable way onto recognised periods of economic distress.[108] Nor is the causative link between writing and changes in poor law policy or organisation inevitable. The initial years of the crusade against outdoor relief clearly coincide with increased writing on the part of advocates and the poor, and the lag between this and a subsequent rise in the number of witness statements would suggest causation. On the other hand, very few of our 102 unions were "crusading," and a careful reading of material from these years suggests no change in tone, causes of writing, or rhetorical architecture. Other waymarkers for the New Poor Law have a problematic place. The able-bodied poor, as we shall see, wrote to contest attempts in the early 1840s to prohibit or make onerous the receipt of outdoor relief, but not in such numbers as to shape the chronologies shown in figures 2.10 and 2.11. Union chargeability and progressive attempts to phase out notions of settlement barely register in the sample, and in general any relationship between changes in guidance or policy and writing by those who might have had a sense of accepted practice or prior entitlement is weak and inconsistent. Momentary, situational, or accumulated everyday experiences, rather than broad policy sweeps, tended above all to generate writing to the Centre and to shape its content, length, and tone.

Overall, the key message is that, even if we strip out witness statements, some four to five hundred letters/petitions by or for paupers and poor writers would usually reach the corridors of the Central Authority annually, and in some years this number would be higher. If we add in witness statements, it is clear that the Centre would have heard an insistent pauper voice. This is not, however, the end of the story.

2.10 *Opposite* The hypothecated pauper voice: Advocate, pauper, and poor persons' letters and petitions; and pauper and poor persons' witness statements, 1834–1896

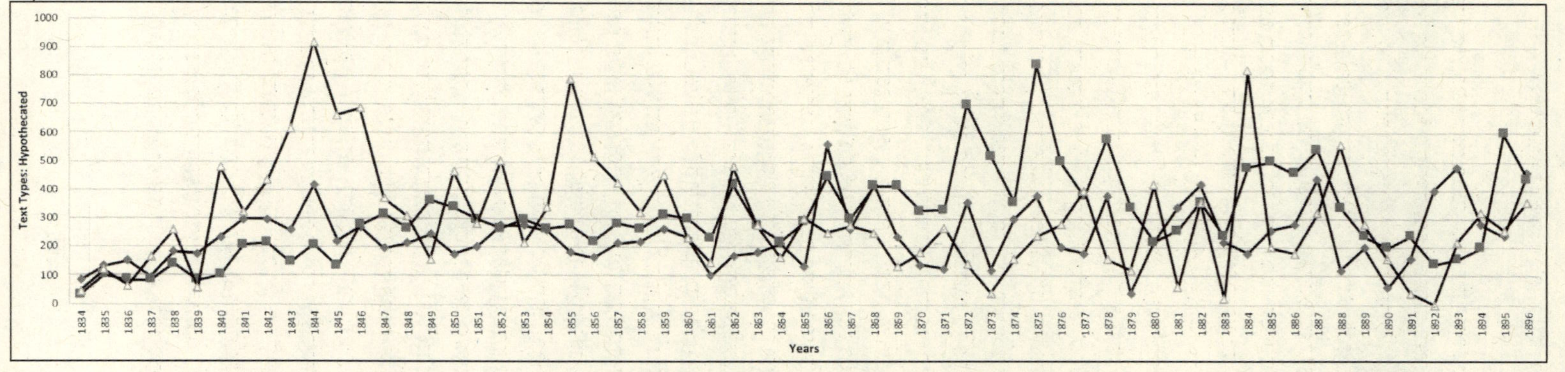
Text Types: Hypothecated
1000
900
800
700
600
500
400
300
200
100
0
1834 1835 1836 1837 1838 1839 1840 1841 1842 1843 1844 1845 1846 1847 1848 1849 1850 1851 1852 1853 1854 1855 1856 1857 1858 1859 1860 1861 1862 1863 1864 1865 1866 1867 1868 1869 1870 1871 1872 1873 1874 1875 1876 1877 1878 1879 1880 1881 1882 1883 1884 1885 1886 1887 1888 1889 1890 1891 1892 1893 1894 1895 1896
Years
Advocate letters and petitions enhancement
Pauper and poor persons letter and petitions enhancement
Witness statement (paupers and poor persons) enhancement

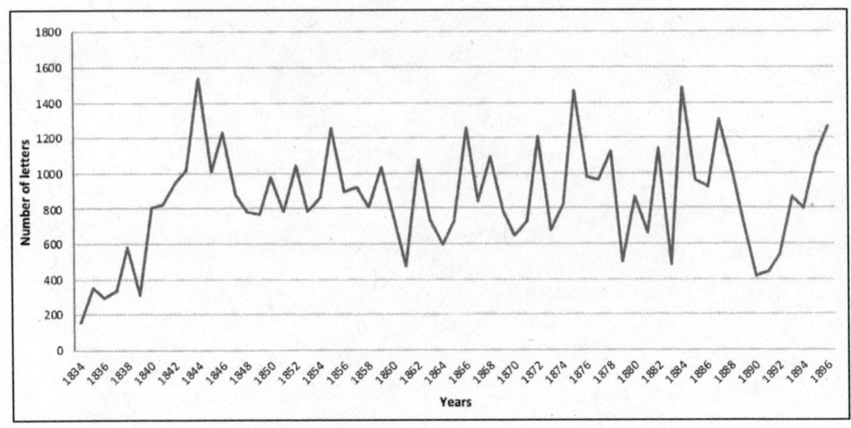

2.11 The hypothecated pauper voice in total

MORE THAN NUMBERS?

In practice, "measuring" the pauper voice means more than just adding up the number of letters, petitions, and witness statements. Some texts were akin to short notes, a little either side of a hundred words, such as that of George Humm of Bethnal Green. He wrote his "few lines" in March 1850 to ask whether the guardians could compel his family to enter the workhouse after applying for relief during his wife's confinement.[109] Jane Maylor, on the other hand, wrote a single detailed letter of varied complaints from Liverpool in 1874 which consisted of 5,074 words covering thirty-six pages.[110] Some pauper voices thus notionally have enhanced significance. Other material refuses to be straightforwardly categorised let alone easily counted. When Henry Jones, late of the Pwllheli workhouse (Caernarvonshire) wrote to the PLB in May 1868, he complained of the diet, bedding, and infestations of vermin. In addition to writing as a pauper, however, he complained as an advocate on behalf of a number of named others. Incorporated into his letter, not as attachments but running as if part of a single text, were two additional letters or notes. These were signed with a cross as their "Mark" by Evan Williams and Owen Owens. Thus this single piece of correspondence could be described in turn as a pauper letter, an advocate letter, and a covering letter for two pauper witness statements, and it has multiple voices of differing intensity.[111]

More widely, "distance" between the voice, issue, and writer adds further layers of complexity to measurement. Some authors, for instance, complained not of their current poverty, but of the impact of local decisions on their *future* welfare. Charles Linnet of Little Wattham (Essex) wrote to the Local Government Board (LGB) in 1884. His father was a pauper and received 2 shillings in money and a loaf of bread weekly but Charles was now asked to pay for both. He asserted that as an only son approaching sixty years of age his "earnings now as a Thatcher is very precarious and I feel quite unable now to support my own and pay 2/– per week to the Parish for my Father." Linnet wrote in small part as an advocate for his father, but in larger part to contest the decisions made, given that he was struggling to make ends meet; *and* he wrote as a future pauper if the costs of welfare were to be transferred to him.[112] Questions of distance become even more focused in the multi-signatory and collective *pauper* petitions outlined earlier in the chapter. In our corpus these count as single documents and were often written in a single hand. Yet most had many names or signatures appended, and so the question as to how the voices captured in such records should be measured is problematic. Their preparation might have been the work of one discontented pauper, with others co-opted into having their names added, *or* an opportunity for a body of people to share their discontent and to convey a collective notion of right, anger, or despair to welfare authorities. In terms of both the meaning of the pauper voice and its scale, the two approaches signify very different things. Sometimes the actual number of petitioners was not specified, as for instance in the case of the "truth Loving test men of Bradford Union," who complained in late 1854 of being put to spade work at a time the weather was so cold that the ground was frozen and could not be dug.[113] This text was collectively conceived but written by a single author and defies easy quantitative analysis.

We also see complexity in the "wider poor" subset of our corpus. Thus, when Thomas Claisse wrote to the PLC in 1842, he complained that stone-breaking being allocated to silk weavers, whose hands were made rough by the task, ensured they would be unable to handle silk in the future, thus closing off future employment. Claisse wrote as someone intimately connected to the trade and those who worked in it, but he was also writing on behalf of a larger constituency:

> Directed by a general and very numerous meeting of Operative Broad Silk Weavers of Bethnal Green Spitalfields and its vicinity to forward to you the following [res]olution unanimously passed after having [been] dispassionately discussed and the [injurious] effects of stone breaking (on those engaged in the Silk Trade) several of whom have been injured by pieces of stone —— their eyes, and the hands of all those [who] have been therein engaged are so roughed as to incapacitate them from handling silk if there was an opertunity for them to obtain [em]ployment.

Such work being deemed particularly cruel to those who worked at the silk trade, Claisse asked "that you will order an immediate exemption of all Silk Weavers [fr]om the same, in all the workhouses of [the] district."[114] How big "very numerous" was remains uncertain but clearly a single letter and signatory could represent a wider group of the poor. Another example suggesting the background involvement of large numbers can be seen in a letter of April 1894 in which Mr Champion, secretary to the Battersea Local Election Committee (Surrey), wrote asking whether the guardians were acting outside their powers by instructing the relieving officer for Battersea and Clapham PLU to cooperate with the Charity Organisation Society for determining who should receive outdoor relief. Champion wrote that this arrangement had been condemned by a large (but uncounted) meeting of local workmen.[115] What we encounter in our sample and the wider hypothecated numbers for all of MH12 are thus the very minimal dimensions of the pauper voice.

Similar observations extend to advocate voices and, although we take up the question of advocacy at length in the following chapter, some discussion of its quantitative nuances is also required here. Superficially, advocate letters were exclusively the (usually single) voice of those willing to put in the time and effort to speak out on behalf of the poor variously defined. Their writers included employers such as Fred Holmes at Wandsworth, who wrote to the PLC in March 1841 calling attention to William Lambert, "aged 64 years (who had been in my employ sometime) [and] is worn out." Holmes claimed that he had "caused him [Lambert] to discontinue work & ... supported him since Saturday week." Holmes had met with the relieving officer on Lambert's behalf but to no avail and it was his dissatisfaction with the local poor law officers that prompted the letter.[116] Magistrates who similarly disagreed with local practice might also take up their pen to write to the Central Authority. Henry Muller, magistrate for Aldeburgh (Suffolk), for example, wrote in May 1842 of an unnecessary imposition on local paupers: the relieving officer had directed that on the death of a pauper, another pauper was to inform him at his house and if he were absent the informant was to wait. On the officer's return the pauper would then be sent with a message to the contractor for coffins, before returning to Aldeburgh. How, asked Muller, could such a journey of twenty miles be "performed on foot by an aged, infirm man, or even an able bodied woman in all weathers and more particularly in winter?"[117] In such cases the advocate voices are clear and powerful. Yet we can speculate that Holmes had spoken to Lambert, and Muller to some aged, infirm, or female paupers, before writing. Such conversations appear likely, given that Holmes was Lambert's employer and that Muller in his role of magistrate would have had many dealings with the local poor at Aldeburgh. In some advocate letters we hear explicitly of these conversations. Thus, Edward Coke wrote to the LGB in December 1874 to complain that Harriet Nightingale, whose husband was "Lying prostrate with sickness, without food [or] money," had to pawn her underwear to secure a medical relief form signed by one of the relieving officers. Coke specifically noted that he spoke from first-hand experience:

> I visited the case myself & saw the husband in bed, the room full of children, the woman with twins in her arms & as they played about in opposite directions "it's almost as much as I can do, Sir" she distractedly exclaimed "to manage these twinnies" if it had not been so sad, it would have been ridiculous.[118]

In such instances we can count the advocate voice, but it is less certain how we can quantify the pauper and poor voices that sit in the background.

What is also clear from our data, however, is that the power and reach of those voices was systematically subject to amplification. Perhaps the most significant elements in this process were the nineteenth-century newspapers. The relationships between poor writers and the different spheres of "the public" require a study in their own right. Nevertheless, the particular place of newspapers in making sure that poor and advocate voices were heard and comprehended, and that they gained traction in seats of local and national power requires elaboration, given the frequency (see above) with which we encounter articles in the corpus. Thus, we see pasted into the PLU correspondence for Bradfield two letters and a note published in *The Times*, all referring to William Weller of Whitworth (Oxfordshire). The first was from "a poor woman" who stated that Weller was between sixty and seventy years of age and had been confined to his house for five weeks with a bad leg. The medical officer attended him (without an order) and provided a note which his wife was to take to the relieving officer, ordering better and more nourishing food. When the case was heard before the local guardians, relief was refused except as a loan. The details of this case were appended to an anonymous published letter from "A Parishioner," who stated that an initial complainant had approached him as a magistrate in the hope of securing redress. He claimed to know Weller and his family, adding that he had "always been industrious and hard-working," and argued that such cases were common "in this notorious union." The writer further confided: "as I know that I should be outvoted at the board if I went there, I prefer sending the case to you, in the hope that it may find a place among Poor Law misdoings." Henry Parker, poor law inspector, annotated the letter and note to the effect that he knew nothing of the case and further that, "In the present temper of the Bradfield B[oard] I do not think it would be advisable to request the Boards observations upon the statements."[119] This situation changed immediately when a letter concerning Weller was again published in *The Times* the following month, referring to the earlier letter as one which the present writer (Henry Philip Powys of Hardwick) had authored. The new letter confirmed that, "The poor man still continues to work [when he can] and has been denied any relief, although the medical man gave him a note stating that more nourishing food was absolutely necessary." It continued that the reason for refusing relief was that Weller had two single sons who should maintain him but: "[it] would not be difficult to prove that if they had the inclination, they have not the means of doing so." Powys thus argued, provocatively given developing criticism of the New Poor Law in the mid-1840s, that:

> according to the law of the Bradfield union, a man with two sons, who cannot or will not support their parent, may … be legally starved; and, hard as this seems, I know of no means of redress, unless you, Sir, or the Poor law Commissioners, will try what public opinion or the authority of Somerset-house may do for him.

On this occasion the annotations at the Centre were less relaxed and it was decided immediately that the PLC should "Call attention to this letter & request [the guardians'] observation."[120] The original voice of the poor person was amplified by that of an advocate and a national newspaper.

In this sense it is perhaps not surprising that a threat by paupers and poor writers that their letters might be or had been published is a fixture in the corpus. In June 1895, for instance, Mark Noble, an inmate of the imbecile ward at the Bradford workhouse, wrote to complain that he was being held against his will. He had entered the house voluntarily, having experienced fits and convulsions, but he now wished to leave. Noble claimed to have been recently examined by the Commission in Lunacy, who pronounced him cured, but that the local officers told him this had been said in jest and kept him incarcerated. Rather than hinting that the letter might be published, Noble stated directly that he had "sent a copy of this to the Bradford Observer for Publication hoping you will take this case into consideration as there is other Patients beside myself."[121] Under what terms the letter had arrived at the *Bradford Observer* is unclear, but in other cases we can see that poor authors seeking an extended audience sought to flatter editors. In 1876 an anonymous pauper inmate had a letter printed by the *Daily Courier* newspaper in a column titled "The Management of the Liverpool Workhouse." The writer had gone to great trouble to be allowed "through the medium of your valued and outspoken print" to provide a narrative of the "painful case of sudden death" of "C _____ D_____," a workhouse inmate who had been admitted in a "weak and delicate state of health." Notwithstanding such ill-health it was a full week before C.D. was visited by a medical officer, and even then he was transferred to a "healthy division of the house." The next day C.D. was taken to one of the workshops for an exchange of clothing and it was here that he "suddenly sat down, and expired in a few minutes." The author considered such cases a frequent occurrence that cumulatively necessitated an official inquiry, but rested the case for the moment: "I leave this to tell its own tale, desiring only to raise my voice in the cause of poor, stricken humanity."[122]

Not all cases were so straightforward. In January 1863 a letter from Thomas Smith of Barnsley appeared in the *Leeds Mercury* complaining of the neglect suffered by Olive Cooper, "whose death from neglect of Mr. Atkinson, the relieving officer, is clear." The writer wished to "respectfully call your attention to that cruel case, and the extreme hardship and severity of a well paid officer."[123] Smith's letter of complaint was at the centre of a pointedly critical piece on the case. Cooper had been heavily pregnant when she had been refused a place in the workhouse, and she died following labour. The inquest found Atkinson "slightly" to blame for her death; however, the guardians exonerated him and passed a vote of confidence. This exoneration had prompted others in the town to demand an inquiry and indeed it was an anonymous published letter which initiated the PLB inquiry into the case, led by the poor law inspector John Manwaring. The local guardians objected to the inquiry, with the chairman stating that: "The Board-room belonged to the Union, and he did not see why such an inquiry should take place there against those who were the legal holders of it." Manwaring retorted that, if they wished, the investigation would be held elsewhere but that he had "a simple duty to perform." Smith's letter noted that in the run-up to the inquiry:

> Private meetings have been held, and I write for fifty or more, and I can say respectfully, but firmly, that the ratepayers, rich and poor, high or low, are highly indignant that the parochial officer are allowed to continue so.[124]

The latter comments highlight again the complex ways in which poor and advocate voices might be rather larger than they first appear. But there was a further twist: the Thomas Smith to whom the letter was attributed wrote later to disclaim authorship. Even so, the published criticisms of an unidentified someone were paraded in front of the *Leeds Mercury* readership and other provincial newspapers which later took up the story. Voices could easily gain wide amplification.[125]

Published letters were likely to attract immediate readership. As we saw above, however, the poor and their advocates also sought to emphasise and enhance the traction of their voices by sending newspaper cuttings to the Centre. An example is the correspondence of Arthur Firth, who wrote in April 1883 concerning the case of Charles Wilkinson, a resident of the Barnsley workhouse who had died shortly after being admitted. Firth cautioned against leaving the matter to be investigated locally, since the chairman of the union had previously (as a magistrate) committed Wilkinson to prison; he therefore asked for an independent inquiry.[126] This letter, which was read out in full at a subsequent meeting of the guardians, was printed verbatim by the *Barnsley Chronicle* as part of its regular union reports and was forwarded by Firth to the Centre. He clearly attached great weight to the newspaper reportage of his words.[127]

Occasionally we see that pauper letters were amplified on several levels in a single instance. In April 1868 Alexander Leslie wrote from the Tynemouth workhouse stating that the master, Mr Watson, had decreed that, "so long as all classes of the male inmates had free access to the garden, a proper classification could not be maintained." It was therefore planned that only the convalescents from the hospital and inmates of the imbecile wards would be allowed to use that space. Leslie argued indignantly:

> There is room sufficient for convalescents near the hospital to walk, and railing could easily be put up to keep them from mingling with the other men. With regard to the imbeciles, they are all working men with two exceptions, and they are the most innocent creatures in the establishment, so the inmates are now prohibited from enhaling the pure "air of Heaven" and cooped up in the North yard, a place not so large as the place allowed for common felons in the County gaol of Morpeth.

The referential architecture of this letter – a sense that paupers were treated worse than prisoners, the fact that even imbeciles were expected to work, biblical references, and the contentious nature of segregation – raises issues to which we return in later chapters. For now, it is enough to note that Leslie was clear that he and other inmates thought the new plans had little to do with pauper classification and more to do with Watson seeking to extend his own privacy into those gardens which up to now had been shared with the inmates. He doubted sarcastically "that the olfactory organs would rob any of Mr Watson's flowers of their beauty of scent when taking a turn or two in the garden in the evening after their day's work in the Oakum-house." Leslie sought amplification of his message regarding peculation and breach-of-process in two ways: first, by claiming that the complaint was a collective one "in behalf of the inmates" of the workhouse; second, by having had his letter published in the *Shields Daily* the following week, affording the story a much wider public airing.[128]

In still other cases we can see the amplification process spinning out of control and taking on a life of its own. In early 1895 complaints abounded in the Liverpool workhouse concerning elderly male paupers. It was alleged that more than two hundred men were regularly required to strip naked and change their underclothes in a draughty cellar room with no fires. Many newspaper column inches were filled with commentaries on the case, including a letter printed in the *Liverpool Courier* from John Joseph Macdonald, one of the workhouse inmates. He referred to a proposed "departure from the present inhuman and indecent mode of divesting the senile inmates of this department of the workhouse for their weekly change of underclothing." Macdonald had a jocularly sarcastic turn of phrase. He headed the letter from the "Subterranean Department, Liverpool Workhouse" and went on to relate the tale of Mr Pickthall, chairman of the workhouse committee, who visited:

> (where he hasn't previously been for God knows how long a time) the paupers' disrobing, discomforting, demoralising, and debasing underground chamber, of which he made a synoptical, and no doubt philosophical, if not philanthropical survey.

Behind this humorous rhetoric was Macdonald's keen and critical perception, which he shared with the *Liverpool Courier* readership. Pickthall, he wrote, had visited the rooms under investigation and spoken only to "three inmates specially chosen for the purpose of interviewing and interrogating them" rather than the more "straightforward, and ingenious way of asking an expression of opinion and experience from the inmates en masse."[129] Macdonald's mockery of the guardians was designed to gain wide attention through the pages of local newspapers and so it proved, with the affair lasting on and off for a whole year and the Liverpool authorities suffering considerable reputational damage.

While it is difficult to trace systematically the afterlife in the press of pauper, poor, and advocate voices, the sense from this Liverpool material that reverberations could last for some time is given weight by numerous other examples, especially from the 1880s as the connection between individual moral failings and poverty weakened in the public eye. Even in the earlier decades of the New Poor Law, however, the amplification process could be very substantial. In late January 1858, for instance, T.F. Parsons complained from Maindee (Monmouthshire) of a "melancholy case of starvation of a pauper having occurred in the parish of Christchurch the particulars of which are enclosed." The enclosure was a cutting from *The Star of Gwent* newspaper reporting on a coroner's inquest under the title "Alleged Starvation of a Pauper," named Clarissa Loveridge. A local inquiry had cleared Mr Waters, the relieving officer, of any blame in the case. However, Parsons was not convinced, and his letter to that effect, which had also been published in *The Star of Gwent*, was enclosed with the handwritten letter to the PLB. The latter fused general criticisms of the union and specific criticism of the small amount of relief allowed weekly to Loveridge. Parsons had not been called by the coroner to give evidence but, he wrote:

> Had my evidence been taken, I was, and am prepared to swear, six weeks ago, or thereabouts, I saw the deceased, not the skeleton I found on the 17th, and there are other gentlemen of the highest standing in Maindee who saw her also.[130]

Through letters to newspapers and correspondence from the Centre we can see that the episode was played out over two years and with a growing insistence in the pages of *The Star of Gwent* (and other English and Welsh newspapers which then carried the story) that a larger inquiry was needed. Paupers, the wider poor, and advocates seemingly had little difficulty in getting their words into print and thus achieving significant local, regional, and national amplification.

CONCLUSION

The development of a central archive and the processes required to preserve and navigate it affords us remarkable insight into the experiences and agency of the poor and their advocates. There are complexities in categorising writers and in understanding how their voices were received, but we may be sure that what can be measured in terms of discrete pieces of text constitutes the minimum likely dimensions of a pauper voice reverberating in the offices of the Centre. Some of the obvious drivers of temporal change in the scale of writing – economic circumstances, changes to poor law policy, radicalism – have an inconsistent or negligible impact until at least the closing decade of the nineteenth century. It is hard to escape the conclusion that the key influences on decisions to write, seek advocacy, or provide evidence were the accumulated circumstances of the individual and individual relationships. We should perhaps thus expect complex rhetorical and strategic approaches to writing on the part of particular lifecycle clusters or pauper groups, and it is this expectation that shapes the agenda in Part Two of our book. In the meantime, we have seen here that there was in a quantitative and temporal sense a strong positive correlation between the writing of poor people and that of their advocates, just as there had been under the Old Poor Law. We thus need to know more about advocates both in their own right and as a potential influence on which of the poor wrote – about what issues and with what registers.

3

Advocating for the Poor

INTRODUCTION

In July 1857 John Griffith wrote to the Poor Law Board (PLB) on behalf of David Jenkins, an elderly pauper from Aberdare (Glamorgan). He would, he said, be glad to learn:

> Whether an aged pauper of 78 loses his rights as to Parochial relief from a union under the circumstances as here detailed? David Jenkins … [a] Pauper of Aberdare receives … ten shillings or twelve shillings from the relieving officer of Aberdare as relief in advance, to enable him to go for one month to visit his friends in Carmarthenshire. The old man goes with the full understanding that he is to return, as I am able to testify. While he is with his friends he is taken ill, & is unable to return for four or five months. On his return he applies, as normal, for his relief, & is told by the Board that he has forfeited all claim upon them; & he has been now for twelve months without any relief whatever. I can hardly imagine the Law to be so severe when there could be no mistake, as I can testify having applied myself to the Relieving Officer on his part, of the animus revertendi.[1]

For this chapter, a number of things are of particular interest in Griffith's letter. First, he was a man of influence and social standing; his position as an Anglican vicar and a magistrate entitled him to sit as an ex-officio guardian. Second, he did not plead for a reversal of the guardians' decision; rather, his letter was a measured request for clarification. Yet, he also brought the full weight of his rank and learning to bear. Griffith used the term "animus revertendi" (literally meaning "intention to relocate"), implying that the guardians were simply wrong in their interpretation of the rules, and invited the Board to confirm his judgement ("I can hardly imagine the Law to be so severe").

This letter and approach is emblematic of our advocate corpus and also has strong links to the nature and content of advocate letters under the Old Poor Law. As Steven King and Peter Jones have argued in this context, seeking advocacy – and in particular seeking it from neighbours, professionals, clergymen like Griffith, and parish officials – was a strategic choice, one that added weight to a claim by demonstrating its veracity.[2] No equivalent work exists for the New Poor Law. In part, this reflects the problems of accessing individual *types* of writers in the poor law union correspondence. More important, the history of welfare in this period has become closely intertwined with wider histories of the rise of experts, social investigation, social workers, and institutional visitors. The broadly construed "social action" of prominent figures has thus been privileged over the daily interventions of ordinary people who advocated for the poor.[3] Similarly, the study of the New Poor Law through the lens of "scandal" clouds any attempt to understand the scale and meaning of advocacy, privileging as it does the voices of after-the-event reflection rather than those of warning, precaution, appeal, and threats of action. Consequently we have little understanding of how, or how far, the poor relied on the advocacy of others, and whether the models we have derived from the Old Poor Law had continued resonance after 1834. Yet, who the poor could rely on for strategic support speaks to their connectedness within communities (even workhouse communities), their place in the circulation of knowledge, and their awareness of continuity and change in the malleability of local and national power. How the poor advocated for *each other* is also an important indicator of agency and of the power of individual personalities in the New Poor Law context. Whether or not some officials actively advocated for the poor (as they did under the Old Poor Law) can tell us something about the continuity (or lack thereof) in the understanding of rights and sentiments toward poor people. And what (and how) such advocates wrote can tell us a great deal about shared norms, and how the poor themselves acquired the tools for establishing, maintaining, and renewing entitlements.

In this context our chapter begins by defining what we actually mean by "advocacy" under the New Poor Law. It then moves on to investigate the nature of advocate writing at the corpus level. Here we implement a new classification for such letters and suggest some of the continuities and changes in advocacy rhetoric. Moving below the corpus level, we then investigate the particular characteristics (and impacts) of letters from five prominent groups of advocates in our sample: "friends to the poor"; social investigators and other serial advocates; poor law officials; the poor themselves; and finally, broad collective associations of workers such as trade unions.

THE CORPUS

For the Old Poor Law, King and Jones have identified a typological spectrum of advocates ranging across close acquaintances, family and neighbours, "middling sort" writers (employers, doctors, and clergymen), and on to poor law officials themselves.[4] In the overwhelming majority of cases, the purpose of these writers was to apply or appeal on behalf of a named person in order to stimulate or contest an individual relief decision. This remains true for many of the writers in our post-1834 corpus; they acted essentially as "friends" to the poor. The notion of "friendship" in relation to eighteenth- and nineteenth-century social relations is complex[5] but in Old Poor Law letters King and Jones identified a tripartite hierarchy of advocate "friends": friends as patrons, friends as close acquaintances, and "good" friends, including relatives by blood or marriage.[6] Under this classification John Griffith clearly belongs to the first: as a clergyman he would have viewed himself as a "friend to the poor," and his intercession on behalf of David Jenkins can be understood as one of benevolent patronage, the result of a sense of moral, religious, and even vocational duty. Indeed, some 26 per cent of advocates-as-patron letters in the post-1834 corpus were written by clergymen like Griffith. The rest came from others within the community whose self-evident "respectability" made their voices both compelling and authoritative: doctors, ratepayers, magistrates, and sundry "gentlemen" (and women) whose wealth and prestige afforded them a particular social standing; in other words, precisely those among the "middling sort" who wrote under the Old Poor Law.[7] Beyond this category, however, our advocate cohort diverges, sometimes significantly, from that in pre-1834 correspondence.

The most obvious divergence relates to writers under the New Poor Law who advocated not on behalf of *a* pauper or poor applicant but on behalf of *the* poor (or a subset thereof) more generally. Here definitional issues become rather complex. For example, some individuals wrote many letters to the Centre which included complaints about the treatment of a named individual, but when we analyse these letter series it becomes clear that they were part of a much wider agenda for which the named person was merely the conduit. The most prolific (though by no means only) example of this type of writer in our corpus is the amateur social investigator Joseph Rowntree, who in the 1850s and 1860s traversed Britain and Ireland probing workhouse conditions and exposing abuse and mismanagement. In common with his more famous namesake, Rowntree was a Yorkshire Quaker. He wrote hundreds of letters to the Centre and between 1859 and 1868 published many more in at least forty-seven national and provincial newspapers.[8] Like other amateur social investigators, Rowntree often began his accounts of local workhouses by outlining cases of the abuse and mistreatment of named individuals. Sometimes, he even persuaded paupers themselves to write and contest local policy.[9] His was a particularly zealous brand of "advocacy," and it served wider objectives than the redress of individual wrongs. Unlike the advocacy of John Griffith and other "friends to the poor," Rowntree's voluminous correspondence can only be understood within the context of a diverse movement which broadly advocated for the reform of workhouses and which took root in the 1850s and 1860s, a movement that influenced many of the shifts in welfare practice that we note elsewhere in this book.[10] Rowntree's activity, and that of less prolific but similarly motivated writers, raises important questions about the nature of advocacy under the New Poor Law and how we interpret it. Undoubtedly, such writers were on the side of the poor, yet the broad agenda of reform or regime change which propelled their activities was not necessarily (and was rarely explicitly) shared by those on whose behalf they wrote.[11]

The discussion of "investigator-advocates" highlights in turn a second category of writer also encountered (but less frequently) under the Old Poor Law: paupers themselves. Our corpus contains letters – often series of letters – from the poor which ranged far beyond their own specific complaints and concerns, and included advocacy on behalf of other paupers or pauper cohorts. Occasionally, they shared characteristics with the correspondence of reformers like Rowntree, developing into campaigns which challenged the entire administration of welfare in a particular institution or locality. So, for example, Mungo Paumier of Bethnal Green workhouse (whom we encounter at length elsewhere in this book) complained often to the Centre about many aspects of his own treatment between 1862 and 1867; but he also took up his pen in defence of aged inmates more generally and, on occasion, on behalf of other named paupers. As with reformer-advocates like Rowntree, these inmates and their treatment served as a conduit through which he was able to mount his sustained campaign.

The distinction between advocates who sought to address their perception of systematic or widespread abuse and/or misapplications of the rules, and those who acted as a "friend" for individuals is an important one. As responses from the Centre consistently made clear, it was not responsible for making, or even arbitrating in, individual relief decisions; although, as we shall see in the next section this did not prevent large numbers of advocates from requesting that they do so. Rather, as we saw in chapter 2, the Centre's role was to formulate and enforce the rules and regulations that unions were to follow, to advise and instruct on the best way to apply those rules, and to intervene, through a process of arbitration and inquiry, in cases of misconduct and transgression. It is therefore unsurprising that advocates who were motivated by a wider agenda engaged in extended correspondence with the Centre. In turn, we find a range of other types of correspondents whose letters melded advocacy with larger concerns, some of whom are familiar from the Old Poor Law period and others not. These range from nonconformist and Roman Catholic clergymen keen to ensure that their workhouse congregations received the same treatment as the Anglican majority, to doctors and physicians who objected to the rules governing medical relief – or, at least, to their local interpretation and application. On occasion, we catch glimpses of internecine conflict between individuals and factions within the poor law hierarchy, where the fate or treatment of particular paupers became inextricably entwined in the threads of claim and counter-claim. This is clear, for instance, in the correspondence of Reverend H. Binney, a dissenting guardian from Newbury (Berkshire), who sent fifteen letters between 1841 and 1858 complaining of the actions and decisions of his fellow guardians and the mismanagement of numerous aspects of relief locally.[12] In cases like this, "advocacy" was woven into currents of personal, political, and/or religious contention, nowhere more so than in the case of letters from political parties, trade unions, and other campaigning associations, which constitute a genuinely new addition to the canvas of advocacy post-1834.

At the corpus level, then, detecting advocacy is driven by a three-strand categorisation of the 1,699 documents first counted in table 2.1: definitive advocate texts (usually single letters or testimonies, most often from "friends to the poor" but sometimes from the poor themselves); serial and "professional" writers (including officials as well as amateur investigators who wrote many times and whose letters contained acts of advocacy); and ambiguous texts of the sort described above. We then classify advocates according to their socioeconomic or occupational background, as figure 3.1 shows. This pie chart excludes the letters of Joseph Rowntree, whose remarkably prolific output (104,000 words in our corpus) makes him truly exceptional and would have the effect of skewing the figures. Even excluding Rowntree, however, serial advocates were prolific. Arthur Firth (a grocer from Barnsley encountered in the previous chapter), for instance, wrote frequently on behalf of individuals within his union, including to the local newspaper, guardians, the Local Government Board (LGB) – and even on one occasion the Prince of Wales.[13] Such potential skewing notwithstanding, we can see from figure 3.1 that professional people, officials, and the poor themselves loom particularly large in the advocate cohort. Moreover, the range of advocate backgrounds under the New Poor Law was considerably wider than under the Old. Landlords and employers or former employers still have a (diminished) voice in the post-1834 corpus, but they are replaced by a rich and colourful array of others, including Chartist organisers, union

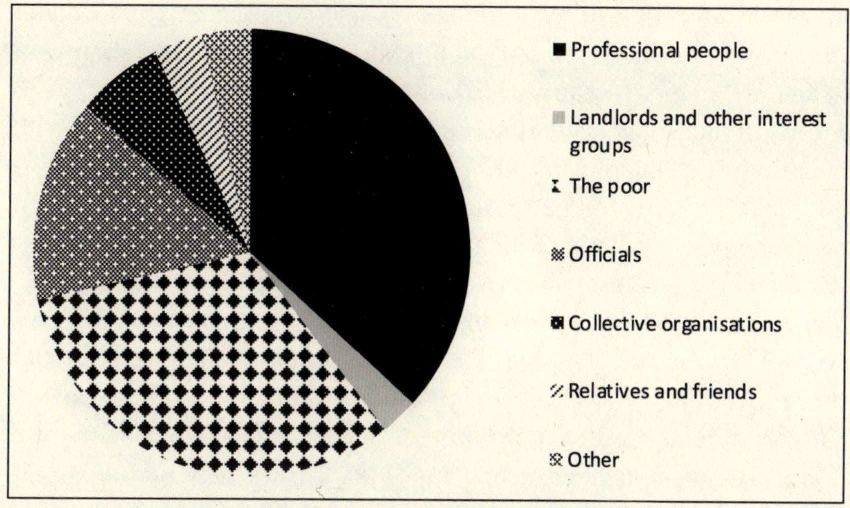

3.1 The distribution of advocate types
Source: MH12. Local Government Board and Predecessors: Correspondence with Poor Law Unions and Other Local Authorities, The National Archives.

officials, jurors, and headmasters. As we know from the Old Poor Law, it is not always easy or obvious to see whether the intervention of advocates was beneficial for paupers and poor applicants. Nonetheless, the frequency of their letters in the corpus certainly suggests that writers, and the poor who sought them out, thought that their concerns *ought* to weigh heavily on the Centre. As with their Old Poor Law counterparts, post-1834 advocates sometimes reacted forcefully when their letters went unanswered or the Centre merely referred the matter back to local guardians. Such men and women had become used to the local and national branches of the state listening to public opinion. Indeed, advocates like John Griffith *were* the "public" of public opinion.

Systematic variation in the scale, type, and intensity of the advocate voice on a spatial, socioeconomic, or urban/rural basis is (perhaps surprisingly) absent from the corpus. Other features are more striking. In particular, and as with the Old Poor Law, men heavily outnumbered women as advocates. Female advocates rarely wrote on more than a single occasion, but when they did so the concerns, strategies, and rhetorical apparatus of their letters were little different from those of male serial writers. Thus Miss M. Philpot wrote from Lyme Regis (Dorset) on three occasions. In May 1837 she sought outdoor relief for Mary Minson of Colyton, a widow of sixty-plus in receipt of one shilling and a loaf of bread per week but who was threatened with the workhouse. In January 1838 Philpot wrote regarding payment of outdoor relief to John and Betty Anning, again of Colyton. Both were aged over seventy and suffering from rheumatism, and she accused the Axminster Poor Law Union (PLU) of discrimination for having provided the Annings with a smaller pension than had been awarded to others of the same age and circumstances. By December 1838 Philpot was writing again, this time concerning Mary Chaffey, who had lived at Lyme until she married, and then went to Castle Carey (Somerset), her husband's parish. After his death Chaffey broke her arm and applied to Castle Carey guardians only to be offered the workhouse. Chaffey fled back to Lyme but the Axminster guardians also refused relief. Philpot acknowledged that the Centre could not interfere in individual cases, but asked how to obtain relief for such a case as this. She stated that the ratepayers would not be "contented to see the poor wanting the necessary assistance," a critique of the wider system that is common ground with male serial advocates.[14]

Figure 3.2 conveys a broad sense of the range of concerns raised by advocates. Its appearance of absolute precision is misleading, given that advocates could and did raise numerous issues in the same letter. Nonetheless, the sense that cruelty or abuse, maladministration, the unsuitability of rules for relief, system failings, and breach of process dominated the strategic intent of advocate letters is clear. We shall see the same themes explored by poor writers themselves throughout the rest of this book, especially in chapter 6.

Once again, as with the Old Poor Law, there is a remarkable spatial and typological continuity to the sorts of concerns raised under the New. The dynamism in the corpus is essentially temporal, with significant changes in the rhetorical construction of advocacy over time. This remains true whether or not we include serial advocates and amateur investigators, and the shift has several clear signatures. First, we can see from the 1840s a decline in linguistic registers of active or passive reportage (as in "I beg to report that" or "I must inform you that") and a corresponding "development

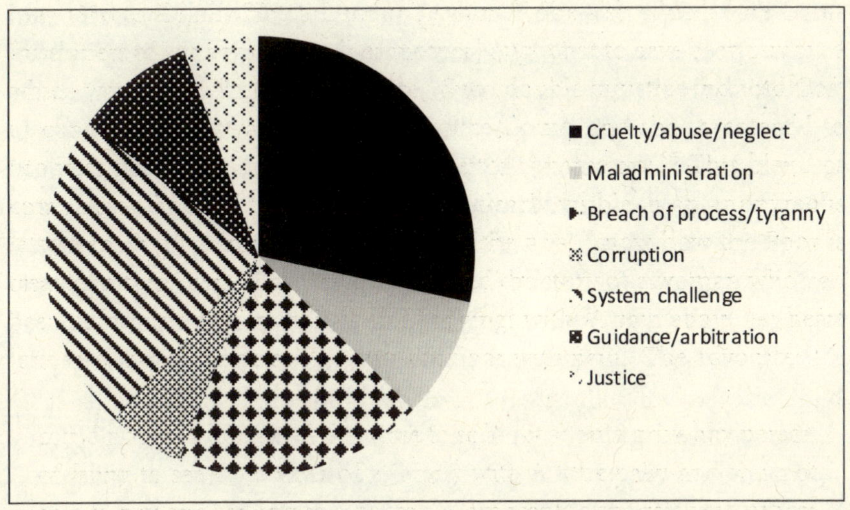

3.2 The range of concerns raised by advocates
Source: MH12. Local Government Board and Predecessors: Correspondence with Poor Law Unions and Other Local Authorities, The National Archives.

rhetoric" signalling expectation of action (as in "I am reporting X and you must act on it"). The analogue of these changes is that we also see a second development: a shift away from registers associated with the harrowing experience of the people for whom advocates wrote, to a greater balancing with rhetoric of the consequences of inaction, silence, or tolerance of a given situation. Against this backdrop, there was a distinct shift away from registers associated with Christian paternalism, humanity, or expedience in favour of those associated with tyranny and abuse. This was particularly marked amongst pauper advocates, social investigators, and serial writers, but gathered pace in the corpus more generally from the 1860s. Inevitably, given this changing focus, we also see a strong shift from language associated with the need for clarity of process in the early decades of the New Poor Law (as in "can you tell me?" or "surely you cannot mean!") to one of process challenge in the middle and later decades of our period.[15]

Finally, there are striking changes in rhetoric associated with what might be understood as "scale and focus." Thus, while advocates in the early decades of the New Poor Law employed language centred on guardians or boards, later advocates (and indeed later advocacy letters from the same person) used more-focused texts to criticise and hold to account officers and staff. Since the conduct expected of officers was increasingly clearly defined and understood, they constituted a weak underbelly for criticism by advocates of all sorts. Equally, while early advocates used a suite of reference points that were essentially inward-looking to the case, we see some shift in the later decades of the New Poor Law to referential models associated with exogenous conditions. This shift partly reflects a change in the composition of advocate cohorts (to include, for instance, trade union officials and others keenly aware of exogenous conditions such as trade downturns) but is also generalisable across all writers. While there was no tendency for the modal advocate letters to lengthen over time (at least once we control for amateur investigators and the paupers we have styled as campaigners), there is no question that such letters became rhetorically deeper, embodying more issues, more reference points, or – above all – more complex registers. These changes are explored at greater length in the rest of the chapter. In the meantime, still looking at the corpus level we can notice that advocacy becomes more dynamic and more confrontational. This is not, however, to imply that all advocates wrote in the same way or used the same linguistic forms in different places and contexts. King has argued that pre-1834 poor writers, officials, and advocates shared the same linguistic register and expectational/referential framework. After 1834 a greater conceptual and linguistic distance between the poor and their advocates is perceptible, and core advocate groups approached their task in different ways. It is to five of those advocate groups that we dedicate the remaining sections of this chapter.

"FRIENDS TO THE POOR"

While the "friends" to the poor were drawn from a diverse socioeconomic and cultural group, they were broadly middling and might be constructed (as under the Old Poor Law and indeed for far longer) as the natural local advocates for the poor. We suggested earlier that their relationship to the poor was rooted in the traditions of moral obligation and Christian duty and that some of the most important and prolific advocates in this category were clergymen.[16] From the perspective of the poor, it made sense to appeal to those who, locally at least, had a degree of influence and who even on a much larger stage had an expectation not only of being heard but of being taken seriously. Yet not all advocates in this category *were* approached by the poor: many wrote of their own accord and often in strikingly direct terms. Thus, in July 1869, Wingfield Homfray, the incumbent of Bintree (Norfolk), wrote to complain about the administration of relief in the Mitford and Launditch Poor Law Union (PLU). He stated that guardians had indulged in "the greatest tyrrany, cruelty, indecency and injustice ever recorded," and went on to ask the PLB to take immediate steps to "rectify the evil." His complaint related to the treatment of some of his elderly parishioners, including William Crowe, aged eighty-two. Homfray wrote that officials wished to turn Crowe out of his cottage (rented to him by a charitable trust) and had threatened to stop his allowance if he would not have a pauper woman to live with him. Homfray complained that even if the old man had accepted the woman into his home, as a Trustee of the charity he would not "have suffered it." As a result of Crowe's refusal to leave, however, Homfray claimed that the relieving officer had given him a note for the workhouse, which was declined, leaving him without any means of support and in a position where he "wished he was dead." The clergyman's strong language was deemed problematic by the PLB, which made a note that the letter was "very intemperate" and even "offensive."[17]

Most writers from this category did not employ such stark language, although it is a consistent thread. Rather, they generally tailored their texts to the capacity in which they wrote, and, although it is difficult to be clear about motivation, three roles emerge from a close reading of this sort of advocate letter: that arising from an extension of a specific or general duty; that generated by genuine sentiment; and that intended to further particular causes. Homfray's role was clearly an extending one, arising from his pastoral duty as a clergyman. Another obvious extending role was held by medical men who acted either independently or as medical officers. Thomas Jackson of Scarborough (Yorkshire), for example, wrote in 1864 to request the intervention of the PLB in the case of a boy named Warren, who had sustained a leg injury and developed an "irritative fever." He had been attended by the "parish surgeon" (probably a union medical officer) but, his condition having worsened, Jackson's opinion was sought and he had resolved to amputate the boy's leg above the knee. The family could not afford sufficient sustenance for the boy to recover either from his injuries or from the surgery, and Jackson argued: "I am afraid of the consequences if he has no better diet and stimulant than 5/– per week can supply."[18] Jackson contacted the PLB as an independent surgeon. Medical officers also acted as advocates, however. J. Matthews of Ampthill (Bedfordshire) did so in 1863 on behalf of an unnamed patient who was suffering "from an illness of an exhausting nature." Matthews had ordered that he should be given port wine to assist his recovery, but the relieving officer refused to act and the man subsequently died. Matthews concluded that "certainly death seems to have been accentuated by the neglect" of the officer.[19]

How far Matthews had any genuine feeling for the pauper patient is uncertain. As with doctors who advocated under the Old Poor Law, their professional position itself limited both the strategic range and the linguistic register likely to be employed, even when there was a personal connection with their subject.[20] Nonetheless, in some cases we can still read "feeling" or "sentiment." This is clearly visible in a letter of E.W. Tinsdill sent from Halton (Yorkshire) in 1858 in relation to Thomas Wellock and his wife. Tinsdill, a surgeon apothecary, wrote that the couple's weekly allowance had been stopped and they had been forced to enter the workhouse. Even after they had discharged themselves, the outdoor allowance was again denied; but, wrote Tinsdill, "the health of the wife is so impaired she cannot live [in the workhouse] & without any wish to make complaints against the treatment says she would rather jump into the river than return to the Union."[21] Tinsdill gave no clear indication that he had treated the couple professionally but did confirm that they were well acquainted, he having "known them both for about thirty years & their parents." He also mentioned that they had "for some time been existing or rather been endeavouring to exist on what he can earn by delivering bills," and that Tinsdill himself had "almost entirely supported them for a while," a situation which, he wrote, could no longer continue. The letter concluded gravely, suggesting that Wellock's "last resort is to appeal to you for himself & wife the latter of whom must fall sacrifice should they be impelled to return to the Union."[22] Under the circumstances, Tinsdill's tone was remarkably restrained. Similar restraint is visible in a letter sent by P.E. Coates, a solicitor from Pensford (Somerset), in 1834. He noted of a parish overseer:

> [he] has lately reduced the pay of many of the aged paupers receiving constant relief & they have complained to me I desired them to acquaint our nearest Magistrate with their case One of them did so but the Justice refused to make any order conceiving he had no longer the power of so doing.[23]

Coates went on to state: "I consider the weekly pay now given to some of the aged paupers too little"; but, he asked, "what can be done if the Justices refuse to act as before & there are no general rules issued by you?"[24] He finished his letter formally, with the expectation that "you will oblige me by informing these people through me how they are to compel the Overseer to afford them proper Relief."[25] Coates's controlled but firm and authoritative tone should not detract from the clear sense that he had feeling and sentiment for the aged parish poor.

Some of the most persistent advocates from the professional and middling classes exhibited our third motivation for writing – the factional agenda or particular cause. Nowhere is this clearer than on the question of religious observance. Upon entering the workhouse paupers were asked to state their religious affiliation and, depending on the number of inmates, an Anglican chaplain could be retained to minister to their spiritual needs. In northern unions and others where dissent was strong, such appointments were resisted locally both because ratepayers considered it an unnecessary cost and because Article 126 of *The Consolidated and Other Orders of the Poor Law Commissioners* permitted guardians to allow any inmates who dissented from the Church of England to attend worship at a dissenting chapel in the neighbourhood.[26] For Catholics, however, the situation was far more complex, and one issue on which both church and chapel-going guardians often agreed was the need to keep Catholic priests out of the workhouse. In places like Liverpool, Wigan, or Sheffield, where there were large numbers of Catholics, the Centre received regular complaints about the lack of access to a priest.[27] Charles Russell took up the cause, writing that the "Catholic body, as an integral part of the community," required assurances that the Catholic poor who were inmates of the workhouse would be allowed to exercise their own religion. He contended that children should be raised in their father's faith and everyone, young or old, should be allowed the "solace" of religious freedom.[28] This was also clearly a view held by Father Burke from Sheffield, who wrote eight letters relating to the spiritual needs of workhouse inmates. His letter of 25 July 1881 sought to provide a full statement of "the Religious questions now affecting our Poor at the Workhouse." Burke complained that the workhouse contained numerous Catholics, including children, whose spiritual needs were not catered for. Although the LGB stated that they could not force the guardians to pay a Roman Catholic priest from the rates, they did think that were "strong grounds for some arrangement" to be made.[29] The guardians, however, resisted and another letter followed in August 1882 in which Burke declared: "I have now used every legitimate means to move the Sheffield Guardians to make some provision for the due & regular supply of the Religious wants of the Catholic Inmates of the Workhouse." Burke claimed that two weeks prior to the date of his letter a Catholic pauper had died in the workhouse without the last rites. This, he argued, was far worse than the normal privations of the poor.[30] In 1884 (when there were 400 Catholics in the workhouse) Burke wrote again. At this point his attention had turned in the main to children, and he argued that while they were now allowed to attend St Catherine's (Burke's own church), this did not provide sufficient religious instruction for their needs. Burke felt that the best solution would be to compel the guardians to place the Catholic children, particularly those unaccompanied, in Catholic institutions.[31] By April 1885 Burke was the visiting priest for the workhouse. The guardians had made the changes as required by law and withdrawn the children from Protestant prayers, but they were not actively being instructed in their own faith. However, by now the LGB had come to believe that at the core of Burke's correspondence was the desire to be paid himself for the children's instruction. It considered that Sheffield guardians would oppose this since, if a paid position of this nature were created, their "constituents would at once turn them out."[32] Moving the children to Catholic institutions was also difficult, as requisite permission would have to be obtained for each child. As the Sheffield union improved its provision for Catholic workhouse children, Burke's letters became less frequent.

It is clear that Burke's campaign on behalf of Catholic paupers was in part born of concern for their welfare, and his advocacy might be viewed in a similar light to that of other clergymen and professionals. Burke's interpretation of his Christian duty compelled him to take up his pen on behalf of the Catholic workhouse poor, just as it was the moral and religious duty of the others described in this section that led them to act as "friends to the poor." However, his advocacy is also distinctive in embodying a particular doctrinal agenda which went far beyond the day-to-day welfare or treatment of a particular pauper or even a named group of paupers. However we read the motivation, Burke's letters share key features with other middling advocates. He implied that the local and national poor law authorities had a duty not only to listen to his concerns but to act on them. This is reflected both in his persistence and in his construction of a sophisticated case (or cases) over several letters. Like other clergymen and professionals we have considered here, Burke's rhetoric was restrained but authoritative; he clearly expected to be treated with respect and consideration by those at the Centre. Anything less would have represented a personal insult and a transgression of the epistolary conventions of the time. This said, and alongside other advocates whose letters were underpinned by doctrinal concerns, Burke also had much in common at the discursive and rhetorical level with our second group of writers: social investigators and other serial advocates who played an increasingly prominent role from the 1850s.

REFORMERS AND INVESTIGATORS

As we saw above, the most prominent and by far the most prolific reformer in our corpus was Joseph Rowntree of Leeds. The range and scale of Rowntree's letter writing certainly set him apart, but it would be a mistake to conclude that he was unique, either in his overarching concerns or in his general approach.[33] In this section we concentrate on other advocate-investigators who were less prolific and whose geographical range was more limited than

Rowntree's but whose correspondence demonstrates key aspects of the role of the investigator-advocate under the New Poor Law. One such writer was R.H.S. Carpenter, a Witney (Oxfordshire) doctor who sent fourteen letters to the PLB between 1857 and 1866. He complained of the actions, attitudes, and behaviour of various guardians and local officials, and chronicled their impact on the lives of the local poor. Carpenter began his campaign in April 1857, bemoaning the neglect of Anna Green and James Neale. Green had been sent to the workhouse while in labour and had arrived bleeding heavily. Carpenter reported that the workhouse nurses had called for the immediate attendance of Mr Batt, the medical officer, who saw Green but said that it was "no case of labour and that he could be of no service." Green subsequently died and Carpenter stated: "it is my belief, that if she had been delivered when Mr Batt saw her, she would have been now alive."[34] James Neale, aged seventy, also died in the workhouse and Carpenter was convinced that this was again a direct result of Batt's negligence.

When Carpenter relocated from Oxfordshire to Durham, he continued his advocacy for a new group of the poor. In 1866, for example, he sent a letter complaining about a relieving officer who not only ignored his unofficial advice that a local pauper required more sustenance but, when he wrote a note to that effect, asked "whether I was drunk."[35] In this and subsequent letters it becomes clear that Carpenter had by that point corresponded with the Durham guardians several times to complain about the conduct of various officers. Following this, he also took up his pen on behalf of specific paupers and their families, as he had in Witney. One key case was that of Thomas Burdess, who was in a "distressed and dangerous condition" as a result of "his having been seriously neglected by the parish authorities ... [and] not having received proper medical attendance during a long illness." Although Burdess was still alive at that point, Carpenter wrote that he feared his case "would soon have a fatal termination" and went on to state that he himself had "complained over and over again to the Durham Board of Guardians and to the Poor Law Board of cases in which serious neglect had occurred to the sick poor of this district, and which cases included instances of death where no parochial medical aid had been given."[36]

As was suggested by the relieving officer's response to his earlier note, Carpenter's intervention was not welcomed by the Durham officials. On one occasion, when he visited Burdess to ascertain what had (or had not) been done for him, he encountered the medical officer's assistant, who threatened to "kick my a— out of the house the next time I went to it."[37] Unperturbed, Carpenter continued to advocate on behalf of Burdess and to complain about the attitude and behaviour of various Durham officials. Eventually, as he had predicted, Burdess died and Carpenter attempted (unsuccessfully) to give evidence at the coroner's inquiry into his death. This led him to issue further complaints and to restate many of the other charges against the Durham officers. Apart from the "campaigning" nature of Carpenter's long correspondence and his advocacy on behalf of the sick poor, one thing that links his activities with other investigator-advocates like Rowntree is his understanding of both the value, and the general tide, of public opinion towards workhouses at this time. More than once he suggested that there was a greater need for openness in investigations of abuse and neglect, and in his first letter from Durham he finished by stating: "I shall publish the case with many more in the London press."[38] In the event, he did publish his concerns, but confined his activities to the local press, specifically the *Durham Chronicle*.[39]

Another correspondent who understood the value of public opinion to a reforming agenda was William Joseph Davies, of Aberystwyth (Cardiganshire). Like Carpenter, Davies wrote a series of letters complaining about local officials and, in common with both Carpenter and Rowntree, did so as part of a wider campaign of publicity involving the press. Davies's letters were all sent in 1869. It is no coincidence that all three investigator-advocates mentioned here were writing in the 1860s, at precisely the point in the history of the New Poor Law when reform was growing into a major national concern and public opinion was being mobilised in a series of formal and informal campaigns for change.[40] Davies began by detailing a broad slate of allegations against local officials, including peculation and corruption, cruelty, and neglect of duty. He concentrated particularly on the guardians and the workhouse master, claiming that "No Union Workhouse in Great Britain [is] worse governed than that of Aberystwith."[41] He later added charges of child cruelty and medical neglect, as well as a host of other accusations, but for the moment the substance of Davies's complaints are less important to us than the manner in which they were made. As with Rowntree and Carpenter, Davies's complaints were exhaustively compiled and scrupulously detailed. Evidence was gathered, names named, and dates verified. They give the impression of a man who had taken great pains to establish the facts and present them in the most convincing way possible.[42] Like Rowntree, Davies questioned the value of allowing the guardians to mount their own investigation, stating that "the offenders will in some measure be constituted their own judges"; and in common with both Rowntree and Carpenter, he all but demanded that the PLB instigate a full enquiry into the way the union was run.[43]

Davies shares one further characteristic with Joseph Rowntree: he was a gentleman of no clear profession who had clearly dedicated a great deal of time and effort to his campaigning activities. Both men encountered abuse for doing so. The *Western Daily Mail*, in its account of a trial on an unrelated matter at the Petty Sessions, described Davies as a "Bohemian" graduate of Cambridge and "a well-known character in this town"; a man with "a very ingenious and disputatious turn of mind … [who had] frequently bearded the law and the lawyers even in the Temple of Justice."[44] The guardians soon tired of his attentions and it was reported (under the title "Mr William Joseph Davies Again") that at one stage they declined even to open a letter addressed by him to "each and every Individual of the Aberystwyth Board of Guardians," on the reverse of which was the note: "N.B. Let Mr. O'Halloran have the contents after perusal to be inserted, or otherwise, in the Aberystwyth Observer."[45] Each of our advocate-investigators probed and inquired with tenacity and zeal into the very heart of the local administration of relief. Davies confined his activities to Aberystwyth; Carpenter divided his attention between Witney and Durham; and Rowntree roamed the length and breadth of the British Isles, documenting abuses of power and the mismanagement he encountered. Each called on the Centre to defend the poor and demanded that unions put their houses in order, and all of them recognised the value of appealing, via the press, to a wider court of public opinion when their private appeals fell on deaf ears. Despite the opprobrium, personal abuse, and sometimes ridicule they received for their efforts, they doggedly pursued their campaigns. They were firmly located among the "middling sort" of Victorian Britain, but their aims and approach were very different from the "friends to the poor" described in the previous section. Rather than appeal against individual relief decisions or on behalf of individual paupers, they mined a much deeper seam of reforming activity positing widespread, even wholesale, change to relief practice. They were, therefore, part of a small but distinctive group of advocates who emerged under the conditions of the mid- to late New Poor Law. By way of contrast, the following section considers an advocate group who were numerically important under the Old Poor Law and continued to be influential (albeit in different ways) under the New; that is, poor law officials themselves.

OFFICIALS AS ADVOCATES

Notwithstanding the unionisation process, local welfare policy and practice continued to be evaluated, shaped, and enforced by officials drawn from the localities encompassed by their union. As we saw in chapter 1, some officials from the Old Poor Law – overseers, for instance – continued to have a role under the New, and the formation of unions saw the appointment of manifold layers of new professional and paid staff, from clerks through to teachers and matrons in workhouses, or medical officers in the community. Under the Old Poor Law, according to King and Jones, officials often strayed beyond reporting facts or the business of administration in their correspondence with counterparts in other places, offering definitive advocacy for paupers and poor claimants. Under the New Poor Law the duties of (and thus limitations on) officials and guardians were more precisely defined both by the Centre and in the many "how to" manuals that codified central regulations. In this sense there was, in principle, less scope for active advocacy. The observation of their continued presence in figure 3.1 is therefore all the more important.[46] We can identify three broad levels of such advocacy: letters in which the core purpose was to play out local politics or personal animosities, and thus where both pauper and advocacy were incidental; letters which focused on local reputation and process, where advocacy was again incidental; and letters which embodied determined acts of advocacy. While all three letter types generally opened in the way familiar from official correspondence of all sorts, the linguistic registers thereafter differ significantly.[47]

It was common for local politics to be played out in correspondence across our sample, and letters with that intent were invariably couched in rhetoric suggesting that the action or inaction of certain parties resulted in the suffering or abuse of the poor.[48] Thus, John Willet (who we later discover was a guardian of the Cardiff PLU) wrote to "the Honorable the Poor Law Board" in 1858 about the failure of the union to appoint an effective workhouse visiting committee.[49] Although there had been "accidental" visits by individual guardians, no "official" visits had been made to the house for years. Because of the absence of oversight, Willet complained, the master had been able to reduce the allowance of potatoes by a third. Moreover, no diet sheets had been posted in the workhouse as required by national regulations. Even worse, the Cardiff board had passed a resolution some years previously forbidding any guardians not on the visiting committee from inspecting the house without their consent. Willet thus stated: "I submit that the time has arriv[ed] when it becomes the duty of your Honorable Board to appoint a paid Visitor to the Cardiff Union Workhouse," and called upon them to support the law, which was intended to "throw a shield of protection" around paupers. Only at the end of the letter did Willet actively advocate for the poor, noting that abuse was inevitable unless the PLB acted.[50] Another letter, sent in 1864 by an unnamed guardian of the Wrexham PLU (Denbighshire), alluded to a newspaper account of their workhouse by Joseph Rowntree in which he had made a number of observations and allegations including inadequate diet, lack of bathing facilities and bedding, and the poor state of medical attendance.[51] The author confirmed Rowntree's observations and went further, charging the chaplain with only attending sick inmates once every three months and reporting having heard the poor complain that they "die like dogs and this is a Union Workhouse in a civilized country with a paid Chaplain." However, the unnamed guardian also hinted that there was more to the allegations than a concern for the poor, posing the question: "How is this for the other officers of the Workhouse are closely looked after" and he answered: "Simply because he [the chaplain] is a friend of the Chairman Capn Panton." The writer asked the PLB to enquire but warned conspiratorially that "it is perfectly useless to make enquiries of any of the following persons because they are all friends of the Chaplains," going on to list the porter, the chairman, the doctor, the nurse, and the master. The letter ended with the dark warning that: "if the Chairman was to know I hade written this my attendance at that Board must for ever, cease … for I should get snubbed every time I open my mout[h] – because [I] have told the truth about his pet (The Paid Chaplain)."[52]

Secondary advocacy of this sort also appears in situations where officers and officials sought to highlight failings of process, or risks to local reputation – although there is often clear overlap between these letters and letters rooted in personal animosities and local politics. Here, even if still not central, the thread of advocacy was usually stronger and more consistent, often extending to multiple intertwining claims of suffering, harsh treatment, and long-term consequence. Thus J.W. Edwards, the clerk at Merthyr Tydfil (Glamorgan), wrote in 1842 requesting central intervention regarding the chairman of the Board of Guardians. In Edwards's opinion the chairman had abused his power and subverted the interests of the union by illegally paying himself "an amount of rent which he had obtained by levying a distress on a poor person's goods" and had "connived" with the relieving officer to enter into the books a greater sum than had been authorised by the local Board.[53] Similarly, "An officer of the B[oard]" wrote from Manchester in 1865 to highlight the poor treatment of children at the union school, insisting that, although the governor of that institution had already resigned, there should be "an investigation into his Conduct and [the] infamous treatment of the Children … as well as of the two late nurses who have died there." The letter continued that there had been systematic bullying of staff, who had been forced to resign, and that the guardians had been "unwilling to listen to any Complaints" against the governor, such that "if steps are not soon Taken Consequences too dreadful to contemplate will assuredly be the result." It is notable that, as with the case of the guardian from Wrexham noted above, the author did not sign the letter, adding only in a postscript, "I will disclose my name when I am sure of your Protection."[54] This highlights very forcefully the difficult position in which even officials and staff who wished to address systematic abuse were placed and, as we shall see in chapter 10, is redolent of the fears of paupers themselves.

Sometimes, though, advocacy from officials was more personal, direct, and determined. W.G. Dennis, a guardian of the Colchester PLU (Essex), wrote in 1842, for instance, describing "a case of great hardship" in his parish of St Michael Colchester. The subject of this correspondence was an agricultural labourer called Gibbons, who belonged to the parish and was unable to support his large family. Dennis commented that Gibbons had always been in employment at the full average wage for the parish and been allowed one shilling of relief per week for a child. This was insufficient, however, for the maintenance of nine persons. Under these circumstances the guardians asked the Poor Law Commission (PLC) for permission to keep part of his family in the workhouse and allow the man, his wife, and the rest of the children to leave. Dennis also added a postscript stating: "I have been endeavouring to raise a fund by means of a voluntary Rate to assist able bodied families who are in distress, but I am told by some of the Rate Payers it interferes with the working of the new poor law."[55] In this sense, rhetorical advocacy translated into practical action much as the advocacy of the "friends to the poor" often came at the end of a process whereby they had exhausted their own means to offer material aid. Sir John Walsham, assistant commissioner, annotated Dennis's letter to the effect that, should the guardians wish to maintain for a time two of Gibson's children without their parents, then the Commissioners would be prepared to assent to the arrangement.[56] As to the voluntary rate, the local ratepayers were deemed right. Walsham annotated the letter: "private Charity which assumes the form and proportion of a rate has an obvious tendency to interfere mischievously with the administration of the legal relief of the poor."[57] The implicit threat of high profile local action by this advocate had thus wrung ameliorative action from the PLC.[58]

As Dennis's case illustrates, some guardians, officials, and poor law staff continued to advocate on behalf of individual paupers, and to insist on a liberal interpretation of the rules, just as they had under the Old Poor Law. They generally did so using the same linguistic architecture as their Old Poor Law counterparts, including registers of mismanagement, abuse, corruption, humanity, and duty. If the letters of poor law officers as advocates were often complicated by personal animosities and local politics, this should not blind us to the sincere efforts made by some on behalf of the local poor, or to the considerable risks to livelihoods and reputations which were inherent in such appeals.[59] Those risks were also keenly felt by our fourth category of advocates, the poor themselves.

THE POOR AS ADVOCATES

Prior to 1834, letters from the poor advocating for other poor people constituted a significant component of advocacy. For such writers neither the quality of the writing nor the frame of reference differed strongly, in general, from the approaches and levels of literacy of officials themselves. While it is difficult at corpus level to quantify "improvement" in literacy, it is nonetheless clear that the incidence of letters in the strongly orthographic form traced by Jones and King for Kirkby Lonsdale between 1809 and 1836 dwindled under the New Poor Law.[60] At corpus level there is also a compositional change in the type of poor advocate, with fewer neighbours and landlords (though the former are well represented in witness statements) and more relatives by blood and marriage. Against this backdrop, three rhetorical forms emerge as central aspects: advocacy arising from duty, fellow feeling, and compassion; the need to confront injustice or rule breaking; and the desire to gain clarity and establish principle (of law, process, or story). Clearly, these are linguistic registers and strategies shared with other types of advocate (as we see above) and with those who provided evidence or wrote on their own account. In investigating the advocacy of the poor, then, we tap into a wider ecology of rhetorical agency, one suggestive of the continuation of Old Poor Law social relations and with common or comparable frames of reference and linguistic registers.

A good example of writing from a sense of duty comes from Bethnal Green, where in 1856 "a Poor Man" wrote that he had been informed by an inmate at the workhouse that "the Schoolmaster of the said Establishment has been Exercising an undue severity upon a boy named Benjn Bishop, a lad of about 13 years of age." The anonymous writer asked the PLB to "see to this and stop this young Schoolmaster from Beating the Boy under his Charge."[61] Similarly, Thomas Simmonds felt duty-bound to write from Whitchurch in 1876 regarding his niece Mary Ward. She was pregnant with a second illegitimate child, and Simmonds explained that her father had washed his hands of her. She had requested an order for the Bradfield workhouse but this had been denied, with the result that "She is destitute no were to go no one to support her." Simmonds insisted that the guardians were "bound to relieve or admit her to the workhouse" and his advocacy worked, at least in part. While the LGB declined to interfere directly, his letter was annotated to the effect that: "The Board would however remark that if this girl is as alleged destitute and in the condition described, the Gdns and their officers will incur a great responsibility should any calamity occur in consequence of the refusal of assistance."[62] Success of sorts also accrued to others and certainly nourished further correspondence. Thus Richard Willden wrote from Bradford (Yorkshire) in April 1843 on behalf of William Chadwick, a seventy-one-year-old coal miner. Chadwick was unable to work and had been removed to Gainsborough (Lincolnshire). On his arrival he was locked up from eight in the evening until nine the following morning:

> and he could not go to the privy to do his Deeds And to do them in the room he Durst not for fear and ... when that he got out to go to the privy the Man that took care of the Doar took hould of him to make him go back and Drue aknife out of his pockit And maid him go to the room and lockt him up a gain the Day and Night.[63]

Willden complained that Chadwick was "so bad that he did not how to live for the pain he had." Although there is no clear indication of any resolution, the letter was annotated to say that an inquiry into the complaint was to be promised to the writer. Willden's is a good example of an *instigating* letter – an initial approach that stimulates or leads to further correspondence, either by the advocate themselves or by others. In this case, it was Chadwick himself who followed up his advocate's complaint, writing two further letters to the PLC.[64]

Many writers who expressed a sense of duty, feeling, or compassion melded such arguments with linguistic registers of injustice and its rectification. Thus, Emma Cost wrote from Bow (Middlesex) in November 1880. She requested the return of five rings taken from her mother when she was an inmate of Poplar workhouse and on the occasion of her transfer on 24

May 1880 to Colney Hatch Lunatic Asylum.[65] She also added: "the Commissioners of Lunacy say that [her mother] ought not to have been removed which was done with great Violence." Such double injustice induced Cost to consult a magistrate at Thames Police Court, and she threatened to progress the matter further with a solicitor if necessary.[66] This blend of compassion and fight for justice is also clearly visible in an anonymous letter sent in 1854 from Burslem "to let [the PLB] know how the Poor is treated in this town." The writer recounted the story of a woman who had been ill for nine days in their shared lodgings with "A pain about her heart [she was] tumbling herself all over the floor with pain." The advocate:

> could not get a doctor all this time to se her it should grive any person of feling to see th mother of a family with A little baby and was not able to pay one shilling to a doctor … we went to the releivein officer Mr Barlo and beged of him to send her a note for the parish doctor and told him the state she was in he told us he would not [let] that person of in a great passion and shut the door in her face.[67]

Once again, it becomes obvious that the boundaries we have imposed between categories and subcategories of advocates are often inadequate to divide them in practice.

A core of writers was also driven into correspondence by the belief that the poor as a whole *should* have been treated better than they were. Perceived discrepancies between national rules and local welfare practice informed such texts, but there were also some who wrote specifically to clarify points of law or regulation. For example, the Burslem cabinetmaker John Walker did not specify precisely on whose behalf he requested clarification when he wrote in 1852, but he asked the PLB to "be so kind as to Inform me at what age a Widow is Entitled to Clame out door Relife from the Parish." The unnamed widow, he continued, "has no Children but what are Marred and have famleys of theire own to Keep [and] I should take it as a grate favour if you will Explain the Law on this point."[68] The neutral tone of Walker's request for information was unusual. Far more frequently, poor advocates who asked to be apprised of the rules did so with a clear sense that an injustice had been committed by local officers. William Worden of

Dartmouth (Devon), for example, asked the PLB in 1865 to clarify whether "such a right by law exists that gives … the Corporation the power to order two corpses to be buried in one grave." Worden's letter was stimulated by the case of his own mother, who had been buried with another pauper when he had been assured of a single grave. He complained to the sexton but in the end, "I was obliged to see my Mother put into a grave upon the top of another corpse, and that corpse a man."[69] Worden's outrage was clear and under the circumstances the tone of his request for clarification was surprisingly controlled. Yet as we have seen, most poor advocates displayed much stronger emotion when they wrote to the Centre. Not only were their letters driven by compassion and a sense of duty towards their neighbours, kith, and kin but they were also fuelled by solidarity, fellow feeling and, inevitably, the sense that they themselves might be the focus of such letters in the future. In our final section here we examine how that solidarity took root in more overt political advocacy.

TRADE UNIONS AND WORKERS' POLITICAL ASSOCIATIONS

In some senses all letters and statements by poor writers and their advocates might be read as political acts. Each criticism challenged the legitimate powers of guardians and their staff, and the very legitimacy of the law itself. Yet, and as chapter 2 began to suggest, we can trace more focused political advocacy throughout the corpus and particularly from the 1860s as the organised poor in their trade unions, those openly out of work and who organised within their various unemployed associations, as well as political movements that allied themselves with this reinvigorated labour movement, all took an increasing interest in poor law matters. Thus John Jones, secretary to the Poor Man's Guardian Society, wrote to the PLC in 1846 pressing the case of Phillis Pavey, an elderly widow living in Poplar but with a settlement at Bridport (Dorset).[70] She had been refused admission to the Poplar workhouse and then instructed to "find her way as she could" back to Bridport. Jones had personally applied on Pavey's behalf but was told bluntly by the same official that "he would have nothing to do with her," prompting the Society to take up the case.[71] Other advocates of this sort acted more directly. Daniel Liddell, a radical involved with education reform and anti–corn law league agitation, wrote eight letters in 1849 concerning the Newcastle-upon-Tyne and Bellingham unions (Northumberland).[72] An initial text contained the confident assertion that Liddell would be looking to bring before Parliament and the public "the treatment by the Bellingham Board of some of their Paupers, which I consider to be cruel in the extreme and illegal." This sense of the power of the public is familiar from other advocate and pauper rhetoric, but Liddell further (and forcefully) asserted that he gave "notice that you may have an opportunity of instructing your Assistant Commissioners to obtain from me the necessary information." Taking Liddell up on his offer, W.H.T. Hawley, the poor law inspector for the district, visited Newcastle to talk through the former's concerns, particularly the case of Widow Frazer. Her relief had been stopped by the Newcastle guardians, who planned to have her removed to Kirkharle (Northumberland), notwithstanding twenty years' residence at Newcastle. Although Hawley appeared at this time to sympathise with Frazer and indicated to Liddell that he agreed she should remain in Newcastle, the PLB were unwilling to translate that opinion into an order. One reading of this situation is that an initial central concern about the influence of radicals should not override the ingrained reluctance of the Centre to coerce localities. Six months of frustration followed as Liddell rehearsed the intricacies of Frazer's case. Having by then lost faith in the PLB he declared: "Our correspondence must be now brought to a close, having extended over a long period to no purpose, and does not appear likely to be attended by any beneficial results." His final act was to send them a copy of a letter published in the *Gateshead Observer* in which he condemned the New Poor Law as a system under which it appeared that:

> a Board of Guardians are an uncontrolled body in some matters, and whether acting from principle, from pique, or from caprice, can set at defiance the recommendations of the Poor Law Board. The country should either be saved the expenses of these Commissioners, or these gentlemen should have power to enforce their decisions or *recommendations*.

The language of frustration and systemic failure of oversight was a feature of much early political advocacy. Thus, in March and May 1850 the Chartist and socialist Isaac Ironside wrote from Sheffield (Yorkshire) on behalf of Emma Mitchell and her brother Hodgson.[73] The latter had been a collier but was unable to work due to ill-health. Mitchell had taken responsibility for the care of Hodgson's youngest child on the death of his wife some six years earlier, for which she had received 2s weekly from the parish. Mr Lorimer, the local assistant overseer, had stopped the child's monies around 1847, for which he was subsequently reprimanded after a magistrate intervened. Sometime in early 1850, immediately following the death of that magistrate, Lorimer again stopped her relief. With no allowance and a sick brother who she feared "will not live many days," Mitchell approached Ironside, who made his views on the Centre's inaction very clear, mixing political, moral, and legal argument with an undertone of utter frustration:

> You may not be aware that [I] hate the centralizing tendency with a most perfect hatred. I do not believe in Malthus nor do I wish to see the poor people starved to death by law. This case is not likely to lessen my hatred. If I could see anything like moral responsibility on the part of the central authorities, I should be inclined to view centralization with more favour. But there is nothing of the kind. Stump orators make perfect laws, and legal response is all that is ever thought of. For instance, you have acted legally I suppose in this case. Lorimer would no doubt say the same, Ditto the Board of Guardians at Barnsley. My first letter to Lorimer was on the 18th Jany. my first letter to you was on the 1st of March, the poor wretch starving all the time – more than 16 weeks.[74]

By the second half of the nineteenth century, as radical political figures like these were joined by groups and working-class associations advocating on their own part, the situation began to change. Thus a group, "Specially deputed by a body of sixteen hundred men of the unemployed Lancashire Operatives," wrote to the PLB in 1863.[75] They characterised themselves, and those they represented as:

> men whose whole lives have been one Continued struggle for manly independence, who have never stooped to mortal man to ask for Charity, men who have banded together in societies to relieve their own distressed, to heal their own sick, and to bury their own dead, men who have (now in this dread crisis for which the history of this County has no parallel) parted with their hard earned savings, jealously hoarded for old age or sickness, sold their clothing, pulled down their household goods, all to put off to the last moment when our pride of independence must give way, and we must perforce ask for assistance or see our wives and children starve before our eyes.

The rhetoric here was not that of pauperised, weak, or wretched individuals but of men who were proud and valued their independence and contribution.[76] They further objected to being prevented from searching for work while they received temporary relief (a matter we take up in chapter 9). And if most of the language was measured and controlled, a clear sense of anger at the irrationality of the relief process is also evident: "The question is frequently put by the relieving officer, 'Have you not got work yet?'… It is a mockery! How can we find work when not allowed time to seek it. We Want Work, a shilling of our earnings is better to us than any bestowal by Charity."[77]

Moving further into the later nineteenth century, we find more permanent established trade unions and socialist political groupings entering the corpus as advocates. In a January 1887 letter for the *Manchester Guardian*, J. Derbyshire ("Secretary to the Unemployed in Salford and Manchester") asked why poor men were forced to be supplicants when guardians and councils could:

> announce to us that work would be given to all that asked, at reasonable wages, and then both the ratepayers and we would be benefited, for there would be no occasion to trouble the Guardians and place them in a dilemma. At the same time pauperism would decrease, a result that all would most strongly desire, both from a moral and physical point of view.[78]

Derbyshire was clearly aware of the then current debates about the physical and emotional toll of pauperism. He also of course implied that the guardians were sympathetic to this essentially collectivist agenda. In 1892 the Liverpool and Vicinity United Trades & Labour Council wrote with an even more direct political text, demanding the abolition of the property qualification for vestrymen and poor law guardians altogether, "as they consider that it is a gross injustice to workmen being excluded from serving on these bodies on account of inability to pay the high rental that is unjustly enacted by the present unsatisfactory law."[79] This demand was followed up two years later by the Liverpool Association of the Unemployed, who enclosed a resolution passed at a mass meeting calling the attention of the LGB to the fact that "no notice has been taken by our local Authorities of the circular issued by the Local government Board 30 Sept empowering them to start relief works and we ask the government to take the matter in hand & compel our local Authorities to perform their duty."[80] This focus on breach of process is a familiar rhetorical backdrop for our book, but here the language of the need for compulsion from the Centre and the undertone of implied corruption gave a distinctive political edge.

At the very end of our period, organised labour was making determined rhetorical and strategic intervention in the local workings of the poor law. In March 1896, for instance, William Davis, secretary to the National Society of Amalgamated Brassworkers, wrote demanding an inquiry "against the Birmingham Workhouse … and especially into the circumstances regarding the death of Henry Fisher."[81] The LGB had already been alerted to the death by Hugh Leonard, a fellow inmate, who noted that Fisher had been in the workhouse for seven weeks, categorised as able-bodied and set to sawing wood. The other able-bodied inmates, according to Leonard,

> wondered at the man being put by their side to work as he looked so ill. The poor fellow had frequently complained to the Medical Officer saying that he was too ill to work but he was ordered by the Doctor to go on with what he was employed at without giving Him any treatment.

Fisher was eventually allowed to sit and bundle wood but other inmates advised him to tell the workhouse staff he could not continue. Indeed Leonard advised him to remain in bed the next morning and ask to see the medical officer. Fisher was unsuccessful in seeing the doctor but the labour master himself thought it prudent to take him later in the morning; and as "the poor dying fellow was being led to the probationary[,] cries of shame were raised by the men in the yard." The death of Fisher an hour later had "caused great excitement all over the building and an inquiry is really the only remedy."[82] The case attracted letters not just from the National Society of Amalgamated Brassworkers, but from the Amalgamated Society of Carpenters & Joiners *and* the Birmingham Trades Council – evidence of concerted advocacy on the part of organised labour.[83]

CONCLUSION

Although we can for purposes of discussion make typological distinctions between categories of advocates, in practice there is considerable permeability between them. Our first category – "friends to the poor" – was largely populated by the professional classes and clergymen, and characterised rhetorically by the obligations of the well-to-do towards less fortunate members of their communities. However, while the levels of literacy and the stylistic approaches of this group differ markedly from those of poor writers (our fourth category), the central purpose of their letters and the registers they employed were in many ways similar. Both groups wrote largely on behalf of named paupers or identifiable cohorts of the local poor; used a broadly controlled form of appeal to highlight what were constructed as significant abuses or misapplications of the rules; and sought the intervention of the Centre to right specific wrongs. When we broaden this discussion to include our other categories of advocates, the similarities between them often outweigh their undoubted typological distinctions. Investigators and reformers – whether semi-professional like Joseph Rowntree, locally active like William Joseph Davies, or personally motivated like Mungo Paumier – blended various public and private agendas with acts of advocacy on behalf of paupers and pauper cohorts, and once again did so using linguistic tools remarkably similar to those of other advocates.

Even poor law officials, whose role was (theoretically, at least) closely circumscribed by the rules and regulations issued from the Centre, continued to utilise similar linguistic tools to advocate for the poor, notwithstanding that their central concerns were procedural, political, or personal in nature. Our final category, trade unions and workers' political associations, moved from the rhetoric and terminology of paupers and relief to a new register of unemployed workers, citizen rights and expectations, and root and branch reform.

How, then, are we to interpret these intertwining threads? It seems clear above all that what King and Jones identified as a "shared linguistic register" among diverse groups of advocates under the Old Poor Law remained influential long after 1834. While each advocate group demonstrates subtly (sometimes markedly) different motives for writing to the Centre, the most striking thing to note is that the concerns they raised, and the manner in which they raised them remained broadly consistent across categories. More often than not they related to the failings and shortcomings of specific local officials or union administrations as a whole. Whether the cases that exemplified these failings and shortcomings related to individual (named) paupers, specific cohorts of paupers locally, or the poor more generally, the appeal was by and large the same: for the Centre to intervene in order to ensure that the rules and regulations were properly enforced on behalf of the poor and, thus, that the rule of (formal or informal) law was re-established. However, the rhetoric of justice, humanitarianism, and natural rights was appropriated by many writers just as it was under the Old Poor Law. This strongly suggests a broad recognition that the law continued to be mutable, and that local practice was, and should remain, malleable. An illustrative case is the appeal of Reverend Charlie Woodcock, vicar of Chardstock (Devon). Having questioned (and reluctantly accepted) the procedural correctness of the decision to remove a chronically sick woman to the workhouse, Woodcock pointed out that the Board of Guardians was deeply divided on the issue. Even the chairman and vice-chairman, having visited her unannounced, declared themselves "quite shocked at the contemplated removal to the Union House." In constructing his appeal, Woodcock asked: "Is it right that a patient severely afflicted for so many years, should without just cause be … driven into the house," and went on to opine: "The whole proceeding appears to me so regardless of humanity, so fatuous & anomalous, that I feel compelled to bring the matter before the notice of the Poor Law Board."[84] This approach – to request procedural clarification from the Centre within a broad appeal for the humanitarian treatment of the poor – is common to all of our categories, and demonstrates an expectation on the part of advocates that after 1834 not only individual decisions, but procedure itself, remained negotiable. This way of proceeding chimes closely with the appeals of paupers and once again demonstrates the broad continuities between the old and new regimes, and between the sentimental and pragmatic approaches of all those involved in negotiations for relief. The question of central responses to this unified rhetorical approach is the subject of the upcoming chapter.

4

Responding to Paupers and Advocates: The Central Authority

INTRODUCTION

Mary Chester, a widow with five children, wrote to the Poor Law Board (PLB) from Arnold on 23 June 1862. She claimed to have brought up her offspring "in an honest way" without any assistance, but stated that she was now too old and infirm to work. Having been offered the workhouse, Chester described an unwillingness to be parted from her children and was convinced that the probability of her dying in a workhouse with "not one Relative to close My Aged Eyes would … quickly bring My Grey locks with Sorrow to the grave." She closed by asking the Board if they would "Condescend to intercede with the guardians."[1] This emotive letter was clearly designed to pull at the heartstrings of the Centre and elicit a favourable response. It is also representative of a view percolating through our corpus that many poor people saw the Central Authority as the highest court of arbitration in matters of poor relief. Not only *could* they intervene in disputed relief cases, but they *ought* to do so.[2] The associated language of intercession runs throughout the material, sometimes very directly. Thus, Edward Lepley wrote to the PLB in 1858: "Hoping you will be Pleased to Intercede with the Guardians of Bethnal Green that I may Receive some Relief for myself wife & Family."[3] William Bennett of Kidderminster asked the Poor Law Commission (PLC) in 1847 for their "Gracaus favour for to Intercede" to get the relief denied to him.[4] Similarly, George Ellis from Basford told the relieving officer that he would "appeal to the higher Power" (the PLB) when his relief was stopped.[5] This notion that the Centre could and would step in is directly at odds with the reality of the Centre's power as set out in its 1862 response to Mary Chester: "it rests with the [Guardians] to decide in what manner relief, where it is needed, shall be given, whether in or out of the Workhouse"; and further, that the Centre was "unable to interfere for the purpose of ordering relief in any individual case, being expressly prohibited by law from so doing."[6]

That there should be such a discrepancy between what the poor and their advocates thought the Centre *should* do and what the Centre claimed it *could* do is perhaps unsurprising. The suddenness of the 1834 reform meant that local officials and magistrates were initially confused about how the New Poor Law was to be interpreted, and confusion spread to paupers and the wider poor in their dealings with them.[7] Writing in its first annual report, the PLC confirmed widespread misunderstanding over its role; some parishes were convinced that, as soon as the Poor Law Amendment Act (PLAA) was passed, all superintendence, control, and management devolved upon the Centre. This forced the Commission to enter into a period of "widely-extended" correspondence as they tried to answer questions about the law and its application to particular cases, as well as more general questions about administration. Moreover, enquiries came "from magistrates, from parochial officers, from rate-payers, as well as from paupers, collectively or individually," and the correspondence continued to increase, forming "a considerable portion of the business of the department, and of the demands upon our attention."[8] The response given to Mary Chester, almost thirty years after the passing of the PLAA, shows that the systemic misconception about who held ultimate responsibility for relief decisions had considerable longevity. The Centre's response also clearly showed an attempt to close down correspondence by implying that further communication would bring no benefit to pauper complainants. The success of this response can be debated and is something to which we will return. Chester's first letter was annotated, "Acknowledge and give the usual answer." However, the nature of a *usual* answer followed different rules depending on how the

Centre characterised a letter's contents; and, more widely, the words of those responses can reveal much about the nature and extent of the power that the Central Authority wielded.

In this chapter, then, we explore the complex mechanics of central attitudes and writing. We ask if all pauper writers received a response or if the likelihood or nature of a reply varied according to whether their letter was written inside the workhouse, whether it focused on individual relief cases or made broader complaints about general treatment, or whether the writer was male or female. The chapter also focuses on the way responses were physically constructed. Our findings can tell us much about the inner workings of what was a huge administrative body.[9] In particular we ask whether texts authored by our three core writer groups (paupers, the wider poor, advocates) were treated any differently to official correspondence from clerks, guardians, and paid officers. Finally, we consider the intertwining issues of how central responses were framed by law and regulation, and how our core writers reacted to replies they considered inadequate.

MAKING SENSE OF THE CORRESPONDENCE

In chapter 2 we explored the size and scale of the poor law archive and noted how the PLC became the classic example of tighter centralisation and co-ordination of government functions. In turn we looked at its ability to "command, filter and deploy information" at a scale which David Eastwood saw as constituting the kernel of a revolution in government.[10] From its inception the Commission tended to keep *all* incoming correspondence and a copy of almost every official letter they sent, developing an organised registry system to maintain control of the resulting archive. Indeed, so important were the various elements of the registry system that the Commission laid out on their responses (or their envelopes) direct instructions for subsequent communications in the form that "the Number as well as the Date of the inclosed letter may be quoted." This ensured that later correspondence could be linked seamlessly to earlier communications and provided a common mechanism for both union officials *and* the poor to approach the Centre.[11] Owing to the extraordinary preservation of material facilitated by the binding process described in chapter 2, we can say with certainty

Table 4.1
Categories of letter to the Central Authority, 1834–c.1900

1. Letters written regarding access to relief: initial attempts to acquire relief, attempts to restart relief which had been stopped, or attempts to increase reduced allowances.
2. Letters of complaint: for neglect, ill-treatment, malpractice by workhouse or wider union staff, or conditions in the workhouse.
3. Letters which bring general complaints and access to relief together.
4. Letters broadly classed under the heading of "other." These tended to be letters which asked specific questions relating to matters of law or process.

Source: MH12. Local Government Board and Predecessors: Correspondence with Poor Law Unions and Other Local Authorities, The National Archives.

that, when it came to the way incoming letters were dealt with administratively, those from our core writer groups were treated very much the same as "official" correspondence. Such letters were invariably date-stamped, allocated union, inspectors', and paper numbers, and had suggested replies annotated on the reverse or appended separately, with pro-forma responses developed for all sorts of correspondence.

It is into this context of quickly developing administrative practices that we must place the draft responses to letters from our three core writer groups, responses that are illuminated by analysis of a subsample of fourteen unions covering the period from 1834 to around 1899.[12] While chapter 2 gave a broad statistical overview of the corpus and archive, this exercise is intended to facilitate the time-consuming process of unpicking the complex threads of writing and response. These fourteen unions generate some 629 items from our core writer groups plus associated responses and (often numerous) prior annotations and directions. Most letters (504, 80.1 per cent) were written from outside the workhouse; of these, 51 per cent were generated by outdoor poor and paupers and 49 per cent by advocates.[13] Only 119 letters (18.9 per cent) were sent by indoor paupers.[14] Further analysis shows that the majority of the letters can be divided into four core categories, as outlined in table 4.1.

An example from our first category is the 1845 letter written by John Lees of Gedling (Nottinghamshire), who noted:

> I have applied to the Basford Union for relief and they offered me the House but I refused to go in being a Man 66 years Old and a Widower and very infirm and not able to do any work. Gent I shall feel obliged to you if you Can do me any service.[15]

This letter may be compared with an example from our second category, a complaint from Patrick McGarry from Burslem in 1859. McGarry begged the PLB's "pardon for this liberty I have taken I hope ye will excuse one as I cannot help makeing this complaint to ye." He accused the relieving officer of neglect in not providing the family a note for the doctor when their children were ill.[16] An example from our third category, where complaint and access to relief form part of a single letter, can be found in Edwin Mills's correspondence from Carlton (Nottinghamshire). He alleged that when he was discharged from the Basford workhouse his old clothes were restored to him but were "as damp as culd be," and he caught a chill while returning home that necessitated a spell in the Nottingham Hospital. He continued that Basford allowed him 1s 6d per week, which he considered not enough to live on.[17] Finally, a representative letter from the fourth or "other" category is an enquiry from Harriet Staples of Gretton (Northamptonshire) in May 1847. She asked whether "A person receiving relief from [the] Parish is obliged to be at or in [her] residence on the time the Relieving Officer bring her the weekly money at the hazard of her not receiving of it." It may be that Staples was herself the person referred to in her letter, though she posed this as a hypothetical request for information.[18] Of course the boundaries between these categories were often blurred. Writers who stated that their current relief was insufficient and requested more were *de facto* making a complaint about relief levels. Direct questions concerning finer legal points of settlement may be taken as questions of relief, as the two were linked and a question about the one would undoubtedly encompass the other. Nonetheless, a close reading of intent at the level of individual letters (itself a reason for this subsample analysis) does allow a definitive classification in the vast majority of cases, and the quantitative distribution of the texts in this

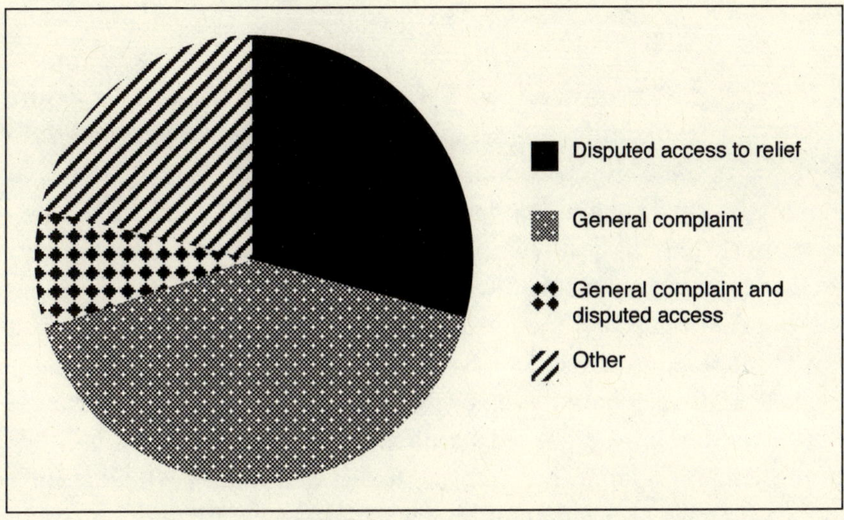

4.1 Distribution of letters and petitions across four category types
Source: MH12. Local Government Board and Predecessors: Correspondence with Poor Law Unions and Other Local Authorities, The National Archives.

sense can be seen in figure 4.1. In what follows we examine the ways in which the Centre responded to writers of these types of letter, fusing together the two categories of complaint letters, given that the Centre considered them as a single canvas.

ACCESS TO INDIVIDUAL RELIEF

Access to relief – its scale and mode – loomed large on the agenda of our core letter writers. Of the 184 letters in this category for our subsample, 181 (98.4%) were written from outside the workhouse.[19] Of these, 147 (81.2%) received an *initial* response, while, of indoor letters, two out of three (66.7%) did.[20] Paupers, poor writers, and advocates seem to have been regarded slightly differently at the margins: of the 127 outdoor letters from paupers and the wider poor, 101 (79.5%) received an initial response, while 46 (85.2%) from advocates received such responses. A look along gender lines reveals that 110 (82.1%) men received initial responses, while for women the figure was 34 (79.1%). For the Central Authority, then, gender had little if any direct impact on the likelihood of responding.[21]

In reacting to letters concerning access to relief for individuals, the Centre created a series of draft responses to streamline their processes. These were explored in the context of seven Midland unions by Natalie Carter and Steven King, and the four key developments which they found in the evolution of such drafts bear revisiting here.[22] First, although the very earliest draft responses were handwritten, by 1836 elements of pro-forma replies had been introduced.[23] These would include the pre-printing of the first line of the response, which initially read: "The Poor Law Commission for England and Wales have to acknowledge the Receipt of your Letter of the ..." Spaces were also designated for the name of the union, parish, and date to be written. Very quickly this form evolved to include a printed section to accommodate the initials of those who drafted, copied, examined, and dispatched the outgoing letter, showing the importance of record keeping and accountability. These forms initially had the printed heading "Acknowledgement Form." Although this heading was dropped in the early 1840s, the form had by then become a staple of the Centre, as it would remain for the rest of the Victorian period thanks to its ability to be used to formulate an answer to all incoming correspondence. Second, by the final half of 1842, we see a significant development in the wording used by the Centre, with the introduction of a sentence indicating that the "Commis [Commissioners] have no power to interfere in any individual case for the ppose [purpose] of ordering relief." These draft responses also stated that a copy of the incoming letter would be sent to the local Board of Guardians for their attention. The third development was that around 1846 the Centre began to use an almost complete pro-forma for the draft response. This printed text took the earlier wording of being unable to interfere, and expanded it with the following addition: "being expressly precluded from so doing by the 15th Section of the Poor Law Amendment Act." Again, the pro-forma included the statement that the Centre had sent the letter to the guardians and that "they do not doubt that the guardians will give such directions as the circumstances of the case seem to require."

The draft letter to the guardians was also largely pre-printed from this time with space to write details relating to the original correspondent and a summary of the subject matter, with further pre-printed text asking for the guardians' observations. Finally, we see another refinement in the pro-forma from 1855. At this point the draft responses to the original correspondent and the guardians were brought together on one sheet of paper, the top half containing the largely pre-printed response to the correspondent and the bottom half being addressed to the guardians asking for their observations. The same pro-formas were used to draft responses for disputed relief cases, whether emanating from inside or outside the workhouse. These developments are instructive. As well as standardising preferred text, the use of pre-printed pro-formas was designed to save the time that the clerks spent working on each response. This is indicative not only of the amount of material that the Centre had to deal with at its inception but also of the fact that this correspondence continued to be voluminous over time. By the mid-1840s letters concerning individual relief cases were commonly annotated, "Usual Answer," in confirmation for us that responding to such letters was a routine part of the Centre's business.

Writers seeking to contest access to relief often put forward details of very specific life events and stories, though they also employed a rhetorical matrix of emotion, appeals to natural law, engagement with black-letter law, and allegations of breach of process and moral obligation in order to emphasise entitlement. We return to aspects of this matrix in the next and subsequent chapters; the point here, however, is that the production of standard textual responses to such individualistic relief letters deliberately ignored these matters. They served as a corrective to the poor's misunderstanding of the Centre's role and to emphasise that further correspondence on the matters raised would be futile. This mode of response had clear roots in the Benthamite ideology which drove many of the initial reforms of the New Poor Law. It took away personal initiative and fixed "responsibilities precisely, to lay down for administrators at all levels clear instructions and guiding lines which would issue from the legislature."[24] Ensuring that the Central Authority was prohibited from discretionary activities on a case-by-case basis prevented relief decisions from being influenced by "partial" or "capricious motives" (or humanitarian grounds), and this was a key aim of the PLC at its inception.[25]

Yet, we should be wary of accepting at face value this prepared structure and content for responses to those contesting relief. Questions regarding individual relief cases, and even questions concerning the intricacies of the law, were not straightforward. Neither were central-local relations. As we saw above, standard-text responses to our core letter writers went together with responses to guardians. From the outset copies of letters disputing individual relief cases were sent to the guardians for their observations. The guardians were expected to respond to these requests for information and so cases would be enquired into locally. This process left the letter writer to some extent at a disadvantage, as guardians, when asked to justify their initial decisions, could do so without involving the writer, leaving the local authorities owning the narrative of individual cases. Thus, when John Fisher wrote from Arnold in November 1847, he noted that he was unemployed except for parish work on the roads, which yielded an income of 8s per week. Fisher argued that this left his family in a starving condition and he thus wrote to the PLC "as my last source" to use their power to relieve his distress. He received the "usual" answer that the guardians would be sent a copy of his letter for their observations.[26] The guardians in turn responded that Fisher was employed at stone breaking and paid 1s 6d per ton for the days he worked and should have been able to earn 15s per week if he worked full time.[27] The implication, not shared with Fisher, that he was shiftless and lazy is clear. On the other hand, such reviews might also result in a favourable outcome for the author. Elizabeth Gatch wrote on behalf of her elderly mother who resided in Axminster and claimed that her mother's relief was insufficient, given that neither she nor her brother could provide additional assistance. She asked the Centre to "interfer in her behalf" and allow additional funds. Gatch again received the "usual" response of non-interference and was told that a copy of her letter would be forwarded to the guardians.[28] The guardians wrote back to the Centre twice, first to say that the relieving officer had been directed to examine the case, and second to report that the case had been before the guardians and an additional 6d had been granted. News of such success was likely exultantly shared by the family and wider community.[29]

The significance of the Centre's sending a letter to the guardians asking for a case to be re-examined cannot be overstated. Even in instances where the poor failed to get previous decisions overturned, the fact that the guardians were obliged to re-investigate their cases sent a powerful message to others who felt they had a genuine claim and ensured that there was a sense, among the poor and their advocates, that local decision makers could indeed be held to account. Each time a re-investigation occurred, it was precisely *because* a letter-writer had put pen to paper. Whenever the process provoked a favourable response, no matter how slight or partial, that message was amplified. It is easy to see why the poor and their advocates took this to be a sign of the Centre doing exactly what they professed they would *not* do – interceding on their behalf – and it explains why paupers, the wider poor, and their advocates continued to write to the Centre throughout the Victorian period. In this sense the Centre's letters to those contesting relief allowed a degree of interpretation of its rules and processes to both the poor and guardians.

LETTERS OF COMPLAINT

Our union subsample yielded 311 letters of complaint or letters combining dispute of individual relief cases *and* complaint (50% of the total). Of these, 197 (63.3%) were written from outside the workhouse and 110 (35.5%) from inside. These figures are to an extent misleading. Some 110 of the total 119 letters written by the indoor poor detailed complaints, whereas of the 504 letters written by or for the outdoor poor only 197 (39.1%) were complaints. This points to an intimate connection between complaint and the experience of the workhouse, something we shall see throughout our remaining chapters. Even so, in our total subsample of 311 complaint letters, outdoor writers received an initial response in 112 (36%) cases, whereas inmates received such a response in only 33 (10.6%) cases. Whether letters of complaint received an initial response thus appears to be strongly determined by whether they were written by the indoor or outdoor poor. It is clear that gender also had an impact, in a way that was not the case with our first category. Of the 258 men and 30 women who wrote such letters, we see that 133 men (51.6%) received initial responses while for women the figure was 10 (33.3%). A more equal distribution is evident, however, when we examine the number of cases being referred back to the guardians for observations. Here, men made up 155 cases (60%) referred and women 19 (63.3%).

The wording of initial responses to complaint letters could be highly variable rather than merely formulaic. In some cases the Centre wrote and promised to make enquiry into the matter; in others they promised that the complaint would receive their attention. Sometimes they simply stated that the matter would be brought to the attention of the guardians, though in practice only 59.9 per cent of complaints were in fact referred to the guardians; much less than the 75.5 per cent of referred relief contestation letters. There seem to be three explanations for this disparity: first, some complaints were dealt with by the Centre's inspectors on their next visit to the appropriate union with no notice given to the guardians, and consequently generated no such correspondence;[30] second, although letters initiating a complaint were likely to be sent to the guardians for comment, follow-up letters often were not; finally, anonymous letters of complaint would sometimes prompt no action on the part of the Centre.[31] Our understanding of the response mechanism for complaint letters is further complicated by the fact that we see a significant change in process for the post-1871 period. In August 1871 the powers and responsibilities of the PLB were transferred to the newly created and far larger Local Government Board (LGB), the remit of which was wider and covered numerous local government responsibilities, including public health as well as relief to the poor. This change of structure seemed to usher in some changes to the administrative processes of the Centre, particularly during the 1890s. What we begin to see slowly from around 1872, but particularly from the 1890s, is that draft responses to either relief or complaint letters were less likely to be bound into the volumes. Indeed, by the 1890s we begin to find instances of letters which were annotated with "Usual Answer" or "Acknowledge" with no surviving copies of responses either to the letter writer or the guardians. Again, particularly during the 1890s (although we do see a scattering in other years from 1871 onwards), a number of letters had a yellow sticker appended with the word "Acknowledged" or "Acknowledged and attention promised" printed on them, along with the date on which the response was either written or sent.[32] However, more significant for us is the fact that during this latter period the number of writers who received an initial response to letters of complaint increased, particularly in regard to indoor writers and just as collective organisations turned their attention to the New Poor Law. Thus, in our subsample there were 164 complaint letters written from outside the workhouse during the years 1834 to 1871 and, of these, eighty-nine (54.3%) received an initial response. However, we then find that there were thirty-three complaint letters written from outside the workhouse during the years 1872 to 1899 and, of these, twenty-three (69.7%) received an initial response. In turn, there were fifty-nine complaint letters from workhouse inmates during the years 1834 to 1871 and, of these, only ten (16.9%) received an initial response. In contrast the fifty-one complaint letters authored by workhouse inmates during the years 1872 to 1899 invoked responses in twenty-three cases (45.1%).[33]

Notwithstanding this change in broadly conceived "success" rates, it is still the case that throughout the period complaints related to the malpractice of staff or workhouse conditions were usually passed back to the guardians as a way of prompting an initial period of local investigation. As with complaints from outside the workhouse, this process handed control of the narrative to local authorities. John Gunn, an elderly Liverpool workhouse inmate, wrote to the LGB in 1881. He complained that Williams, the workhouse tailor, had pushed him back into his bath, the shock almost causing him to drown.[34] Gunn received no response to his letter but the LGB sent a request to Liverpool that they be "informed of the result of the investigation which the Select Vestry no doubt will make into the complaint of this pauper."[35] An investigation was made and the LGB was informed that the evidence was contradictory enough to indicate that the assault did not take place. Further, they believed instead that Gunn, whom they described as an "irritable and obstinate old man," had wanted to leave the bath before he was properly washed and Williams had been stopping him from doing so, with the result that Gunn had stumbled and fallen into the water before being assisted by another inmate. The LGB was satisfied by the response and annotated the report: "his Complaint has been attended to."[36] As often the case with pauper complainants, the local authority used its response as a chance to undermine the character of the original correspondent and cast doubt on the pauper's narrative of events. Sometimes the writer's character was already known to the Centre and, although the usual response mechanism might be followed, the outcome was already predetermined. Johnathan Middleton wrote from the Berwick workhouse (Northumberland) in 1843 complaining that although he was suffering from palsy he had been sent out to work in bad weather, which aggravated his condition. He also complained that the master, a dissenter, sent a "madman" to attack him because he belonged to the Church of England.[37] The annotations show that Hawley, one of the assistant poor law commissioners, did not believe Middleton, whom he understood to be "a troublesome dissatisfied person." Nevertheless Hawley suggested the guardians would be "quite ready to institute a searching inquiry into his complaint, on being requested to do so by the Commissioners – There is no Board more anxious to have their workhouse in good order than that at Berwick." The guardians carried out an investigation and concluded that the charges against the master had no foundation, and "that Middleton is a Man of the most worthless and depraved character." The report was annotated by Hawley: "This explanation turns out precisely as I expected, and is quite satisfactory."[38]

It is perhaps this vulnerability to having their appeals dismissed on the basis of an unfair assessment of their character that partly explains why the poor turned to advocates, with 111 complaints (17.6% of all complaints) reported by them.[39] We have already considered advocacy at length but it is important to revisit the theme here, not least because in this subsample advocate letters received a slightly higher percentage of initial responses than those of paupers and the wider poor. Thus Charles Woodcock, rector and magistrate of Chardstock (encountered already in chapter 3), wrote a letter of complaint to the PLB on 6 October 1865 reporting a case of "medical severity." He related the case of Edith Matthews, who had been bed-ridden for some years and "from a prodigious growth of adepose matter (the cause of, & the remedy for which has puzzled & set at defiance 4 medical officers in succession) has become perfectly unwieldy." She had been receiving weekly outdoor relief but the guardians had stopped this and it was feared that she and her able-bodied husband would be removed to the workhouse. The medical officer disputed the order and, following investigation, her relief was reinstated. It was then removed again on the following board day by a majority of two, at which time Woodcock alerted the PLB, who wrote to the guardians requesting their observations.[40] The guardians responded a month later, stating that they were convinced that their earlier resolution was correct and believed that strict attention to diet would cure her. Edward Gulson, poor law inspector, annotated this letter, noting that it was "a very hard case – & one which will not stand investigation & exposure." He further stated: "I know the Revd Chas Woodcock to be a very intelligent, able, & discreet clergyman & Magistrate & he would not make such a representation as that contained in his Letter on slight grounds," and he suggested that the PLB should write to the guardians questioning their decision.[41]

The guardians did not answer the Board's letter until 10 January 1866 (prompting an intervening annotation to ask the guardians for an explanation of the delay), when it was reported that two medical officers had visited Edith Matthews and concluded that the workhouse was the best place for her.[42] A further annotation to this letter, addressed to Gulson, questioned the utility of further correspondence unless he could make it "convienient to attend the Axminster Board and induce them to take a different view of the case." That notation was followed by yet another note suggesting once again that the guardians had exceeded their discretion, that it was unlikely any change in diet would help, and that Matthews would be very wretched if forced to leave her husband, friends, and home.[43] Thereafter, Gulson reported that he had attended the guardians' meeting and they were unanimous in their refusal to increase the allowance.[44] The guardians stated that the woman had a son earning 18s per week and that she was an "idle undeserving person."[45] A letter was drafted by the PLB to Woodcock, the original correspondent, stating they had been in communication with the guardians, who would not alter their decision regarding the family's relief, and adding that it rested with the guardians to determine how relief should be afforded.[46] Ultimately, then, Matthews's case was played out over many letters, annotations, and replies which showed the extraordinary complexity of the correspondence process and the ambiguous role of the Centre. Woodcock was promised that the case would receive attention, but the guardians ultimately maintained their position, questioning the pauper's character in the process. It is clear that the Centre supported Woodcock's view that the initial decision should be overturned but, crucially, they were powerless to change the local decision and Woodcock's status as a known, trustworthy, and diligent individual did not alter the final outcome. Even so, the lengthy process of contestation and inquiry would not have gone unnoticed in the community: it demonstrated that the guardians could and would be held to account for their decisions, and it was an important caution to them about their actions in the future.

"OTHER" LETTERS

In our subcorpus for this chapter there are 134 letters (21.3%) which we categorise as "other." These are for the most part letters asking specific questions about matters of law or process, the rhetoric and strategy of which are addressed at length in chapter 6. Even so, a brief rendering is necessary here to capture the full canvas of responses from the Centre. Thus, some 126 (94%) of the letters were written from outside the workhouse.[47] Of the outdoor letters, 110 (87.3%) received an initial response, while for indoor letters the response rate was much lower (50%). Along gender lines some 124 (92.5%) of the letters were from men, and the gender disparity compared to the wider subsample points to differences in the use of rhetoric of law and process between men and women. This disparity notwithstanding, men received responses in 107 (86.3%) cases and women in six (85.7%). These writers queried relief decisions or issues of ill-treatment and neglect couched as more dispassionate enquiries, but they also asked questions across a broader range of subjects. Thus, in 1887 Adam Hall wrote to the LGB asking if they could help find his sister, who had been "taken from the Industrial School Liverpool by a person named Miss Rye." His sister had been sent to the Western Home for poor orphans in Ontario, Canada. He had tried to contact her and had "applied to the magistrate of Bolton but said that he could not aid me being advised by the master of the Industrial School to seek your aid."[48] A different kind of example would be the case of union officers advocating for central regulations to be moderated in specific cases. For example, in 1864 William Goodacre, clerk of the Mansfield Poor Law Union (PLU) requested sanction to grant outdoor relief to Samuel Spalton, who was able-bodied, a widower, and a father of small children earning only 7s per week. Goodacre's letter was one of a series across our whole corpus which sought to challenge the 1844 Outdoor Relief Prohibitory Order. Indeed, Goodacre's letter is heavily annotated and the Centre considered that: "These cases are probably selected for the purpose of agitation."[49] This case brings to the fore the different attitudes that might divide central and local poor law authorities, a matter to which we now turn.

CENTRAL AND LOCAL RELATIONSHIPS

When the Centre passed along letters which disputed relief decisions or otherwise complained of the treatment of paupers and the wider poor, they did so in effect as part of their surveillance and supervision of local unions.[50] The Centre had a duty to monitor local officers, put in place procedures to encourage professional practices, and suppress reported malpractice. It was painfully aware of the criticism and departmental damage that would follow reportage of poor law press scandals or instances of neglect.[51] The passing of complaint letters to local boards reinforced the fact that guardians were under central surveillance and gave the Centre the opportunity to highlight irregular practices. Thus, William Saxton wrote from Hucknall Torkard (Nottinghamshire) to the PLB in 1853, stating that his relief had recently been stopped and that he and his family were refused both outdoor relief and the workhouse.[52] Saxton received the usual response that the Board was "expressly precluded" from interfering, but a copy of his letter was sent to the Basford PLU for observations. The guardians responded they were content that Saxton was able to maintain himself "if he had the disposition to do so."[53] The PLB was dissatisfied with the answer. An initial annotation by Lord Courtney, one of the Board's secretaries, read: "The cases are but few in which it is safe to refuse all relief: should not the WH have been offered?" The question was directed to Robert Weale, poor law inspector, and he responded in a further annotation that: "the PLB should write to that effect + remind the Gns that the offer of the WH is the best test of destitution." The letter from the Board to Basford stressed that the guardians "incur considerable responsibility in refusing all relief, in whatever form, to a person who represents himself to be destitute … and they are of opinion that in a case of doubt the safer course would be to offer relief in the Workhouse."[54] The message was clear: the guardians were being put on notice to act.

As we have already seen, contested cases relating to individual relief decisions tested the relationship between central and local authorities. The annotations and draft responses to the guardians expose this often-fragile relationship and reconstitute the thought processes behind the Centre's more nuanced responses. When asking the Kidderminster guardians for their observations on a letter from an elderly couple who applied for outdoor relief but were offered the workhouse, for instance, the PLC stressed that they: "wish the Gns to understand that they have no desire to influence the Gns in any way in their decision on the case."[55] This is common wording across the archive. Indeed, the desire to keep good relations between the Centre and individual unions was sometimes so strong that the forwarding of complaints was *discouraged*. In 1877 Mary Ann August, an inmate of Poplar workhouse, wrote to ask that the sum detained from her for her maintenance be restored so that she could gain employment as a needlewoman. Her letter was annotated by Robert Hedley, poor law inspector, to the effect that August had obtained relief under false pretences. Having 3s 8d in her possession rendered her not destitute. Hedley thought the money should be withheld and, moreover, that "no encouragement ought to be given to correspondence by individual paupers with this Bd." He further stated "I can see no reason for sending a copy to the Gns. they dislike these sort of letters very much." A further annotation questioned this response, stating that it seemed only right that the Centre, having being acquainted with the facts of the case, "should give the Gns also the opportunity of learning them." A third and final annotation – "Put by" – would suggest that Hedley's view prevailed and the letter was perhaps never forwarded.[56] This, however, seems to be a rare course of action, and in the main the strength of administrative procedure won out even on occasions where there was some reluctance to forward copies of pauper complaints. Thus, Joseph Fleming wrote from Bethnal Green to the Centre alleging (among other things) that Dr Knox, the workhouse medical officer, had "tried to caus my death" by ordering other inmates to "drag me … in the mad house."[57]

At the time of this letter, in October 1895, Knox was already the subject of an informal investigation as a result of an earlier complaint by Fleming (much to the same effect) and a further accusation of mistreatment by another inmate, Richard Wyatt.[58] In annotations to Fleming's second letter, it was noted that the guardians reported Fleming to be a "'silly' sort of man upon whose statements little reliance could be placed," a comment which resulted in several further annotations suggesting that it should be "put by." However, regardless of the fact that he "should hesitate to take any steps which might unjustly prejudice the position of a professional man" under such circumstances, W.E. Knollys, assistant secretary to the LGB, still resolved that the letter should "go forward to the gdns" for their observations, following which further investigations by the Centre ensued.[59] We can see in these examples that administrative procedures were to a significant extent put in place for the Centre's protection. The PLC was the first public body to have systematic oversight of local government officials. With that came a public responsibility to inspect and maintain surveillance and supervision of local authorities – a responsibility for which the public would indeed hold them accountable. Not having the numbers of inspectors to painstakingly investigate individually disputed claims, the Centre used its power of administrative process to oblige unions to initiate their own investigations. This, however, merely extended and deepened the reach of local-central engagement for all concerned.

RESPONDING TO RESPONSES

The response mechanisms used by the Centre were, as we have seen, designed to discourage cumulative correspondence from the poor and their advocates. For many writers, however, the receipt of a negative response – or no response at all – did little to end their writing, not least because either action was regarded as both insulting and inadequate. We see this across all subsets of the corpus and all genders, with the poor and their advocates subtly or forcefully expressing their dissatisfaction. In December 1837, for instance, Humphrey Hutchins wrote from Llandyssil (Cardiganshire) to say that he and his family were in distress with no food or money due to irregular work. He had received out-relief but this had now been discontinued.[60] Unusually, Hutchins received no response, but the PLC wrote to the guardians for their observations and they replied that Hutchins was an "Idle good for nothing fellow."[61] Hutchins, having been sent a copy of this response by the PLC, was prompted to write in indignation:

> It is very mortifying to me to find that, after all my and my wife's hard labour for our numerous family we have been misrepresented to you as "idle good for nothing fellows," which all my neighbours will most unhesitatingly disprove.

Hutchins included testimonials written by two Baptist ministers, a farmer, and a vicar confirming both his distressed state, and the fact that he was a sober and industrious man. He was also well connected in his community, which in itself should have been a signal of respectability.[62]

Other writers were even more direct. When Jane Mullarkey wrote from York in July 1867, she stated that her husband had recently become unwell, and her language inferred urgent need: "my husband has taken ill [only] last Thursday night." The couple were "living in the most abject and extreme poverty" which necessitated her calling for a medical officer, "who stated at his second visit that my husband had death on him." Mullarkey applied for medical care and food but this was refused "to the Great astonishment of the neighbours who – knows that there is no one in the world in greater misery than I am, and who also knows that we had neither bit nor sup to taste for the last seven days."[63] Naturally, her letter was annotated to acknowledge and write the usual letter. It was additionally annotated to send a copy to the guardians requesting their immediate attention to the case, "which appears to be an urgent one – Request also, to be furnished with the ~~observation~~ explanation of the Relg Offr as to his proceedings in it." While still following its usual pattern, the Board appeared to insist that some speed should attach to the case. Mullarkey, however, only received the usual answer that they were prohibited by law from interfering in individual cases and had no idea that her sense of urgency had been noted. This led her to write again with greater intensity at the beginning of August:

> Gentlemen this murderous way in which justice is connived at surpasses understanding … A person gets ill suddenly … he calls on they commissioners to interfere, they only do so by making the – apology that the poor Law prohibits them, does not the poor Law Commissioners know that the Relieving officer is intitle to give relief in case of a sudden immergency like mine and dont they know that the Doctor is intitle too [to use] why it has been done in many cases here to our knowledge use this, we say why not they commissioners be able to cause the relieving officer and Doctor to exercise the authority vested in them in such cases independant [of] the Guardians to such a patient.[64]

Mullarkey demonstrated her knowledge of the law and her belief that the PLB could and should have insisted that the powers and responsibilities vested in relieving officers in cases of urgent necessity be followed. The sense of precedent (and thus the exercise of tyranny in her case, this precedent not being followed) is important here too. It is also likely from her narrative that the Central response (both the letter and its contents) was shared with neighbours and that "they Board of Commissioners wont take trouble to stop these horrid abuses and therefore everybody may look on the poor law here with the most indignant abhorance."[65] The Centre's letters were thus public rather than strictly private pieces of correspondence, and we return to this and other issues raised here when we consider rhetoric at the level of the whole corpus in chapter 5.

Meanwhile, it was sometimes the process of response itself that drew the greatest criticism. John Rutherford wrote on 4 December 1885 with a series of complaints about conditions and treatment in the Poplar workhouse.[66] A week later and having heard nothing, Rutherford wrote again asking to be informed of the results of the charges he had made. This letter was annotated to be held for one week while the LGB waited for a reply from the guardians.[67] No response was sent to Rutherford, who thus wrote again on 21 December to complain that the more time elapsed the less easy it would be to prove his charges:

> This is my <u>fourth</u> letter to your Honourable Board, And I have given abundant time between each letter for the right sort of answer to come. However the receipt of my first letter was simply acknowledged and that was all; even though a succeeding letter contained a very serious charge against your official Workhouse Visitors. I am strongly inclined to think that my letters have been repressed in the hope that I would abandon my charges in disgust. But I shall do nothing of the sort.[68]

The LGB replied[69] that they had forwarded his previous letters to the guardians for their observations and this response prompted Rutherford to write again with a series of outraged questions:

> Why field to my last letter, such as it was, the information denied to the earlier ones? When were the copies of my letters of the 4th & 7th transmitted to the Poplar Guardians, & with what object? Was it intended to make them judges in their own cause? Was it intended that my charges were to be disposed of in my absence? Were they to be allowed to "square" witnesses in this case, as I charge them with doing in other cases? … Is there to be a real investigation when I shall be able to meet these gentlemen, call my witnesses, & analyse their defence if they have any? If there is to be no investigation – what is the value of the superintendence which your Honourable Board [– – – – – – – –] to exercise of these people?"[70]

This reply gets to the very heart of the problem faced by the Centre in locating the boundary between too much and too little intervention, as well of course as highlighting the stridency of some paupers. Meanwhile, advocates also showed an unwillingness to accept negative or non-responses from the Centre. In 1835 the Reverend Hugh Matthie wrote from Worthenbury (Denbighshire) on behalf of a seventy-five-year-old man named Edward Humphries, who was sick and unable to work. On Matthie's suggestion Humphries saw the overseer of Kiddington, his parish of settlement, to secure outdoor relief. When this was refused, Matthie wrote to complain.[71] The Centre responded that the overseer was within the law to refuse relief and included the standard text that the 15th section of the PLAA prohibited the Centre from interfering in individual cases.[72] Matthie responded that he had referred to the 15th section of the Act and found that the PLC did have the power to make rules for the administration of relief to the poor; and, though they could not interfere in any individual case, a general rule issued by them would apply to individual cases. Furthermore, Matthie pointed out that according to the 27th section of the Act two justices of the peace could order relief to an aged person disabled from work outside the workhouse.[73] His response once again illustrates the clear grasp of law and process that the poor and their advocates had.

A final example of the way that writers conceptualised and used responses from the Centre highlights many of the themes that will emerge in the rest of this book. Thus, James Oliver, a workhouse inmate, wrote an initial letter from Tynemouth in 1865 complaining of the staff "impeaching me things I knew nothing about and punishing for the same." He stated that he was locked up in a cold draughty room, that numbers of elderly sick paupers had been found dead in their beds due to neglect, and that "poison was administered by Carelessness to two Children & a Man." Oliver's knowledge of the processes of the New Poor Law was evident in his final assertion that "many other things I can prove *if I had a hearing.*"[74] Oliver received no response but as usual a copy of his letter was sent to the guardians for their observations. That his letter had been discussed by the guardians was discovered by Oliver via a local newspaper report giving a verbatim transcript of the guardians' meeting at which the PLB request for information had been considered. Oliver sent them a second letter enclosing the newspaper report so that they could see the kind of derogatory language the guardians had used about him. In the report, the chairman said he did not believe a word of Oliver's accusations, and a guardian named Mr Salkeld stated:

> I think it is a very great pity we are bound to take any notice of such communications. In my opinion we have in the workhouse some half-hanged scoundrels, who really ought to be dealt with in a very summary manner.

The report continued that the chairman considered it the best course of action to refer the matter to the workhouse committee, although Salkeld felt that there was "too much significance given to those sort of things." Oliver claimed it was useless for him to go before the internal guardians' committee as they had already made a determination in his case and he again voiced a hope that the PLB would instigate "a proper enquiry."[75] The PLB wrote to the guardians, forwarding this second letter and its enclosure and asking for a copy of the report made by the workhouse committee when ready, but purposefully refrained from censuring the guardians for the language used in their meeting.[76] In turn, the guardians replied that a workhouse committee had been appointed but that, since Oliver had "expressed dissatisfaction" to be examined by them, the guardians had decided that he would deem unsatisfactory any report they might make, and they therefore asked that an inspector be sent to conduct the inquiry.[77] By holding his ground, therefore, Oliver managed to force the local board and the Centre to act on his request for an official investigation. Oliver's agency would undoubtedly have been noted by other inmates and demonstrated what writing to the Centre could achieve. Although Oliver's charges were found on inspection to be unproven, it was at the same time noted that nursing in the workhouse was inadequate, and that one or more additional paid nurses should be appointed to secure proper attendance at all times. Hurst, the PLB inspector, described Oliver as a "a shrewd old man, 80 years of age, but apparently in robust health" and recommended that if Oliver were willing to accept some level of out-relief "it would probably be advantageous to the discipline of the workhouse."[78] The Tynemouth guardians were informed of the outcome of Hurst's investigation in a letter which also pointed out a number of management infringements.[79] Only a month later the master and the matron submitted their resignations, and, although their departures were not connected in the correspondence to the recent criticisms of workhouse management, Oliver and other inmates would undoubtedly have felt that his letters of complaint and the official PLB inquiry had contributed to their decision.[80] This detailed process of correspondence flags the strategic themes and rhetorical matrices employed by poor writers, emphasises the importance of personality to an understanding of the New Poor Law, and provides a detailed dissection of the sorts of agency that we will encounter through the rest of this book.

CONCLUSION

A significant feature of the Central Authority archive is that it captures regular correspondence with union officials (both staff and guardians), district auditors, wider local and regional government officers (magistrates, coroners, parish officers), and also with paupers, the wider poor, and their advocates. Because the texts of poor writers immediately became part of the same administrative process as more official correspondence, it was clear not only that the poor had a right to approach the Centre but that the Centre had a duty to respond. The poor and their advocates recognised this right to correspond from the inception of the New Poor Law and indeed were instrumental in establishing it. The Centre found itself caught (almost in the bureaucratic headlights) between the necessity of responding to our core writers in order to monitor local activities, and the desire both to close down conversations, particularly around individual relief cases, and to disabuse such writers from insisting that the Centre should intervene in such cases. The poor followed the administrative rules of the game, adopting suitable rhetoric, acknowledging earlier letters from the Central Authority, and referring to earlier correspondence via administrative paper numbers. Through experience, receipt of letters back from the Centre, and reading the same guidance as officials, the poor and their advocates quickly learned the processes of the poor law system of correspondence, much as they had under the Old Poor Law.

Letters from paupers, the poor, and their advocates became part of a complex web of communication and information passed between the Centre and localities, and thus were perceived to be as ordinary for the Centre as the people who wrote them.[81] Standardised response mechanisms sought to remove discretion and individuality from central dealings with the poor (and indeed with unions in some senses), but it is apparent that in this system personalities mattered. From the commissioners and their inspectorate, through the local guardians to the poor writers and advocates themselves, the way responses were handled and cases followed up could depend on the perceived characters of, and relationships among, those involved. Power and authority were important in this respect, and for letter writers concerned with contested individual relief decisions it is clear in law and in practice that the discretion of the guardians outweighed many concerns of the Centre. Even so, agency is not always determined by positive outcomes and it is clear that despite a centralised response that emphasised its inability to directly intervene and repeatedly put the narrative in the hands of local guardians and union officers, people were not dissuaded from writing. They continued to exert their right to correspond and were unwilling to accept what they felt were unsatisfactory responses. In such writings we find tenacity, determination, and exhibitions of sheer willpower. Such attributes were essential in a situation where the poor and their advocates often argued from a point of weakness. Yet, as we have seen, their voices broke through and secured local and central inquiries, led to the dismissal or resignation of poor law union staff, and sometimes won additional relief resources. Such successes (for this is what they were) tell us much about the way in which the poor had a sense of expectation in regard to their treatment and about the agency they often pursued and realised through their correspondence with the Central Authority. It is to the rhetorical and referential infrastructure framing this correspondence that we now turn.

PART TWO

Pauper Agency

5

Rhetoric and Strategy: A Corpus View

INTRODUCTION

In June 1855 Samuel Templeton wrote from Carlisle (Cumberland) asking the Poor Law Board (PLB) to:

> give me your opinion on what to me, is, an important case it is as follows – Eight weeks ago I applied to the Board of Guardians for the Carlisle Union for relief. I am 65 years of age my wife is 68 years of age. I am a hand loom weaver & for some time previous & since my earnings are about 4/– per week. I have a Grandson. a little boy aged 8 years I have him to support out of my own earnings.
>
> I never in my life got any relief from any Poor Law union. & I wish I could do without it now; but I cannot I applied, as I have before said, but they have refused me. & offered me work at the stone heap I only wanted a little out door relief to help me along with what I could make by weaving. which for an old man would do better for me than [the] stone heap.
>
> I have been employed with the Messrs Discons in Carlisle during the last 21 years. And [my] [character] is well known to them. I know that they will speak [for] me. It [is] also well known to some of the Guardians but they said they could not help further. I was born in Ireland [and] my family likewise.

> Necessity compels me to appeal to you for your kind assistance, [Your] influence would be very [valued] and be much [appreciated] by your grateful. & humble [petitioner]
>
> PS I was obliged last [term] day to part with my [shop] I could not keep it S.T.[1]

Templeton's letter contains some key examples of the rhetoric and strategy that we will encounter in later chapters of this book: he presented a *case* and asked for an opinion, both linguistic vehicles linked to indirect knowledge of the law and its processes; he conveyed his age and that of his wife with the clear implication that deservingness and age should be linked; and he explicitly questioned whether he could be regarded as able-bodied *enough* to work in lieu of outdoor relief. Templeton's depiction of these aspects of his case were conditioned by the fact that he was Irish and thus would have had (at least in the eyes of local guardians) an uncertain eligibility for any relief at this date.[2]

The letter also begins to hint at some wider rhetorical and strategic approaches to establishing deservingness that require further consideration by way of framing for our later chapters. Templeton expected his correspondent to know and appreciate that by 1855 almost all branches of the handloom weaving trade were in structural decline, such that 4s per week probably represented full-time work.[3] Exogenous circumstances washed over Templeton and old-age dependence was thus to some extent inevitable.[4] Some of his linguistic infrastructure was consistent with that employed by paupers and claimants under the Old Poor Law, including familial duty (Templeton was supporting a young grandson),[5] a desire to be as independent as possible in the future, and the narrative of inevitable decline into greater or total dependence, given that he had been obliged to give up his weaving shed. Character, and the fact that it could be externally verified rather than simply claimed, was also a rhetorical tool that had great resonance with poor writers from decades earlier.[6] Some reference points are rather less familiar in relation to this older material: Templeton equated deservingness with a long history of independence, presumably since he had arrived in England. He also sought to emphasise his reputation (as opposed to just his character) in the locality, having been employed by the same firm for twenty-one years, a history which also spoke to the centrality of labour in establishing a moral case whatever his legal status as an Irishman. Emphasising this belonging, but also elaborating on it in the sense that his case was well known to "some" of the guardians, Templeton tried to convey to the Board that he had a public persona and that people had a favourable opinion of him.[7]

Concentrating on the corpus as a whole, but using case studies for detailed elaboration, this chapter begins to change our focus from questions about the scale and nature of the voices in our material to issues relating to the construction and employment of that voice as the poor sought to exercise agency and negotiate the explicit power imbalances inscribed into the very processes of the New Poor Law. As we shall see, some of the rhetorical approaches of poor writers had continuity with their counterparts under the Old Poor Law, even into the 1880s.[8] The chapter also focuses, however, on new or intensified rhetorical and referential modes post-1834, and the sorts of temporal, spatial, and other patterns that can be found in the data. Analysis at corpus level provides a broad context against which we can understand the meaning and significance of cases such as that of Samuel Templeton over the remaining chapters. Ultimately we conclude that the core feature of this remarkable national corpus is how consistent, over time, place, and union typology, the registers and strategic practices and understandings of poor writers were.

PRESENCE AND ABSENCE

Taking a corpus view of the development of rhetoric and strategy across several million words and numerous categories of poor voice is an inherently difficult task. Large-scale auto-coding is rendered problematic not only by the flowing and unstructured narrative of our sources, but also by the irregularity of their punctuation, the substitutability of their terminology, and the orthographic nature of some texts from poor writers even well into the 1890s.[9] Given these inconsistencies, and as we saw in the preface, two options were available to us. First, we undertook a very large series of lexical searches of the corpus using the software package *WordSmith*. Such an approach allows the location of all instances of words/phrases like "able-bodied" and morphologically related terms. Extending the search to equivalences ("fit," "short of work," "unemployed," "half-time," for instance) can give a quantitative sense of the presence of letters by or about able-bodied people in the sample. It also provides a means of fragmenting the dataset so that we can focus in on text sets that have this theme as a central or core motif. Since the underlying data is date-defined, coded for gender, and organised by spatially located unions, it is possible to further analyse or fragment the data so as to bring out chronological, spatial, or other patterning. These approaches do not, however, easily foster semantic searching whereby we can try to discern the intent of the writers as opposed to *merely* the words they used. To go further requires us to engage in the manual coding of data by topic, a procedure that inevitably limits the potential sample size.[10] This is, however, necessary. Thus, for our argument it matters whether: the term "old" was co-located with the adjective "very"; whether the word "sick" was linked either to signifiers of continued decline or prospective recovery; and whether the different manifestations of "service" (to country, military, family, or community) were co-located with linguistic registers of citizenship. To this end we conducted a topic modelling and coding exercise on a subset of the data from nine unions and used the n-gram functions of the software package *Sketch Engine* to draw out some of the rhetorical patterns reported below.[11]

In an endeavour of this sort, there are striking things that we do *not* see, but which might have been expected, given the tenor of the secondary literature for this period. Thus the linguistic register of masculine citizenship is almost completely absent from the corpus even by the 1880s. Nor do we detect the emergence of a new register of "honest poverty," even if its sentiment is found in the words of people like Templeton.[12] This partly reflects the fact that, when drawing the linguistic signature of this position widely, we found that concepts of honest poverty were alive and well at the end of the Old Poor Law. It is also likely that the various (and more passive) linguistic registers of vulnerability (to the impact of unemployment or sickness on capacities for independence, for instance) which are found repetitively in the data mask some broader sentiment of citizenship.[13] Nor do we see any substantial or consistent presence of the language of radicalism. Rhetorical modes of natural justice carry over from the Old Poor Law, and there are episodic examples of paupers and union officers *labelling* people as Chartist or trade union activists, but the language we might associate with these groups and their wider petitionary culture is largely missing from the corpus. What we do find seems to be more passive, in the sense of a forewarning that unless problems were remedied, the poor would be driven into the arms of radical thinkers.[14] Robert Harrison, writing from Bradford in January 1849, is typical in his view of the New Poor Law as:

> a system so diametrically opposite to the Poor law or Charter of England … a system very unwarrantable by the principal and design of the [Old] Poor Law – a system productive of every evil that can befall human nature … and will in the end produce anarchy and revolution because it is seductive and destructive of … all good that human language can express.[15]

Finally, we see no changes to the mechanisms of claim, complaint, and appeal around the times that the Centre was re-organised and renamed, when the laws of welfare changed significantly, or at times of supposedly "national" movements such as the crusade against outdoor relief in the 1870s and 1880s. The absence of such change is striking and reinforces the sense of the complexity to temporal change in the corpus identified in chapter 2.

Other linguistic registers and rhetorical strategies have a transient, episodic/particular, or fleeting presence in the corpus. These usually go unnoticed for individual unions but are more obvious in aggregate and are often inter-correlated with wider economic, sociocultural, or other events, structures, and processes. Thus references to external workhouse visitors and voluntary visiting committees are relatively uncommon before the 1870s but deepen in the 1880s and 1890s as the number of such visiting committees increased and became integral in campaigns to elect women and working-class poor law guardians.[16] References to weapons in the workhouse (sticks, whips, and even pistols, usually but by no means always carried and used by workhouse staff) are never common but they concentrate discernibly in the first decades of the New Poor Law. After this, weapons for punishment and allegations of the mistreatment of children often become co-located as topics in texts. Other episodic linguistic strands include those attaching to the moral threat of vagrancy and homelessness (which hove into view around the time of the nineteenth-century moral panics over vagrancy[17]), and complaints about particular sorts of officers (especially medical officers) which have a striking domino effect amongst unions, possibly connected to publicity over cases of neglect, abuse, and death at the hands of officials.[18]

There are also of course long-term continuities in the presence and density of some rhetorical devices to establish agency and thus eligibility – or eligibility on better terms. Most obviously, poor writers demonstrated a familiarity with law and process. We are able to trace, carried over from the negotiation structures inherent to the Old Poor Law, an increasingly formalised knowledge of the law and its deployment in letters after the 1840s. There is also broad consistency over time and place in the construction of deference, humility, gratitude, and an unwillingness to become a burden. Permutations such as "humble"; "humble and obedient servant"; "I take the liberty"; "thankful"; "servant"; "obedient"; "I beg leave"; and "Sorry to trouble you" dominate open and closing statements in letters from the poor, as well as petitionary-style narratives that intersperse the corpus.[19] In many ways continuity is to be expected, given deeply ingrained traditions (British and European) of formulaic writing both in familiar letters and in those embodying imbalance of power.[20] Yet, such opening and closing statements also masked their writers' concerted attempts to claim agency or employ other rhetorical and strategic vehicles that were the opposite of humility, obedience, or deference.[21] When Elizabeth Burke wrote from Manchester in September 1862, she opened her letter: "Honoured I take the great liberty of addressing you with these few lines to lay before your humane consideration my misserable situation of Life." The language then became more combative, however. Burke claimed that "if her Magesty knew I am sure she would allow me A something that would enable me to go home." This assertion of implicit duty on the part of civil servants who in effect embodied Her Majesty's Government was a subtle but important claim to agency. Moreover, a postscript to the letter actively sought to contest the notional power of the recipient, Burke writing: "I can send you My character from My parish Minester that will show that I am no imposter."[22] These words might betray a fear of being disbelieved but it can also be read as an assertion of locally recognised deservingness, much as with Samuel Templeton. None of this is to suggest that we do not find angry, rude, or blunt openings – Emma Dorse, for instance, writing from the Mitford and Launditch Poor Law Union (PLU) in July 1889, opened tersely: "I now complain to you the tretment that has been Given to me last week after my days task I was called abon to goe and sleep with too wimmon which was in a filthy condishon & not in there write minds"[23] – but merely to note that deviation from this pattern tended to be individual and individualised, situational, and in most cases some way into a set of correspondence by or about the same person.[24]

Other established linguistic registers extended and deepened after 1834. Thus, while the rhetoric of parenthood and the inability to fulfil familial roles can easily be detected in Old Poor Law letters, for much of the time it was latent.[25] This pattern changed post-1834, perhaps not unexpectedly, given that workhouses sought to separate parents from their walking children.[26] Constructions of the proper role of mothers in relation to their children were particularly powerful in this period and extended to the outdoor poor and those threatened with the workhouse. Moreover, at corpus level there was an increasing tendency for that rhetoric to be yoked to youths rather than merely "children." Mary Powderley, writing from Barnsley in February 1856, is typical. Her "humble application" noted that she was a "Widow with one Daughter who is in a very bad state of health and not able to follow constantly her employment I am allso afflicted and can only casuly perform labour which leaves me in a very depressed condition." With a soldier son on duty and as a former ratepayer herself, Powderley asked to "be saved from going in to the Union house in Barnsley." This was not a request underpinned by law, character, or revulsion of the workhouse itself, however, but by the duty of a mother to her daughter and mindful of the contribution that her daughter might make in the future:

> the house if offered to me whereas my daughter would be left homeless or be compelled to go in with me, She is seventeen years of age and by proper attention she may become more able to labour after she passes her most critical years.[27]

Set within the whole corpus, such words are part of a wider linguistic register of compromised motherhood, one to which we return in chapter 7.

At the other end of the life-cycle spectrum, both the whole corpus approach and the more focussed subset analysis at union level point to a nationwide development of an increasingly complex rhetoric of old age and decline. This is unsurprising. While the connection between advancing old age and dependence has often been overplayed, by the 1890s some 59 per cent of all those aged seventy-plus had at least a passing connection with the welfare system.[28] As we might expect from the work of David Thomson and Pat Thane, the gender and age focus of such dependence varied according to the socioeconomic composition of the unions surveyed.[29] Nonetheless, we find striking regularities to the rhetorical construction of old-age dependence. These are explored at greater length in chapter 8, but the letter of David Jenkins, a sawyer from Aberystwyth is broadly emblematic. Writing in January 1847, Jenkins noted that "in consequence of the Advanced Ages of my Wife & Myself added to infirmity Myself 76 and Wife 74," he had been unable to earn more than two shillings per week. Acknowledging the inevitability of old-age dependence, the Aberystwyth PLU granted 2s 6d in outdoor relief but then removed the allowance. Jenkins noted that "whenever we make an Application we are ordered to the Poor House." Now, with "My Wife a Cripple and Myself too infirm to follow my usual occupation," he asked that "your Lordships will have the humanity to intercede in our behalf."[30] This sense that those who represented government and taxpayers ought to know and understand the impact of old age becomes increasingly strong in the later nineteenth century as wider philosophical and policy conversations about the aged turned to the need for formal pensions and a different framework of treatment.[31]

Both Powderley and Jenkins wrote about particular life-cycle situations. Equally, however, they referenced issues of disability and (permanent or temporary) inability, and sickness, just as those who wrote to parishes under the Old Poor Law had.[32] Yet, from the very earliest letters to the Centre we see evidence of a hardening and extension of this linguistic register and strategic positioning. Disability, inability (the writer's own or that of family members), and extended sickness became a reason for, *inter alia*: the granting of outdoor relief; more favourable treatment in the workhouse; enhanced visiting and workhouse leave rights; sustained attention by medical officers; and above all for disputing the conduct and language of officers inside and outside the workhouse. This deeper and more extensive rhetorical engagement was to some extent inevitable. Certain disabilities became more obviously remediable after the 1860s, and the fact of their not being remedied for poor people generated a narrative of the need for better treatment in the meantime.[33] The rise of specialist medical institutions and treatments raised expected standards of treatment and care.[34] As the medical specialty of gerontology grew from the 1850s, loss of capacity due to old age became increasingly understood.[35] And of course enquiries into factories, mines, and other employments led to better understandings of the precarious position of workers and their susceptibility to accident and occupational health issues.[36]

More widely, sickness was one route through which exceptions to New Poor Law rules and guidance relating to allowances could be claimed and granted, such that strategic use of the language and actuality of sickness was a core part of navigating the system. From the start of the New Poor Law, rhetoric of helpless children at the mercy of abuse, inadequate treatment, less able men and women who were subject to the petty tyranny of workhouse staff, inappropriate workhouse fabric, and poor practice and active neglect or abuse in relation to the needs of the sick became common. Juliana Cox, for one, wrote from Great Yarmouth (Norfolk) to the Centre on 27 December 1851, "With tearful eye and heavy heart" on behalf of her husband, Thomas. The family had entered the workhouse on 7 November, and notwithstanding her "husband being afflicted on the left side with paralasis [he] was passed into the able bodied ward." Days later, Thomas:

> was set to pick rope into oakum and because he would not do it the Governor put him on bread and water then the Surgeon declared him unable yet the Chairman justified the Governor because it was a board order my husband was then set to work at the Pump until he lost the use of his limbs even those on the right side.

Recognising that even severe disability did not at the time obviate the requirement for the poor to work (whether outside or inside the workhouse),

Juliana recounted cases of others with seemingly minor ailments who had been placed in "the infirm ward" and hence exempted from labour. Thus:

> I complain not Sir Geo [the Home Secretary, to whom the letter was addressed] because others are in the infirm ward but to show that it is prejudice from party feeling to put one so afflicted as my husband to work while others could do it with pleasure and without pain and yet they must on the truly afflicted to labour beyond his ability and now Sir Geo my poor afflicted husband [cannot] walk erect I Sir Geo something will be done in this case that the miss called Guardians be not allowed to treat with cruelty and contempt those whose misfortune it is to come to their notice.

She hinted darkly that such treatment was more likely "if the person [so] unfortunate are or have been of a different opinion in view or religion."[37] However it was to be explained, the linguistic register of sickness, disability, inappropriate treatment leading to further disability, injustice to the disabled, and inconsistent treatment towards sick people in what was supposed to be a rule-driven classificatory system is clear.

Cox's strategic deployment of the rhetoric of injustice and unequal treatment finds parallels throughout the corpus, particularly on the part of the sick but at times among all classes of the letter-writing and evidence-giving poor. Indeed, the very words "unjust," "injustice," and "unfair" collectively figure in almost 15 per cent of all pauper and advocate letters, as in the case of the able-bodied poor of Caxton and Arrington workhouse who complained that:

> the Old men & women and Children and Sick are to have their fare of their Christmas Dinner as usual but the able bodied men & women are to be Deprived of it and not have any at all which is causing a great disturbance all throughout the union and we think it a very unfair thing.[38]

Here precedent, not regulation, was invoked in the name of fairness, but the writers nonetheless expected the Centre to understand the sense in which fair play and the rights of free-born Englishmen extended to all, no matter how unfortunate. To be punished for writing in the first place was rhetoricised as particularly unjust. This theme is taken up at length in chapter 10, but is emblematised by Mungo Paumier, who complained that his customary liberty had been stopped for six months as a result of persistent complaints to the Centre. In doing so he highlighted the arbitrary nature of this curtailment, writing that:

> In fact the Guardians have no valid ground whereon to base their Punishment as I have not violated any of the Rules or regulations [and] Have never been classed as a Disorderly or Refractory … Because I am now no longer on the Sick or Dangerous List I am supposed to be one of those entitled to go out on Sunday.[39]

Paumier's strategic comparison of his own treatment with that of other paupers in the same situation is typical of those, like the Caxton and Arrington petitioners, who complained that customary or long-established rights and privileges had been withdrawn arbitrarily, and it finds echoes throughout the corpus. James Kitsell, writing in July 1871 on behalf of the inmates at Chelsea workhouse (Middlesex), complained that they, too, had had their "liberty stopped [for] 6 months & the privilege of seeing our [friends] for the same period," and that this "confinement for a long time has become intolerable – [and] very prejudicial to our health." In this case, the ostensible reasons for the restriction was that smallpox had been recorded in the area; but, like Paumier, Kitsell countered by noting that "the inmates of Kensington, St Georges, & other Houses have been let out for some weeks past – therefore we cannot understand why our confinement is still continued."[40] Paupers not only knew – but were keen to demonstrate that they knew – how a well-regulated system was *supposed* to operate.

This broad rhetoric of injustice in turn finds its analogue in the Old Poor Law linguistic registers of humanity, Christian paternalism, and duty, all of which maintained a presence as the nineteenth century progressed. These phrases, or their equivalents, occur over 4,700 times in the corpus.[41] This presence is to some extent linked to wider patterns of evangelical revival, Christian social work, and a basket of religious "interventions" in the inner cities and de-industrialising areas.[42] Quakers, too, were actively expanding their engagement with the New Poor Law in this period.[43] Yet the broad linguistic register of Christianity took on specific connotations when deployed by the poor themselves. An unsigned and undated (but c.1839) appeal detailed arbitrary, cruel, and callous treatment by the workhouse master at Nantwich (Cheshire). In one instance:

> he took hold of the man by the shirt Collar he Draged him out of bed on his Back and floged him naked as was all but shirt and kicked him and Drew him all Round the Room so that any Christian man would not use a Dog we sapose the man to be Nearly 60 years of age and not quite so Bright as many is But that is no Rule he Should be so abused.[44]

These words keyed into wider contemporary concerns about the mistreatment of the mentally ill[45] and suggest a real connection between paupers and wider public debates, a matter to which we return below.[46] The author went on to suggest that the ratepayers, paupers, and reputation of Nantwich would be better served by dismissing the master and replacing him with a genuine Christian. From the perspective of writers, assertions that they were good Christians and that the good Christian men of the Centre should assert themselves in favour of the downtrodden poor were common. Episodic and persistent fights between clergymen and workhouse inmates on the one hand, and between guardians and workhouse staff on the other, over who should and should not be allowed to minister to the poor (see chapter 3) were an important backdrop to these observations.[47] So, of course, was a resurgence of philanthropic endeavour in the post-1850 period, given that in certain areas much of it was led and inspired by nonconformist groups.[48]

A final element of continuity with or development from the Old Poor Law linguistic registers is in the area of emotions. While it is difficult to quantify definitively, there is a sense that the New Poor Law corpus is more "emotionally charged" than its pre-1834 equivalent. Registers of hopelessness, fear, predation, despair, happiness, frustration, and anger all become more extensive and deeper. To some extent this reflects the presence of the workhouse as a focus for the emotional journey of poverty, and there is no doubt that many constructed it as the end of a journey of decline, to be avoided at all costs.[49] Yet there is more than this. In a New Poor Law system where local administrators seemed to have more power than had adhered to them pre-1834, and where the treatment of poverty had clearly become more ideological and less pragmatic than in the closing decades of the Old Poor Law, there was an inevitability to poor writers' confronting their situation on a more emotional level. The language of this rhetorical infrastructure is complex and multi-faceted, as others have also found.[50] Nonetheless, Elizabeth Gatch, whom we encountered in chapter 4 seeking outdoor relief for her almost blind mother, captures the essence of our point about emotion. Elizabeth's "prayer, earnest, and respectful to your Honors" was that the Centre would have "the great and merciful Goodness to interfere in her behalf" so as to secure "the commonest necessaries." It would have been possible for Gatch to end the letter at this point, leaving the age and disability of her mother to speak for themselves. Instead, she continued that it "grieves my heart to know, that she is suffering sad privations – I will not encroach on your Honor's time by saying more, only anxiously and imploringly begging your attention to this afflicting case at the earliest moment." Her letter was, she wrote, "wrung from an anxious Child by her parent's distress."[51] Such words speak to a wider sense of the nineteenth century as a period in which the self was reinvented, bringing a new interiority that also drove the rise in working-class autobiography and literature.[52]

NEW REGISTERS

Perhaps most important in the corpus work is the fact that other rhetorical and strategic vehicles for constructing or asserting agency are *particular* to the New Poor Law period or undergo a dramatic increase in presence and intensity. Some of these categories are familiar from our other published work and do not require detailed elaboration here. Peter Jones and Steven King point to the intensification of a workhouse reform movement from the 1850s and there is a corresponding increase in demands for the systematic and systemic reform of rules and practices.[53] An alternate linguistic register demanding that the Centre rigorously enforce the law and previous guidance to unions can also be detected as an adjunct of this strategy. This is most often seen in relation to longer-term workhouse inmates, but is also shared by advocates and other third parties. Thus, when George Last encountered problems in gaining regular access to minister to two orphaned Catholic children in the Chelmsford (Essex) workhouse, he engaged in a long and detailed correspondence with the Centre. Last sought to bring the matter to a head in January 1860, noting that in a reply to him of 29 December the Centre was "mistaken in supposing that the Chelmsford Board of Guardians have not thrown, and do not throw obstacles in the way of my access to the two Stubbings, admitted by them to be Roman Catholics, as well as to the two Charlesworths, also named in mine of the 13th of December." Frustrated at again being turned away when attempting to visit the children, Last demanded that the Centre "secure me the access that your Recent Orders would wish to secure to the Catholic Priest."[54] This sentence is comparable in intent and basic architecture to other letters written by clergymen (of all denominations) seeking access to their flock, as we saw in chapter 3.

Another rhetorical means, familiar from the work of Steven King and Carol Beardmore, is the strategy of focusing on the treatment of children both in their own right and as a mechanism by which adult paupers contested wider workhouse regimes. A linguistic register that speaks to the softening of attitudes towards children developed progressively after the late-1860s as public and professional opinion coalesced to construct the importance of an age-defined "proper" childhood that increasingly did not involve work or undue discipline.[55] A balancing register can be found in letters or witness testimonies that contested the power of workhouse staff to neglect or actively chastise children, and focused on constructing people who did so as unmanly, inhuman, or out of control. Those with power who failed to challenge such treatment were morally bankrupt, cowardly, and corrupt. Considered in the round, registers associated with the proper treatment of children intensify and deepen markedly across the New Poor Law period.[56] It is also notable, however, that this concern with the experience of children was located in and partly explained by a much stronger set of rhetorical notes of "the family" under the New Poor Law. Thus, good and bad marriages, grief for the dead, and above all the idea of families straining every sinew to support each other emerge as strong threads. A sense from the historiographical literature that responsibility for the aged and other groups of the life-cycle poor shifted sharply towards the state under the New Poor Law is problematised by our material. Guardians and their officers certainly pursued families to augment or remove the burden of poor relatives from union finances. Yet the emergence of a substantial and sustained linguistic infrastructure of the family after 1834 suggests that the poor became more confident and rhetorically skilled in underplaying the potential for kin support. The poor under the Old Poor Law tended to ration or drip feed references to family. Their New Poor Law counterparts tackled the issue head on. Indeed, sometimes family was the *cause* of a dependency problem, as was the case for Richard Moore of Manchester. His letter of 14 July 1844, written from prison, asked the Centre to "interfere" on his behalf, explaining that:

> after Bring up a Family in Decency and Credit; (their Mother Dead) I had the Misfortune To Marry an old Woman in Nov[r] 1837 Before I had Been Married one Month; she and her Daughter and Son in Law Took all out of the House and Whent away I knew Not Where – at the End of Five years and Nine Months (after Making all away Even till it Came to the Ring that I Bought her) she Made her appearance; she found I was neither able Nor Willing to keep her she apply[d] to Manchester Overseers for Relief I was Taken With a Warrant before Mr Mand the Chief Majestrate I Told him I was Not able To keep Myself I was Liberated in a short Time after My sons Door was Broke open on the Dead of Night I was Take out of Bed Taken Before another Majestrate and sentenc[d] to 14 Days Imprisonment For Neglect of Family.[57]

Whether Moore was released is unclear, but in a corpus of pre-1834 pauper letters collected by Jones and King there is not a single instance of this sort of rhetorical and strategic construction of need.

Other new strategic signals in this period reflect the organization of relief, particularly in terms of workhouses, and the nature of poor law process. Linguistic registers associated with the breaking and enforcement of rules, treatment, and mistreatment of those subject to mental illnesses, sexual abuse, punishment, incarceration, poor food quality, clothing inadequacy, and inappropriate work tasks all become more frequent and more intensive. They are related (directly or indirectly) to understandings of the proper functioning of a centrally regulated system. Workhouse regimes operated on inadequate staffing and complex or overlapping layers of responsibility and power. Historians may differ on the degree to which these regimes were disciplinary and depended on strict discipline, but it is still the case that the propensity for things to go wrong or to be seen to go wrong was considerable. Thus, workhouses increasingly provided significant education opportunities, but schoolmasters were often accused of abusing children, peculation, and religious indoctrination. Parents in the workhouse had responsibility for their children and yet were physically separated from them and could only learn about punishments or illnesses through gossip and rumour. Workshops and gardens provided training and pseudo-recreation spaces for children but they were also places of sexual abuse, as for instance in the case of thirteen-year-old Elizabeth White, a workhouse inmate at Beverley (Yorkshire). She claimed in February 1867 that the workhouse master Mr Hudson had on several occasions "put his hand up my clothes." Notwithstanding the fact that she had told others in the workhouse and threatened to inform Mrs Hudson, the master then "did [it] in the Garden when me and Polly Freebury were pulling Rasps – this was last summer – I told Sarah Boston a woman in the House – I told Emma Jessop a woman, also."[58] This language of telling, yoking witnesses to the case, the precision of the charge, and the emphasis of Hudson's operating in plain sight and thus with contempt, was deliberate and deliberative. An organised, institutionally focused and directed welfare system created new layers of language for the contestation of those structures.[59]

More broadly the emergence of markers associated with the rise of the information state and new or reinvigorated understandings of how ordinary people could and should communicate with government is clearly visible in the corpus. Under the Old Poor Law there was both an exponential decline in the presence of petitions as a means through which poor writers addressed welfare administrators and (more significantly) a sharp decline in broadly "petitionary" language.[60] In the post-1834 period such rhetoric has a more concerted presence. There is an obvious link to be made here between the now familiar rise of petitionary cultures of all sorts in the nineteenth century, and the nature and extent of pauper and advocate writing.[61] On the other hand we have already noted the absence of the registers of radicalism in the corpus and find no obvious relationship between the presence and intensity of petitionary rhetoric and spikes in petitioning activity in wider society. While prior knowledge or the experience of joining collective petitions may have increased the confidence of writers, it seems likely that any direct relationship was "slow burn" and that other fora in which petitionary forms and language were required – in particular court and legal systems – were more important influences. Moreover, poor writers, advocates, and those who gave evidence also drew language and strategy from other features of the relationship between the people and the nineteenth-century state. These include the emergence of a language of time, timing, and timeliness, mimicking the increasing focus of the Central Authority on timely correspondence, response, action, and inspection. Thus, when James Holmes wrote from Calverton (Nottinghamshire) on 29 August 1846, he claimed that he could only get relief if he worked "upon the Roads," but that his "Constitution was so impaired" by military service "that I am quite unable to bear any Exertion." Bringing immediacy and drama to his case, Holmes claimed the situation was now perilous and "I cannot die in the Street." He called for the "prompt attention and timely interference" of the Centre, urging them not to "delay to attend to my Very distressing Case."[62] Equally, the poor and their advocates rapidly came to understand that the New Poor Law was conceptualised as an economic, and not merely an administrative, system.[63] Their response was to forward evidence, to quote from reports, and to rhetoricise quantitative indicators of need, hopelessness, and deservingness.

Two further compelling changes to the rhetoric and strategy that post-1834 poor writers, advocates, and witnesses deployed are also apparent. First, while authors under the Old Poor Law tended to refer infrequently and often obliquely to public opinion, their New Poor Law counterparts were much clearer that they understood themselves to be operating in a public sphere both as recipients and as agents. This growing awareness is to some extent expected. The presence of an increasing number of amateur investigators and workhouse visitors at the margins of the poor law provided channels for the poor to contest their treatment over and above the advocates they had always used.[64] Moreover, we know (chapters 2 and 3) that the poor and their advocates were increasingly aware of and connected to the world of public opinion through newspapers and magazines. An implicit acknowledgement of this trend is found in the correspondence of George Scott, Curate of Colyton (Devon), who specifically emphasised that he was "not one of those that like to set people against the laws, or to write letters in the newspapers agst them" before going on to lay out his complaints.[65] Scott's willingness to support the principles of the law while questioning its local operation is a familiar part of the emergent post-1834 rhetorical infrastructure. Hence, H. Bruce Campbell wrote in 1841, on behalf of himself and "several other gentlemen" of Nottingham, that the poor treatment of John Henson, an elderly pauper at Basford, must surely have been the result of officials misapplying the law:

> carrying out the provisions of the New Poor Law with a degree of cruelty and harshness which the legislature in framing that law did not contemplate and which it was our unanimous belief the commissioners would not sanction.[66]

There is, in this appeal (and many others like it), a clear sense of the locally well connected "calling out" practices they deemed anomalous to the way the new law *should* work; but also a much wider sense of the "counter-surveillance" of local practice by individuals and communities under the New Poor Law. Awareness of public opinion and public audiences, and the interlinked conception and construction of the Centre as a public body, fundamentally shifted the writing of the poor after 1834. If we strip witness statements and other minutes of evidence out of the corpus, it is possible to see a subtle but marked transition in the nature of reportage. Thus, the traditional linguistic registers of seeing, speaking, experiencing, and hearing ("I saw"; "I heard"; "I need to tell"; "I report"; "I am") inherited from the Old Poor Law were augmented and sometimes replaced by a broadly construed distancing language. This includes: "I Call your attention"; "I read"; "you know"; "It is well known"; "nobody could"; and "I speak for." Such phrases came to be co-located with the provision of "evidence" rather than merely with reportage of a situation; the linguistic register in effect separates the predicament from the pauper. By the later 1850s this shift is clearly visible in the corpus and, read in one way, it signals awareness that writing for "public consumption" was a different exercise to "merely" writing to welfare officers or even the Centre.

A second notable rhetorical development is the emergence of the dichotomous registers (often in the same letter) of cruelty or tyranny on the one hand and kindness, decency, or other *de facto* yardsticks of good and expected behaviour on the other.[67] Nowhere are these more powerful than in the construction of tyranny on the part of individual officers. Thus, when John Hankinson wrote from the township of Timperley (Cheshire) on 10 July 1858, he alleged that:

> I was Badly used By Hard labour and tirany used Me in abruit Manner honr I ~~Begs~~ Belongs to timporly But Knutsford was our union workhouse I Been ahand loom wever Poverty compelled me so I's had to go to the workhouse I Been 64 years ~~yage~~ of age wife 63 Cathirin hankison-honr Sir I Been three times after trying it I had rumitic Pains and when I could not work the Sumoner.

Locating the source of the problem very precisely, Hankison claimed that "Since Mr Lloyd [the workhouse master] Died Paupers is used with all Cruelty I am Stating all correct to your honorable Secretary hoping that your hon' would feel for my ill usage."[68] This particular letter reminds us about the importance of individual personalities to the effective and humane running of workhouses even as the New Poor Law moved into middle age. Yet the language – ill usage, brutality, irregularity, forced labour, compulsion, cruelty, and mistrust – develops strongly in the corpus from the 1840s onwards, suggesting a wider change in the philosophy of poor writers. We see it powerfully displayed in the letter of Hannah Ingrey, writing from Chesterton (Cambridgeshire) on 24 August 1840. She sought the "aid" and "powerful and immediate protection" of the Centre:

> against the oppressive conduct towards herself her husband and family of the Earl of Hardwicke & the Board of Guardians of the Caxton and Arrington Union of which the said Earl is the Chairman Conduct

> which has deprived ~~her children~~ your Petitioner of her house & home & comfortable livelihood which latter her husband once obtained for her, himself & family ... Which Oppressive conduct occasioned her & husband to be turned into the Street where they had nine nights and day to remain exposed to the inclemency of wintry [weather] which said conduct has lead also to incarceration of the whole family in the Union House of Caxton & Arrington aforesaid ... your Honourable House never intended that the New Poor Law should thus be made the instruments of so greatly oppressing an honest and industrious family[69]

Phrases referring to "oppression" (and its equivalents) recur over 3,300 times in the corpus, further pointing to the sense that writers could elaborate a positive notion of what a "good" regime might look like.

The word "tyranny" and its equivalents locates the construction even more clearly.[70] Advocates, serial writers, witnesses, indoor and outdoor correspondents, religious ministers, and sometimes even officials themselves employed this linguistic register, again with the clear indication that "proper" behaviour was well understood. If we turn our attention back to the Great Yarmouth union, the register of tyranny was codified in the 1850s. Between them, Frances Land, Thomas Cox, Juliana Cox, and Thomas Lorick (a mixture of genders and serial and individual letter writers) employed the word "tyranny" ten times between 10 February 1851 and 14 August 1855. They also generated twenty-nine other equivalences. When the aged Lorick wrote on 14 August 1855 he crystallised this sense of tyranny, claiming that he ought not to have been forced into the workhouse since the law allowed other options. Now he was there, Lorick wished to call the attention of the Centre to the character of the "Governor & Patron who it seem are only fit to peep listen & bear evidence agreeable to tyrannical desires." Cataloguing a series of tyrannical decisions linked to work, drudgery, withholding of food, and the separation of husband and wife, Lorick contrasted the "Manly Conduct" and "sound Judgement"[71] of the workhouse surgeon who saved his wife after a fall, with the actions of the "Governor Matron & Porter." In their cases:

> cruelty to old age is tyranny & oppression which with Princely wickedness is about to be justly punished for God never intended the blood thirsty to suck or trample on the weak or needy but oppressors like Shuckford Isaacs & the notorious Cufande with some of the G[uardians] & relieving officers thier undue practice prove them unfit for the society.

Warming to his task, Lorick went on:

> I am inform my Lord the Poor Law Board was framed to protect & not oppress I think if you refer to your Report Book that Mine is not a solitary case from this Muse governed Town where truth is smothered & people galled by error a few fine clothes & other peoples cash & a [obscured by Seal] of bluster which to men of understanding must command contempt & Disrespect awaiting your Lordship reply before laying the case before The Public.[72]

Lorick, then, conveys a fine sense of some of the changing rhetorical approaches to the Centre, pointing not only to tyranny, but to increasing knowledge of the organisation and the meaning of welfare, the rise of the information state and its mechanisms, and a growing awareness of the power of the public. He had been informed about the law, understood that the Centre kept such cases on file, and claimed that the actions of the union could and should be held in contempt by the "men of understanding" who shaped the local public opinion to which he now threatened to appeal. Moreover, Lorick's letter also suggests something more, showing how paupers and writers jumped from finding fault with the individual and the individual institution, to seeing systemic failings with the framework of welfare at the organisational and philosophical level.[73]

RHETORICAL COMPLEXITIES

This broad attention to continuity and change at the corpus level masks some important granularity in the material. Thus, as we have seen, there were no tangible shifts in the linguistic infrastructure of poor writers or their advocates at or around the times that the Centre was reorganised in 1847 and 1871. Nor were there changes either in the volume of letters sent or in their rhetorical infrastructure at or around times of widely publicised (and broadly construed "national") poor law scandals.[74] This observation fits seamlessly with our wider sense that such widely publicised scandals were atypical, with most local disputes either resolved well before they erupted into formal scandal territory or administratively managed and hidden. On the other hand, stepping back from the clumsy category of "the poor" and considering (in the coded sample) writers as individuals with stories and histories, it becomes possible to detect the post-1834 emergence and increasing prominence of a linguistic register relating to what we might broadly understand as "contribution." Its particular imprint is to be found in words and phrases that signal knowledge of the poor law, "proper" behaviour and standards, the insolence of officers and guardians, the impact of lost position, accumulated social, economic, or cultural reputation (as for instance with Samuel Templeton), and the humiliation occasioned by dependence and notably by workhouse residence.[75] Such linguistic footprints were usually co-located with snippets of stories of a past life or a sense of the character and reputation of the writer prior to dependence.[76] Thus, George Lawton wrote to the Local Government Board from Barnsley on 6 September 1886 to complain that the relieving officer had "oppressed" him, making up stories to get him ejected from the relief list and thrown onto the meagre resources of "my Lads." Explaining that the two boys had highly variable wages from colliery work and lived miles away, Lawton launched an intriguing attack:

> The Relieving Officer uses too much polemic and too little concern for pure truth. He has called me more than once A Begging Imposter whether he used the falsehood for his own sake ~~that I am offered~~ with pretension that I am offered the Union House by the Guardians as yet I will not write The Guardians right to offer is surely by consent of the Paupers.

This idea that a pauper had rights and should be consulted is important. In Lawton's case, it was no doubt informed by the fact that "my solicitation is honourably made for Relief where I have paid the Rates Contributions but at this the Relieving Officer has made dissension rather than agreement." Lawton went on to claim that he was fifty-five years old and had paid rates:

> for nearly 24 years to 1876 Probable total of Poor Rates £19. 0. 0 and I may have received as Relief about £10. 0. 0 There is nothing magical about this simply I have a Credit Balance with the Guardians in the Rates paid a/c The Relieving officer has tried to deny this as if in Mockery of my poverty through affliction. The Guardians no doubt will discharge their legal and Moral obligations.[77]

Here, then, a respectable man made a simple calculation that an accumulated contribution entitled him both to relief and to consideration.[78]

The obvious conclusion to draw from such examples is that, rhetorically, matters of "contribution" were heavily skewed towards the so-called shamefaced poor, those falling down the social, occupational, and residential scale. There is substance to this contention; some 60 per cent of the coding related to this linguistic register adheres to letters written by those we know or can assume to have once "been someone." The frequency with which we encounter workhouse residents whose occupations denote men and women of prior status suggests that these observations are likely to have wider resonance in the full corpus.[79] Yet, even allowing for the fact that writers are difficult to classify, it is certainly the case that some of those experiencing lifelong marginality also employed linguistic markers of contribution. This rhetorical complexity is not accidental. Claiming and evidencing prior contribution might be read as suggesting that the writer was not so very different from the reader and that mere chance could render the same consequences. More than this, the language of contribution may be understood as having its analogue in the rights of a citizen who has contributed at whatever level, and the duties of the state to its welfare citizens. Finding those rights and duties broken apart spoke to a basic failure on the part of the poor law to secure the dignity of those who belonged to their society and community and had just claims upon them. As Samuel Templeton (the poor writer whose story opened this chapter) reminded the Centre, the fact that he was an Irishman should not detract from moral rights accumulated through years of sustained work for the same employer. We have seen throughout this chapter that the poor and their advocates quickly came to focus on failures of process under the New Poor Law as they recognised it to be a rule-based system. But Templeton's focus on his moral right to decent welfare treatment as a hard-working citizen reminds us that a much older, and in many ways more insistent, referential framework regarding the relative duties of the state and the individual was never far from the surface. Even so, when we locate "our" material in wider cultures of petitioning and writing for this period, we see that the poor and their advocates were skilled at generating new registers and meanings of identity within an expanding state system susceptible to and requiring new narratives of welfare citizenship.

A further complexity relates to regional patterning within the corpus. The New Poor Law was imprinted on a pre-1834 system with distinct spatial or regional dynamics in terms of the nature and meaning of poor relief.[80] As we suggested in chapter 1, the Centre had a mandate through the exercise of soft and hard power to leaven regional dynamics, something that historians agree it failed to do. In part this failure reflected the inherent contradiction of the New Poor Law: a system largely designed to deal with structural unemployment in southern and eastern arable communities was imposed on all of England and Wales, such that an *acceptable* level of local variation in policy and practice was inevitable. This is most clearly visible in the case of Welsh unions, which have been understood as conducting a long and subtle campaign against any extension to the practical powers of London.[81] Such opposition was cultural, but also practical. This is emphasised, for example, in authors' differing rhetorical treatment of the sick and disabled. Mary Jones of Ysgoldy-bach Llannon in the Newcastle-in-Emlyn PLU (Cardiganshire) is typical. Writing in July 1854 "to acknowledge the receipt of two Official communications from you," Jones wanted to say that she was: "deeply grieved and greatly surprised at the Result of your communication and correspondence with the Guardians of the Board of Union in Newcastle Emlyn," the culmination of which was the denial of an allowance for two nieces that she had taken in. It was, she assured the Board, "painful to me to find fault with my betters," but the granting of relief was "a matter of duty," given that the children were destitute, had been committed to her care, and that "The youngest girl is in the 10th year of her age and is almost blind." In the particular context of that disability, Jones hoped that "your suggestion and direction lead to a better, a more just and more liberal conclusion."[82] We rarely see this sort of multi-focal register of family and duty in England. Yet even in England the linguistic registers of claim and appeal differed subtly between north and south. The language of exogeneity (crudely "I am in this position because of circumstances which are beyond my control") was denser and more frequently deployed in northern and midland industrial and commercial communities than by writers from agricultural areas. It was also shared by officials themselves in their own correspondence with the Centre, and Welsh officials in particular were prone to write of the way in which circumstances beyond anyone's control meant that poor law rules should not be enforced.[83] These rhetorical particularities in turn map comfortably onto the older spatial patterns that shaped relief under the Old Poor Law.[84]

As some of these examples begin to hint, it is also possible to find distinctive rhetorical patterns linked to community type. Some of these are obvious, in particular the way in which the nature of work might shape structures and languages of appeal in places where economic activity was highly concentrated. Coal-mining areas, for instance, disproportionately generated rhetorical patterns centring around disability as a potential justification for outdoor relief, something we might have expected from the work of David Turner and Daniel Blackie.[85] Similarly, unions dominated by industry and commerce episodically encountered situations where the need for welfare rapidly and comprehensively outpaced workhouse capacity, shaping both who wrote for welfare and how. In such cases and at such times, writers and witnesses focused particularly on breaches of rules and process, egregious cases of confinement and punishment, failings in the material culture of provision, and the use of "trusties" (paupers favoured by hard-pressed workhouse staff) to manage the workhouse. Urban unions and those coalescing around transport and trading hubs were more likely to have a "vagrancy problem" and to generate letters (by claimants and advocates) referencing vagrancy, and not least the fact that shabby, improper, or misguided treatment might force an otherwise respectable person into a vagrant life. One such, for instance, was Henrietta Egerton, the subject of a letter of 19 August 1843 by John Barker, writing from Nantwich. She had applied for assistance to go to Manchester and seek support from relations. This request had been denied and Barker asked her:

> how she intended to get to Manchester and [whether] she had any money – She said she must walk there and that she had not a farthing – [It] appeard to me next to an impossibility for a delicate female to walk 40 Miles in bad weather (for it was very rainy at the time) without rest [or] refreshment, and for which she must trust to the uncertain hand of Charity – or pawn clothes – or commit an act of Vagrancy or be tempted to something worse.[86]

Other more subtle patterns were associated with particular community types. Thus, the broad linguistic register of abuse, punishment, and neglect was more often and more forcefully applied in urban than in rural contexts, with a clear sense that overcrowding and poor staffing levels were interrelated.[87] Similarly, the register of rights, anger, and breach of process was more common in urban then rural unions. And, of course, there were also highly localised particularities: unions that kept more of their insane and imbecile poor in workhouses tended to generate more extensive and complex rhetorical platforms of punishment, resistance, and abuse;[88] unions with larger workhouses tended to generate more rhetorical constructions of hunger; and unions with more unbalanced age and gender structures tended to be associated with a clearer rhetoric of humanity and inhumanity, failures of duty, and demands for formal investigation rather than informal solution.

Two final complexities are also important for the rest of this book. The first is a link between the linguistic ecology of letters and serial letter writers. Many paupers wrote more than one letter, but relatively few wrote more than two (only about 8 per cent of the sample) and only half of these wrote four or more letters. Jones and King have noted that the fundamental concerns – and, indeed, the general rhetorical structure – of serial letters were the same as those that were sent singly or in pairs,[89] but a number of important strategic patterns are particularly associated with this group. For one thing they accumulated large bodies of evidence in support of complaints over the course of their correspondence. Unlike their counterparts under the Old Poor Law, where stories were developed through a process of slow epistolary "accretion," New Poor Law serial letter writers would generally overlay many different complaints (and, sometimes, even different types of complaints) as their letters progressed.[90] For example, in a series of eight letters and a detailed police statement sent from Great Yarmouth between February 1851 and January 1869, Frances Land complained about, *inter alia*: the cruelty of the "governor"; the "stinking state" of the food; physical abuse of female children by the schoolmaster; withholding of rations; the immorality of workhouse staff; corruption of the guardians; and the inadequacy of medical relief.[91] Although many of the complaints related to her own treatment, Land advocated on behalf of other paupers and pauper cohorts. As we suggested in chapter 3, serial letter writers in the corpus had as much in common with advocate writers as they did with paupers who wrote only one or two letters. But there is also a clear sense that those who wrote substantial numbers of letters quite consciously took on the mantle not only of advocates, but of campaigners for local welfare reform.[92] Despite the risks associated with widespread and consistent complaints, serial letter writers used the platforms that they developed, formulating sophisticated and detailed critiques of local practice. They hold a special place in our corpus, openly straddling the line that was only implicit in the letters of most advocates and paupers between the expression of personal grievances and the systemic criticism of the New Poor Law.

A final complexity relates to the primacy of the written word and rhetorical or epistolary agency in our study. Following the work of James Scott, it would have been possible to focus on non-literate forms of protest.[93] Witness statements – but also the letters of paupers, poor writers, and even advocates – provide complex evidence of staged scenes, glances, acts of vandalism, stealing, hiding things, the making of gossip, cross-dressing, lewdness, chanting, loitering maliciously, escaping with food, and simply refusing to do things. Some of these were acts of resistance and contestation in their own right, while others – damaging or stealing union property, for instance – were a sort of secondary agency where the primary intent was to appear in a court or other forum in which wider complaints could and would be heard. Focusing on these stories would have given even more depth to a New Poor Law history from below. It would also have established a false dichotomy. Those who wrote also saw, confected, convened, and undertook non-literate forms of resistance and protest. This was often admitted, implied, or reported by others and sometimes it was recorded in newspapers and other public forums. Just as the illiterate found voice, the literate called for, observed, and participated in action. The individual and individual personalities are important in this scene, but it is important to understand a wider point: material and emotional actions, whether fleeting or sustained, irritating or disruptive, welded the story of the individual to the local superstructure of the state. Small material and emotional acts made the conduct of the local poor law inconvenient and time-consuming, but only rarely did they reach the critical mass to burst in sustained fashion onto the public scene. The letter and the intent of epistolary agency, on the other hand, was all about breaking the story apart from its local context. Its aim was to address a different and wider public in the sense of a public body. Thus, while many of the stories in this book speak to the presence and importance of material acts of resistance, it is the embodiment of those acts in writing that we see as having primacy in the development of concepts of entitlement and the search for moral justice.

CONCLUSION

Ultimately, what is surprising about this corpus is not its segmentation by period, changing legal frameworks, community type, or county and country. Much as with the Old Poor Law, the strong variations in linguistic and strategic framing of appeals that might have been anticipated along these lines do not transpire – or not to the degree that might be implied from the existing literature. Whether we consider the corpus as a whole, order it by period or document type, or disaggregate it into a subset of union data coded for more detailed corpus analysis, it is clear that poor writers, witnesses, and advocates were enmeshed in a well-understood, rehearsed, and relatively unyielding rhetorical ecology. Even when their orthography was barely tenable – what Ivor Timmis calls "uncoached" literacy[94] – writers understood and were able to implement core linguistic registers and strategic tropes. We see this played out in the letter of James Franklin, writing from the Newbury workhouse in February 1846. His letter opened with the humble "request [of] the favour" of being informed whether a man of sixty, who was effectively disabled because he was "much afficted with a Ruptur, and unable to much Manual Labour," could be forced into the workhouse. Franklin pointed out that confinement in the workhouse (as opposed to an outdoor allowance) meant that "if we remain in the Union Long, all our goods are gon for Rent." There was injustice here, not least where:

> a Poor Man [such as himself] which have always Paid Poor Rates untell this above named time, Sir its for our benifit us and the said Parish also, to relive us wont when at liberty the is a cause of finding some Employments that our strenght will admit its.

Franklin concluded as the obedient servant of the Poor Law Commission, and thereby demonstrated many of the rhetorical and referential models encountered in this chapter. It is too much to argue that poor writers adopted a common template, but on the other hand this consistency across time, space and community type is compelling and perhaps points to the existence and transmission of a common pool of knowledge about who to write to, what to write, and how to write it. In turn, we know that Franklin received a reply from the Centre because the unnamed poor law commissioner who annotated the letter told the clerks to: "Explain to the Writer that if his case is of the nature described his case is within the discretion of the Gns."[95] While the guardians in this case may well have had discretion to impose the workhouse, the fact of any reply would almost certainly have cemented the effectiveness of particular rhetorical and referential tropes in the eyes of the writer and his wider marginal community. The rest of Part 2 deals at rather greater length with some of those tropes, starting first with the invocation of law and process.

6

Knowing the Poor "Law"

INTRODUCTION

On 1 February 1842 Thomas Henshaw wrote to the Poor Law Commission (PLC) from Ilkeston (Nottinghamshire). Choosing his words carefully, Henshaw sought to "beg … most humbly to submit my case."[1] He wrote not of charity, nor of begging for relief. Rather, he asked for consideration: "that you will afford me that redress" which he felt his "case" demanded. A framework knitter, Henshaw said that unemployment had left himself, his wife, and their three children "completely destitute of food." Moreover, he had already taken active measures:

> I applied on the 3rd to the relieving officer, Mr Stotten for relief or an order to the union workhouse and he refused to do either – I then applied to Mr Bennett assistant overseer and he refused likewise. I then applied to Mr Radford A Magistrate at Smalley who sent A positive order to Mr Bennett to see to my case as I was destitute, according to the 54 clause in the poor law amendment Bill.

In deploying this fusion of narrative and legal reference Henshaw was clear that he had done what was expected. He had followed the procedures laid down by the commissioners to claim relief, and local officials had denied him what he considered a right as established under the 54th clause in the

Poor Law Amendment Act (PLAA).[2] And Henshaw took this language even further: "I saw A circular sometime ago from Mr Chadwick clerk to the poor law commissioners stating you would hold officers responsible for any [bad] consequence arising out of such neglect." In short, Henshaw had not only heard of Edwin Chadwick but knew his official position and demonstrated a clear understanding of the administrative process by which the Centre issued its rules and regulations; that is, via the orders and circulars outlined in chapter 2. Indeed, he claimed to have *seen* the circular which held relieving officers to legal and procedural account.

What, then, was the outcome of Henshaw's complaint? In a further letter we find that he applied again on 10 February and received an allowance of bread plus a shilling, for which he chided the Commission, writing, "I cannot supose that the law requires that A family shoud be all that time before it makes any provision for him."[3] The following August, Henshaw and his family were more securely listed in a return of able-bodied paupers on outdoor relief.[4] The sense that Henshaw had agency and knew he had it, and that other poor families were likely to know it too is unmistakeable. This is a theme to which we return throughout our book. For now, Henshaw's letters of 1842, less than eight years after the New Poor Law was functionally established, point to the presence amongst paupers and poor applicants of a practical and rhetorical knowledge of laws, rules, and regulations, and a definitive sense of the existence of a right to relief. This should not surprise us. Steven King has established that a similar familiarity with the law existed before 1834.[5] Indeed, there are good reasons to expect knowledge and use of the law to have deepened in the Victorian period, including the growth of the press, poor law scandals, increased literacy, and the intrusion of the law into many aspects of work, family, and environment.[6] It is this broad theme – what did poor writers and their advocates know of the rules, orders, regulations and the law itself of the New Poor Law; how did they come by that information; and how did they use it? – which informs this chapter. We argue both that the poor exhibited deep knowledge of the "poor law" and central regulations, and that they deployed such knowledge in subtle ways so as to promote an organic sense of a "right" to relief stretching across the period. The coming section considers the extent to which the legal underpinnings of the poor law granted a right to receive relief as opposed to a right merely to apply for it. We then move on to consider the presence of legal registers and strategy in the corpus as a whole, building on the analysis in chapter 5, before offering a new way of framing the depth and nature of legal language and considering the matrix of sources that informed the choice of rhetoric by the poor.

RIGHTS AND DUTIES

The question of whether individuals ever had a legal entitlement to relief is a thorny one which is fundamental to writing a New Poor Law history from below. To probe the matter, we must first turn to the Old Poor Law. The Elizabethan Act of 1601 was silent on the matter of individual rights. It merely stated that the collected parochial stocks and monies raised through the poor rate were to be expended in setting the unemployed poor to work, and that "competent Sums of Money" should be set aside "towards the necessary relief of the Lame, Impotent, Old [and] Blind."[7] The legislation was vague enough to ensure that questions as to who should be relieved, the methods by which the unemployed should be set to work, and the level of relief which should be given were open to considerable interpretation. The act missed the opportunity to assign positive rights to the poor. It also introduced numerous layers of confusion which would be the source of tensions within and between parishes. Such tensions ultimately led to what Peter King has called a "remaking of justice from the margins" as magistrates and judges accumulated case law in an effort to test the balance of the rights of the poor and the obligations of parishes.[8]

The PLAA was couched in similarly vague language. It was (as we saw with Thomas Henshaw) unlawful for relieving officers to give further relief than was ordered by guardians unless there was "sudden and urgent necessity," in which case they were:

> required to give such temporary Relief as each Case shall require, in Articles of absolute Necessity, but not in Money, and whether the Applicant for Relief be settled in the Parish where he shall apply for Relief or not.

The same section of the PLAA also empowered any magistrate to provide orders for medical relief cases, again only where there was "sudden and dangerous Illness [that] may require it."[9] But how sudden might "sudden" be? Could a case deserve urgent action even if the situation from which a person's destitution arose had grown steadily over several weeks? How long might "temporarily" be? What were "Articles of absolute Necessity," and which articles were proscribed and which might be prescribed? Definitional issues such as this are crucially important. Appeals by paupers or the wider poor to magistrates and the Central Authority would be read against the meaning of words and phrases, and elicit subtle interpretation of law. Henshaw traversed the territory for negotiation created by this vague language. Others in our sample found themselves confronted by the contradictions and complexities of law and practice on issues outside the scope of the PLAA. Thus, we have already seen that, in the early decades of the New Poor Law, settlement continued as a thorn in the flesh of guardians and the Central Authority. So did the meaning and scope of legal obligations of kin to support family members.[10]

Yet it is also important to understand that the "poor law" was more than mere statute. Just as magistrates made "local law" under the Old Poor Law, so the Central Authority made "informal" law under the New. It held a suite of executive powers over unions and therefore over the local poor. However, rather than specify the detailed management of poverty and paupers in the legislation itself, the 15th section of the PLAA provided the Centre with sweeping powers: "to make and Issue all such Rules, Orders, and Regulations for the Management of the Poor." This provision allowed it to introduce new and supplementary rules and regulations as necessary and on a timetable of its making.[11] There was consequently a continuous process of emerging regulations and rules set down and circulated in official orders. Many were contained in, and conveyed by, tangential Central Authority publications such as their annual reports, and these gained a *de facto* legal status. Such directives fell into two types: the first were styled "general orders" and their contents applied to more than one union. All general orders were to be laid before Parliament at the start of the following session. The second set were "special orders," and the rules and regulations contained within them were directed towards specific unions and required no political involvement. In the first few years after its establishment, the PLC sent out multiple copies of special orders to individual unions, thus eliminating the need for general orders and keeping the business of the Commission away from the prying eyes of Parliament. Special orders were often revised more than once and reissued over the years, creating a sometimes dizzying complexity of poor law rules. The Centre also began disseminating precedents of their decisions to unions via official circulars, strongly akin to the way in which magistrates made local law. In 1847 a collection of the Commission's orders was revised and reissued as the *Consolidated General Order*. Naturally (and as we began to see in chapter 2), the complexity of New Poor Law regulations and rules encouraged a huge private publication industry of guides which sought to bring together and interpret the law and its current directives for guardians, workhouse masters, and others throughout the Victorian period.[12] The frequency with which such guides were reissued and the sheer volume of Central circulars point not only to the scale of the making of informal law, but also to its organic nature and the fact that rules and laws had constantly to be reinterpreted in the light of wider societal changes.[13] The rise of social investigators in later nineteenth-century England and Wales, for example, led slowly but surely to a reshaping of views on the causation of poverty. The ascription of fault was incrementally transferred in the public imagination from the individual to the socioeconomic system, generating new rules on relief for the able-bodied from the Central Authority.[14] In short, there was no such thing as a single "law" of the New Poor Law.

Given this background, welfare historians are decisively split on the question of the existence of rights, either under the New Poor Law or over the longer term. Steve Hindle concludes that for the period prior to 1750: "the Elizabethan statutes did not in themselves confer entitlement. The 'right to relief' was negotiated in the course of local" engagements.[15] More recently Steven King has developed this idea in relation to the last decades of the Old Poor Law, arguing that while the poor had a right to apply for relief in a place of belonging, they had no right to receive such relief.[16] Lynn Hollen Lees, in her magisterial survey of the English and Welsh poor laws, likewise concluded that discretion was an Old Poor Law leitmotif.[17] On the other hand, Lori Charlesworth (tapping into a wider palette of earlier welfare history)[18] has asserted that the poor did have a legal and individualised right to welfare, concluding that welfare historians have forgotten that poor law *was* law and afforded "doctrinal black letter right."[19] In particular such rights were "located within the possession of a legal settlement" and they continued, even if in diluted form, through the New Poor Law.[20] David Englander also claimed on a similar basis that "the able-bodied poor had a statutory right to relief" in England and Wales.[21] In practice, however, the question of what obligations were imposed upon parishes by settlement law is fiendishly complicated. Keith Snell reminds us that "[t]he right to poor relief … once gained by settlement, could not legally be withheld, unless of course the person became settled elsewhere."[22] Yet at the same time it is clear that "[s]uch a definition [of settlement] does not of course mean that the settled poor had a legal right to poor relief on demand, even if they sometimes believed that."[23] Turning the argument on its head, David Feldman suggests that the fact that some 36 per cent of all relief was spent on the irremovable poor by 1864 (up from 21 per cent in 1855, and 18 per cent in 1802) gives a sense of the scale of "effective disentitlement" immediately after 1834.[24]

For the New Poor Law, just as for the Old, it is clear that many poor people *felt* they had a right to relief. Moreover, it is possible to read decisions by unions to "offer the house," in the hope that applicants would refuse and thus forfeit support, as a *de facto* acknowledgement that they had to act in the first place. Certainly Thomas Henshaw, with whose story we opened this chapter, believed that was the case. Conversely, the considerable dataset underpinning our project gives a compelling sense that most of those enmeshed in the New Poor Law understood welfare, just as under the Old Poor Law, to be essentially discretionary.[25] Here we take the view both that no individual "black letter law" afforded a legal right to relief in Victorian England and Wales, and that no such right was created by the accumulation of local practice. It was not until the Liberal Welfare Reforms that we can speak effectively about rights to welfare.[26] This contention is important for the rest of this chapter and our book. It means that while formal (black letter) and informal law (orders, regulations, and accumulated practice and local court cases) was fact, it was also an artefact: that is, "law" was not only a legal precept but a rhetorical tool to be assembled in a negotiation process much as it had been under the Old Poor Law. The key questions for this chapter thus relate to what poor people and their advocates knew of the law, where they gained that knowledge, and how they used it in their engagement with the powerful.

THE CORPUS

As chapter 5 has shown, the use of whole corpus quantification provides us with a broad sense of the presence of legal registers in the material. Here we deepen that analysis, since a particular patterning to such rhetoric might be expected from a reading of the literatures on Victorian literacy, urbanisation, law, petitioning, poverty, democracy, and the rise of the press. Thus, we might assume that London would generate more and deeper legal language than other cities and rural areas. As David Green reminds us, London came to account for much greater activity and expenditure under the New Poor Law than had ever been the case under the Old.[27] Keir Waddington also suggests that formal and informal law were simply more complex in London, and we know very well that the London press came to dominate hostile commentary on the New Poor Law.[28] We might also expect urban areas generally to sustain more legal commentary simply on the basis that literacy rates are often perceived to be higher in such places and that information on the formal and informal law of welfare would circulate more readily.[29] Moreover it is logical to assume that certain themes and topics would be particularly susceptible to a narrative of "the [formal or informal] law,"[30] and that certain periods, or key transition points, would generate denser and more sophisticated narratives of the law than others. The latter could include such transitional periods as: when the number of assistant commissioners was reduced, thus freighting unions with more discretion;[31] immediately after local and national scandals, given the publicity that "the law" might get; or as the democratisation of Boards of Guardians created alternative power structures at the heart of unions in the 1890s.[32] We might also perhaps expect definitive temporal trends (progressively as knowledge of "the law" filtered through communities and gained traction) and spatial patterns (for instance, less legal rhetoric in Wales, given the precarious hold of the New Poor Law there).[33]

In practice, corpus analysis suggests that these hypotheses have limited reach. Focusing on letters from paupers and poor applicants (and using *WordSmith* to count a basket of phrases that might indicate knowledge of the law at any level; see discussion of classification below) suggests a relatively consistent engagement with the legal arena. Removing the years 1834–38 from the analysis (that is, the obvious point at which we would expect queries about a brand new law) suggests that 39 per cent of all letters employed some legal rhetoric broadly defined. There was a small but consistent increase in the number of letters using legal reference points across the period covered by our book, but much of this was related to the increasing tendency for writers to refer to their stories as a "case," notably after the mid-1860s. At this level of analysis there were no discernible differences between unions of different socioeconomic complexion (at least once we control for serial writers) and no peaks in legal registers associated with changes to the organisational structure of the Centre. In a simple quantitative sense, men were more likely to employ direct and indirect legal references than women, but since male letters were on average longer this difference may reflect inter-correlation effects. Finally, there were minor spatial differences in recourse to the linguistic registers of the law: lower in Wales and the southwest of England, and higher in the midlands and northwest. These variations are broadly in line with those implied by King for the Old Poor Law, suggesting that we may be witnessing long-run cultural and linguistic patterns rather than something specific to the post-1834 period.[34] Running the same basic counting exercise for advocate letters suggests that those who actively wrote on behalf of the poor were more likely to use direct and (particularly) indirect references to "law" than poor authors, but this difference to some extent reflects the presence of particularly prolific and litigious advocates like Joseph Rowntree in the sample.[35]

The figures above measure only the overall number of letters containing legal rhetoric, rather than the number of "hits" in each letter. Switching from a flat counting method, we can use other corpus tools (see chapter 5) to probe the material more deeply.[36] Three key observations stem from such analysis. First, if we order the material by letter length and then exclude the very longest (simple probability in language use and repetition would suggest that long letters will inevitably generate more references), then it is clear that the density of legal references increases over time, rising from 1.7 mentions in 1840 to 2.6 in 1871, and 3.6 in 1900. That is, the poor who used the rhetoric of the law became more confident over time in its frequent deployment in the same letter. Second, while legal language could be scattered through texts there was a tendency for "the law" to appear toward the start of letters (as in "I beg you will consider my case") or towards their conclusion (as, for instance, when writers quoted an Act or asked for the opinion of the Centre on the interpretation of its own regulations). Such positioning suggests that writers invested particular authority in this referential structure. Finally, two distinct linguistic registers emerge from the coding exercise. In one, writers sought to use "the law" in a positive and directed sense to change their situation and experience or those of others. Alternatively, writers might use legal rhetoric in acts of avoidance – avoiding kinship liability, the workhouse or responsibility for their position for instance – at the local level.

At base, then, we can understand the poor and their advocates as having a significant knowledge of the formal and informal law of the New Poor Law, much as has also been argued for the pre-1834 period. The law was repackaged and repurposed to claim agency with the Centre. While few of our writers sought to actively challenge the validity of poor "law" (though some did), they were willing to employ legal references to try and improve their experience of its operation. In the remainder of this chapter we delve more deeply into the specific nature of this language in *individual* texts and explore how the poor came to build on the knowledge of the law that they carried over from the Old Poor Law.

CLASSIFICATION OF KNOWLEDGE

A classification analysis suggests that the texts dealing at some level with the law fall into three broad types. First, those which, while not using legal or rule-based terms, were nevertheless concerned with the formal or *informal* (rules, regulations, and process) law. Mary Smith, for instance, wrote from Reading (Berkshire) in November 1838 because she was unsure how to proceed concerning the discontinuance of "pay" for her child: "I have [spoken] this day to Coll. Blagrave, one of the Magistrates who signed the Order for Wm. Parsons to pay the 1s/6d per week to the Parish of Tilehurst." Her child's "pay" was, in fact, maintenance due from Parsons (the child being illegitimate) which was supposed to have been channelled to Smith via the relieving officer of Tilehurst. In a stunning act of theatre, Parsons refused to give the money directly to Smith, and the officer refused to take the money from Parsons to give to Smith. Blagrave had in his recent meetings advised Smith to write, which she did: "I shall therefore feel obliged by your Honors informing me by what means I am to receive the Childs Pay, or in what manner it is to be supported as I am not able to keep it myself."[37] Her case highlights one of the commonalities – family issues – in letters of this type. Thus, the lime-burner John Jones wrote from Trefechan (Cardiganshire) in April 1865 to ask for legal and procedural advice. He wanted to know if the Aberystwyth guardians could "demand me to pay 1s/6d a week to my mother," explaining that he had earlier paid £2 5s towards his mother's costs on the understanding that he would not be asked for more.[38] We see a similar request for clarity in the letter of Jonas Bush in April 1877, asking whether the Mitford and Launditch guardians had a right to compel him to pay one shilling per week towards his mother's maintenance. Bush was a labourer with a wife and child and was already voluntarily providing his mother with 6d a week but the guardians wanted an additional 6d, which he claimed he could not afford.[39] While the extent to which legal provisions for certain categories of family members to provide welfare to kin were or could be enforced in this period is uncertain, letters like these provide a pointed reminder that the law could nonetheless be contested.[40] The fact that paupers and poor applicants felt *able* to challenge it, and that they afforded the Central Authority the status of a legal rather than an administrative arbiter, is also important and carries lessons to which we shall return.

How far writers like Smith and Jones were fully representative of others in the same positon is uncertain. We can be rather clearer, however, about another group of writers who used this first, "soft," narrative of the law: those who complained that they had been refused outdoor relief and been offered only the workhouse. With more paupers maintained on the outdoor relief lists than indoor throughout the Victorian period, the compulsion to enter the workhouse was broadly constructed as unreasonable. In particular the aged showed tenacity in their use of soft legal narratives.[41] Thus, in February 1857 John Hartshorn, a sixty-eight-year-old framework knitter from Woodborough (Nottinghamshire), wrote to the Poor Law Board (PLB). Hartshorn explained that he could not maintain himself "at my trade and therefore … went to the Relieving Officer to get A little or small relief but he refused me any and gave Me an Order to go to the Union House at Basford." His parting question was replicated across the spatial and temporal dimensions of our corpus: "Can they Compel me to go to the House at my time of Life?"[42] Jane Harton similarly wrote in February 1848 from York, explaining that having applied for relief she had been offered the house, and stated: "I wish to know if the Guardians can compel me to go in as I am nearly 64 Years of Age."[43] In practice, of course, guardians *did* have the legal and administrative power to order relief in the workhouse but the fact that the poor wrote to seek clarity on this matter is itself revealing of a fund of contradicting "knowledge" at local level. Even when such people were forced to enter the house they continued to contest the decision. Robert Alderidge, an inmate in the Newbury workhouse in November 1858, wrote for the first time a few days after he entered, seeking to clarify the legality of the decisions made. Moreover, he noted: "I have paied all Poor Rates in Newbury for thirty years I have a few household good, being in the Union my Rent go on and soone the Landlord take goods for his Rent, this is trying Case against me."[44] Alderidge felt himself to be under a dual legal cosh – the poor law and the law relating to debtors – and clearly believed that his paying the poor rates in earlier years ought to afford him some kind of insurance against later claims. The latter was not a legal narrative *per se*, but it reached to the heart of the moral justification for the New Poor Law at a time when a wider narrative of criticism of the workhouse was gathering pace.[45]

Soft narratives of law and process were employed not only when a pauper entered the workhouse but also in regard to the work regime once there. William Walker, a sixty-seven-year-old inmate of the Bethnal Green workhouse, wrote in April 1850 that he had been discharged from the army "having been … a considerable time afflicted with giddiness in the head." This medical condition prevented him from securing employment. Once in the workhouse Walker was ordered to work at the pump for ten hours per day "on pain of being locked up in the cells or his usual food substituted by Bread and Water." He complained of ill-health midway through a shift on the pump and notwithstanding the threats of punishment refused to continue, resulting in just such a punishment. After setting out the facts to the PLB, he asked them (in the third person, perhaps to give a sense of objectivity) to "interpose your authority in his behalf and that you will be pleased to direct that he be not compelled to perform that which his affliction renders him unfit to do so."[46] Similarly, in 1852, an anonymous pauper wrote from Chelmsford workhouse to ask: "[under] the poors laws if you plese to send us word wither they can put us to hard labour or not after they are 71 or 72," adding that "their is one man their [in the workhouse] was put on bread and water 8 and forty hours because he could not do his work." The writer requested that any reply be sent "not direct to the govenor but to the board," presumably because they felt that the workhouse master may have been interpreting (or misinterpreting) the rules in this way without the knowledge of the guardians.[47] This was not a direct invocation of statute or informal law, yet the linguistic register "feels" legal and the writer was again asking the PLB to act as a court of arbitration.

In turn, we see a variant of this indirect soft narrative in cases where poor people wrote *prior* to contacting local officials, wanting to be armed with a "judgement" from the Centre before making such contact. A typical account can be found in the letter of Joseph Fletcher, written from York in early 1859, about his daughter "whose Limbs are Paralized." She had been "Born in that state, and has no use whatever of herself she cannot talk nor anything, and is likely to be a burden as long as she lives." The family had cared for the child with no assistance but their fortunes were now in decline and Joseph asked for guidance:

> [A]s I am but a working man, I have not much to stir on, therefore I beg to ask your Advice about applying to the Board of Guardians, for a little support for her, I wish to know if they can take her from me, I have not yet applied to them nor do I intend untill I have your Advice on the subject … therefore I ask your Advice whether I must

> Apply for myself or the Child, an Answer will greatly Oblige your Humble Servant.[48]

This rhetoric of good fatherhood is by now an important strand in the secondary literature and was part of a moral case for relief.[49] But more than this, while Fletcher did not refer to the *terminology* of law, regulations, and rules, his letter is nonetheless saturated with legal and procedural concerns. At the corpus level, the importance of different sorts of "soft" legal narratives rises and falls over time and, overall, 51 per cent of legal rhetoric falls into this broad category.

A second letter type embodies much more direct use of terms such as "the law," "the poor act," "regulations," and "rules," though without any specificity. We see this in a letter written by William Morgan from Pontypridd (Glamorgan) in May 1852 with a series of complaints, including, *inter alia*: malicious gossip about inmates on the part of union staff; elderly and infirm paupers being forced to undertake strenuous work; the unfair treatment of Irish paupers; failure to provide clean clothing; and the "inhumain" treatment of sick paupers by the surgeon. Morgan specifically wrote for clarification of the rules governing the house, stating: "I take the libberty of writing these few lines in the way of asking a few questions Respecting the rules and regulations of the Cardiff Union."[50] Letters like these seem to have gained particular traction and sophistication in the later New Poor Law, perhaps a signal of the deep permeation of a general knowledge of law and process.[51] John Brydon of Bellingham, for instance, wrote in 1892 concerning an unnamed cousin who was an inmate of the workhouse. He had been to see her once, and then sought to see her on the following day only to be told by the master: "I had better take and keep her myself as [*illegible*] her so much. Now I simply asked him the question; was it against the regulations to be allowed to see a relation." Brydon went on to request that the Local Government Board send him notice of "any restrictions as to people going to visit any of their own relations who through misfortune be at the Union."[52]

Sometimes writers of this letter type encroached on long-standing legal or process questions. In September 1893, John MacDonald, an inmate in the Liverpool workhouse, described how paupers were forced to immediately open any letters they received for official inspection. Any stamps the letters contained were confiscated or withheld. MacDonald believed that this was "contravening not only the Orders and Regulations but the generous, mild and beneficent spirit of the Poor Law as embodied and represented by the Local Government Board," itself a clear inference that the Centre was the ultimate legal arbiter. He claimed the right to hold "the means in the shape of a little money or postage stamps, for epistolary communication with my friends and kindred in the outside world" free from official control. MacDonald's claim of a right to correspondence had, by 1893, deep historical roots.[53] Local authorities had long sought to intercept incoming or outgoing correspondence or, failing that, to reduce opportunities for paupers to write. As early as October 1843 the PLC was asked by an unnamed union about the legality of opening paupers' incoming correspondence. They replied (to every union) via the official circulars that neither the master nor any other officers had any authority to do so.[54] Yet the legal right to send or receive letters was contested throughout the nineteenth century. When Henry Jemmett wrote from the Witney (Oxfordshire) workhouse infirmary in March 1849, for example, it was to complain that his earlier correspondence had been suppressed by staff. He wrote that "the Master & Mrs of this House … labor under the erroneous impression, as I hear, that they are authorized (by your Board even) to open [or] detain any letters the Inmates may wish to be posted."[55] George Lester Puttock made a series of complaints about the Poplar workhouse in April 1873. In the body of one letter, presumably worrying whether the staff would be given the name of the complainant, he asked if the workhouse master "has any liberty to open the letters you send to an inmate."[56] In all these cases the poor presumed that there was, or *ought* to be, a legal right to privacy and they constructed the Central Authority as the body whose responsibility it was to provide legal clarity. More widely, while the poor who wrote this second type of letter may not have made specific reference to formal and informal law, their texts were nonetheless essentially framed as legal or procedural enquiries. In other words, they understood that law and process afforded the opportunity for redress as well as subjection. In the corpus as a whole, this approach accounts for 33 per cent of all traceable legal rhetoric.

Those who wrote a third type of letter were much more specific and demonstrated a more intimate and detailed knowledge of poor law–related legislation and the various orders and regulations which established "informal law." Henshaw referred directly to the 54th clause in the PLAA. Across the chronological range of the New Poor Law, many other poor writers demonstrated a similarly detailed knowledge of specific laws and central regulations. In November 1845 John Fin, a sick inmate of the Tavistock (Devon) workhouse, wrote to point out that a burden of responsibility had been placed in the PLB by the Queen under the PLAA, "of great importance to the pauper as well as the ratepayer." In criticising the Tavistock guardians, Fin claimed that no visiting committee had ever been appointed to hear complaints despite "the 56th article of the Poor Law act."[57] He noted that the Board sat every fortnight but no complaints were heard and it thus appeared to the ratepayers that everything was as it should be. Claiming to speak on behalf of his "fellow paupers," Fin stated that detrimental changes were made to the diet, no support was given to the aged and infirm, some paupers had eaten meat off the bones brought in for crushing, and that the overall effect was to expose pauper inmates to premature and inhuman deaths.[58] The PLB responded to Fin the following week, acknowledging his complaints and explaining that an enquiry would be made into his statements, a response that would have demonstrated the value of both writing and a knowledge of the law to those who knew Fin.[59] The guardians, however, responded that Fin was "a worthless man, totally unworthy of credit – a convict just returned from transportation." They also stated that that he had previously been at Andover, which is where they believed he got the story about the bones. But the fact that he had "previous," in terms of his run-ins with the poor law authorities and the wider legal apparatus, suggests that he, too, had gained knowledge and experience in this sense.[60] He later asked for protection from the board during an investigation into his allegations, pointing out that the guardians had the best legal advice whereas the inmates were mostly "poor, ignorant and unlearned and have no means whatever of purchasing that part of the Poor Law Act which <u>contains the articles for the Internal Regulation of a Union Workhouse</u>." He concluded by asking the PLB to furnish him with a copy.[61]

This broad knowledge of the law of welfare so soon after the effective implementation of the New Poor Law is not unusual, as we have already argued. John Cartwright, from Wolstanton and Burslem Poor Law Union (PLU), in October 1848 referred to a recent change concerning emigration:

> Understanding, that in the House of Commons on the 4th of August last past you consented to the introduction of a clause in The poor law union Charges Bill, bearing directly on emigration: I submitted my case to The Guardians of this Union as to the propriety of being assisted by them as set forth in the said clause.

Cartwright had been unsuccessful. Joseph Lowndes, the union clerk, informed him that poor rates could not be used to assist emigration until the applicant had gained a settlement by five years' residence in the union. However, Lowndes continued, if a sufficient number of applications for emigration came forward which justified the necessity of levying a special rate, then something might be done.[62] Cartwright stated that he did not "question the ability of the Guardians to determine matters in general, yet I most earnestly request you to inform me if this construction of the clause is in accordance with its legal meaning." However we interpret it, Cartwright clearly signals a near contemporaneous knowledge of legal changes.[63]

The sense from the detailed corpus analysis that knowledge and rhetoricisation of formal and informal law deepened as the Poor Law was consolidated is given weight by three further examples. In July 1851 Thomas Cox and his wife, Juliana (both encountered briefly in chapter 5), began a series of correspondence consisting of eight letters over two years concerning his treatment at the hands of the Great Yarmouth guardians.[64] His second letter, sent not to the PLB but to the home secretary, Sir George Grey, claimed that he had been to see the mayor in order to get outdoor relief. The mayor suggested that Thomas should "write to you [Sir George] and any abuse or wrong was done it would be attended too."[65] His case was not attended to, and in March 1853 Thomas wrote to tell the PLB that the "severe prejudice the Chairman Governor & Porter of the Poor are inbearable." Cox had been ordered to go to the workhouse but "given My dread of unfair treatment th[r]o' starving" had turned down the offer. He explained: "Gentlemen by accident I [discover] that Justice may order out door [relief] to aged & infirm persons unable to [work] &c &c New Poor Law Section 27."[66] Cox was quite correct in his understanding of the law: Section 27 of the PLAA did allow outdoor relief for the elderly and infirm in preference to the workhouse, providing that an order was obtained to that effect from two magistrates.[67] Whereas Cox had complained about the refusal of outdoor relief, Thomas Snelgrove, an inmate of the Exeter Incorporation workhouse (Devon), was concerned with his treatment as an indoor pauper. In March 1868 he wrote to complain that, having sent for his medicine as agreed by the doctor, the master had then rescinded the order. Snelgrove took this up with the master, who called the police, and he was arrested and charged with assault, having been so "excited at such illegal treatment and pushed him [the police officer] from me." Snelgrove was then taken before the magistrates at the Exeter Guildhall and sentenced to twenty-one days' imprisonment for insulting language to the master and an additional fourteen days for assaulting the policeman. He was able to question the master at the time of his conviction, who confirmed that Snelgrove was not placed in confinement as disorderly, brought before the visiting committee or been denounced "to the committee of nine as disorderly or refractory." Hence:

> Gentlemen has not the master exceeded his duty? had the magistrates power to act in my case previous to my haveing a hearing before the guardians of the boardroom of this house and my receiving a punishment from their hands and the masters. I refer you to articles 127. to 131 for disorderly and refractory paupers which are hung up in the various wards of this house and signed Geo. Nichols. George Cornwall Lewis, Edmund W. Head. we have no protection from your hands when the master is allowed by the guardians to act so illegal.[68]

A claim of illegality similar to that of Snelgrove was made in relation to pauper punishment in March 1872 by Frederick Rogers, an inmate of the Poplar workhouse. Rogers admitted committing an act for which he would be deemed refractory and that "according to an article 128 the master was empowered to punish me by giving me Bread & water in place of any other food that I might have been entitled to otherwise."[69] However, this did not happen. Instead, Rogers claimed, the master:

> illeagally used Art. 131 by confining me in a cell not 12 hrs as stated in the Art. but 13 hours in addition to which he kept me without food & water 10 hours bsides which according to an Article not here to be seen a person so confined behond a given number of hrs is to be accommadated with a bed in the said cell which was not done in my case. I was confined in the said cell from ½ past 9 a.m. till ½ 10 p.m. The time for bed being 8 p.m.[70]

He went on:

> Now Sir I ask is it possible the master can plead ignorance in this case. He being an educated man & receiving out of the rate a large salary in recognition of his services being considered as in the case of a magistrate well qualified to administer justice. Had I so pleaded before punishment was inflicted would he the Master have accepted such plea To that I say no. Then why in the name of common sense should such plea be accepted from him. It appears to me Sir that a man being poor is to be crushed & visited with a penalty even heavier than the law allows with impunity. I admit I have broken the law in one instance & have been punished illigaly, now – Sir in my humble opinion the Master as broken the law in 4 instances. May I ask Sir is he, being an educated man to escape punishment. It appears to me Sir that a man being poor is to be ground down there is an old Adage which says give a dog a bad name & then hang him. [71]

The increasing density of legal rhetoric in the corpus as a whole is well illustrated in Rogers's sophisticated response to his treatment.

These are important individual cases but, in constructing our three categories as essentially discrete and by focusing on individual letters, we underplay the complexity of the use of legal registers by the poor. Two observations are thus important. First, individual letters were sometimes part of a series which included advocates, as we have already seen. Judged in the round, a set of correspondence has a deeper legal "feel" than any of its constituent parts. For example, in July 1851 Robert Cooper wrote on behalf of the aged William Petty and his wife, who had been refused outdoor relief and were confined in the workhouse at York.[72] Petty had previously written to complain in his own right, citing "Gray Hares" and infirmity, but Cooper's letter took this argument a stage further, once again alluding to the right of the elderly to be relieved outside the workhouse upon obtaining a magistrate's order.[73] "[N]ow sir," he wrote, "this is a breach of the law [and] you as a chief magistrate of England and a law maker ought not to allow the law to be broken in this way."[74] In January 1860, however, Robert Cooper the advocate became Robert Cooper the applicant when he wrote to the PLB asking for their assistance in securing his own outdoor relief from the York PLU. He described himself as sixty-two years old and suffering from asthma, adding that as a result of his poor health he had been unable to work for the previous five winters. Cooper added that his wife was also unable to work. The couple had been removed from York to the Sculcoates PLU (Yorkshire) the previous year but returned the same day, as Sculcoates "would not give me anything and I cant think of going into the Poor house to be treated worse than a felon."[75] Echoing his earlier defence of Petty, Cooper wrote:

> I know the law allows relief to persons our age when not able to work and if you will be so kind as to assist me to get it I shall be very grateful as I am in great need my name is Robert Cooper I belong to Cottingham near hull but I have been in york 20 years and 3 years in St Savaurs parish yours respectfully Robert Cooper.[76]

In the event, the PLB declined to intervene, but the key point is that throughout the Victorian period the Centre received complex constellations of letters framed with a basic legal infrastructure.

A second nuance is that across letter series written by paupers or poor applicants it is possible to see writers traversing all three of our rhetorical approaches to law and process, and not always in a strictly linear way. Occasionally, we can even watch them enfolded in a single letter such as that written by Joseph Smith of Sheffield in 1883.[77] Like the pauper from

Chelmsford cited above, Smith initially used a "soft" approach to the rules regarding the employment of the elderly in workhouses, complaining that: "I am 71 years of age [yet] They put me to very laborious work, heavy washing and wringing," and that on querying this he was told that "I must do it wether I was able or not." As an ex-serviceman, Smith was entitled to a service pension of 9d a day, but this had been withheld from him by the relieving officer in lieu of his keep, even after he had discharged himself from the workhouse. At this point, he demonstrated a keen understanding of the process by which, as a pauper, he should have been able to get redress, writing: "I went to the relieving Officer again and asked him if he had received my money. He said yes [and] I then asked him to put my name down for me to see the Guardians." The officer refused and simply said that "he would admit me any time into the House." Having failed to gain satisfaction through due process, Smith went to a higher authority to clarify the legality of his treatment:

> I went to the Magistrates in Sheffield & stated my case to them. They told me it was not legal for them [the Sheffield PLU] to make me work for my food, & also receive my pension as well, but they said they had no jurisdiction, but must apply to you & see if you could not recover the whole – or part of that money back.

Navigating all three of our approaches to the laws and regulations governing the application of relief, Smith finished his letter with an appeal not to legal but to natural justice: "It seems rather hard that a man who has fought and endured many hardships for his country & Queen should be swindled out of his money & can get no redress." As with writers under the Old Poor Law, none of these approaches happened by chance. Employment of different strands and densities of rhetoric and strategy focusing on law and practice was a choice, an expression of agency whatever the outcome.

SOURCES OF KNOWLEDGE

If an extensive and increasingly dense matrix of legal language exists in our sources, the important supplementary question is: how did the poor gain and maintain that knowledge? Some of the individual stories in the last section provide a clue. Like their counterparts under the Old Poor Law, writers could draw on the knowledge (and appropriate the voices) of advocates. It has already become apparent that local magistrates could be important sources of legal and regulatory knowledge. Both Mr Radford, the Smalley magistrate in Nottinghamshire who was probably the source for Thomas Henshaw's legalistic assertions, and Colonel Blagrave, the Tilehurst magistrate who had advised Mary Smith to write directly to the PLC, provided information and advice in their respective cases. The two applicants may have seen the letters written and then recycled that advice. Other third parties were important too, as we saw in the example of Thomas Cox, who drew on information given to him by the mayor of Great Yarmouth. Social investigators likewise sometimes provided direct advice to the poor, rather than merely observe their plight.[78]

This is not to argue that poor writers were incapable of "getting" the law in their own right. Peter Jones and Steven King have noted the increasing presence in workhouses of vociferous individual paupers who engaged intensively with the Central Authority not only on their own behalf but also as representatives of a wider pauper body. These writers went out of their way both to collect and read legal tracts, circulars, and orders, and to deploy that reading in their engagements with the powerful.[79] Such knowledge inevitably percolated through pauper and poor applicant populations, leading at the very least to the sorts of letter we see in the first type of our three-strand typology above. Even where such individuals were not present (or after they had left), a cursory look at census material gives a clear sense of workhouses populated in part by teachers, ex-ratepayers, clerks, and even former parochial or union staff, all of whom would have had the literacy and knowledge to acquire "the law." More widely, it is clear from recent historiography, but even more from the considerable data analysed here, that the poor were also able to glean something of formal and informal law from the occasions when they were called to give evidence to central and local inquiries at the union level.[80] As Oz Frankel reminds us, the reports of these sorts of inquiry were a form of "orature," material that "transcends the dichotomy between literature and orality" and rapidly made the transition to a common store of knowledge.[81]

Inquiries were often the subject of intense local and national press coverage, and we have already established here that poor writers read newspapers and were thus likely to pick up legal knowledge by osmosis. Moreover, it is now clear that, while newspapers such as *The Times* (and London-based newspapers more generally) maintained a hostile brief on the New Poor Law and its workhouses throughout the period covered by this book, the press more generally sustained and accelerated a movement for workhouse reform, one which again must have percolated through the poor and pauper populations. If newspapers were part of the "connecting tissue between the state and its citizens," then it is important that the poor seem to have gained increasing access to them.[82] In turn, Acts themselves were published and circulated, and the "informal law" (established through orders and circulars of the Central Authority) was widely advertised and reproduced in official poor law periodical publications, annual reports, and commercially published advice for union and parish officers which we know the poor managed to obtain. And sometimes, of course, formal and informal law was literally given to the poor. Thus, in terms of punishment, workhouse masters were supposed to make copies of articles 127 through to 131 available by having them "suspended in the dining-hall of the Workhouse, or in the room in which the inmates usually eat their meals, and also in the Board-room of the Guardians."[83] Indeed, we saw in Snelgrove's letter that he referred to the copies hung in various wards in the workhouse. Such rules were there as reminders to inmates of their behavioural obligations, but they also defined the powers of workhouse employees and thus provided paupers with the limits of legitimate staff intervention, and laid out routes for complaint where such limits were exceeded. When Robert Cooper wrote to the PLB on 5 January 1860 to say "I know the law," he was literally writing the truth.[84]

Nor should we forget that the Central Authority was itself a source of knowledge. This theme was explored in chapter 4, but we have seen here that when John Jones and Jonas Bush asked whether they could be forced to pay toward their family members' upkeep, and when John Hartson and Jane Harton asked whether the local guardians had the right to compel them to enter the workhouse, they did so on the understanding that not all family members made such payments and not all paupers lived in the workhouse. In other words, if the "law" was in play, it was being inconsistently applied. If the responses from the Central Authority "taught" individuals the law, then it is likely that the teaching travelled deep into the villages, towns, and cities in which the poor lived. We also witness within the underlying corpus a spread of the notion of "rights" far beyond the most basic, and perhaps the most important, relating to whether indoor or outdoor relief was to be offered. The entitlements claimed in the corpus include the rights of poor people: to visit their inmate relatives; to receive and send private mail; to not be allocated work that would affect their health; to make complaints to visiting committees; to be considered for emigration; to retain care of their sick children; and to be provided wholesome food. As the New Poor Law and the workhouse became a settled and permanent feature of mid-to-late Victorian welfare, so paupers extended the "rights" which they claimed. In responding or not responding to their claims, the Centre inevitably "made" informal law and invited its rhetoricisation.

Finally, it is important to remember that the indoor and outdoor poor were rarely, at least until old age, *merely* paupers. Some noted in their letters that they had once been independent and hoped to be so again in the future. In that other life, aspects of and perspectives on law were easily accrued. By the mid-1830s, public anti–poor law meetings and radical anti–poor law newspapers which advertised such meetings undoubtedly provided much knowledge of the poor law and its workings.[85] Chartism and trade union activism were also underpinned by core narratives of the law. Indeed, in the middle of the 1842 general strike Robert Weale (an assistant poor law commissioner) wrote to the PLC. He was then investigating allegations that several people in the Wolstanton and Burslem PLU had received relief under false pretences. Weale reported that one of the able-bodied applicants, a man called Hamlet Booth, was a Chartist and had been haranguing the men in the workhouse grounds and condemning the poor "Law" in very strong language intended to create dissent. Working-class meetings on the poor law were thus taking place in the heart of the system itself and this might have intensified narrative engagement with "law" even if we see little of the language of radicalism, Chartism, or public petitioning in the corpus.[86]

CONCLUSION

Crossing the normative spatial and temporal divisions usually pinned onto the New Poor Law, we have been able to trace a pauper and applicant population with sustained knowledge of formal and informal law and a determination to rhetoricise that knowledge as they sought to influence eligibility for and the scale and form of welfare. With some writers, the linguistic footprint of "the law" was light, almost transient. Others had such a detailed control of the legal narrative that they could reference legislation down to the sectional level. All those who referenced the law to some degree assumed, asserted, or claimed "legal" rights (just as they had done under the Old Poor Law) as a way of trumping the overseer, guardian, or workhouse master who refused relief applications or treated the poor other than the way they wanted (or even expected) to be treated. Formal and informal law certainly did not give the poor a legal and individually personal right to relief; it did ensure that poor relief practice in an essentially discretionary system was not arbitrary or merely inward-looking. For these poor writers, the rhetoric of the law was ultimately an anchor for local and national accountability. Of course, the law favoured the authorities, and claiming rights could be dangerous, as most complaints to the Central Authority were relayed back to the local guardians for initial investigation. Yet, public knowledge of such laws ultimately gave poor writers a powerful linguistic register and strategic apparatus which they shared with the general public and the communities from which they were drawn. How far the Webbs were right to argue that the New Poor Law "gave a dogmatically uniform direction to English poor law policy" is still a matter of debate.[87] But in its issuance of codifying orders and circulars, the Centre provided a uniform and easily knowable mechanism – an informal law – by which staff, guardians, and the Centre itself could be held to account. In this context, limited successes like those claimed by Thomas Henshaw and others ensured that writers continued to develop narratives of "the law" throughout the nineteenth century and that those increasingly extensive and dense narratives became part of a continuing moral challenge to the legitimacy of the New Poor Law.

The fact that paupers and poor applicants grasped the language and process of formal and informal law meant that they inserted themselves into an interpretive community. Here, the poor, central administrators, guardians, and local staff understood and reacted to a common stock of knowledge and dealt in similar linguistic currencies. This common stock related narrowly to the poor law, but it related also to a wider suite of legislation and process and to what Lawrence Goldman understands as a wider intellectual canvas of social reform broadly defined.[88] In turn, their language and strategy connected the Old and New Poor Laws and must be understood as a single chronology of pauper agency, one in which the central theme is the appropriation of the language and structures of the powerful to the services of the dependent poor. Situated (as it must be) in the emerging contexts of social investigation, new understandings of the causation of poverty, new narratives of contributory citizenship, and fears of national decline, this language of the law is an important footprint of the increasingly concrete obligations of the state to its less fortunate members. One of the most notionally dependent and powerless subsets of this group were women, and it is to the particularities of their rhetoric that we now direct our attention.

7

The Female Voice

INTRODUCTION

In November 1853 Harriet Cross wrote to the Centre laying out her case and asking for their intervention. She had applied to the Leominster Poor Law Union (PLU) in Herefordshire to obtain relief for the three youngest of six children. Her husband's recent trial, conviction, and twelve-month sentence at Hereford "for misconduct" had robbed the family of its main wage earner, and the response to the application was that she and *all* six children were offered the workhouse. Cross wrote that she took it "very hard":

> as I must take them [her eldest three children] out of imploy as is able to get little to live with and I cant work and pay my rent to keep a home for them and all I wanted was aliving for them as is not able to work as I am not able to maintain the 3 children

Income from her three working boys was minimal: the oldest two received three shillings per week each, while the youngest earned only his food, and all three "comes hom to sleep." Having explained her situation, Cross claimed: "I am a bliged to go in as we shall be famished me and 3 children I am treaded very hard Gentlemen." Her key point was: "I does for them as a mother ought to do I am not take them into the house."[1]

There is much here that is common across the corpus: a narrative of income not keeping pace with rent and other outgoings; an unsuccessful application for outdoor relief; and a concluding question concerning the rights and wrongs of the poor being forced to accept relief under the circumstances stated. However, there are also *particular* elements of the text which mark this out as a woman's letter. Most people tried and convicted through the criminal justice system in England and Wales were poor young men, and the system thus had a huge effect on young wives and children.[2] Here the father was imprisoned and Harriet had both parental roles to undertake. Unable to earn enough to keep the family in his absence, she drew upon rhetorical constructions of the duties of motherhood in relation to her youngest children ("I does for them as a mother ought to do") and upon wider understandings of the role of parents in physical and moral protection of all children ("I am not take them into the house"). The register used clearly marks this as a letter from a female family head but also a woman with agency: she did not ask for relief but "a living," pointing very strongly to a sense of natural right and a reward for maternal citizenship.

The ubiquity of circumstances like these makes it all the more surprising that women occupied a liminal position in the law and practice of post-1834 welfare and that there has not been more engagement with female experiences in the historiography.[3] As we have already seen, the Poor Law Amendment Act (PLAA) stated that, apart from some exceptions regarding medical attendance and apprenticeship, "all relief whatever to able-bodied persons or to their families otherwise than in well-regulated workhouses … shall be declared unlawful."[4] In this context, and as Sidney and Beatrice Webb emphasised in their analysis of the New Poor Law, neither the Poor Law Commissioners' Report of 1834 nor the law itself afforded much by way of practical guidance or clarification for guardians as to how women were to be treated. Married women, with or without children, were implicitly regarded for relief purposes as children themselves; they were appended to the aged, impotent, or sick male, or refused relief along with the able-bodied male.[5] In relation to able-bodied single women, even those with illegitimate children[6] or widows, there was less guidance. This situation reflected complex contemporary views on the purpose of welfare. Lynn Hollen Lees persuasively argues that the labourer of previous generations was perceived as understanding the connection between improvidence and his family's sufferings, and appreciated his responsibilities towards parents, wives, and children. By the time of the 1834 Report it was contended that men would desert their dependants, demand "parish pay" as of right, and as soon fight for those rights as earn their money legally and thankfully. The 1834 Royal Commission thus looked at the challenging nature of pauperism and declared it male.[7] In turn, the explicit location of the case for poor relief within a male breadwinner model meant that the poverty of women and children would best be ameliorated by confronting idleness and increasing the earnings of male household heads and other workers. Even though we have come to see the male breadwinner model and the associated breadwinner wage as an organic concept,[8] Marjorie Levine-Clark has argued that the New Poor Law at the close of the nineteenth century still privileged and embodied the male breadwinner as the norm and ideal. Earning the family wage bestowed the male head of house with a respectable independence. Women were thus seen as dependants and their wage-earning capacity was not taken into account in terms of family support.[9]

Yet, on the other hand, we have become increasingly aware of the importance of women's work and earnings to the prospects for the family economy under both the Old and New Poor Laws.[10] For many households the loss of the wage-earning capacities of women through accident, illness, pregnancy, childbirth, or death could have disastrous economic consequences.[11] Under the Old Poor Law both women and men rhetoricised this fact in their negotiations with parish authorities, with the "cover" of lost female earnings used to obtain relief in situations that might not otherwise have called for it.[12] The picture is less clear for the post-1834 period. Jane Long's astute contention that in dealing with the female poor in the northeast of England, constructing "labour" as a male activity would push the female working-class experience of poverty to the periphery, remains starkly true.[13] More widely, women comprised a large part of most workhouse populations except during intense trade depressions and, while significant recent work has been done on the plight of illegitimate children and their mothers, it is still true that for every other category of pauper and poor applicant we know much more about the experiences, rhetoric, and strategy of men than of women. Addressing this situation has consequences for the way we write and understand a New Poor Law history from below. Focusing on women who wrote or gave evidence might tell us much: about the continuing purchase of localism in policy execution (David Englander has asserted that a mother applying for relief could never predict what the outcome of her application might be[14]); about the susceptibility of masculine authority to arguments about motherhood, protection, and vulnerability; and about the wider rhetorical matrices of citizenship, contribution, fragility, and responsibility that women in particular employed when dealing with men.

Thus, the current chapter will look at registers, strategy, and agency specifically in relation to women like Harriet Cross. Exploring the different circumstances that impelled women to write to the Centre or to offer evidence in their own defence or that of others, the chapter considers whether the rhetoric and strategy developed by women focused on concepts different to those that engaged men. The reach, range, and complexity of the female voice – a voice that fused concerns and language drawn from the time of the Old Poor Law based around notions of dependence, deference, respectability, and their roles as mothers and wives, with new referential and linguistic models – will become very apparent.[15]

THE CORPUS

Although the 1834 Report and legislation were often silent on the female pauper, women were not silent in regard to their own welfare concerns. The corpus contains numerous letters, witness statements, and other documents from, by, or about single, married, and widowed women.[16] Chapter 2 dealt with the quantitative dimensions of that corpus, and here we pick up on a particular feature: numerically and proportionally the female pauper voice is stronger in witness statements than in letters. Meanwhile, the nature of this voice, as chapter 5 began to show, is complex. In the 1830s and 1840s backward-looking rhetorical models and reference points predominate. Even at later dates there remain long-term continuities as women addressed and sought to negotiate with male authority figures.[17] Thus women variously appealed to and for the protection of male correspondents, enjoined recipients to imagine the emotional turmoil of mothers and wives faced with sickness, desertion, and death, and pointed to the fact that poverty and exogenous circumstances compromised the role constructed for them. As mothers they suffered, fretted, and regretted. Clearly following rhetorical threads established under the Old Poor Law, women spoke of multi-layered dependence (on husbands, brothers, fathers, systems, and processes) and on occasion constructed themselves exactly as the New Poor Law intended – which is to say as children seeking the guiding hand of a parent. Sometimes the linguistic register spilled over into anger, and in our earlier chapters we have seen instances of women writing confrontational letters about the treatment of parents, children, and husbands. For much of the period between 1834 and the 1850s, however, the corpus exhibits a distinct rhetorical note of resignation, a sense that there was an inevitability to dependence which should be recognised, accepted, and treated outside the workhouse. Corpus level analysis also reveals that women shared in some of the referential and rhetorical models of all paupers, or at least those in similar circumstances. Old women – single, widowed, or married – wrote of decline and increasing inability much as did old men. Younger women hoped to become independent again if given a little help in the present, preferably outside the workhouse, just as working-age men did. And while women were disproportionately likely to use "soft" narratives of the law throughout the period, they were more likely than their male counterparts to deploy rhetoric that pointed to abuse of process and the systematic failings of institutions.

These are all important observations, and they point persuasively to female involvement in the basic linguistic and strategic architecture required to actively navigate the New Poor Law. Yet we can also see other distinctive developments, especially from the 1850s. Some are subtle and speak to the sense that women were well connected to proximate contemporary debates. Rhetorical construction of the moral as opposed to the physical threat of homelessness for women is relatively rare before 1850, but thereafter we see more direct and indirect engagement with this theme. By the 1860s the inference that failure to offer relief, or alternatively to force people into workhouses, might result in female vagrancy and prostitution is strikingly clear.

Similarly, in a simple statistical sense, women were more likely than men to rhetoricise or threaten public exposure of grievances and policy or process failings. This reflected a core historical reality – there was a greater public appetite for the stories of suffering women and children than for tales of men's misfortunes. At the same time, women writers made strategic decisions to frame their texts in terms of public and private spaces and faces. Such rhetoric was often co-located, and usually intricately entwined, with a rhetoric that constructed experiences of poor females with failings of humanity, masculinity, and dignity.

One further distinctive element of female rhetoric (established from the very start of the New Poor Law) is what might be understood as "community," which included referential modes of friendship, protection, connectedness, and group identity. Such language was often co-located with and situated in a rhetorical framework that dripped with vulnerabilities: to punishment, sexual abuse, hunger, loss of family and status, nakedness, and various forms of casual tyranny and neglect. We see this clearly in the case of Phillis Pedder, an outdoor pauper in Flitwick (Bedfordshire). In 1841 Pedder was a forty-year-old widow who headed a family consisting of herself, her sons John (twenty) and Thomas (eighteen), and her daughters, Ann (sixteen), Mary (thirteen), and Rachel (six).[18] She was a poor woman who at this time was in receipt of weekly "widow's pay" of 2s 6d. By October 1844, Phillis briefly took on the mantle of a pauper *cause célèbre*. She had died, apparently "from Starvation and Neglect," and the case was extensively reported in *The Times*.[19] A correspondent visited Flitwick the day after her death and ascertained that "that there had been a great deal of talk" about Pedder's case. The reporter collected testimony from friends, neighbours, and children. Among those commenting on Pedder's death was Mr Fane, a local farmer and churchwarden who claimed that a great many in the parish were dissatisfied with how Pedder had been treated. He recalled a conversation with a woman named Deacon, who told him that "she never saw a poor creature lie in such a state in all her life."[20] Elizabeth Fowler, a close neighbour who had "Attended her backwards and forwards for a month or six weeks before she died," was herself a pauper. Ann Langley, a neighbour, was another regular visitor to the Pedder household, attending every day over a period of weeks. She saw Mr Chapman, the surgeon, exiting the house a couple of days before Pedder died and pressed him on the case. Mary Spendelow,[21] Pedder's sister, lived at Pulloxhill, a little over two miles from Flitwick. A couple of weeks before Pedder died, Spendelow went to the Ampthill guardians for relief on her sister's behalf only to be turned away. Spendelow said that she visited her sister every week, when in Flitwick to sell straw plait, and confirmed that Pedder's relief had been stopped because she had refused to go into the infirmary. She claimed that Pedder knew she was going to die and for that reason did not want to leave her family and pass her last days surrounded by strangers and potentially susceptible to the terms of the Anatomy Act.[22] Forced workhouse residence, she had said, "shall break my heart."[23] Spendelow was not the only female member of the family who had sought assistance for Phillis. Her thirteen-year-old daughter Mary Pedder went to Ampthill to speak to Mr Chapman, who sent her to the relieving officer for an order that would allow him to attend on her mother, but in the end it was too late. The case here demonstrates the importance of female friend and family networks for the very poorest of women and goes some way to explain the prevalence of female voices in witness statements. Any case of disputed relief, especially outside the workhouse, would likely be known about by, and involve, large numbers of women who had a detailed knowledge of each other's lives and volunteered help in times of hardship. More than this, we can see a sense of the particular vulnerabilities of poor women and their daughters.

The problem with this level of analysis, however, is that we risk treating women as a uniform group and thus missing subtle rhetorical or referential models which were broadly patterned onto life-cycle or situational variables. Our corpus analysis suggests that we should explore the experiences of six broad categories of poor and pauper women, as summarised in table 7.1. The letters and statements allotted to categories one to five came overwhelmingly from female outdoor paupers or poor applicants, and they are consonant with the ways in which we can classify women's writing under the Old Poor Law.[24] Our final category of writers – women in institutions – was vanishingly rare before 1834 and we might thus expect new layers of rhetorical engagement with male office holders.

Table 7.1
Categories of women writers

Category 1	Women acting as head of the household by virtue of the death or desertion of the husband or cohabiting/casual lover.
Category 2	Women living alone or as head of family household who had suffered the temporary loss of their husband; for example through his incarceration following conviction, being in military service away from home, or having travelled to secure work elsewhere.
Category 3	Women whose husband was incapacitated from writing (perhaps from ill-health) or who lacked writing skills.
Category 4	Women writing jointly with men, sometimes in multi-signature petitions but mainly as part of a couple writing a "husband and wife letter."
Category 5	Women writing as advocates, either as other poor women or as wealthier and well-connected women.
Category 6	Women who were pauper inmates.

Source: MH12. Local Government Board and Predecessors: Correspondence with Poor Law Unions and Other Local Authorities, The National Archives.

CLASSIFYING WOMEN'S WRITING

Our first category consists of women who assumed the role of the head of a household following the death of, or desertion by, a husband or a lover. Mary Ann Taylor of Nottingham (Nottinghamshire) wrote in July 1863 complaining that her husband was dead and that "My health is very bad & I cannot work very little at all." She referenced her status as a mother with small children and described herself as destitute without the means of providing for her family, implicitly assuming that the circumstances of compromised motherhood would be well understood.[25] In July 1878 Maria Butterfield wrote from Dereham (Norfolk). Like Taylor she was a widow with three small children. One of them had been placed in an orphan school, and she had been allowed one shilling and a flour allowance for each for the other two.[26] On seeing a vacancy for a nurse at the Mitford and Launditch workhouse she had applied for and secured the post, which yielded an income of

£25 a year. During a trial month her father had looked after the children but this was not a long-term option, he being "an old man & nearly 70 years of age." At the end of the trial month the guardians stopped the relief for the children, leaving Butterworth having to put them "out sepprate & had to pay 4s per week for each child beside there clothing, this i found i could not meet the exspences so was Oblidge to leave & take my children again." Butterfield thus had to apply for the renewal of her children's relief from the very guardians by whom she had just been employed. Their response was that she must enter the workhouse with her children as paupers; her appeal to the Local Government Board (LGB) was that she would have "been glad to have stoped for the sake of my children had i been able to meet demand for the keep of my children." This emphasis on the welfare of children is a continuation of Old Poor Law strategies, but the linguistic effect was given added reach in circumstances where an assumed male breadwinner had been permanently lost.[27] Indeed, Butterfield reinforced her mothering credentials by concluding, "if any thing can be done for my children will you kindly let me know."[28] The case also points, however, to other strong rhetorical signals for this category of writer, including contribution against the odds (she had obtained a job), hoped for and evidenced potential of renewed independence, family support at a time of *extremis* and, of course, explicit and implicit appeals to masculine authority figures.

The circumstances of a second category of women – those who experienced the temporary loss of husbands to prison, military service, or working at distance – had very different connotations for both writers and recipients. Welfare officials exhibited ingrained hostility to the families of convicted men or those they suspected of dumping families on the poor rate, and to women they suspected of complicity.[29] The oratorical engagement of these women was thus complex. Margaret Wallace appeared before the Durham (County Durham) guardians following her husband's conviction and imprisonment for poaching in February 1870.[30] She later wrote:

> when I were *before you* on the last occasion making an application for outdoor relief, I were very *timid* and in fact afraid to speak, never having appeared in my life before such a number of *public Gentlemen*, and I now respectfully beg leave to inform you that I have a small house

> together with two young children neither of whom can assist me in gaining an *honest* livelihood to support ourselves.[31]

Wallace illustrated her deference to the status of the local guardians ("public Gentlemen"), as well as the links of dependence and inter-dependence of her children to herself, and of her family as a whole to the union. She also gave voice to the respectable desire for an honest income which would support the whole family and stood in contradistinction to the strategy of an errant husband. Some of these rhetorical approaches were traced in chapter 5, and we also see here linguistic registers of dependence and deference which link with those of the Old Poor Law. There was, however, more to it than that. Wallace claimed that she and the children would have voluntarily entered the workhouse but that this would entail the rent for their "humble dwelling" falling into arrears and her husband's goods being detained and sold at a fraction of their value; something she "durst not take upon myself to sell … without my Husbands' sanction." The duty of a wife to an absent man (as opposed to the responsibilities of an ex-wife when a man was dead) was a powerful strategic trope in this period.[32] Wallace also deployed two histories of past contribution as a way to nullify moral suspicion, arguing that she had done everything "since I were before you to gain an honest livelihood, but find it utterly impossible to do the required to gain the necessaries of life," and that her husband had in fact been a respectable ratepayer of many years. Her case with the guardians having failed, Wallace asked the Poor Law Board (PLB) to intervene and help her obtain 1s 10d weekly for rent and rates to supplement the money she could earn, thus allowing an independent future. As with Butterfield's letter the emphasis was on the impossibility that a single female parent could earn enough to supply family necessaries. Indeed, this theme is consistent across the spatial and chronological dimensions of the category, as we see from a joint petition from Elizabeth Lester and Ann Merryman of Alvenchurch (Worcestershire), whose husbands were committed to Worcester jail in December 1853, also for poaching. Both women, being destitute, applied to the local relieving officer. He took their application to the Bromsgrove (Worcestershire) guardians, who in turn offered only the workhouse. This would entail both mothers' losing their existing employment and the homes they shared with their young children. The two women emphasised that with a little assistance they would be able to survive until their husbands were released.[33] Returning to the case of Wallace, however, we see that she went further, drawing attention to failings of due process. The letter enclosed the copy of another text:

> which I gave to Mr Thomas Gowland, relieving officer of this parish, whome promised to lay the same before the "Durham Board of Guardians" and he did not only refuse to do so, but likewise prevented my appearing before them on the same day in question[34]

Such a rhetorical approach points to the ability of women in this category to balance backward-looking models of dependence and deference with a newer sense of right defined by regulation or law.

Some of the same approaches were adopted, and adapted, by women with very different circumstances. Jane Hewitt, writing to Warsop (Nottinghamshire) from London in April 1838, stated that her soldier husband James was:

> now on his way to Canada with his Battalion. I assure you he made every exertion in his power to get the two children into the Duke's School but the girl being half an idiot & the boy having a deformed chest they could not be admitted. I am now destitute & write to know wether you would be pleased to allow grant me the same allowance I had before or wether I shall apply to the parish here & be passed up to Warsop. Mr Griffiths of Friday Streets, in the City, says he is willing to advance to me weekly whatever you may please to allow, as he did before, earnestly requesting an early answer. I am Sir Your Obedient humble servant Jane Hewitt.[35]

This is a non-resident relief letter of the type and texture familiar from the closing decades of the Old Poor Law.[36] It also, however, carried more sophisticated and specific layers of linguistic direction: Hewitt's husband was serving his country and prior to his departure had also tried to serve his family; his absence left a mother alone trying her best to care for two disabled children, a strong rhetorical theme across the post-1834 corpus; Jane Hewitt had been in this position before and asked whether she was to have her old allowance, highlighting precedent, obligation, and even right; and she was trusted and known in her community. While Hewitt applied for the protection of the "male" Central Authority, there was bite to this text. The Poor Law Commission (PLC) acknowledged receipt of the Mansfield clerk's letter and contended that "The course to be adopted is *the same as that if the women had lost their husbands or if they were in the custody of the law.*" This was a clear recognition of the impossibility that any female-headed household could achieve economic security. The clerk was also told that the union might apply to recover any allowance from the husband's pay but that they could not claim this as a right, conveying in effect a precise right for wives temporarily separated from their husbands to obtain unencumbered relief.[37]

Hannah Roberts, whose husband was in the Monmouthshire militia, adopted a very different approach in similar circumstances. She wrote from Aberystwyth in July 1854 noting that her husband had been stationed at Newport, some seventy miles distant. Roberts, writing in the third person as did many earlier Old Poor Law paupers, claimed that she was now sick in the Aberystwyth Infirmary and:

> In such Calamity, do most Humbley Implore your goodness to Inform her where she is to aply for Rilief, whither to the Parish her Husband was Chargeable to before he married your petitioner or the parish he Inlist in since he was married:– The former is the parish of Llangarnvelin, 7 miles distance from Aberystwith the later is the parish of Brydwelltdy 80 miles distance from Aberystwith.[38]

Here, then, Roberts conveyed a strong sense of the impact of an absent husband and assumed that the Centre would understand the necessity for her application and her right to apply for relief. In this context she wrote with a simple question of process and in so doing she highlights, to us and to the PLB, the complexity of settlement law for married women in general and women married to militiamen in particular. Should she apply to the settlement place of her husband, she asked (having lost her own settlement after marriage), to the place for which he was serving as a militiaman, or to the place in which she lived? The implicit message in this question – that Roberts had moved long distances repeatedly across Wales and thus lacked kin or neighbourly support – was clear.

Our third category encompasses women whose husbands were incapacitated from writing (due to sickness, for instance) or who lacked the necessary writing skills.[39] Relatively uncommon under the Old Poor Law, such letters became more frequent post-1834, a reflection in part of the growing literacy of women.[40] An example is Harriet Robbins, who in December 1865 wrote from Stowey (Somerset) stating that her husband, Edward, was suffering from heart disease. She had already successfully applied to the Clutton PLU for relief, and the family had additional income "from his Club."[41] Three months earlier her husband's health had begun to improve and the allowance was removed. Still struggling, Robbins "Was ablige [to] Make My Aplication Again Last friday Week they Alowed me 4 lovs of Bread for a fortnight and no more." She now wrote to the Centre not to ask for relief for her husband (who was nonetheless still sick), but for the children:

> please to Alow me Something for my 3 Children. I have one a Cripple and deaf She is 23 years old [and] incapable of earning any thing the gentleman about have very Kindly Subsribed and got my [husband] a donkey and cart But he is not about to earn more than 3 shillings a week [*illegible*] from his Club and gentleman we cannot live and pay rent

Here, then, a woman robbed of full male earnings pointed to both character and prudence (they had subscribed to a friendly society) and the suffering of a mother trying to do her duty to a disabled child. The ultimate rhetorical basis for her appeal, however, was not these things but the chilling effects of sickness and a clear knowledge that medical relief was a contestable element of New Poor Law process. Robbins thus finished: "I have 1s and 6d a month for my husBands Club [1] shilling a year Doctor and 3 shilling a year for myself for Doctor so I try all I can to keep from the parrish *But I cannot help Sickness.*"[42]

Emma Farr of Glasbury, a small village near Hay-on-Wye (Brecon), used sickness in a different rhetorical mode. Writing in October 1869, she would "humbly and earnestly … implore your immediate interference to prevent the untimely Death of my husband Jabez Farr." He had been summoned in May 1869 to appear before the magistrates for non-compliance with an order to contribute one shilling per week toward supporting his parents. At the time Jabez had told the court that in consequence of his own bad health he was in debt and struggling to get a living from shoemaking. Now:

> notwithstanding his delicate state of health his imbecile appearance and the certificate exhibited He was not allowed to return to his own home but was taken in custody there & then and committed to the county Prison at Hereford for the Day in lieu of the Prison for Radnorshire [which] was under repairs.

Emma pointed to the poor treatment he received in prison, adding that a letter from one of the prison officers informed her that unless he was immediately freed he would not survive. Through the financial intervention of a neighbour, Jabez was brought home and confined to bed, but following a second demand for maintenance she asked if the "Law require that when a Man is poor and afflicted and cannot pay he must be thus punished."[43] The case here conforms with the evidence found by Levine-Clark that relieving officers sought out sons to assist elderly and chargeable parents and not daughters, though that process is relatively uncommon in the corpus as a whole.[44] More significantly, Emma Farr established herself in a rhetorical sense as a woman making every effort for a husband whose life-long disability left him unable to either write or earn a "family wage." She (and their case) was well known in the neighbourhood and the established power dynamics of the family were thus legitimately reversed due to sickness. As with other women, Farr wrote with a question of process, linking sickness to the potential for local officers to legitimately step away from the full force of the law of the New Poor Law.

A fourth category comprises women writing jointly with men. Sometimes they participated in multi-signature petitions, such as that of fifty-five inhabitants of Grantley (Yorkshire) who wrote in February 1851 asking the Centre "to take into serious consideration the present extreme distressed state of Agriculture, (on which this Township is entirely dependent) and not bring upon us at a time like this, the almost ruinous Expence of forming this District into a Poor Law Union."[45] The petition, deeply infused with a notion of exogeneity, was headed by the local land agent and a sprinkling of farmers, tradesmen, and labourers, but four paupers were named, all of them women: Margaret Place, Ellenor Brown, Isabella Dixon, and Ann Brown.[46] It is possible that the active recruitment of such women was meant to convey a message about suffering and dependence to the Centre. Most joint writing was, however, smaller in scale and more personal, and often (as under the Old Poor Law) consisted of letters from a husband *and* wife. Thus, in January 1842 James and Mary Cox wrote from Barton (Kent) stating that:

> your Petitioners being at the advanced Ages of 76 and 72 years, and totally incapable from infirmities and age to perform any laborious employment; and having no means of support, would humbly pray that the wanted Benevolence of the Poor Law Commissioners by granting them a similar Grant of Out Door relief, as bestowed on others.[47]

Fusing together rhetoric of age and partial inability, and calling for the protection of the Centre, the couple used referential tropes that are central to the whole corpus. However, they also dealt in linguistic currencies of precedent and comparability, in effect questioning the process of the poor law as other writers encountered already in this chapter also did. This letter had no clear gendered voice. The same is not true for others. In March 1852 Edward and Sarah Linning wrote, partly in the third person, from Stoke Prior (Herefordshire):

> to inform you that we old people Edward and Sarah Linning are living in the parish of Stoke prier and are inferm that we are not able to waite on one another and this winter we have been ill and so bad off that we was nearly lost for want and our pay is too shillings a week a peace and we cannot live on that

The couple had applied to the Leominster guardians and were granted an extra shilling, but this was only for two weeks. The Linnings stressed their age, inability to provide mutual support, and – an implicit risk to future health – not being able "to pay any one to wash us clean." The tone, pace, and referential model of the supposedly joint letter was clearly masculine.[48]

We might compare this with a letter signed by William and Mary Ann Ward and written in June 1876 from East Dereham. Here the text was written in the female first person. William's widowed daughter from an earlier relationship had returned to live with the couple along with her three children. Mary Ann's stepdaughter made a claim for relief and was allowed 3d per week and a flour allowance, to last one month. However, when Mary Ann went to collect the relief at the month end, the 3d per week was taken off and only the flour allowed. Arguing that the family was unable to cope with this level of relief, she was given an order for the workhouse. By the time of her letter, two boys were in the workhouse and a little girl still with Mary Ann; their mother was then at Gorleston vicarage at Great Yarmouth and presumably in service. Mary Ann described her husband as a sixty-eight-year-old farm labourer who earned 14s per week and had brought up a family of ten children, all of whom were living. In relation to the two boys she poignantly asked the LGB: "Gentlemen will you kindly return me some help as it is breaking the poor man's heart at haveing them in the workhouse."[49] A dutiful wife (caring for relatives by marriage for whom she had no responsibility), married to a man who had made a substantial contribution to society (raising ten children without poor relief) now wrote to the Centre about breaches of process and humanity that had resulted in emotional suffering for her husband, and in a wife having to write in her hour of need to a male authority.

The final category of women writers considered in this chapter consists of female workhouse inmates, a new group in the post-1834 period. We have seen in the case studies employed thus far that the threat of the workhouse was ever-present, and it is unsurprising that the vast majority of female-authored letters were written in an effort to avoid becoming an inmate in the first place. Once the principle was lost, and in common with men, women complained to the Centre about their confinement and sought to reverse it. Joanna Maddon, for instance, wrote to the home secretary from the Liverpool workhouse following the death of her husband in Brompton Hospital (Middlesex). Maddon recounted that she had travelled to Liverpool to find some friends (a creditable example of self-help), but was unsuccessful in that endeavour and had then been placed in the workhouse rather than being sent back to London. She argued that her four children could get into the Duke of York School, detailed her husband's service in the army and (subsequently) the War Office, and stated that she herself would be able to secure employment if she could only get back to London.[50] This complex fusion of second-hand status (her husband's service), prior good character, dependence, motherhood, and concern for her children shows very well that some of the core rhetorical infrastructure of women outside the workhouse made a seamless transition to the workhouse context.

There were, however, more situational and gendered linguistic registers and strategic modes. All workhouse inmates were subject to classification: conceptual, physical, and spatial. Females were to be classified as: aged/infirm; able-bodied women and girls over thirteen years (raised to sixteen in 1842); girls aged from seven to thirteen; and (all) children under seven. Not only did such classifications and associated internal walls and workhouse yards separate husband from wife but they also kept parent from child.[51] We have seen in the case of the outdoor poor that mothers wrote often about their maternal duties of protection and part-provisioning for children. However, when they entered the workhouse their ability to perform such roles was severely curtailed. Children above seven years were separated from their parents and housed in a separate section of the workhouse, and even though the regulations allowed mothers to sleep with children under seven and have reasonable access to them at other times, some guardians would separate mothers and babies so that the women could work.[52] Children thus became a particular rhetorical and strategic flashpoint for workhouse relations. In February 1852 James Danby Affleck of Dalham (Suffolk) complained that one of the major causes of tension in the local workhouse was "that Children as early as 18 months old 1 year ½ old are separated from their mothers, the whole day until night … I would suggest that none be so separated under five years."[53] Collective letters (often but not always anonymous) also point to this tension by focusing on the health consequences of parent-child separation. In February 1857, for instance, an anonymous letter was sent from the Bethnal Green workhouse stating that:

> it is right, you do cum and see oure children bad for munths with hich [scabies/ringworm][54] and gets wors the Master nor Gardans wont see to it and if we giv our names we shall get loked up hask to se all, and sum name Sarle and Sisil – soon as you can a Mother[55]

This sense that the Centre was seen as an arbiter on contentious matters is familiar from earlier chapters. There are many cases, however, of direct action. In 1856, while giving evidence to an inquiry established to examine whether Elizabeth Dawson, the Ampthill workhouse matron, had served poor and sour food to pauper inmates, Sophia Heathfield referred to a punishment she had received the previous year. That punishment was a sentence of three weeks' imprisonment imposed by local magistrates for the non-literate protest of breaking workhouse windows. Heathfield noted: "I broke the Windows because my Baby was locked away from me, I was suckling the Baby at the time I was kept on Bread & Potatoes for 10 days At that time & had no Meat this was a twelve month ago."[56]

The physical divisions and management regulations inherent in the segregated workhouse tore up accepted family relationships and disrupted gender roles. The subjects common to outdoor letters – requests to secure relief outside and provide for a family, the description of varied attempts to make ends meet to secure rent and food, and so forth – became less relevant for the pauper inmate. Letters from female workhouse residents thus represent a real shift in style and content compared to those from women outside. They tended to write longer and more frequent letters, and to use a range of supplementary rhetoric. For example, the letter which Jane Maylor (encountered already in chapter 2) wrote from the Liverpool workhouse to the LGB in November 1874 was some thirty-six pages long. The text rambled and covered a multitude of complaints concerning the treatment received by various patients (herself included) at the hands of staff in the Mill Road Hospital. Maylor closed her letter by asking for an official inquiry as it would "be a pity such conduct would be allowed," a sentiment that picked up the increasingly powerful rhetoric of breach of process that we have traced in several chapters.[57] Similarly, Jane Rosier wrote five letters over a two-year period from the Chelsea workhouse complaining of the actions of Daniel Sutton, the workhouse master. Though these letters were rather scatalogical, one of her repeated complaints was that Sutton had tried to prove her a lunatic. Rosier wrote that she would "suffer death from starvation in the streets before they shall the advantage of so doing," and further noted in later letters that Sutton tried to wear down her resistance by repeatedly placing her in the Westminster Bridewell and stealing her personal effects.[58] In this way Rosier entwined the quadruple narratives of vulnerability, need for protection, tyranny emerging out of a breach of workhouse rules, and the character of its staff.

This rhetorical infrastructure is particularly well defined in the correspondence of Hannah Berry Pearson, who wrote five letters over a period of six years from the Dorking workhouse (Surrey). Her first was written to the superintendent of police in Dorking in April 1886. Here, she charged Dr James Moody with cruelty and illegally detaining her two years earlier in the Cane Hill Asylum at Purley (Surrey). In addition she accused him and others of conspiring to keep her closely confined in the Dorking workhouse so as to reduce her to a state of insanity; and charged Mr Woodley, the workhouse master, of lying about her "to try to excite me in the said Workhouse."[59] The themes of incarceration linked to wrongfully diagnosed mental health issues and vulnerability that we saw in Rosier's letters are replicated here. However, Pearson also wrote lucidly and with some style concerning the lack of sanitation in the workhouse: "I suppose sanitary reform has not reached Dorking Workhouse up to the present time … My manner may be rather blunt. But as a thorough English woman I am none the worse for that."[60] Like other writers we have seen, Pearson was keenly aware of contemporary debates, in this case the sanitation concerns and reform movement arising out of typhoid and other epidemics at this time.[61] Her final letter, of 20 November 1892, ranged over a collection of complaints from insufficient accommodation for the sick, inadequate staffing levels, and the mixing of "lunatic" and sane paupers, to bullying amongst the inmates. Her letters appear to show a woman ground down after many years of living in poverty and many years of writing her grievances. It is tempting to see the accusations as the ramblings of an elderly and perhaps mentally ill or disabled woman. Certainly this was surmised by the LGB clerk who annotated one of her later letters: "Hannah Pearson is an old correspondent of the Bd, + was formerly classed as imbecile."[62] Yet the final letter shows her to be articulate, observant, and exhibiting a concern for fellow inmates of the sort which we also see in the case of serial male writers. Thus, she began by stating: "This letter is not written to exite sympathy nor Charity But simply in the cause of justice and good order in one of the Workhouses in Her Majesties Dominions Namley Dorking." Oratorical threads of fairness and the need for unions to work within the framework of rules and regulations set for them by the Centre are clear. So is the implicit rhetoric of Empire and a sense that, as with the populations of other dominions, protection and oversight were required domestically as well.[63] Pearson claimed such protection not as a woman but as a citizen of the nation widely defined. Her closing statement was equally powerful as a rhetorical artefact:

> It would be in vain for me to apply to the Guardians as they have other business to attend to. I am only a simple minded country woman not used to Dignitaries But if you will kindly send this letter where it ought to go [the letter was addressed to the Lord Mayor of London] I will ever pray for your health, comfort, and well being.

These closing words convey a sense of the struggles occasioned by six years in the workhouse and they might be understood as signifying that Pearson was on the verge of exhausting all her outlets for agency. Read in a different way, however, the letters indicate that Pearson constructed herself as a country woman struggling in an unfamiliar urban environment, ignored by the very officials who were supposed to look to her welfare, and subtly trying to elicit the very sympathy and feeling of charity she claimed at the outset not to seek.[64]

These three women – Maylor, Rosier, and Pearson – received varied outcomes to the requests for inquiries into their cases.[65] More widely, however, female voices are disproportionately represented in successful attempts to confront workhouse regimes.[66] Theirs are the voices of alleged victims of sexual harassment or rape,[67] impropriety, abuse of power, and cruelty at various levels. Charlotte Newman, following Anne Crowther, contends that workhouses "consistently segregated paupers by gender, ensuring there was no contact between male and female inmates in the workhouse," although some intermingling might be allowed between elderly couples, elderly women and children of both genders, and occasionally between elderly men and boys. Only rarely, she contends, were segregation rules broken leading to pauper sexual relationships.[68] Such instances were by no means as infrequent in our corpus as this definitive statement implies, but even without this perspective, gender segregation did not stop male staff and female paupers from coming into regular contact. Some female inmates were treated like servants and given duties which saw them working in close proximity to male members of staff. Thus, in July 1855 Ann Birkbeck, an inmate at the Reeth workhouse (Yorkshire), deposed that she had gone upstairs in the staff quarters to turn down the beds and here she encountered the workhouse master. Birkbeck alleged that he pulled her into one of the bedrooms and raped her. She "begged of him to give over but cannot remember what he said I begged of him to let me go when he was fighting of me … the Master then had connexion with me on the Bed – he had tried this a good few times before."[69] This very precise quote highlights the vulnerability of some female inmates to both rape and concerted pressure for sex from office holders. It also, however, contains the language of resistance ("fighting of me") and it prompted a long train of witnesses, many of whom attested to a deep history of other alleged breaches of process, morality, and humanity in the workhouse.

There are also examples of consensual or opportunistic sex that led to similar outcomes. By early 1862 Mary Ann Chamberlin had been an inmate at the Great Yarmouth workhouse for three years. She had been allocated work duties which included delivering the officers' linen and cleaning the room of Mr Brownjohn, the workhouse schoolmaster. It was on one occasion when she took the linen up to Brownjohn's room in August 1861 that Chamberlin later claimed her son had been conceived.[70] In 1868 Elizabeth Rudd, a pauper of the Mitford and Laundich workhouse, claimed to have had sex with Mr Bradfield, the schoolmaster. She was responsible for cleaning the schoolmaster's bed sitting room, and stated that on one occasion he "expressed what his feelings were to me and said he had thought about it a score of times but he never dare attempt it before. He then pulled up my clothes and had connexion with me."[71] This encounter may not have been coercive, with witnesses noting that Bradfield and Rudd would make up petty excuses to be in each other's company, yet the relationship of power lay convincingly with Bradfield.

As well as female paupers having access to male staff areas in the workhouse, some workhouse officers – medical officers, chaplains and porters, for instance – had access to workhouse areas more commonly understood as female spaces. In January 1851, for example, Ann Hodgkinson, who was pregnant with an illegitimate child and resided in the lying-in ward of the Nantwich workhouse, was approached by Reverend Wilson, the union chaplain. After asking how she was, he pulled her from her chair and indecently assaulted her.[72] Other spaces were more liminal. In November 1850, Mary Ann Wilson, an inmate of the Great Yarmouth workhouse alleged that John Harboard, the porter, had sex with her in the laundry resulting in pregnancy. Although the laundry might be regarded primarily as a female workspace within the workhouse, one of Harboard's duties was to lock it up once work had ended for the day, and it was as Wilson was leaving and Harboard arriving with the keys that the space overlapped. Wilson stated to the guardians that: "The connection took place in the Laundry once or twice before the time she was in the Family way – Will swear the Porter is the Father."[73] Extensive further witness statements implicating both the schoolmaster and the porter point to extensive currents of gossip about all parties in the wider community, and suggest the remarkable complexity of some of the relationships between female inmates and male staff.

These detailed cases point clearly to criminality and a range of abuses of power and position. Women were vulnerable (and were able to rhetoricise that vulnerability) both to opportunistic sexual and other harassment and to sustained profiling or targeting of specific individuals. Many (but by no means all) of the instances were cases of young women or the mothers (and mothers to be) of bastard children. The latter group seem to have been especially vulnerable because, in order to make a complaint and be believed, they had to overcome sustained reputational bias and thus may have been more likely to let instances pass. There is substance to this view in the corpus. When Ann Skerratt and Ann Sadler accused Nathaniel Bryan, the Nantwich workhouse master, of a sexual assault, Charles Mott, the presiding assistant commissioner, voiced his opinion that Sadler, who had had three illegitimate children by three different men, was a poor witness. A former employer stated that "from what he knew of her character, he would not believe her on her Oath." Mott also considered Skerratt thoroughly untrustworthy and stated that "a more abandoned creature can not be found than this young woman." Moreover he thought that her previous conduct established "beyond doubt that Skerratt is utterly unworthy of belief."[74] Such views, allied with a well-known process of investigation in which a woman would have to relive the event under oath, often cross-examined by the alleged offender, means that it is likely that only a small fraction of the instances of sexual abuse and harassment that occurred would have made their way into an archival artefact. In particular, if a complainant was the mother of illegitimate children her character would systematically be brought into question; she would have been asked why she did not make an immediate accusation, why part of her initial recall was confused, or why she did not fight back during the event. Alternatively, investigations would be much more cursory and assume the innocence of officers, as was the case with Elizabeth Rudd who had "four Bastard children living The eldest is about 24 years of age and the youngest is upwards of 12. They are not all by one man."[75]

Yet we should be careful, here, of painting a picture of hopeless vulnerability. Female inmates knew very well that, apart from the abuse of children, there was no subject more likely to excite local public opinion, advocate intercessions, and staff unease than accusations of sexual abuse, depravity, and moral failing. In other words, the system (national and local) was itself vulnerable in these terms. Some stories were certainly invented to exploit this vulnerability.[76] Others were heavily contested, pitting pauper against pauper, staff against other staff, and union establishments against the communities of which they were notionally part. In such cases, the abuse of or cruelty towards women was the touchpaper for smouldering grievances, long-established doubts about the very validity of the workhouse, and wider concerns about the quality of staff and the nature of the welfare process. Some instances were not contested at all, yielding a uniform pauper "view" of the workhouse. When set against a parade of witness statements, the particular vulnerabilities of female inmates are still writ large, but a wider picture of agency, some of it gendered, also appears. Giving evidence in the inquiry at Great Yarmouth into how she became pregnant, Mary Ann Wilson subtly changed her story to implicate the schoolmaster as well as the porter, recounting that: "West [the schoolmaster] said there was a fine talk about the Town – She asked what about – West said he heard I was with Child and it was by him – I said whoever could have spread that nonsense about." Two men in positions of power were thus implicated in a case that gained ("there was fine talk") wide local notoriety, in effect undermining the position of both of them.[77]

CONCLUSION

Most women writers make their appearance in the corpus under circumstances in which men were not present or were separated from them for a variety of reasons. Like men, their main concern was to secure outdoor relief and avoid the workhouse. Women's letters emphasise their care, protection, and responsibility for children while stressing the complete impossibility of their being a sole family breadwinner. Here and more widely, the similarity of rhetorical and referential modes to those of the Old Poor Law is striking. Once in the workhouse women wrote to contest their care, to advocate on behalf of others, and to highlight abuse of process. They also wrote and deposed in cases of vulnerability to sexual harassment, impropriety, and abuse. The scale of sexual abuse in the nineteenth-century workhouse is a significant (though so far understudied) factor in the overall history of institutional welfare, and it finds a clear and consistent outlet in the female pauper voice in our data. This new rhetorical and strategic element (there are almost no instances under the Old Poor Law) is important at corpus level.

There were, however, other gender-specific or dominant registers in addition to motherhood, children, and vulnerability, and they are inscribed in a much more complex rhetorical ecology. Thus, female writers fused symbolism (nakedness, tokens of belonging), the rhetoric of direct and derived contributions (their own wage earning, family care, prior payment of rates by a husband or father), claims to citizenship and right, and claims to humanity and masculine duty, in order to shape welfare decisions or to reorder them. The sense that male respondents should feel a sense of responsibility – and, at times, even shame – about the circumstances that writers described is palpable, even if female writers rarely asserted it. Within and between letters and (for serial writers in workhouses where we can more effectively trace this issue) over a welfare life-cycle, women created a complex rhetorical matrix. To this mix might be added episodic witness statements and a deeper analysis of the failings of process, law, and duty at union level toward individual women. However, although they have long been recognised (and portrayed) as economically, socially, and legally vulnerable in any number of ways, the women writers in our corpus also demonstrated an acute awareness of the power of narratives of vulnerability and were highly adept at mobilising them in negotiations with the Centre. It is ultimately impossible to say whether letters from female writers were more effective or "successful" than those of men, but what we can say is that women generated some of the most complex rhetorical infrastructures in formulating their complaints, appeals, and statements. Nonetheless, despite these gendered differences, there are also many striking synergies with male writers and this is particularly true in terms of the rhetoric of ageing and decline, the topic of the following chapter.

8

Becoming Old

INTRODUCTION

In January 1861 John Hankeson of Stockport (Cheshire) wrote the following appeal to the secretary of the Poor Law Board (PLB):

> your right honourable secretary Sir honourable Sir I am stating this few lines to your honourable Secretary hoping that you will be Generous Enough to Show the poor distressed man humane relief destitute of any means for a prisent liveing him Self and his poor old woman has no way of Getting livelyhood his old woman made application to the relieving officer and the answer he gave he would not without She Both go inside the house the poor old couple did not like to part their little sort of place the would see an [answer] from your honourable Secretary hoping that you will have humane feeling to order the poor old man and wife to stop at their own fire while the can keep it and By so doing the are duty Bound the poor old man Been a hand loom weaver and is poorly this two month and do nothing and did not like to leave his little place untill all would fail him.[1]

The subject of Hankeson's letter is hardly unique in the correspondence we have been considering. The central complaint – that he had been refused outdoor relief and ordered to the workhouse – is familiar in every union we have sampled, across the period under review and for all life-cycle groups. However, the way that his appeal was constructed, and the rhetorical architecture and motifs that were used to press his case are of particular interest. In the first place, without actually specifying their ages, Hankeson wrote that he was "a poor old man" and consistently referred to his wife as an "old woman."[2] In the second, he pointed to the fact that, although a handloom weaver by trade, he was now "destitute" and had "no way of getting [a] livelihood," partly because of being ill for some time but also, by implication, because his age and capacities told against it.[3] Third, from a stylistic perspective, he wrote that "the poor old couple did not like to part [from] their little sort of place," and appealed directly to the secretary's "humane feeling to order the poor old man and wife" to be allowed to "stop at their own fire while the can keep it." Hankeson appeared (though his distancing language may have been a strategic device) to acknowledge the inevitability of workhouse residence at some point; he did not overtly question the guardians' logic, only their timing. Others, as we shall see below, questioned the very principle of indoor relief for the aged.

Hankeson's appeal was couched in the kinds of complex, multi-layered rhetoric we have come to expect from poor writers. He was a supplicant ("a poor distressed man") who, if his plea was successful, would be "duty Bound" to the PLB. He was unabashed in using the sentimental imagery of domestic contentment at life's end to drive home his case – the "comforts of a private fireside," to use Jeremy Boulton and Leonard Schwarz's evocative phrase.[4] Yet he was also fully expectant that the secretary of the body responsible for the oversight of welfare for the whole of England and Wales would not only respond to his request (Hankeson "would see an answer" to his letter, almost as of right), but that he would act on the couple's behalf.[5] What was it, then, that enabled Hankeson to knit together a sentimental appeal to the "humane feeling" of the PLB alongside an assertive expectation that his request should be granted? What was the vital ingredient that gave his entreaty its strength? In this case, it was not a distinct rhetorical model but the framing of the case with old age – the rhetorical power of the grey head.

In this context it is striking that, while the number of case studies dealing with the welfare experiences of the aged in the post-1834 period has accumulated, there is limited agreement on how the aged poor understood their "rights" and how guardians constructed their obligations. David Thomson argues that in the nineteenth century "between one-half and three-quarters" of women aged seventy and older, and "slightly less than one half of all men" in the same age bracket, were in receipt of a regular pension. More than this, because these pensions were maintained at pre-1834 levels (Thomson suggests a "standard payment" of 2s 6d per week until the 1870s) most old people "were maintained by the poor law … [at] a relative value in excess of pensions paid by late-twentieth-century welfare states."[6] They were also maintained largely at their own firesides or in the houses of relatives, with Thomson suggesting that between 1851 and 1891 the proportion of the aged poor in English and Welsh workhouses never rose above 8 per cent for men and 5 per cent for women. Thus, "institutional care for the aged was not important."[7] By contrast Edward Hunt suggests that a picture of the relative generosity of the New Poor Law is "obviously incompatible both with popular conceptions of what it meant to be old and poor in Dickensian England and with the considered assessment of [other] poor-law historians";[8] and it is certainly true that others have interpreted similar evidence very differently to Thomson. Pat Thane, for example, claimed in her seminal book *Old Age in English History* that the attitude of the poor law authorities toward the aged in the nineteenth century "was benign only in comparison with the treatment of able-bodied men," and that "the old restrictive rules still applied. Poor relief remained a strictly residual safety net for those unable to survive on other resources." As a result, she concluded: "Throughout the nineteenth century a large minority of old people received poor relief, but they often received very little, very late in life and grudgingly."[9] The sense that relatively few of the elderly poor were forced into workhouses has also attracted considerable scepticism. Nigel Goose suggests that in Hertfordshire (1851) and Kent (1881) almost a third of workhouse inmates were aged sixty-plus, despite the fact that this age group constituted only around 8 per cent of the total populations of each county at these dates.[10] More recently, Alistair Ritch has shown that in Birmingham, "older inmates constituted 22 per cent of all inmates in 1851, rising to 52 per cent by 1891."[11]

Indeed, most commentators have implicitly agreed with Anne Crowther's early assessment that the New Poor Law workhouse, initially conceived as a deterrent to the able-bodied poor, "soon began to fulfil the functions of hospitals and asylums," and, one might add, adult social care facilities.[12]

These very different perspectives are underpinned by complex evidence. The meaning and "value" of allowances must be interpreted against a background of ingrained regional traditions of relief.[13] In any case, as many welfare historians have noted for the Old *and* New Poor Laws, outdoor relief, whether in the form of temporary payments or regular pensions, was never intended to be sufficient for subsistence on its own, and was only considered a supplement for other resources in the "economy of makeshifts."[14] The point is well made by George Boyer and Timothy Schmidle, who suggest that at the end of the nineteenth century, "the minimum necessary weekly expenditure for an elderly person was 6s, and for an elderly couple 10s."[15] That is, the majority of the elderly poor had to work hard to provide between half and three-quarters of their own subsistence income, depending on the availability of other resources such as kin, friendly societies, and the generosity of neighbours.[16] Moreover, it has become increasingly clear that some of the aged poor actively used and navigated the workhouse as part of their strategy for making do.[17] In fact the tensions and ambivalence that were generated by the form and function(s) of the nineteenth-century workhouse, particularly in relation to the elderly, have not been frequently explored in terms of the lived experiences of paupers themselves. Studies have instead tended to rely on familiar cultural tropes dredged from accounts in newspapers, fiction, and social commentary.[18] For example, when Keith Snell wrote that "[s]ome of the most embittered and depressive writing of the nineteenth century covers the treatment of the elderly" in workhouses, the sources he pointed to were the semi-fictionalised impressions of George Sturt and Alexander Somerville.[19] Even Crowther, when identifying a growing sense of disgrace on the part of the "respectable" aged poor for being compelled to go into the workhouse, used the campaigning voices of "notables" such as trade unionist and later MP Joseph Arch and social reformer Charles Booth to illustrate her point.[20]

In practice, the nature of the care that was available in workhouses and the conditions experienced by the elderly within them proved to be some of the most controversial features of the New Poor Law. They have contributed strongly to popular views of the workhouse as a penal institution, rigid and severe in its restrictive regime, and often cruel in its treatment of the innocent poor, such that workhouse residence was to be avoided at all costs. The purpose of this chapter is to take a fresh look at some of those familiar tropes and some of our key understandings relating to the experiences of the elderly poor after 1834, through the words of the poor and their advocates. It will address several key questions: how were the elderly poor affected by sentimental and administrative shifts in welfare policy between the Old and New Poor Laws, and as the century wore on? How generous, or otherwise, was the relief that was offered to them outside the workhouse, and did this change over time? How far did they *feel* themselves forced to resort to the workhouse against their will? How did they experience the workhouse once there? And, crucially, how far were they able to mitigate or influence their experiences of relief through the exercise of practical and rhetorical agency of the sort that John Hankeson sought to deploy? We will see that the aged outside the workhouse shared much of their rhetorical infrastructure with other life-cycle groups, but that underpinning their correspondence was an ingrained sense (with deep chronological roots in the Old Poor Law) that old age and advancing incapacity conferred a right to favourable consideration. We see relatively little change in this rhetorical architecture, even from the 1880s onwards as a new sense of the absolute responsibilities of the state to the aged grew and prompted modified policies, precisely because this sense of right on the part of the aged poor had always structured their interactions with the notionally powerful.[21] Those inside the workhouse had to confect a more subtle linguistic mode and seem to have been relatively successful in confronting the regimes to which they were notionally subject.

OLD AGE AND "DESERVINGNESS" UNDER THE NEW POOR LAW

The elderly poor have always occupied a somewhat privileged space in the welfare landscape. They unquestionably fulfilled the main criteria for "deservingness": their indigence was likely to be highly visible when they approached the "decline of life" (as some Old Poor Law writers styled it[22]), and it was the result of the natural processes of ageing rather than any personal moral or practical failing. In the early modern period, when society was "concerned to direct all charitable efforts into the hands of the deserving,"

> [t]he aged poor fulfilled this brief with distinction. No one could blame them for their failing physical abilities, for their loss of labour, or their eventual need of aid: they were poor through no fault of their own. The elderly formed, along with widows and orphans, a trinity of worthy poor.[23]

On the basis of this status, Susannah Ottaway tells us, under the Old Poor Law "care of the aged and impotent poor remained one of its most closely guarded principles, one of its least controversial doctrines."[24] This is not to suggest that the aged were guaranteed support within a discretionary welfare system, that the support they received was always what they asked for, or that it was on its own sufficient to meet all their needs.[25] Yet in terms of public sentiment at least, the elderly ostensibly had less need to justify their claim on common resources than other life-cycle groups. Under the New Poor Law, however, the imperatives of the Central Authority clearly threatened the long-standing privileged position of the deserving poor, within which the elderly figured prominently.[26] Whether there was a sustained and systemic assault on the regular relief given to the aged post-1834 is still uncertain, but our corpus provides evidence that cuts were made, and in some places they followed hard on the heels of the Poor Law Amendment Act (PLAA).[27] As early as October 1834, for example, Peter Coates wrote that officials in the Clutton Poor Law Union (PLU) had "lately reduced the Pay of many of the aged Paupers receiving constant Relief." He went on to complain that he had advised those affected to approach the local magistrate for redress, but "the Justice refused to make any Order conceiving he had no longer the Power of doing so."[28] A similar story was reported in 1837 from Colyton, where the widow Mary Minson found that her reduced pension was "not sufficient to subsist upon, being now very helpless."[29] In 1852, Clifford Shirreff claimed that the guardians of Axminster, "in their zeal to keep down the Rates," had "curtailed a poor womans (named Sarah

Hooper) allowance so that she must starve if not relieved." The writer, himself an ex-officio guardian, went on to state:

> She is 70 or 71 years of age and not capable of earning any thing, she has complained to the Relieving Officer several times, and he says he cannot assist her She now complains to me, saying she cannot exist on the allowance She has been obliged to sell her bread to pay her rent. I trust you will cause an enquiry to be made into her case.[30]

Letters such as these, which complain of pensions or regular relief payments being refused or reduced, are consistently found throughout our sample. Although they began soon after the PLAA was enacted, there is no sense that the issue affected the elderly more during one particular period of the New Poor Law than any other, or that it affected those in any particular geographical or typological location. As late as 1895, for instance, James Clitheroe of East Dereham complained that he had been refused relief and told "I must make my own living," despite being seventy-five years of age and incapable of doing so. Clitheroe claimed the support of many advocates locally, including a farmer who had advised him to apply for relief in the first place, a policeman who told him, "they ought to allow you half a crown a week," and a local ratepayer who reportedly said, "they ought to allow you [relief], we pay the rates."[31]

Given this background, as well as utilising many of the corpus level referential modes outlined in chapter 5 (including contribution, humanity, sympathy, and Christian paternalism), the aged outdoor poor sought to exercise agency through a well-tested and familiar rhetorical mode.[32] With strong connections to the Old Poor Law, the elderly thus repeatedly entwined the ideas of a *de facto* right accruing naturally in old age with the associated rights that declining health and physical capacity *always* conferred upon old people as they tried to maintain their independence. Like their Old Poor Law counterparts, these writers implied – and sometimes stated – the injustice of refused applications in the circumstances described. In December 1853, for example, John Mark wrote from Llanengan (Caernarvonshire) to complain that, despite being eighty-one years of age, "having been receiving a nominal relief of One Shilling a week during eighteen months … in the Spring in the year 1852 I was deprived of the above relief." But he also wished to make clear that there was nothing else he could fall back on other than poor relief: "I have no relations in any position to aid me only day labourers."[33] Mark's reference to a lack of kin support makes sense, given that he was of an age at which it would seem unreasonable to have expected independence. But most of those who considered themselves to have reached advanced years acknowledged in their communications that they would still be required to contribute toward their own maintenance *if* they were able to do so, regardless of their age.

As we saw at the start of the chapter, John Hankeson indicated that, on account of old age *and* illness, he was unable to earn his subsistence as a handloom weaver. Charles Burchell of Kidderminster similarly noted in 1876 that his seventy-seven-year-old wife was unable to walk, and that he himself had "been ill for the last 5 months with Broncites and not able to do any labours."[34] William Sturton and his wife, in complaining that their weekly allowance had been cut by one shilling, and later by a further 1s 6d, noted that they were both over eighty, but that he still did "what jobs I could" to top up the five shillings they had originally received.[35] The sense that old age did not preclude the poor from being productive members of the local community – indeed, that even the very old had an obligation to demonstrate that they were making every effort to shift for themselves – and the impression that poor writers knew that this issue had to be treated rhetorically, comes through very strongly throughout the corpus. George Ellis of Arnold wrote to the PLB in 1862. Despite being seventy-four, he still identified himself as "being a Frameworkknitter" who had "nothing to earn a livelyhood [because] trade is in such a state of depression that there is scarcely anything for anybody to do." He added that even if trade had been good, "I am not able to earn much" because of old age; a man who was far beyond what would today be considered his productive years still recognised the value – and even the necessity – of demonstrating his willingness to work when negotiating the terms of his relief. Productivity, alongside a wider sense of the importance of an enduring contribution to the local community, is thus an important rhetorical strand in the subcorpus for the aged poor, and it closely mirrors the linguistic construction of similar letters from the Old Poor Law period.[36]

These observations speak to Steven King's sense that "[t]he question of what constituted old age" before the advent of a national state pension "is extraordinarily complex."[37] Despite the fact that local officials under the New Poor Law generally accepted sixty as the dividing line between middle and old age (as Pat Thane has also argued), in practice this distinction had only a marginal impact on their decisions regarding entitlement to relief.[38] For example, Catherine Baker wrote to the Poor Law Commission (PLC) in 1843 to complain that her widow's pension had been cut by the Camelford (Cornwall) guardians from 2s and two loaves of bread weekly to 1s 6d and one loaf. She also informed them: "within that time they have ordered me to nurse and wait upon one Grace Garland of this parish who is unwell, and also to look after the family, and upon my refusal to do so the Board of Guardians have stopped my pay altogether." The guardians clearly considered Baker to be fully equipped for the arduous (and perhaps onerous) task of nursing and housekeeping for another family in the parish.[39] However, Baker herself believed that being beyond the accepted threshold of old age meant she should have been exempt from such demands: "I would not object to look after the family and the sick woman were I able to do so," she wrote, "but I am at present sixty three years of age, and have more need of some one to look after me."[40] Baker offered no further mitigation for her refusal to do the allocated work beyond the simple fact of her advanced years. She was unusual in this respect: most writers between the ages of sixty and eighty took great pains to include details of disability, sickness, and other misfortunes to emphasise their inability to make shift, as we saw in the cases of John Mark and Charles Burchell, above, and that of John Hankeson which opens this chapter. Thus, James Hoare of Colyton wrote: "I am now arrived at the advanced age of 64 years and totally dissabled with rupture and loss of one eye," and he asked the PLC to ensure (in a strong assertion of right) that "what is allowed [by] the Poor Law act … be paid to me weekly."[41] George Caffin, vicar of Brimpton (Berkshire), wrote on behalf of Timothy Marshall and his wife, an "aged and infirm couple." Marshall, he explained, was "upwards of 60 years & very infirm from Rheumatism," but an order had been given for them to go into the workhouse. Intriguingly, in the context of this discussion, Caffin also wrote: "It is the first time I have heard the term 'able-bodied' applied to a man upwards of 60 years of age … and on that account refused out-door relief," indicating once again that the treatment of those with grey hair remained a topic of public debate and that space remained for the negotiation of relief terms as a result.[42] Being "worn out" by the cumulative impact of age and infirmity thus becomes a core rhetorical model in the corpus, as in the case of Evan Williams of Penrhos (near Pwllheli, Caernarvonshire) who noted in 1855: "My Occupation is as a Labourer, and [I] am now 76 years of age and my Wife is 73 – I have been very industrious through life, until worn out by age and bodily infirmities."[43]

As these examples begin to suggest, the interactions between the poor law authorities and the elderly in relation to outdoor relief were framed in rhetorical structures familiar from the writing of other life-cycle groups or which had a much longer provenance in the Old Poor Law. There was little that was truly distinctive in the way the aged and their advocates sought to construct deservingness, right, and obligation beyond the dual argument of age and inability. And even this could be shared with other life-cycle groups. When it came to indoor relief, however, a very different set of practical and rhetorical constructions seems to have been placed on the issue of old age. As Patrick Joyce reminds us, the workhouse potentially struck at the heart of individual and community identity. Resistance to such a threat was "made up from the materials to hand, and if these are not solely rhetorical in character then they are very importantly so."[44] It is to the subject of resistance to indoor relief that we now turn.

"CONFINEMENT" AND THE AGED POOR

Witney Union House
March 28 [18]59
Gentlemen
If you would favour me with a answer to this and lett Me know if I cannot have my pay out for the confinement does not agree with my

health I am 72 years of age a erly answer will much oblige
I am Most Obdnt Servt
John Phipps[45]

It is clear from our corpus that, in common with John Phipps, there was widespread, and genuine, uncertainty among the poor, their advocates, and some officials throughout the whole of the New Poor Law period about whether the elderly could be *compelled* to enter the workhouse, or if they had a right under the law to outdoor relief. We began to explore this issue in chapter 6, but the theme is so significant that it begs further analysis. Thus, John Hankeson asked the PLB as late as 1864: "whether Sir robert peell Enacted a law when a man is arrived [at] 60 that they have no law for to order him into the house But he is allowed 3s a week."[46] Similarly, when Mr Philpot wrote in 1837 on behalf of Mary Minson, who was "upwards of 60," he stated: "I understand that no one at her age can be compelled" to go into the workhouse. His interpretation of the law was almost identical to that of Ann Willson, who thirty-five years later complained that her aged husband had been ordered to go into the workhouse: "I have not the means to suport him [as] I am 78 years of age and I was informed that the Act of Parliament did not give the Guardians the power to send the Paupers to the Work House after a Certain Age."[47]

There was of course no explicit ruling or order specifying that elderly paupers must be maintained outside the workhouse, or that they could not be sent there when in need of relief. There are, however, compelling reasons that such a belief persisted so strongly amongst the elderly poor and their advocates. The primary reason is found in the original legislation, which allowed for an appeal to the local magistrates if an aged pauper was ordered into the workhouse *unwillingly*. In such circumstances, two justices acting in concert were empowered to overturn that ruling and order outdoor relief.[48] This provision is one indication that, even if not enshrined in law, exceptionalism in the treatment of the elderly was recognised in principle by the architects of the New Poor Law, as well as by the commissioners who oversaw its application. Indeed, in their first *Annual Report* (1834), the commissioners specifically condemned cases of the elderly being harshly treated by local officials under pretext of implementing the new regime, and urged officials to exercise caution in such cases. "In instances of voluntary change [in relief allocations] made by the parish officers," they wrote,

> it was stated that the most severe alterations were too frequently adopted towards the aged and infirm persons, they being the least capable of opposing a powerful resistance. In this communication, as in most others relating to the first alterations of relief, we [deem] it necessary to urge caution as regards this class of paupers, and to endeavour to extend protection to them.[49]

The problem for paupers, as the commissioners further noted, was that, despite those cautionary words, "[b]oth the amount and the quality of [outdoor] relief which is to be assigned to the [aged poor] is to be decided upon and awarded solely by the Guardians, by whom alone, by the 54th section of the Act, the power of ordering and regulating the relief of the poor is to be exercised." Such was the case even when an order for the workhouse had been overturned by local magistrates.[50] In the event, this anomaly proved to be a loophole in the legal and administrative apparatus of the New Poor Law. It explains the radical differences between counties and unions in the preponderance of the aged in their workhouses and their gender characteristics. And it simultaneously addresses the issue of why so many of the letters and witness statements from the elderly poor and their advocates in the corpus relate both to outdoor relief being reduced *and* to being forced to go into the workhouse.[51] More often than not, an elderly pauper who complained of one of these issues also complained of the other. From the qualitative evidence of the letters, it seems clear that some unions consciously reduced regular relief as a *de facto* workhouse test for the elderly poor, a measure which, if applied directly, was explicitly prohibited under the law.[52] The fact that the commissioners generally adhered to the ruling that they were prohibited by the same law from interfering in individual relief decisions seemingly left elderly paupers and applicants between a rock and the proverbial hard place.

Yet, even here, it is evident that paupers and advocates were far from lacking influence. Their letters to the Central Authority were consistently – and consciously – written within the kind of rhetorical framework the commissioners would recognise from their own cautionary advice to local officials, and which also had clear roots in the pauper letters of the Old Poor Law. H. Bruce Campbell (already encountered as a serial advocate in chapter 5), for example, wrote from Nottingham in 1841 on behalf of John Henson, an eighty-one-year-old widower from the parish of St Alkmund in Derby. Bruce Campbell laid the foundations of an appeal by explaining that Henson had "been for some time past from age and bodily infirmities unable to do anything towards maintaining himself," adding that his daughters were too impoverished to be expected to look after him. He then went on to establish the man's deservingness, explaining that he had "brought up seven children and had borne a good character through life for honesty industry and sobriety." But, he wrote (with a degree of incredulity given this evidenced citizenship contribution), "the parish … actually refused" his claim for outdoor relief, and instead "offered the workhouse!" Henson, we are told, soldiered on for some time outside, but was eventually forced to resort to indoor relief. Shortly afterward, however, having:

> suffered severely in mind as well as body … His poor daughters … resolved to suffer every misery and even starvation rather than allow this cruel separation from their aged infirm … parent to be continued: they though suffering most severely by the effort have ever since maintained him.

Bruce Campbell concluded his letter by forcefully informing the commissioners that "This case appeared to the gentlemen who heard it [to be] one where some degree of out door relief, however small *ought* to be granted."[53]

Bruce Campbell's letter, in common with so many others from paupers and their advocates under both the Old and New Poor Law, is a complex and multi-layered document. It is both a record of an old man's suffering (verified in this case by the involvement of his respectable neighbours) and a sophisticated piece of negotiation, deploying all the rhetorical tools available, from familial and husbandly duty through to the emotional consequences of the actions of officials. The letter sits on a spectrum of appeals from the elderly and their friends ranging from those which invoked statute law or the Centre's own advice, to others that leaned even more heavily on an appeal to sentiment and the principles of "humanity." Amongst those invoking statute law, we could place the complaint of seventy-year-old John Tarby, who wrote from Ditchampton, near Wilton (Wilshire), in December 1842 to say that his request for outdoor relief "was conveyed by a direct refusal accompanied with an order to go into the House," whereupon he simply observed, "that such was never contemplated by the Poor Law Amendment Act needs no comment and I therefore call on You in your Official Capacity to pervert this order."[54] Amongst those appealing more to sentiment are the many letters that point to the inhumanity of the separation clause, whereby married couples, even in old age, were forced to live apart in single-sex wards. Daniel Rush, for example, wrote that he and his wife (seventy-one and sixty-eight respectively) had been refused relief and ordered into the workhouse, where "they insisted in Sepratin me from my Wife wich I have had 49 years or turn us out." But, he declared, in an appeal to humanity and natural justice, "soner than We Would be seperated We will Perish for Want."[55] John Hankeson, with whose story we opened this chapter, also made use of the emotional pull of separation, claiming: "I am informed that there is [a] law for not Separating an old couple."[56] In this instance, Hankeson was not far off the mark: in response to widespread criticism of the Separation Clause in the original legislation, the PLC subsequently allowed – but did not compel – unions to offer elderly couples shared accommodation in workhouses.[57] James Ward, writing from Stockport in July 1866, made an even more emotional appeal, claiming that his wife, Maria, was "frightened to be left by herself or to be separated from me whom she knows will do all I can for her," and he demanded that the PLB "see that we get our Poor Relief … [and] has we have lived together so long you will let us die together at our home."[58]

Ward's use of domestic imagery to further press his case is typical of many letters from, or concerning, the elderly. The appeal of "home" was often used in relation to those, whether married, widowed, or single, who claimed they were being forced into the workhouse. Charles Uggles of Chelmsford (Essex) complained in October 1850: "I have a home and a bed to lay on but no victuals," implying that it would be hard for him to lose his domestic independence in old age simply for the sake of a small weekly allowance.[59] Others deployed the imagery of home to build a compelling case for special treatment. Harriet Johnson, writing from Grinstone (Norfolk) in September 1851, appealed on behalf of her sixty-seven-year-old mother, who, she described as "respectably brought up" but "must be sent from that home she has lived in for the last 30 years" because the Mitford and Launditch guardians had refused her outdoor relief.[60] William Ardington Cooper of York wrote in March 1861 on behalf of William Kitchingman and his wife, asking the Centre to "allow them to remain outside the workhouse as it is very hard for people who have always been hard working people, when they get old to have to break up their Homes and go there."[61] There is little doubt that the elderly and infirm were more fearful at the prospect of being transported from a place of domestic security to a workhouse than the able-bodied, or even the sick. Such a move was freighted with the danger that they might never again achieve any degree of the independence they had long cherished and tenaciously fought for, and that the workhouse would end up being their final refuge.[62]

As we have noted, however, the elderly *did* end up in workhouses, and in large numbers. Given the by-now well-established rhetorical strategies they employed to establish a right to humane treatment as outdoor paupers, it is natural that there would be equivalents among the indoor poor. It is ubiquitous across the geographical and chronological range of our corpus that old age was the first gambit in an elderly inmate's appeal, whatever the further details of their complaint. So, for instance, Anthony Perey wrote from the Berwick workhouse (Northumberland) in March 1843 complaining that: "I have been most Cruelly used here by the Master and almost Crushed to death by him throwing me down and l[y]ing on me ... so that I Can hardly draw my breath." But he then immediately laid down the key detail: "I am an Old man Sixty nine years of age an not able to bear such usage." In a similar vein, but more than fifty years after Perey's letter, George Batlock wrote from the Mitford and Launditch workhouse to advocate on behalf of an unnamed "old man of 72 years" who was "locked up" by the labour master with "what outsiders called unnecessary violence ... by order of the Matron in the absence of the Master ... thereby injuring his back."[63] In cases of both "cruelty" and the general inadequacy of workhouse conditions, the letters of the elderly clearly convey that they not only deserved, but had a right to expect differential treatment on the basis of their grey hair. These expectations were undoubtedly reinforced over time by advice and directives from the Centre which gave them weight in specific ways, such as that relating to the separation clause, noted above. When Thomas Lorick of Great Yarmouth, from whom we heard at length in chapter 5, wrote in August 1855 that "cruelty to old age is tyranny and oppression which with Princely wickedness is about to be justly punished," he was exceptional only for the flourish of his prose: the essential sentiment – that "cruelty" and poor treatment towards the elderly were unconscionable and would be punished – was widespread.[64] Thus, an anonymous correspondent wrote in 1857 that he had: "lately heard that the old inmates of Bethnal Green a[t] Spitalfields Workhouse are very harshly treated, the poor old men being set to break stones, which is quite beyond their strength, & the old Women being very scantily clothed and fed." Despite the denials of the guardians, the writer concluded in a similar vein to Lorick, warning that the aged poor should "be treated in a becoming manner by those in authority: or assuredly the latter will hereafter be called to account."[65]

Pauper correspondents for whom old age and infirmity formed a central rhetorical strategy, account for around 25 per cent of all those in our sample who wrote as workhouse inmates. Nonetheless there is no doubt that, by and large, the elderly would do anything to avoid becoming inmates. As we have seen, concerns about losing one's home and forfeiting one's domestic independence were central to the "rhetorical armoury" which the poor used to negotiate with the central authorities and to fight decisions by local officials that were never explicitly sanctioned by those authorities.[66] Indeed, there are clear parallels here with notions of "home" and "belonging" that were deployed in Old Poor Law pauper letters, although the circumstances under which they were written – and therefore the manner in which such notions were deployed – are subtly different. Under the Old Poor Law letters relating to "home" almost always originated with the out-parish poor who asked for relief so that they could remain away from the parish of settlement, their notional home under the law. When these writers offered to come "home," as most did, they were in effect offering to comply with the law. Their letters, however, were invariably orientated toward showing that they "belonged" to (and thus had a functional home in) the place where they were currently resident. In the letters under consideration here, as we have seen, the notion of "belonging" was in general applied in its domestic rather than geographic meaning, and the familiarity and security of "a private fireside" placed in direct contrast to the cold comforts of the workhouse. Occasionally, however, these differential meanings of "home" and "belonging" came together in the correspondence of elderly paupers in particular, and one excellent example of such a letter relates to our old friend John Hankeson.

NON-RESIDENCE AND THE AGED POOR

In his second letter to the PLB, dated February 1859, Hankeson (who wrote in two distinct voices) began by informing them that:

> John Hankeson Pauper from Stockport Brinksway Cheshire hill resides in Stockport But Belongs to Altrincham Union when it comes to the Point of old age he and wife living in Stockport 22 years and Still we are in a destitute State at present;

and he went on to ask that the Board:

> allow me what … your honours thinks Proper to allow the[m] outside Being that I reside in Stockport so long the old woman gets a little washin from old customers and therefore I hope your honour will allow Me an outside relief. [67]

Part of Hankeson's complaint was that he and his wife had been forced into the Altrincham workhouse by sickness the previous year and had discharged themselves prematurely because of "ill usage" by officers there. He even added that his wife told him "that if She Clamed to Death in the Streets that She now Shall go no more" to that place. But the fact that they were not resident within the boundaries of their own union added a very important dimension to their appeal.

Although allowances to the non-resident poor were fundamental to the organisation of relief under the Old Poor Law, this changed significantly under the New – in principle at least. Taking their lead from the original architects of the PLAA, the commissioners were keen to discourage outdoor relief to the non-resident poor because it was felt that officials under the old system had used it to keep many of their paupers at arm's length, and thus without sufficient scrutiny of their real circumstances. In particular, non-residence was viewed under the New Poor Law as a means by which the potentially independent poor might avoid the workhouse test.[68] It was mainly for these reasons that George Nicholls, one of the most influential voices advocating for poor law reform from the 1830s and later the PLB's permanent secretary, described non-resident relief early on as "particularly open to misrepresentation and abuse."[69] As with the workhouse test more generally, however, elderly non-resident paupers were especially vulnerable to the new rules. They had often lived in their parish of residence for many years by the time they fell into hardship, raising children and developing networks of friends and neighbours on whom they could to some extent rely in times of need. To be taken from places of long-standing residence and familiarity and be "confined" to a workhouse in a distant (and often unfamiliar) place as a result of the natural hardships of old age could be a personal as well as practical tragedy. It was often treated as such by poor writers and their advocates.

In 1838, for instance, Peter Garnett wrote to the PLC on behalf of Richard Cook and his wife. They were living in Otley (Yorkshire), the parish to which Richard had moved thirty years earlier, where he married his wife and worked for most of his adult life. By the time of Garnett's letter, the Cooks were "very infirm, quite unable to work." For three or four years previously (under the Old Poor Law) they had been allowed 2s 6d weekly out-parish relief by the overseers of Newcastle-under-Lyme. Shortly before Garnett wrote, however, that relief had been stopped and the old couple were obliged either to starve in Otley or enter the workhouse in Newcastle-under-Lyme, a place that held no practical or sentimental attachment for either of them. Garnett wrote: "they are suffering the most extreme privations selling which little furniture they have rather than go into the workhouse at Newcastle." It was a particularly hard case, he added, "the parties being so infirm … the woman especially cannot bear the idea of being torn away from her native place." Indeed, just the thought of the workhouse "seemed to break the poor old woman's health."[70]

Similarly, John Wise wrote for Nancy Higginson, a widow aged seventy-eight, who had lived at Bridgeford (Staffordshire) for half a century, but whose legal settlement was also within the Newcastle-under-Lyme PLU. Wise visited the local guardians on the old woman's behalf and was told that, because she had a daughter – she was a single mother providing for two illegitimate children – they would not reconsider a decision to stop her weekly pension. Wise's letter is particularly intriguing. Not only was he a magistrate but he was also the chairman of the Board of Guardians of Stoke PLU, where Higginson resided. In a letter that he had earlier sent to the Newcastle guardians and later copied to the PLC, Wise stated that:

> The mal-administration of the old Poor Law caused me to hail the new Act with pleasing expectations, as I believed it would improve the Condition of the People, if administered by tender and benevolent Parties but when I see its practical working, in a case like the present, where there appears to be a total absence of sympathy and feeling for the Poor I feel it my duty as an Englishman and as a friend to the destitute to protest against such practises.[71]

Wise's emphasis on the differential treatment of paupers by proximate unions is important here. Despite the fact that the bureaucratic landscape had changed dramatically following the passage of the New Poor Law, the interpretation of the rules at the local level remained surprisingly malleable, and nowhere was this more marked than in the treatment of the non-resident elderly poor. Wise's view, as chairman of the Stoke Board of Guardians, was that any inflexible administration of the non-residence rule in connection with elderly paupers was unnecessary, inhumane, and inconsistent with rational action, and that "[t]he inevitable consequences of such harshness must be fatal to the good working of the Act."[72] However, his view was at odds not only with that of his brother guardians in neighbouring Newcastle but also with the official line that he received from the commissioners: that they "entertain so strong opinion of the cost result from granting relief to non-residents … [that] they cannot approve of the [Guardians] taking such steps."[73]

On the other hand, there is plenty of evidence that the Centre remained systemically ambivalent about applying the rules regarding the non-resident elderly poor, even as those rules changed in complex and patchy ways over time – at least until the beginning of the "crusade against out-relief," as of the late 1860s.[74] Thus W.E. Goodacre, clerk to the Mansfield PLU, whom we have already encountered advocating for other paupers, wrote in 1850 that Mary Wright, aged seventy-one, had recently been removed from Ecclesall Bierlow (Yorkshire) by a magistrate's order. But, he continued: "She is now very desirous of returning to that place to end her days amongst her children who are become residents there, and the Guardians are wishful to comply with her request." He added further assurance: "The woman is of good character & conduct & the Overseer who brought her stated that the authorities of the removing parish [Ecclesall] was perfectly willing for her to return & be relieved there."[75] Given that the officials in both unions were willing to continue the arrangement, quite what the confusion was in this case is not clear. However, despite previous objections to paying non-resident allowances, the response of the Board's inspector, H.B. Farnall (appended to the letter), was: "I beg to recommend this proposal be sanctioned," and the PLB followed suit.[76]

We hear from Goodacre again fifteen years later, this time on behalf of widow Margaret Sansom, aged seventy-two, who was living in East Stonehouse (Devon). She was, he wrote, "a native of Devonshire, where all her friends and connections reside," and her only connection with Mansfield was a technical one, because it was her late husband's place of settlement. Goodacre emphasised the guardians' willingness to comply:

> Unwilling to separate the poor woman from her connections to spend her few remaining years and die amongst strangers, the Guardians are willing to relieve her at her residence parish provided the authorities consent to her remaining and to advance relief on account of this Union and provided your Board will approve such a course.[77]

Once again, the PLB official, whose remarks were appended to the original letter, agreed to the arrangement in this case, stating: "I see no objection provided that the Guardians of East Stonehouse concur."[78] Despite occasional pronouncements and responses to appeals of this sort which echoed the reformist sentiments of the original architects of the PLAA, the Centre in its various guises was happy to sanction such arrangements in individual cases when consulted by local unions, and to overlook instances where they occurred without explicit sanction.[79] Their most consistent line when contacted by the poor and their advocates on this issue was to fall back on the familiar refrain – that they were prohibited from intervening in individual cases and so were unable to overturn decisions which had already been made. But given their willingness to intervene under other circumstances, and allow relief at a distance when asked to do so, it is not hard to see how the expectation persisted among the elderly poor that non-resident relief could be claimed as a right, in the same way that a right to outdoor relief rather than compulsory workhouse residence was. Added to this is the clear evidence from our corpus that officials interpreted the rules very differently from one another, even in neighbouring unions and potentially in the same union at different times or under different circumstances. It is no wonder, then, that the elderly poor and those who wrote for them continued to negotiate so doggedly on this, as on so many other issues.

CONCLUSION

Many historians have suggested or implied that the aged and infirm poor occupied a "privileged space" in the welfare landscape under both the Old and New Poor Laws. The evidence presented here suggests that they (and their advocates) continued both to have and to believe they had such status throughout the nineteenth century. Along with widows and orphans, they formed a "holy trinity of the worthy poor" whose claims were hard for local and national administrators to ignore completely. It is something of a paradox, however, that the strength of those claims lay in the particular social and economic vulnerabilities of the "worthy poor" when it came to fending for themselves, and this is perhaps truer of the aged poor than it is of even the other groups in this "holy trinity." In a discretionary welfare system – of which the New Poor Law was a prime example, regardless of the apparently rigid framework of rules and regulations after 1834 – that vulnerability was particularly exposed during times of retrenchment and reformism. Hence, the frequent cries of unfairness and inhumanity which were voiced by the elderly immediately after the passing of the PLAA as some local officials sought to use regime change as a way of instituting immediate and swingeing cuts. However, even at times of retrenchment, there were plenty of advocates locally who were prepared to speak out on behalf of the elderly, and what becomes clear from this correspondence (including from paupers themselves, and from the responses and directives of the Centre) is that guardians and officers were up against a considerable body of local and national opinion (including from within the commission itself) which did not support cost-cutting measures being extended to the elderly poor.[80]

Nonetheless, the New Poor Law did change things fundamentally for the elderly, just as it did for all claimants on the public purse. The general workhouse, conceived as the centrepiece of the reformed system, was never specifically intended as a social care facility, but this became one of its central functions as time wore on. There was no specific intention to punish the aged through the strictness of the regime even if this was how it felt at the local level. Indeed, the rhetoric of the architects of the new law – and the bodies of oversight who administered that law throughout the nineteenth century – was clear in absolving the elderly poor of all blame for their situation and assuring them and the public that the workhouse was a place of refuge not torment. The PLC even claimed that the much-hated separation clause was "requisite for their comfort and appropriate treatment" in relation to the elderly, whereas for the able-bodied poor it was framed as a necessary measure for the maintenance of decency, and for instilling habits of abstinence and self-control.[81] Yet, from the letters it is clear that the aged normally had an intense hatred, and heightened fear, of the workhouse and avoided entering it at all costs. In this, they paradoxically found plenty of support in the official pronouncements of the Central Authority, which in 1845 specifically advised guardians that:

> With respect to aged married couples (whose residence in the workhouse is likely to be of longer duration than that of able-bodied persons) the Guardians may, by observing the forms prescribed in this proviso, place them in a separate sleeping apartment. Moreover, the

> Guardians can allow out-door relief to any aged couple whom it may be inexpedient to separate.[82]

This remained the approach throughout the remainder of the nineteenth century.

The problem for the poor and their advocates was that "exceptionalism" in principle did not always lead to exceptional treatment. The directives of the PLC and its successors, even when grounded in the intentions of the original legislation, were almost entirely designed to *enable* unions to treat the aged with a degree of compassion, to allow them to give out-relief, and to mitigate their workhouse experience. Local unions were under no legal compulsion to do so, and our corpus shows clearly that local officials could if they wished easily ignore the sentiment behind these directives. Once again, however, in this they were opposed not only by the great majority of commentators on the operation of the poor laws but by elderly paupers themselves and by their advocates. The complex rhetorical and referential architecture of the resultant correspondence and the associated strength of the claims of the aged on the public's consciousness meant that both central and local authorities were often obliged to react. The elderly were the one group able to fundamentally challenge the rules regarding relief to the non-resident poor, and more widely to claim that their emotional and practical well-being trumped political economy and reformist ideology. In this, as in so many other grey areas under the New Poor Law, the elderly continued to negotiate for, and occupy, their privileged space in the welfare landscape. At the opposite end of the spectrum, in terms of their believability and their presence in public sympathies, were the able-bodied poor. It is this group that we discuss in the following chapter.

9

The Able-Bodied Poor

INTRODUCTION

In April 1835, less than a year after the passage of the Poor Law Amendment Act (PLAA), the commissioners in London received a petition from the ratepayers of Newbury objecting to the very existence of workhouses:

> by an Act of Parliament made and passed in the last session intitled "An Act for the amendment and better administration of the Laws relating to the poor in England and Wales a most alarming expense is about to be incurred in erecting numerous Workhouses in which many of the agricultural labourers may be collected which your petitioners cannot see any probability of being advantageously employed And they can not but lament that the late parliament instead of endeavouring to raise the condition of the labouring population should have devised the means of depressing and depriving them of their liberty with the professed view of reducing the poor rates ... (but ~~which~~ part of which is applied for other purposes) and is applicable to the Relief of the whole of the poor in England and Wales and for which much labour is done.[1]

One can only imagine how this petition was received by the "Bashaws of Somerset House,"[2] and particularly by their secretary, Edwin Chadwick. It may have caused great indignation, challenging as it did the whole notion of the workhouse test, the central tenet of the New Poor Law in relation to the able-bodied.

Yet, on further reflection it might also have been interpreted as a vindication of the stance of those who framed the 1834 legislation. Newbury was after all the town which contained the tithing of Speenhamland and, if we were to take a reductionist view (as many did at the time), it could be said that the "Speenhamland System" was the reason the PLAA was passed in the first place. In 1795 a number of Berkshire magistrates had gathered at Speenhamland to address the problem of male, able-bodied poverty in their county. They were concerned specifically about the large number of agricultural labourers whose wages were insufficient to keep their families. Their solution was to set a "bread scale" for the county – in effect, a family allowance paid on a parish-by-parish basis from the poor rates, administered on a sliding scale according to the price of bread, the wages of the individual labourer, and the size of his family.[3] Over the next three and a half decades, the "Speenhamland System" came to signify all that was wrong with the late Old Poor Law for its critics. It has arguably had a correspondingly disproportionate influence on debates about welfare history ever since.[4] In reality, the Berkshire magistrates' ruling was merely the codification of a set of practices that had been established in individual parishes over the best part of a century, particularly in the agricultural south of England. Nor was the scale ever adopted in any systematic way in Berkshire, let alone as a country-wide expedient.[5] This is not the place to rehearse the many nuances of the debate over Speenhamland, but whatever today's view of its impact, there is no doubting its symbolic importance for those who wished to see a radical redrawing of the welfare rules after the 1820s. Much of what the PLAA set out to do was – rhetorically, at least – designed to rectify the damage perceived to have been done to the "morals" of the able-bodied poor by such schemes. In supposedly rewarding idleness and demographic profligacy, allowances were said to have destroyed the independence of agricultural labourers and created a huge escalation of relief spending.[6]

Given its central place in debates about welfare reform, one might have thought that by the 1830s it would be difficult to find anyone prepared to stand up for the bread scale – which makes the petition from the Newbury ratepayers particularly intriguing. Not only did the signatories object to the forcible incarceration of able-bodied labourers and their families in the new workhouses (mirroring views from northern England, though for different reasons) but they did so explicitly because, in their view, there was no prospect of the inmates "being advantageously employed." Furthermore, they went on to contrast this situation with that of the "Speenhamland System," under which labourers on short-time or inadequate wages received relief while working for local landowners or tenants. "[F]rom 1795 until within these few years," they wrote, "[a labourer was] allowed the price of two gallons of Bread and one shilling over for his bare sustenance not including House Rent and Clothes or medicine when ill." In case the commissioners should still have doubts as to their commitment to the old ways, the petitioners closed by asserting that poverty "should have intitled the labourer to the consideration of parliament instead of rendering him subject to the discipline of a Workhouse and Separation from his family."[7] It seems almost incredible that, after thirty years of opprobrium and reformist ire, the Newbury ratepayers – the nearest thing to the direct heirs of the Speenhamland magistrates – were still insisting on the benefits of giving outdoor relief to the able-bodied, and even supplementary allowances when necessary. That they did so brazenly, addressing their petition directly to the body charged with implementing the new system, suggests strongly that we should look again at the relationship between work and relief under the New Poor Law, and examine how that relationship was understood and mobilised by the able-bodied poor and their advocates at different times.

One thing that stands out in the Newbury petition – and something shared with other letters across the socioeconomic range of the sample – is the fact that it self-consciously highlighted the tensions between ideology and pragmatism in the post-1834 welfare world. The signatories clearly felt that the architects of the PLAA, in their reformist zeal, had sacrificed the interests of all classes. Tenants were forced to pay for expensive workhouse accommodation, they argued, and labourers were not only detained against their will "without any means of regaining his goods or returning to home," but the work they were forced to perform was meaningless and unproductive. What's more, the children of labourers, who were more than willing to do work outside the house if it was available, even for a bare subsistence, were denied a direct example of industry and thrift because the workhouse was a place of sterile and meaningless drudgery in contrast to even the most basic gainful employment on the outside. This was, of course, an intriguing (and very telling) inversion of reformers' long-standing concerns about the demoralising effects of wage subsidies and outdoor relief on the labouring poor, and particularly on the children of those who depended on the supplementary allowances of the "Speenhamland System."[8] Of course, the insistence that it was the ideological needs of reformers that underpinned the New Poor Law and the workhouse test, rather than the pragmatic needs of ratepayers and paupers, has informed much of the debate since the Webbs first published their Fabian analysis in 1929.[9] But just how the able-bodied poor and their advocates understood the workhouse test and the wider relationship between work and relief, and how this understanding informed, and even framed, the correspondence they sent to the to the Central Authority has not been closely examined. This is the central purpose of the current chapter, turning first to the corpus level.[10]

THE CORPUS

It has become clear from our earlier chapters that outdoor relief continued as the modal form of welfare and that workhouses were largely spaces of containment for groups such as women, children, the sick, and the aged.[11] In this context, the able-bodied made up a small proportion of all paupers relieved outdoors even in the 1840s as the New Poor Law became well established.[12] By 1901 this group constituted just 3.5 per cent of *all* paupers relieved, though a much higher proportion of outdoor recipients were able-bodied but (supposedly) temporarily sick.[13] The accuracy of these figures is of course questionable, and we return to the issue of how the recording system could be manipulated below. What is more evident is that there were long-term geographical patterns to the scale of able-bodied poverty and pauperism, and that such patterns were also episodically punctuated by crises (trade cycles, for instance, or the crusade against outdoor relief) which increased the number of able-bodied applicants or raised their visibility. There is also evidence (as we have seen earlier in this book) that guardians in some unions used the advent of the New Poor Law to systematically reduce per capita outdoor allowances, thus putting pressure on the family economies of all paupers.[14] In short, we might expect both that the scale and intensity of writing by or about the able-bodied poor would vary over time and place, and that the declining importance of the able-bodied in the overall pauper population would change the way officials viewed them. Equally, there are good reasons to expect variation and change in the rhetorical architecture of writing by or about the able-bodied, reasons that include developing concepts of citizenship, changing understandings of unemployment and philanthropy, the rise of trade unions, and the intricate sphere of public opinion.

Yet, notwithstanding such potential influences, there is striking regularity and uniformity to the presence of the able-bodied in the corpus. Despite the fact that they called into question the very foundations of the new law, complaints similar to those made by the Newbury petitioners occur surprisingly often and, just as significantly, they continue well after the first flush of anti–poor law sentiment in the 1830s and 1840s. Advocates and guardians episodically revisited the supposed futility of cancelling small allowances, sometimes at exactly the time as they themselves *were* reducing the value of those allowances. We return to this matter in the next section, but the rich seam of opposition at the local level reflects and creates a complex and fluid patchwork of local practices, including actively misleading the Centre, using the exemption clauses of legislation and guidance, and openly continuing wage and family allowances.[15] In the same vein we see the consistent presence of the able-bodied as poor writers, many of whom shared the underlying rationale of the Newbury ratepayers, a fact that poses a fundamental challenge to our current appreciation of the way in which those who were subject to the New Poor Law's most stringent disciplinary measures understood and responded to the law and its application. Our evidence demonstrates quite clearly that, in subtly altered form, the allegation that the threat of the workhouse militated against the independence of able-bodied labourers and, by example, took from their children all hope of a productive future, grew in strength after the 1830s and formed the cornerstone of an implicit critique of the New Poor Law that struck at its ideological core. What emerged was a linguistic and referential register shared at several levels: between the able-bodied poor and advocates/officials, with other pauper groups, and with letter writers under the Old Poor Law. As we have seen throughout this volume, loss of independence was central to the grievances of a large proportion of paupers and advocates who wrote to the Centre. It was, after all, the most obvious practical and symbolic penalty suffered by the poor under the new regime, as it was always intended to be. But enforced confinement and the rigours of workhouse life were rhetorically appropriated and utilised by the able-bodied quite differently to the way they were used in the claims of other more "deserving" groups such as the sick and the elderly. Whereas these groups tended to question the justice of incarcerating those whose poverty was the result of unavoidable physical misfortune or inevitable decline, the able-bodied engaged directly and forcefully with the basic principles of the New Poor Law itself (and its practical application) and often with considerable rhetorical force. In particular, they directly challenged the Central Authority to defend a practice which, they believed, was not only unjustifiably punitive but inherently self-defeating.

There are thus a number of rhetorical regularities across the corpus. Those shared with other groups and to some extent with the Old Poor Law include: struggle and prior suffering, particularly in the context of family income,[16] the promise of resumed independence if supported now, exogenous circumstances, time (often in the sense of predicting a timescale over which a better position might be achieved), public opinion, and of course prior character which should assure the reader that the current state of affairs was genuinely temporary. Alternatively, and working within a broad framework emphasising faults in the basic principles of the New Poor Law, distinct rhetorical threads are perceptible. Thus, the able-bodied equated current deservingness with a prior record of, or future commitment to, trudging and moving in order to improve their lot.[17] And more than any other group, they and their advocates sought to use logic to argue a case, including calculating the costs of action versus inaction on the part of local guardians and portraying relief in the requisite mode as a form of investment rather than of welfare. Such calculating and controlled approaches were often fused with a wider suite of rhetoric which amounts to a narrative of fragility. This included the fragility of mind and body, of family integrity and even of able-bodiedness itself, with writers, advocates, and officials co-locating such statements against a sense of the ominous arrival of tipping points such as hunger, nakedness, or distraint for rent.[18] Finally, across the corpus and all its spatial, typological, and chronological dimensions, the able-bodied, their advocates, and sometimes even officials consistently used markers of moral citizenship. The able-bodied were proud, had worked hard for themselves and their families, had contributed, and were never meant to be dragged down by a system with which their contact was often fleeting. They may not have had rights to welfare, but they did have a right to an ear, respectful treatment, and logical decision making.[19] This was not exactly the citizenship associated with honest poverty of the sort found by Marjorie Levine-Clark in the English midlands, but might rather be understood as the citizenship of contribution and consideration, with an analogue in compelled dependence.[20] The rest of this chapter explores some of these corpus themes.

"PERPETUALLY PAUPERIZED": THE ABLE-BODIED AND THE WORKHOUSE TEST

James Archer, an unemployed silk weaver, wrote from Shoreditch (Middlesex) in 1848 that he had been unemployed for seven months, and received outdoor relief for the whole period: "I have received Parochial Relief to the amount of Thirty Two shillings … and it would be useless to say that this did not support five persons [even though] I was compelled to sell part of my Tools for money to Traffic [to buy stock] with." Yet, when he applied to the Bethnal Green guardians for a loan to recover his tools in the belief that his prospects of work were improving, he was instead told that his family would have to go to the workhouse.[21] Archer's response was to "pursue another course which was to apply to you [the Poor Law Board] hoping you will not allow me to be perpetually Pauperized without affording me a chance of Striving against it."[22] Nowhere in his letter did Archer use the language or sentiment of natural justice that we have become accustomed to in other pauper appeals. Rather, he simply let the facts speak for themselves and questioned the logic of sending his family into the workhouse, rendering him (and them) "perpetually Pauperized," at precisely the moment when he might get back into work. George Dovey of Poplar was even more succinct in 1872, telling the Local Government Board (LGB): "I have been to the board [of] popler union and they wont give me no cloths and I not got no box nor no brushes to work [with] and I wont go to the house [where] I cant git no worke."[23]

Thomas Smith of Exeter took a similar approach in 1861 but pursued it even further than Archer had done. With work promised a fortnight hence, he approached the guardians for temporary relief but was told that he would be given nothing "other than as an inmate of the Workhouse." Undeterred, "I stated some hardships, and I had a Wife & 5 Children, but to no purpose." Smith reasoned that:

> I am without employment or means but am shure of work in a short time, therefore it would not be just to put any body of ratepayers to so great expense, as unnecessary to send me an Inmate of the Workhouse, particularly at such a time of grievous complaints of over taxation from the Ratepayers I only earned 8 [shillings] last week. <u>I have a Wife and 5 children under age</u>. It would be wicked and unjust in me to consent to such a proceeding while I am able to work, entaling the support of such a Family upon the Ratepayers for a long time, besides Law & other incidental expences, when a little temporary relief only is necessary.[24]

Smith's is a particularly interesting example of how a partially employed labourer with a large family – the bugbear of the New Poor Law – could still negotiate its apparent rigidities with reason and a great deal of rhetorical sophistication. The guardians, he complained, had put him in an intolerable position, forcing him to contemplate a "wicked and unjust" act in becoming a permanent burden on the ratepayers, and his letter is either full of understanding for their plight at a time of "grievous complaints" over the tax burden or a skilful piece of rhetoric which positioned him on the side of the ratepayer. Nonetheless, its most forceful expedient was once again the simple implicit message that by refusing him short-term outdoor relief, not only would the guardians be condemning the ratepayers to support his large family in the long term, but it was in breach of its own principles by denying him the opportunity to take on any work that might become available.

Occasionally, this message was pursued with such doggedness that it conveys incredulity on the part of the writer that the gulf between principle and practice could be so self-evidently wide. Thus John Gowland, a law clerk, wrote to the Centre in 1866. Through sickness and misfortune he had been forced to apply to the Durham Poor Law Union (PLU) for relief.[25] He too was refused and offered the house. In this context Gowland was keen to emphasise that he was actively seeking work, writing: "I have daily watch'd the advertisements &c in various newspapers & through [this] I have this day succeeded" in securing a position. However, his new job would not begin for another two weeks, and "I know not how we shall live for the next fortnight, as I shall receive no wages until a week come Saturday night." Still, the Durham guardians had refused his application for temporary relief. At this point, Gowland spelled out the situation for the benefit of the Poor Law Board (PLB). "Now I may here further state," he wrote:

> that if the said "Guardians" acting had have taken into their Consideration the difference of "Tempora[ry] out door Relief" instead of determining that we were to enter the said "Union House" as they wished to force, it would have been a very great saving of expenditure to the Ratepayers of this City … And which is easily explained, I.e. the wife & Children of Self would have cost at least 3s/6d a head [in the house] and if they had granted us but 1s/ a head out door tempora[ry] relief it would have proved at least 10s/ per week advantage and to the interest of the Ratepayers of this City for whom they act. And further I would then have been held in such a position by an entrance [into the house] that I might (with Wife & Family) have been detained the whole of my (& our) Life therein and have been prevented to have any Employ And even could I have applied for a situation (when If I were) within their Union House, it would very probably have always been said by people to whom any application might have been made to – Oh! I or we cannot engage a Pauper or a man out of a Workhouse however well learnt, or whatever an exceptionable reference could have been supplied by recent Solicitors under which I have worked well I am certain that any reasonable person or Gentleman of understanding would hold or take a similar view or opinion as stated.[26]

Gowland's reasoning is clear, but there is something long-suffering about it too, as though he were explaining an obvious truth to a child. Not only were the inconsistencies of the law and its application plain for all to see, but he also recognised that the stigma of workhouse residence was a penalty that could blight the prospects of the able-bodied long into the future, especially in the case of the temporarily unemployed "respectable poor."[27]

The inherent inconsistency of confining the potentially productive poor was not lost to others, either. On occasion, the kind of exasperation betrayed by Gowland surfaces even in letters from poor law officials. An early example, clearly echoing the petition from the Newbury ratepayers, was sent by Richard Lewis, the overseer of Shocklach Oviatt, a small hamlet on the Cheshire side of the English-Welsh border and part of the Wrexham PLU. Shortly after unionisation, Lewis wrote to the Poor Law Commission (PLC), ostensibly to complain about the behaviour of the Wrexham guardians in relation to rents. As a landlord with several local cottages, he had been assured by the chairman of the board (of which he was part) that he would "be paid without grombleing" for cottages rented to paupers. Later, however, after his request for payment had been refused, he wrote: "I took [the paupers] in Expecting such gentlemen as them would naver Diviate from there Worde." But in the course of his complaint, Lewis made it clear that the rules prohibiting payment of rent and other outdoor relief to the able-bodied poor made no sense at all from the point of view of anyone local with an interest in the matter. "If I Distress these poore piple," he wrote, "and take the bed from under them and the[y] go into the workhouse it will cost the Township at lest one twelve shilling per week and the oather ten Shilling and sixpence." This was above the cost of his accrued rent, and "will be a w[e]ighty matter for the Township to bare." Moreover, he wrote, "these poor piple are willing to Strive if the[y] eate potatos and Sault every day so the[y] had a house to keep the frost and Snow from starving them to death." Finally, despite his dissent from the principles of the new law, he signed off as "your Most ob[edi]ant and humble servant and well wisher to Queen and State."[28] For Lewis, as for the Newbury petitioners and all those who objected to the treatment of the able-bodied, it seemed self-evident that to keep the employable poor in a workhouse offended both the good sense and the economic prospects of everyone concerned.[29]

Over time, poor law officials recognised the futility of challenging the principle of the workhouse test head-on, and strongly worded appeals like Lewis's become less frequent in our sample, particularly after the issuing of the Outdoor Labour Test in 1842 (see below). But guardians across England and Wales did still seek the sanction of the Central Authority to allow relief to the outdoor poor beyond the published exceptions, and in doing so they continued to use a very familiar logic. In July 1868, for example, the clerk of the Mitford and Launditch PLU wrote to request sanction for a pragmatic solution to the plight of an unnamed able-bodied labourer with a wife and ten children who was "unable to maintain himself and family." Wright went on to explain that, "[t]he Guardians being unwilling to break up the poor mans home by admitting him & his wife & children into the house are desirous of affording him some temporary assistance." Rather than suggesting that he be given outdoor relief directly (something that would be refused) the guardians asked if they might take two or three of his children into the workhouse temporarily. As a solution, it must have seemed eminently sensible to them, and they therefore went on to request that they might be given the power to do the same thing in any similar cases that arose. Across our corpus and the wider historiography we have examples of unions that took exactly this action without even consulting the Centre. Yet, having been asked, the PLB's response was to "decline to assent" and to explain that "although this case may be a hard one the ratepayers might have just reason for complaints if [the Board] acceded to the request." They went on to emphasise that the workhouse could not be used in this way as it would have constituted "relief [in lieu] of wages," not unlike the Speenhamland allowances. In doing so, they were simply reaffirming the principle of "less eligibility" which was by then more than thirty years old. The workhouse was not there to be used as a means of improving the condition of the able-bodied poor, a rule that should already have been well known to the Mitford and Launditch officials.[30] As a correspondent from Cambridge noted as early as 1839: "I am well aware as an ex officio Guardian of this Union that the Law will not allow us to put the whole or part of any family in the House" without the breadwinner.[31] The fact that this knowledge did not prevent the Norfolk guardians from proposing it as the most sensible solution to an intractable problem almost thirty years later speaks volumes about the way the workhouse test was viewed by many of those who were charged with applying it. These observations stretch across the chronological and typological divides in the corpus, encompassing for instance mining and industrial areas, port towns and older market towns as much as rural areas such as Mitford and Launditch.[32]

Explaining this systemic shared approach between the poor (in both witness statements and letters), advocates, and guardians is a matter of some complexity. At base, however, we need to take a step back and recall that this remarkably consistent critique of the workhouse test was nothing new even in 1834. It is too easily forgotten that the deterrent workhouse was a product not of the New Poor Law but of the Old: its form and function were first codified in the Workhouse Test Act (or Knatchbull's Act) of 1723, which allowed parishes to "purchase or hire any house or houses … for the lodging, keeping and employing the poor."[33] Just as the 1834 legislation ushered in the principle of "less eligibility," the 1723 Act intended that a "workhouse test" should ensure that life inside the institution was at least as arduous as the meanest life outside it in order to deter the idle and feckless from living on parish charity.[34] Although the measures contained in the 1723 Act were not compulsory (it was merely an "enabling Act" sanctioning the building of a workhouse by a parish or union of parishes should they wish it), large urban and metropolitan workhouses were built before 1834 with internal structures and regimes that would have been very familiar to those who met them after that date. In many London and Westminster parishes in particular, the deterrent workhouse became a familiar part of the welfare landscape from the 1720s, and by the end of the century Liverpool and the Corporation of Bristol both had well-established institutions with regimes based on strict classification of inmates and hard labour.[35]

The important issue here, though, is not that deterrent workhouses predated the PLAA, but that the broad critique of them that we see repeated time and again in our sample by the able-bodied and their advocates was also of very long standing. Wherever deterrent workhouses were established in the eighteenth century, they were the subject of much soul searching about their effects on the morals, independence, and long-term prospects of the industrious poor, as well as the cost-effectiveness of institutional relief. This deliberation only increased as the century wore on.[36] For John Thelwal, a radical: "a workhouse is but a gaol; and, therefore, a fit receptacle only for those paupers, whose infirmities make confinement necessary to their preservation."[37] The baronet and social reformer Thomas Bernard (who had established the Society for Bettering the Condition and Increasing the Comforts of the Poor) described workhouses in 1797 as "objects of terror to the honest and industrious, and at the same time the favourite resort of the dissolute and abandoned."[38] But for many commentators, there were sound economic and practical reasons for opposing them, too. As an anonymous contributor to the *Annals of Agriculture* noted in 1815:

> it appears natural to me that a pauper should be more easily supported in his own family than in a workhouse, where the expense of management, buildings, &c. must be considerable, and the food more costly than that he contents himself with in a poor cottage; and yet he prefers the latter to the best house of industry, though it cannot be the labour that deters him; as the earnings, by the reports of overseers, are very trifling, and give but little hope that children educated in them are to become industrious.[39]

Another contemporary calculated in 1807 that it cost almost three times the amount to keep an industrious family in a workhouse than to relieve them in their own home. With reference to the "useful work" which they could do from home when compared with the "useless toil" of task-work in a workhouse, the article concluded that "every institution which tends make the poor depend on any other support than their own industry, does them a great disservice, and is highly injurious to society."[40] It was for this reason that the Whig MP Samuel Whitbread declared, also in 1807: "I am an enemy of the workhouse system, it has almost universally increased the burthen of the poor rate; and instead of adding to the comfort of the poor, or the improvement of their morals it has furnished seminaries of idleness and vice."[41] The distinctive rhetorical signatures that we see in relation to the able-bodied in the corpus can thus be understood as a product of deeply ingrained and long-term public discourse about the place of the able-bodied in English and Welsh welfare philosophies.

By the early years of the New Poor Law, then, the Central Authority ought to have been well prepared for the kinds of rhetorical approaches seen so far in this chapter. The staff of the PLC and their successors may even have congratulated themselves on the fact that the "workhouse system" seemed to have an immediate impact on levels of relief spending after 1834.[42] Whether or not (as Fraser and others have argued) expenditure was falling before the passage of the PLAA, there seems little doubt that the combined effect of the new law's various clauses, with the workhouse test at its core, forced many able-bodied who may previously have sought relief to think again or at least to delay their engagement with the guardians.[43] Nonetheless, the Centre was also acutely aware that welfare practice in relation to the able-bodied was far from uniform, and nowhere was this truer than in the application of the workhouse test. As Steven King has argued elsewhere, "we should speak not of a workhouse system but of several systems."[44] The most obvious inconsistency was in the attitude of unions in the north of England and Wales, many of which resisted applying the workhouse test with varying degrees of rigour, and some of which refused to apply it all. But the evidence from our sample demonstrates that even *within* individual unions the test could be applied or not applied in arbitrary ways. Humphrey Moneypenny, for instance, wrote letters from Bethnal Green to complain about the Board's refusal to allow him temporary relief, noting in March 1841: "I don't see why I and my family should be forced into a Workhouse any more than others there is them that has had 4 months relife and I had but 1."[45] However, he also noted that if they were forced into the workhouse "the Rags that is on our Backs is to be taken of[f] … and then when we come out a gane we are to have them on our Backs agane and then We Shall be Place[d] in the same State as we are at the present time."[46] In this way, the arbitrary application of the workhouse test could be incorporated into a wider seam of criticism that focused on its many inconsistencies. Yet, the core of this rhetoric was always the clear message that, despite its deterrent intentions, the long-term effect of the test was to destroy the independence of the able-bodied poor and thus to "pauperize" them still further – precisely the situation it was explicitly designed to prevent. In turn, this broad and consistent message from and regarding the outdoor poor was also a motif mobilised by the able-bodied who were already workhouse residents. It is to this group that we now turn, and we continue to focus on Bethnal Green as an archetypal workhouse when it comes to the presence and agency of different groups of the able-bodied poor.

"NO LIBERTY WHATSOMEVER": THE ABLE-BODIED CONFINED

In July 1841 John Vickers wrote to the PLC and explained that due to the "Depresed state of my Trade" he had been unemployed since April and thus been "Gected [ejected] from my miserable Dwelling on the 26 of June." Now in the Bethnal Green workhouse, he further reported having been told by the guardians that he must do "as mutch worke has would support me and my wife and familly" whilst there. Worse, he had been deprived of the liberty of going out of the house, even to go to church on Sundays.[47] However, the core issue for Vickers was that a potential employer had written to the workhouse Master to tell him that he had work for Vickers, who would have been glad to accept if he could get a little relief to set up home again. Despite the fact that (as he had told the guardians) "i did not wish them to keep my Family" in the workhouse any longer than necessary, "they Refused me and my Employer has Waited since the 28 of June and he cannot wait any longer." Vickers ended the letter by insisting that "your Petioner begs to most earnestly … inform you that sutch an Opertunity may not meet his View for Months to come," and warned that "[as] i am to have no Liberty whatsomever i am likely to Remain here during my Life."[48] The crux of Vickers's case, then, was that he could have a job but the only chance of improving his condition was for the union to assist him temporarily while he built up reserves from his own labour in order to establish an independent household. This predicament was the reverse of that of the unnamed male pauper on whose behalf the clerk of Mitford and Launditch wrote in 1868 (see above). In that case, the PLB refused to sanction short-term relief for some of his children in the workhouse to lessen a financial burden at home. Here, Vickers was specifically prohibited from going out of the workhouse to earn his living because it would have meant leaving at least some of his family behind and effectively making them chargeable to the union in the long term. In practice, of course, many unions used the workhouse much more flexibly than they were supposed to and the Centre allowed,[49] but this should not detract from the point that the essential contradictions of law and official regulations notionally placed the able-bodied in an almost intolerable position.

It is thus not surprising that, just as local officials and guardians occasionally complained about their inability to offer temporary outdoor relief to the able-bodied, so they also raised the issue of the indoor poor who were forced to become a long-term burden on the rates because the guardians were, in effect, prohibited from allowing them out to work. In a long and detailed response to the *General Workhouse Order* issued by the PLC in 1842, L. Chalke, the Chelmsford PLU chairman, argued that it was in no-one's interests to maintain every member of a large family indoors. Using an example of the pauper Joseph Clarke, Chalke patiently explained the deficiencies of the commission's ruling when applied in the real world. Clarke, he said, was "brought up by an indulgent father in a farm house was [bred to] no trade; he is a small man, and not accustomed to hard labour, the utmost he could earn under a liberal employer is 10/– a week." Clarke and his wife had a family of ten children between the ages of a few months and sixteen and any wages he could earn were likely to have been inadequate on their own to keep his family. Chalke went on to point out that:

> if this pauper is to continue [in] the workhouse until means are devised to enable him to earn sufficient to maintain such a family, his fate is sealed, and [it is] clear that he must remain where he is at the expense of the parish for an indefinite period.

In case the logic of his argument should still be lost on the commissioners (and in common with poor writers who also entered into extended logical discussion) he added: "but if he is allowed to go out and such of his smaller children as may be termined by the Board, I have no doubt in that case places which he cannot procure will be found for such of his children are of a proper age." Finally, as if to anticipate a refusal, he wrote that if Clarke did indeed abscond and leave his children in the care of the union: "the parish should not [be at a] greater loss than they [would be] by your

[plan]."[50] In other words, if Clarke had been allowed to take his wife and some of the smallest children out of the house, he may well have been able to subsist without relief.

The structural conditions of workhouse life that militated against the able-bodied regaining their independence occasionally became the subject of strident contestation. In 1853, for example, five young men between the ages of seventeen and twenty-three wrote from Bethnal Green workhouse, stating: "We the undersigned petioners have been in this House some time [and] not being able to get any Work out of the House Hope you will if it lays in your Power … assist us to get Abroad being able and willing to do anything to earn A honest Living."[51] Thirty years later, a solicitor's clerk named Frank Burge made himself notorious by waging a one-man crusade against the policy of not allowing family men out of the workhouse to seek employment. So extensive was Burge's correspondence with the LGB that it deserves a volume of its own.[52] For now though, he entered the Poplar workhouse in July 1883 with his wife and four children, where they remained for two years. Very little is clear about his earlier life, but we know a lot more about certain aspects of it once he was there because he wrote at least nine letters to the LGB between February 1884 and December 1885. The first two of Burge's letters appear to have been mislaid and are no longer in the MH12 correspondence, but this is less significant that it might otherwise have been because in September 1884, he sent a third letter with enclosures in which he made extended reference to his earlier correspondence and covered much of the same ground. This single item ran to thirty-five pages and over 10,500 words. It becomes clear that Burge had applied for, and on several occasions been granted, short periods of absence from the workhouse to seek work between July 1883 and January 1884. On most of these occasions, and against the long-term policy of the Central Authority, he had been permitted to go out of the house without his wife and children. However, in January 1884 he applied again to go out on his own and was refused. This simple refusal precipitated his letter-writing frenzy and an extended campaign to get the rules changed.

On the first occasion when Burge was refused leave of absence, in January 1884, he had obtained a written guarantee of work with a firm of solicitors;

namely, Broad and Broad of Laurence Pountney Lane in the City of London. In his fourth letter, he even sent a copy (in his own hand) of a further guarantee from Broad and Broad in which they confessed themselves "rather surprised" that leave of absence has been refused by the guardians because "it seems that he would in all probability have been able to effect the reestablishment of a home."[53] The LGB wrote back much as we would expect from the analysis in chapter 4, to say that the form of relief: "is entirely within the discretion of the Guardians." Nonetheless, this was far from the end of Burge's correspondence. He wrote further letters both to the Centre and to the local guardians which were assiduously copied and sent as enclosures to the LGB. Often (and echoing John Gowland, another solicitor's clerk from whom we heard earlier in the chapter) in the most painstaking and long-suffering tone he explained that his requests for leave of absence were solely "to avoid permanent pauperism" and to prevent the family from becoming an "aimless burden on the ratepayers." At one point, Burge sent a detailed calculation of the likely cost to the ratepayers of his family's remaining in the workhouse, arguing that if he and his wife lived to the age of seventy-five, and each of his children stayed in the workhouse until they were sixteen, the net cost would be around £1,200, "all of which might have been saved if the Board on the 29th January had permitted the applicant to … acquire the means to take the expense on himself."[54] Finally, towards the end of his second letter, Burge stressed that a direct effect of local decisions (and the refusal of the LGB to overturn it) was to render him utterly incapable of regaining his independence:

> With regard to the suggestion that it is open to a man at any time to seek employment by taking his discharge with his wife and children and that he would thus "somehow or other" make a home, Does this mean that his Workhouse experience will invest him with superhuman energy or divination to that end or is it to be implied that the mans new home is to be started by the charity of some private individual. A man must not steal or beg[,] and when he is without relations (as in the applicants case) it is impossible to borrow. The only hope then for such a man is that some benevolent person seeing his

> plight may take compassion on him and may assist the ratepayers by giving him a start. A lame conclusion truly considering the vast amounts compulsorily extracted from the ratepayers.[55]

It is hard to imagine a clearer or more persuasive argument against the blanket application of the rule that prevented the relief of some members of a family inside the workhouse while the breadwinner(s) were permitted to seek work outside. Indeed, Burge's case even made faint ripples in the legal fabric of Victorian society: in 1887, he took his case to the Royal Courts of Justice, suing members of the Board of Guardians for slander and for depriving him of his liberty. In the event, he was deemed "non-suited," meaning that the case was thrown out before it could be considered in detail. The judge suggested that Burge might have had a stronger case if he had targeted the local board as a whole. However, events still rumbled on and in Parliament the following year a question was put to Charles Ritchie, the president of the LGB, by Cunninghame Graham, MP for Lanark North-West. He asked if "the Guardians of the poor of the parish of Poplar exceeded their duty in refusing Mr. Frank Burge, an inmate of that parish, three weeks' leave to provide a home for his family on being offered employment." The answer – predictably, perhaps – was, no. Ritchie confirmed that "during earlier years of his stay in the workhouse the Guardians repeatedly allowed him to leave the workhouse without his wife and children; but the continual recurrence of these applications tended to interfere with the discipline of the workhouse," which is why his final application had been refused.[56] Despite the extent of Burge's agency both in writing and in court, the attitude of the LGB remained lofty and dismissive: the last letter he sent from the workhouse (December 1885) was annotated by the clerks with a single sentence: "Annex to the previous communications from this man … Burge's letters are not as a rule worthy of much consideration."[57] Even so, Ritchie's reply confirmed that Poplar, effectively in dissent from the LGB line, *did* routinely respond to pauper agency and release the able-bodied from workhouses so that they might find work. This observation reflects in part the complex and organic relationship between work and welfare that was "worked through" under the New Poor Law and it is to this issue we now turn.

"TOSSED ABOUT WORSE THAN ANY DOG": THE OUTDOOR LABOUR TEST

So far in this chapter, we have focused on the (shared) words of poor writers, advocates, and officials who wrote to the Centre complaining about the denial of outdoor relief or the fact that the workhouse test effectively prohibited work as a supplementary form of income for the able-bodied poor. However, and unlike most of the scenarios we have explored in this book, it might be argued that the very existence of such texts actually reflects the ideal operation of the New Poor Law as far as the Centre was concerned. After all, the principle of less eligibility meant that the able-bodied were not supposed to gain any advantage from the conditions that were imposed on their relief. The fact that the poor complained about them could not therefore have been interpreted other than as proof that the law was operating correctly. Thus, rather than draw attention to the local misapplication, or even to the overly harsh interpretation of the rules governing relief, the questions posed by our writers addressed the fundamental philosophy of the New Poor Law as it pertained to the able-bodied. They did so not because authors necessarily wished to see the system dismantled (although many of them undoubtedly did) but because this was the only response that was available to them.

Yet, despite the presence of a consistent thread of grievances from the able-bodied poor and their advocates throughout the nineteenth century, their letters do not tell us the whole story about the way the law was applied locally. As we have seen, not only did large numbers of able-bodied paupers continue to receive relief outside the workhouse after 1834 but, as Michael Rose and others have pointed out, the "allowance system" which had underwritten much of the reformist debate leading up to the PLAA continued to operate in altered form in many places.[58] In some cases, Boards of Guardians circumvented rules forbidding outdoor relief to the able-bodied by applying the "exceptions" written into them on a grand scale (and failing to inform the Central Authority that they were doing so); in others, they simply reinterpreted the term "able-bodied" to suit the circumstances they faced.[59] However, in yet more cases, especially (although not exclusively) in manufacturing and mining districts, guardians made little attempt to hide the fact that they had no choice but to give relief to the un- and under-employed poor. Periodic trade downturns and low wages in the 1830s and 1840s meant that labourers had little opportunity to insure themselves against the threat of hard times, and unions complained that workhouses were simply unable to accommodate the numbers who came for relief. This was certainly the case in many of the out-working areas, and it is clearly reflected in a letter sent in 1837 to the Basford PLU by the Reverend Alfred Padley of Bulwell Hall (Nottinghamshire). Padley explained that framework knitters in the glove trade locally were "either wholly out of employment, or obtaining such small weekly profits … as will not even maintain themselves and their families in the most ordinary food." As a result, he went on to plead that the guardians would "not drive the poor to desperation" by the strict application of the law prohibiting outdoor relief, and would "relieve every case before it becomes one of complete destitution and beggary."[60] It is clear from recent research by Chris Grover that, across the landscape of the New Poor Law, pleas like Padley's were often answered. Revisiting the returns made by unions to the PLC between 1840 and 1847, Grover suggests that the proportion of those who were given outdoor relief on the grounds of insufficient wages never dropped below 50 per cent of all of those relieved outside the workhouse in that period, and in certain years this figure was as high as 60 per cent.[61]

It was in large part for this reason that the Central Authority issued three key directives from the 1840s: the Outdoor Labour Test (1842), the Outdoor Relief Prohibitory Order (1844), and the Outdoor Relief Regulation Order (1852). As with so much *ad hoc* English and Welsh welfare legislation, these directives were intended to codify existing practice but to do so in such a way that the Centre was able to retain (or, at least, appear to retain) a degree of control. The latter two measures – the Outdoor Relief Prohibitory and Regulation orders – were specifically aimed at clarifying eligibility and ensuring that only able-bodied applicants for whom there was absolutely no alternative would be temporarily maintained outdoors. However, each Order contained exemptions (as did most poor law orders and regulations) which allowed Boards of Guardians to interpret them in their own and, at times, in paupers' interests. Specifically, guardians had discretion to order outdoor relief in cases of "sudden and urgent necessity," a subclause whose wording allowed for the broadest possible interpretation.[62] The first measure – the Outdoor Labour Test – was, as Elizabeth Hurren has noted, a far more pragmatic measure which recognised that "seasonal working patterns forced large numbers of unemployed labourers to apply for parish funding" and provided a mechanism through which officials could allocate outdoor relief without breaching the principle of less eligibility.[63] In theory, the Outdoor Labour Test was analogous to the workhouse test: in circumstances where it was absolutely necessary to relieve the unemployed outside the workhouse, unions were now required to ensure that the poor performed long hours of unpleasant and arduous work for the minimum remuneration that would just about keep body and soul together.[64]

Whilst it encoded the principle of allowing outdoor relief to the able-bodied, the conditions of labour attached to the Outdoor Labour Test generated many complaints from those who were subject to it. Samuel Marriott, for example, objected in 1858 that, as an unemployed widower with two small children, the guardians had "put me to work gathering stones," which meant that he "had to go 5 miles to work [and] the same distance back," and all he received for his labour was 7d per ton of stones gathered. "Sir," he continued, "to go 10 miles per day give a poor man 7d per ton trusting to rainy days" was intolerable, and because he still had to find 2s a week for his lodgings the pittance left over meant that: "I Remain in Starvation me and my Children." Despite his appeals to them, Marriott was clearly in no mood to appease the PLB with deference, writing that "a poor man is tossed about worse than any dog" and ending, "God help the poor man." His situation was made more desperate because "they will not allow me to go into the union House Neither but compeld to live in Complete Starvation."[65] The fact that Marriott had been refused indoor relief suggests one of two things: either the workhouse was full to capacity or the guardians were conscious of the expense involved in maintaining a family inside the workhouse and were using the Outdoor Labour Test to drive down costs. The latter interpretation gains weight when we consider that his complaint about being refused indoor relief and placed on the labour test is far from unique in our corpus. For example, Thomas Gresham, vicar of Mansfield, reported in 1846 that Louis Francoise, one of his parishioners, was refused admission to the workhouse, and (like Marriott) was instead ordered to break stones for one shilling a day, which necessitated a journey of "twelve, fourteen, sixteen, and as far as eighteen miles a day to his labour." In this case "it too frequently happened that from the badness of the weather and from lameness occasioned by the distance he had to walk he lost a day or two in the week," which was deducted from his earnings.[66] Similarly, Edward Cooper, another vicar, this time of Burford (Oxfordshire), asked in 1844:

> whether the plan of sending a poor man (either as a kind of punishment or for some alledjed offence in word or deed, or otherwise) 5 miles in the morning and 5 at night, to the Union House – to be there by 7 o'clock in the morning and remain till 5 or after in the afternoon – to labor all day there without food & receiving at the end of the week 3s – partly in bread – the man having to pay 10d per week for a lodging is a [plan] which … receives your sanction.[67]

Almost as an afterthought, however, he added: "I [wager] to mention also that the man is not allowed to go into the House." Finally, Charles Leonard complained as late as 1886 of similar behaviour by the Manchester guardians. Having been put to work breaking stones, work for which he steadfastly maintained he was unfit, Leonard was then refused permission to go into the house, where he would have been employed in oakum picking, as an alternative to having to rely on the Outdoor Labour Test.[68]

The refusal to admit the able-bodied poor into the workhouse in favour of a work regime outside perhaps challenges our understanding of the ways that relief was organised, and the uses to which it was put, under the New Poor Law. Nonetheless, at the heart of these complaints was the punitive nature of the work and the inadequacy of the remuneration that accrued, and such themes are expansively developed throughout the letters of those who were forced to submit to it. Thus, in 1855 a group of unemployed cotton operatives in Stockport were compelled to clean the streets for 11 hours a day for "6d up to 1 shilling [and] no more," despite often having large families to feed. Not only that, but they were placed under the supervision of an appointed official with a "Tyranical disposition," a situation they felt was clearly "inconsistent with reason."[69] Fifteen years later, another group of men from the same union complained that they were put to work on the roads in the middle of winter, and were forced "to work in the hardest weather ... or else [they] give us no payment which they have not done for the last two days." The letter went on to allege that their treatment was nothing short of scandalous: "There has been a Delicate man sent to the same work," the men wrote: "he was not able to wheel they barrows until he got a rope round his neck to assist him[.] Still he was compelled to work [and] it helped him on towards his death he died last week."[70] The assistant commissioner who investigated their complaint responded: "The allegations contained in this letter have been enquired into," and concluded: "it is not necessary to do anything further in the matter."[71] We can see how easy it would have been for the local interpretation of national rules to mushroom into scandal and conflict, or for central and local authorities to administratively "manage" complaints. The able-bodied poor were thus at some times and in some unions severely disadvantaged by a simple question of interpretation of the workhouse test and the outdoor labour test. What these paupers and poor writers considered to be a clear case of inhuman and unreasonable treatment, a punishment merely for being victims of circumstance, could be (and was) interpreted by guardians and the Centre as deterrence working exactly as it should. Where officials were so minded, there was very little the poor and their advocates could do to mitigate their treatment except write to the authorities in London and to confect the potential for scandal. Yet, this did not stop the able-bodied, their advocates, and even officials from mounting a consistent moral and logical case against many of the most fundamental injustices allowed for and embodied in the rules for relief, at least in part because they knew very well that most unions did not apply – or inconsistently applied – an outdoor labour test. Despite the structural disadvantages they faced, the able-bodied poor in particular continued to exert a strong seam of agency and to ensure that their voice was heard. And it *was* heard: the Stockport operatives got their inquiry even if the outcome was not as they might have hoped.

CONCLUSION

We began this chapter with what, at first sight, appears to be a counter-intuitive defence by the Newbury ratepayers of the Old Poor Law practice of supplementing the wages of un- and under-employed labourers. The "allowance system" formed the cornerstone of reformist critiques of the Old Poor Law, and opposition to it was therefore fundamental to the ideology behind the New. It was, by the 1830s, much discussed and widely condemned in debates about the future of poor relief. Yet not only were the gentlemen of Newbury quite open in their defence of allowances (and, conversely, in their opposition to the incarceration of the potentially employable poor) but their petition broadly set the tone for the complaints sent to the Centre by and for the able-bodied for the rest of the century. In particular, those complaints closely followed the Newbury petition in questioning a system that was supposedly designed to foster independence but which, in practice, prevented labourers from accepting paid work. As we have suggested, the able-bodied poor reacted to their position using much of the same rhetorical infrastructure as the rest of the life-cycle poor, but they could not easily draw on the kinds of rhetorical strategies centring round deservingness that were open to other groups such as the sick, aged, orphaned, and widowed.[72] They had in a sense been finally and officially de-legitimised by the PLAA and so their access to sentimental or humanitarian appeals (often very successful under the Old Poor Law) had largely been cut off. Nonetheless, the emphasis on the practical inconsistencies of the New Poor Law with regard to the workhouse and outdoor labour tests were also their great strength: put simply, the able-bodied made it clear that they wanted to work when work was available, but that the structural conditions of New Poor Law, applied locally by Boards of Guardians and both confirmed and sanctioned by the Central Authority, prevented them from doing so. This was a narrative not of "honest poverty" but of "constructed dependence," a dependence which was morally and practically wrong.

The anger – and at times even incomprehension – in these letters from the poor, advocates, and officials reveals the huge ideological and experiential gulf between those who framed the legislation and those who enforced or experienced it. This gulf, though often assumed in the literature, is largely invisible in the sources that historians are used to dealing with. The poor – and in particular the able-bodied poor – were rarely able to make their voices heard in national debates about welfare, let alone in the official reports of commissions of inquiry or the printed papers of the poor law authorities. But as we have seen throughout this chapter, those voices are loud and clear in their correspondence to the Centre. The message they convey is remarkably consistent over time and place: an insistence that, given the structural conditions under which they lived, economic independence, though something that labouring families could and did constantly strive for, was too often impossible to achieve or to make permanent. Under the Old Poor Law, the measures that were so unpalatable to the 1834 reformers were precisely those that enabled the labouring poor to survive episodic waves of sickness, incapacity, misfortune, and economic downturn. By the early years of the nineteenth century they had become a vital – even central – part of the "makeshift economy" of the poor as large parts of England and Wales experienced the huge demographic and economic disruptions associated with rapid industrialisation, urbanisation, and agrarian transformation.

It is, of course, precisely the costs associated with these measures that the New Poor Law was intended to curtail, so one might expect that, as the industrial economy matured and the nineteenth century moved on, the labouring poor (and those who wrote on their behalf) would recognise the reality that they lived in a different "world of welfare," one where that older makeshift economy no longer applied and under which they were expected to shift entirely for themselves. But the message that emerges most strongly from the corpus is an altogether more pragmatic one: whatever contemporary reformers (no less than historians) might have extrapolated from Britain's considerable economic growth between 1834 and 1900, the lot of large groups of the labouring population remained highly insecure and periodically precarious. In this lived reality, a welfare system that denied the poor an opportunity to ride the waves of labour insecurity without total economic collapse was, they argued, in no-one's interest. There is a sense from the material too that most unions at most times understood this basic issue,[73] which should lead us to think carefully about the symbolism applied to the New Poor Law through its assumed hostility to particular groups. The same might be said on the matter of punishment of paupers within the workhouse system, another core symbolic trope of the New Poor Law literature. This is the theme that we now take up in part 3, devoted to forms of contestation and challenges to agency amongst those who needed their voices to be heard by the administrators of the New Poor Law.

PART THREE

Contestation

10

Punishing the Pauper Complainant

INTRODUCTION

Daniel Dixon, an ex-inmate of the Hungerford (Berkshire) workhouse, wrote to the Poor Law Commission (PLC) in early 1845 from Clapham (Surrey). He complained of his recent treatment. Describing himself as an aged "cripple," Dixon explained that he had been an inmate of the workhouse at Hungerford over the previous Christmas period but had been supplied with insufficient food and medical assistance during his stay. He also bitterly complained on behalf of other paupers, declaring, "I was witness to the Pauper Inmates dying with want and neglect which urged me to get out." The inmates experienced overcrowding, an intermixing of the healthy and contagiously sick, lack of soap, and inadequate food. Indeed, the letter was signed off with the hope that the case would be taken into consideration for "the sake of the poor sufferers" in Hungerford. At a personal level Dixon noted that he was currently starving and unable to secure a living of his own, a particular injustice given, he added, that "I have fought for my Country & worked hard for my living." Such strategic motifs and rhetorical infrastructures are not uncommon across the corpus. Yet Dixon also set out a further and more particular concern, asserting that the act of complaining itself was no simple undertaking for a pauper and that "if any one complain he is sure to meet with ill treatment from the Governor of the house & taken before a Magistrate and Committed."[1]

The theme of punishment has wide resonance in the poor law literature. Anne Crowther suggested some forty years ago that the history of the New Poor Law, and the iconic workhouse in particular, abounded with reports of illegal pauper punishments. Contemporary accounts of floggings, starvation, denial of decent funerals, harsh punishments, and the forced separation of mothers from their babies or the dead from their relatives persisted throughout the period considered by our book.[2] Indeed, it has been suggested that workhouse spaces were purposely built as disciplinary structures, displaying and embodying the visible administrative power of the newly centralised poor law.[3] A disciplinary regime appears to some extent inevitable, a function of persistent understaffing on the one hand and overcrowding on the other. Inevitable or not, there is no doubt that punishment could be harsh and tagged onto a variety of offences. Crowther in her statistical investigation of pauper committals, for instance, found that the disciplinary charges of the New Poor Law's early years were dominated by drunken and disorderly behaviours, wilful damage as an act of protest or resistance, refusing to work, and absconding from the workhouse (sometimes in union clothes), as well as smaller numbers of theft, assault, breach of the peace, and family desertion cases.[4] More recently David Green (for London) and Samantha Williams (for a widely distributed study of workhouse punishment books) have both confirmed the rich colour to the multitude of disorderly or refractory behaviours that were punished.[5] Yet (and as chapter 2 began to suggest) the formal punishment books that were kept or survive can provide a misleading picture of both who was punished and why. Some recap of that argument is required here. As David Green points out, young women were a particular problem for workhouse staff both in terms of their disruptive behaviour and the inability of officials to impose meaningful punishment.[6] More recently Paul Carter, Jeff James, and Steven King, focusing on the Southwell workhouse, have noted that only a fraction of likely rule-breaking was officially punished. The authorities concentrated their limited resources and punishment capacities on cases and individuals (such as the insane or children) which posed the greatest risk to the running of an ideal well-regulated workhouse.[7] In turn, wider dispute and confrontation of authority overwhelmingly occurred when the culturally accepted norms of workhouse management were broken by staff or guardians.

Overall, then, the picture of workhouse punishment is an inconsistent one in which the injustices and cruelties that undoubtedly took place in some unions and at some times were counterbalanced by an almost constant atmosphere of contestation and the pushing of boundaries by certain cohorts of paupers.

This chapter focuses on the punishment of one particular subset of those who posed a systemic threat to the authority of workhouse staff and guardians: the pauper complainant.[8] That this group could be systematically, if erratically, targeted is suggested by stories such as Dixon's. His point was not that punishment would have been *officially* linked to any complaint made – after all, paupers were allowed to make complaints. Indeed, the establishment and development of the workhouse visiting committee, one of the regular subcommittees of guardians, made the examination of pauper complaints a standard function of workhouse management processes, at least notionally.[9] Rather, what Dixon asserted was that the guardians and staff of Hungerford sought to contain pauper complaints through the misuse of local power structures – in this case the authority of the workhouse master to impose punishments and the abuse of the local criminal justice system. Such a state of affairs, he felt, would undoubtedly deter complaints and result in minimising any reports of pauper ill-treatment. In this chapter we will see that allegations of punishing the pauper complainant were chronologically and spatially widespread. The poor who wrote to the central authority were routinely identified to the relevant authorities, as we have consistently seen. The subsequent process of official investigation in the first instance through the use of the local authority itself left the pauper complainant open to reputational damage – being marked out as a rabble-rouser, troublemaker, agitator, irritant, or nuisance – or to retributive informal punishment such as stopping, reducing, or otherwise changing an individual's relief. This was a situation well understood by paupers, advocates, and even some officials, and we have already seen it across letter sets and witness statements.[10] Complaining was an activity that involved risk, and writers knew it. Our chapter thus analyses both the nature of retributive actions and the ways in which paupers mitigated such acts while still engaging with the Central Authority.

THE CORPUS

The fact that paupers were well aware their identities would be revealed to local officials has three potential consequences at corpus level. The first is to dampen the number and narrow the type of letters sent to the Centre, something we have already discussed in chapters 2 and 5. A second (at least when we consider the material in the round) is the privileging of an administrative voice, one focused on conveying models of efficiency and humanity. Official local renderings sought to minimise internal tensions and causes of complaint. Even when newspaper accounts of mismanagement and neglect were sent directly to the Centre, the usual course was to ask the local guardians to investigate and send their observations. Assistant commissioners (later, inspectors), who also investigated complaints of ill-treatment, neglect, and general mismanagement, often developed a particular tonal quality to their reports.[11] This included latent assumptions that anecdotal instances of relief refusals and reductions along with mistreatment and neglect by local staff were *merely* instances of union employees acting according to the rules, or at worst being too zealous, over-enthusiastic, or passionate in relation to their duties.[12] Thus, when our old friend the Great Yarmouth workhouse inmate Thomas Cox (see especially chapter 5) complained of his treatment in 1851, the inspector, John Walsham, wrote, with no comment on the truth or falsity of the content:

> I should be unwilling to refer this letter to the Board of Guardians unless the P. L. Board should consider it absolute necessary to do so, – for the present Guardians (who are steadfastly endeavouring to remedy the evil results of the very the loose administration of their predecessors) will possibly relax their meritorious exertions to reform abuses if every dissatisfied person may involve them in a correspondence with the Poor Law Board, – 3 or 4 complaining communications have already been referred for their explanation since the end of April.

Internally, Walsham's concerns were understood by the Centre. The letter was annotated: "I quite agree with you that nothing should be done to discourage the Gns in their efforts to reform the system at GYarmouth – There does not appear to be any … feature in this case which would require a reference to the Gns." A further annotation read: "Send copy to G^NS stating that the allegation appear to imply nothing more than a judicious enforcement of regulations which are an essential to the maintenance of order and discipline."[13] Such narratives would be better received than conceding that the poor law inspectorate had lost elements of control to individuals willing to practise a version of tyranny over the local poor.

The sense that the punishments for writing reflected particular local circumstances and particular combinations of pauper and official has some basis in our material. However, there are important regularities and signals at corpus level which should inform the chapter. The vast majority of those who complained about being punished for writing were men, mirroring the fact that most letter writers were men. Paid officials and guardians may have thus perceived and genderised such complainants in terms of being "disruptive males." In addition, there was no sustained tendency for this sort of letter and associated witness statements to fall off over time as the quality of staffing across the poor law improved, case law accumulated, and the "rights" of groups most likely to attract other forms of punishment (children, youths, idiots) were extended. This in turn may suggest lingering fears on the part of workhouse staff and guardians about their ability to maintain control of the workhouse and their ability to exercise the extensive powers over the lives of the poor notionally assigned to them. While it is difficult at corpus level to separate out the rhetorical signatures of punishment in general from those associated with informal punishments attached to complaining, a detailed exercise on a subset of unions suggests that those who wrote or gave evidence to resist such punishments used two distinct approaches.[14] The first was to employ rhetoric also used by other groups of the poor – terms signalling injustice, tyranny, and inhumanity or lack of Christian sympathy, and those calling on logic, claims to truthfulness, helplessness, lack of fault – which we might expect in the sense that the punished complainants were drawn from other subsets of the poor. A second rhetorical architecture was more distinctive. In letters and witness statements, punished complainants emphasised outrage, hurt or damage, breach of process, intense suffering, and the moral fragility of officials and the workhouses they oversaw. They also found various ways to express tenacity. Much as with the serial letter writers that we have encountered elsewhere in this volume (of which those punished were a notable subset), they did not simply report punishments but implied and stated a desire to confront and challenge harsh treatment both in relation to their own case and more widely as advocates fighting for a principle, at whatever cost.

THE PUNISHED COMPLAINANT: PRINCIPLES AND PRACTICE

An example of one of these tenacious paupers was John Cowles of the Chipping Sodbury workhouse (Gloucestershire).[15] He had absconded and been apprehended by two policemen who took him to a magistrate in nearby Horton, where he was sentenced to six weeks' imprisonment for stealing his workhouse clothing.[16] This could have been an interesting footnote in an article on workhouse discipline, but for our examination of pauper rights and agency it is a much more important case. The background was, as set out in Cowles's later witness statement produced for an official investigation into the events, that towards the end of 1842 the quality of food in the workhouse had deteriorated. Cowles stated that on 21 December 1842 the bacon and cheese had been very bad and paupers had dripping instead of butter. In fact he alleged that no butter had been used during the nine months he was there and although he had complained about the food no notice had been taken. Thus Cowles determined to leave the workhouse, taking samples of the bad food with him to confront a local magistrate, with the express aim of complaining of the dietary conditions at Chipping Sodbury. Thus, on 1 January 1843 he asked for leave of absence but the workhouse master refused; so on 2 January Cowles walked out of the workhouse grounds wearing his pauper clothing and taking the food samples with him. He made his way to Lawfords Gate at Bristol (Gloucestershire; a round trip of nineteen miles), to present the food. When he returned, the relieving officer, William Limbrick, refused him an order for re-admittance to the workhouse and abused him verbally, stating that he was a "lazy idle fellow – sponging on the Parish and able to earn his own bread." At the request of the master, two policemen subsequently came and escorted Cowles from the workhouse on a journey culminating in his imprisonment. The case thus far clearly signals the importance of personality to the way that the New Poor Law operated at union level, as we argued in our first chapter.

This was not, however, the end of the story. William Mirehouse, one of the magistrates at Lawfords Gate, wrote to the PLC and explained that he had met Cowles there and commented on the food he had brought: "I believe every person who was in the room [fellow magistrates] thought it unfit to be given to a human being."[17] Furthermore, Mirehouse continued, the fact that Cowles was sent to prison:

> utterly precludes a pauper from making a complaint before [a] Justice ... I will only add that in the Union where I have the honor to be Chairman [I] sho' not only make no objection to a pauper leaving the W.H but would encourage him to do so if it were for the purpose of making a complaint before a magistrate.[18]

In short, Mirehouse indicated that the actions of workhouse staff constituted a serious breach of process. An initial inquiry by the commission concluded that the case should be revisited once Cowles was out of prison. However, that date was brought forward when Mirehouse wrote again, stating: "I have this day received a communication from Sir James Graham [Home Secretary]," who had recommended Cowles be given a free pardon. The resulting official inquiry found bad food (bacon) had been sent to the workhouse and should have been returned to the seller rather than being served to inmates. In addition the master was found to have acted improperly in sending for a policeman without a warrant and for this he was officially censured. Limbrick had behaved improperly and, "It would have been certainly better if the RO had immediately given John Cowles an order to the W.H." Other allegations were dismissed, but Cowles's determination resulted in the arbitrary actions of Chipping Sodbury Poor Law Union (PLU) being held up to scrutiny not only by neighbouring advocate magistrates and the PLC but by the Home Office as well. Victories such as this, both in terms of the original complaint being validated by a neighbouring magistrate and union chairman, and the punishment accruing for that complaint being quashed by the Home Office, would doubtless have made their way into a stock of community knowledge and fostered confidence in others.

Since this was a case driven by external advocacy, it is not hard to see why the poor invested faith in this route to contest local power.

Yet, the rhetorical impetus of complainants and the principles and practices of punishment emerge more clearly when advocates are absent. Thomas Hartley (encountered already in chapter 2 appending his name to a multi-signature petition) was a long-term inmate of the Kidderminster workhouse. His numerous letters to the Centre suggest a different kind of retributive action. In April 1848 he wrote to complain that, despite earlier protests made to the local authorities (that the inmates' stockings were infrequently washed, elderly men were not provided with tea and butter although entitled to them, and some elderly disabled men were incorrectly classified as able-bodied and set to hard labour breaking stones including one man "80 years of age or upwards forc'd to the stones sometime carried up on a mans back some [times] Weeld down in a wheelbarrow"), the situation had not improved. These sorts of practice are familiar from earlier chapters, but Hartley also added that the sick were sometimes intermixed with the able-bodied and that, "Idiots [are] in places below the earth," both clear signals of administrative chaos and inhumanity.[19] This was, he concluded, enough information to warrant an official investigation.[20] A second letter from Hartley was received two weeks later, following just such an investigation by John Graves the relevant poor law inspector. Hartley began with his thanks:

> for your kind endeavours in Regard of my last to you & I have confidence to say that every inmate who is a rational man is thankful for the same, what it as Produc'd and what the Future Result may likely be the Commishoner who came to Kiddr I imagine could not help witnessing that I was rather annoy'd in the Room with the guardians[21]

The annoyance he referred to in this moment of triumph stemmed from an altercation with the workhouse master during the investigation. To counter Hartley's complaint of being left with no clean stockings for three weeks, the master noted that he himself wore the same stockings for three weeks, to which Hartley "answer'd more shame for you to say so." Hartley was called to order by the guardians for criticising the master directly in front of the inspector and one of them suggested that he should quit the workhouse if he did not like it. As Hartley was about to leave the meeting he heard a guardian ask the master what work he, Hartley, was put to in the workhouse and the master replied, at the stone block. The guardian, Mr Fletcher, responded that the master should "keep him to it," something that Hartley considered "a Clandestical threat" and, since the words came from a clergyman guardian, he contended they were "neither moral or spiritual." Warming to his task, Hartley then gave a further account of an inmate named Bates who was assaulted in the yard by another inmate and, having informed the matron, was later told by the master, "you may Report that to the commishoners if you like." Hartley responded that he would, to which the master, "Returning down stairs said I will look after you, which I consider a threatening." Aware that general workhouse complaints were easily rebutted by local guardians and union officers, he gave his view on how PLB inspectors should undertake their regular visits:

> When you come to these kind [of] places the best way is to come on an unexpected way if they have the least notice they will be prepar'd for it if taken on a Sudden you will find its General state, the general way of this place when anyone in Authority comes is sweep that place put Clean bedquilts on those beds there put clean sheets there change those beds wich are dirtyd through & though among those Ideots, such running in all quarters like as if an Ennemy was coming at the same time its friend.[22]

Clearly emboldened by his success, Hartley even felt he could offer the Centre advice on process.

Meanwhile, Kidderminster is an example of a union that generated a number of similar complaints. In early 1853, for example, William Miles, another inmate and a contemporary of Hartley's, complained of widespread "cruelty to thez Children and injustice to they Inmates." He claimed that the vegetables were "kept until they were spoild and not fit to eat," but that they were nonetheless cooked and served to the inmates.[23] Miles noted that on occasion between December 1852 and January 1853 over a dozen young boys were punished with dietary reductions because they could not eat them. Their punishments had not been mentioned by the inmates during a visit by one of the poor law inspectors, and Miles explained that:

> you will think it very strange that i did not make my complaint to the Commissioner when he was here a few weeks back. but the Govenor did not take him all over the house and i did not see him. and most of these inmates were afraid to speak their mind.[24]

The sense that inmates found themselves unable to complain because of fear is a key theme across the corpus and throughout the nineteenth century.[25] On the other hand, we can also trace anger and determination in the letters of the poor, even though they well understood the potential consequences. Thus, P.J. Cusack wrote from Brownlow Hill workhouse in Liverpool in 1886 noting that he had been discharged from the hospital to the "main body of the house" on the orders of the visiting committee, despite the fact that he was in no fit state and that "the nurses in Brownlow Hill had nearly Killed [me] as I can prove." On complaining of his treatment he was "Kept in a cellar 10 feet below the road way with cold flags under me all the time," as a result of which his health declined still further. He also alleged that there were many men who were fit and able to work – much fitter than he – who were suffered to remain in the hospital, and that "I was most brutally treated & badly neglected by all … and because I took the only course open to me to complain I am practically deprived of my rights in a hole and a corner way by the committee." His sense of anger and injustice at such treatment is clear. "The place is officially rotten," he wrote, "& nothing but exposure or a public inquirey before your inspector will purify it;" and he again insisted that "I look to you for justice which a poor patient cannot get in there [because] if he complains he is punished, and if he is quiet he is allowed to suffer."[26]

These sentiments are also found in Wales. Thus, Henry Jones, a retired seaman and then an inmate of the Pwllheli workhouse was even more resolute and tenacious. His six letters between May and July 1860 outlined a litany of allegations including: poor bedding, a lack of clean clothing, inadequate medical attention, and food often contaminated with insects.[27] Jones also recounted earlier verbal complaints he had made to union officers on behalf of fellow inmates and the wider workhouse. These included Owen Owens, a sick pauper who was given vermin-laden underclothes; Mr Thomas, a pauper lunatic whose clothes were full of vermin; William Thomas, also a pauper lunatic, whose bed was "thick with vermin"; John Thomas, an elderly inmate, who was losing blood and left to clean his own underclothes; and John Jones who was denied fresh clothing and at one point described himself as "swarming with vermin."[28] Jones's letters included transcribed statements from James Hughes, a fellow inmate whose sore leg had been neglected resulting in its "rottening off the whole time till it got so bad that the stench of it was unbearable"; and Ann Owens, who told of her food having being contaminated with "black beetles And other insects."[29] However, a considerable portion of these letters in terms of wordage and structure dealt with the treatment Jones received because he *was* a pauper complainant. Thus, he related an account of one of the workhouse servants (and a pauper herself) who had given Owen Owens the filthy underclothes noted above. Jones asked if "she was not ashamed to bring such a filthy article for a man to put on." She said no, swore at him and called him "nothing but a poor Miserable pauper," and then reported their argument to the master and matron.[30] With his two daughters in attendance, the master later enquired of Jones why he quarrelled with the women servants and said that if he (Jones) had a complaint he should bring it to him directly. Jones said in his letter that the master abused him in front of his daughters, one of whom reportedly said at the time: "come away father … let us go for a policeman and put the [fellow] In confinement." Jones then reported that the master threatened to take him before the guardians at their next meeting, to which he replied that he was ready at any time to go before the board and defend himself.

This readiness to argue his case, as well as to advocate for other inmates, infuriated the local officers, something which speaks to the fragility of their control in the workhouse as well as the importance of personalities for the nature and meaning of workhouse life. After the vermin-ridden bed of William Thomas was examined following his intervention, Jones was "warned by the matron that one pauper has no right to Interfere with another so the poor idiot man was left to their Mercy in a most miserable state no one [dare] say a Word on his behalf." For raising these complaints, Jones wrote that he was brought his clothes, and ordered to change immediately and leave the workhouse. He "dressed myself And went out. having no home nor any place to go Depending on the world for something to eat & also [shelter]." Although an official investigation was held, Jones turned his ire on Andrew Doyle, the poor law inspector who ran it:

> I even asked Mr Doyle Himself at the sham or mock inquiry they Held at Pwllheli Union work house When I was not allowed to have all my witnesses brought there. It seems to me that It is useless to me to seek or ask for Mercy or justice done to me and others If I and others dare to have presumption to say that we are entitled to any mercy Or justice in this world there is but very Little of shown to us here at Pwllheli.

Angry invective, here centred on accusations of central complicity in the task of treading down the poor, is not unique to this group of writers, but it is strikingly regular. Jones did not reference law, although that does not mean he believed he had no rights under the law. Rather he spoke in terms of natural law, invoking human rights over arbitrary authority. He asked if paupers were entitled to "Justice, as human beings":

> if it is Just or reasonable of Guardians of the said Pwllheli Union workhouse to stop payment of my weekly relief and likewise of James Hughes, And Ann Owens. Because we have made our complaints Known to the poor law board at London And that we should suffer and be punished For it to the state of starvation for having the presumption to speak about any justice Or mercy As it was mentioned in Ann Owens Complaint that the women were under Heavy yoke and [cruelty] which Mr Doyle Did not very well comprehend at the Inquiry In plain speaking it is this. If the women made the least complaint to the Matron about anything not being right That the Matron would revenge on them By compelling them to do to more work than They were able for [so] to And so that they had no Time to look after their own children as they Should so I think that this is quite a hard A yoke and cruelty as ever Pharaoh King of Egypt exercised over the Children of Israel.[31]

A central lesson of our material is that petty vindictiveness often constituted a tipping point for pauper sentiments. One of these centred on work, and particularly the assignment of an onerous and even impossible task in revenge for complaining, often in the first place about work the pauper was already unable to perform. In November 1862 Thomas Swingler wrote to explain that he had been a Birmingham Incorporation workhouse inmate on numerous occasions over several preceding years. He was a mechanical draftsman until, his "eyes being weak," he entered the workhouse and then found the stone-breaking tasks impossible due to a "weakness of the loins."[32] As a result, the meat in his diet was stopped for ten days and Swingler eventually discharged himself. Before this he attended a guardians' meeting to explain his inability to do the work and to complain about the punishment he had received. Swingler's letter asked if "Her Majesty's law provides that men shall be punished for not performing that which is impossible," and he made an explicit comment that he was further punished for threatening to write to the PLB:

> since I intimated my design of writing to you they have used me still worse I am placed in a ward set apart for criminal and defamed characters but I have never dishonoured my name at present – they have done all they [can] to induce me to break the laws They have kept letters from me that was delivered at the office of the House for me – I laid my complaints before the Board of Guardians and they entered into a sham enquiry[33]

Claims to honesty, the rhetoric of being pushed to the very edge of tolerance, the breaching of established process (his letters should not be stopped; the inquiry was not in earnest), and a resentment of tyranny play out clearly here and more generally in the texts of this sort of writer. By the following week Swingler was a Birmingham workhouse inmate again, and this time he was keen that workhouse officials no longer knew of his complaints. In a nervous, and very telling, postscript to a further letter he requested that "you will not refer me to the Board of Guardians of Birmingham."[34]

Not all those who wrote or gave evidence made immediate connections between their complaints and later punishments; some process of reflection, consolidation, and very probably discussion is suggested. Joseph Brentnall of Carlton wrote three letters in the mid-1860s. The first was in May 1865, when he introduced himself as "a poor disabled boded man" who had lost the sight of one eye and was losing the sight of the second.[35] He explained that for some time he had received outdoor relief of 4s and 8lbs of bread as well as his rent paid but that the local board had reduced his relief by one shilling. Brentnall asked: "sir What is 3 shillings for free Persons to live on take 8 Pence from free shillings What is thear to live on tenpence for one tenpence for a nother and 8 Pence for another." This reduction in relief – one apparently endorsed by local magistrates – imperilled the family and he now asked if the union could be allowed to "clem" the poor to death.[36] To emphasise his point about vulnerability he claimed that no local farmer would employ "What is almost blind When they can get Plenty of men that can see to du thear Whork."[37] Thus far Brentnall's letter seems unexceptional. In response to an invitation to comment on the case, the Basford PLU claimed that although suffering from impaired vision, in all other respects he was sufficiently able-bodied to work.[38] However, the guardians also added a further comment that was to have consequences – that Brentnall's "quarrelsome disposition" meant he was unemployable.[39]

Brentnall disappears from the correspondence record until February 1866, when he wrote that the union had dismissed his appeal for outdoor relief and offered him the workhouse with his "Wife and child out to du for themselves." Dissatisfied, and by now a reluctant inmate again, Brentnall threatened to complain to the PLB but claimed that officials sought to keep pen and ink away from him, and this he considered a clear breach of due process. More than this, he wrote that the guardians had threatened to "punish all those that Write to the … poor law board" to ask for investigations into their complaints. This, he now gathered, was pointless because the Centre was complicit in allowing such tyranny: The poor "Write to London to find a friend he finds his enmey in sted of a friend because the Poor law has not got any power to interfere with the guardians and thea can du as thea like With them and put them [in] the Whork house all thear life for it." In his particular case, and having reflected, Brentnall concluded that "thea have swear venges a gainst me for Writen in 65 to the poor law board is not the poor law board to … prectet the poor in sted of geting them in to truble."

Indeed, he accused the Poor Law Board (PLB) of systematically getting paupers into "truble With a poor man Writen to them for thea har made a foot on With Written to them and troden down under foot with the gueardians." The rhetoric here is that of an incensed person. He condemned the guardians for their spite and the PLB for its complicity and for not confronting men like John Goslen, the relieving officer who had menacingly told him: "thea Would make me remer Writing to london When then thea got me in the house."[40] Brentnall revisited this theme in a third letter, which acknowledged receipt of the Centre's response to his previous one. Here, he stated that he "was sorry to see that it was the old tail over again that the poor law board has no powr to interfere." He accused the Centre of refusing, rather than being unable, to act and forcefully claimed that the refusal to give outdoor relief was based on his prior allegations that John Gaslen and Henry Smith (relieving officer and assistant relieving officer respectively) had defrauded ratepayers.[41] To be seen as quarrelsome and publicly complaining clearly entailed considerable risk for paupers, as union staff seemingly targeted particular writers so as to make a wider point and caution others.[42] The effectiveness of that caution, and a sense of the chronological reach of poor writers being punished for the act of writing, can be ascertained in a letter of February 1891 from H. Minion, who wrote to complain to the Local Government Board (LGB) about the treatment of elderly male inmates and specifically about the quality and quantity of food in the Birmingham workhouse. Minion, like many paupers before him, noted the fear of retribution which prevailed and inhibited pauper complainants:

> When the inspector comes he asks us if we have any complaints and if we are comfortable none of the paupers ever speak to him there is not one man in A Hundred that durst speak to him because there is always some of the officers of the House with him very likely they would get punished for doing so the inspector might come hear a many times and go away without knowing very little about the place I mean what is desirable for him to know.[43]

Yet Minion *was* a man in a hundred, and it is to the actions and reactions of people like this, on their own account and more widely, that we now turn.

REACTING AND RESISTING

The workhouse conditions and staff-pauper relationships emerging from the texts used so far in this chapter give weight to pessimistic readings of the New Poor Law. Yet, paupers were not powerless or lethargic in resisting and contesting either the conditions of relief or the punishment they might receive for that contestation. Our letter writers were enmeshed in a rhetorical infrastructure that included appeals to natural justice, logic, biblical exegesis, sarcasm, anger, appropriation of the voices of others, and languages of persistence and determination. They also adopted very specific strategic and rhetorical avenues. Some paupers, for example, wrote collectively as a group rather than as individuals, as we have already seen. Thus, in late March 1835 some twenty-seven inmates of the Blything Incorporation workhouse (Suffolk) complained that they were not allowed to leave the workhouse, friends were not allowed to see them without a note from the relevant parish officers, and family gifts were banned.[44] The focus of the complaint offers an interesting commentary on what workhouse inmates might have considered normal or a matter of right, but for our purposes the key thing is that a collective approach meant that no single individual could easily be punished. We can find similar instances across the spatial and chronological dimensions of the corpus, suggesting that the collective approach was a well-known backstop for the poor. In July 1849 a petition signed by sixteen inmates of the Kendal workhouse (Westmorland) complained that, contrary to central regulations, the weighing and measuring of pauper meals was not carried out and that inedible oat bread was provided.[45] In May 1860 a petition from sixteen Liverpool workhouse inmates complained that their accommodation was a cellar some ten feet below ground and that their living spaces were consequently damp and cold.[46] In March 1862 six able-bodied paupers from Carlisle complained of being set to work in the stone yard but were unable to earn any more than 7½d per day or 4½d per day and a loaf of bread which was "at times scarcely fit for use." Furthermore, the work was set at too great a measure per person and lateness was punished by being disallowed any work and thus payment.[47] For this notionally least deserving group of the poor, collective signatures made it more problematic for the authorities to identify and target ringleaders, and added weight to the force of the charge. A hybrid strategy was to adopt the style of a formal petition complete with multiple-signatures but then seek to ensure that no-one's name was at the top of a list. An example would be the thirty-one male inmates of the Chelsea workhouse (Middlesex) writing to the Centre in March 1871 complaining about loss of liberty, and who (see figure 10.1) appended their signatures as a round-robin.[48]

A second strategy, and one associated with piercing rhetorical, legal, and procedural precision on the failings of workhouse regimes, was the collective but anonymous petition. These once again occur across the spatial and chronological divisions of the corpus. Thus, an anonymous petition from the Faversham workhouse (Kent) in 1851 complained that new male entrants were being ordered not to a probationary ward until seen by a medical officer as the regulations specified, but to areas designated for able-bodied paupers. This petition also detailed a further set of complaints, including: the master omitting roll calls; that not enough soap was supplied; that the seats in the dining area were never cleaned; and that the master and matron provided their personal visitors with workhouse supplies – all failings that broke central or local regulations. The complainants, unwilling to put their names to such accusations, signed the document from "the whole of the able bodied men." The writer(s) also asserted (in common with others confronting punishments) that: "what we have here stated are facts which we can give our affidavits if required" – clearly an invitation to the PLB to undertake an official investigation.[49] Similarly, in 1852 an anonymous text from the Plomesgate workhouse (Suffolk) protested that (amongst other failings) the master would not allow paupers to attend the local chapel. The letter was signed: "the inmates of the union House."[50] The fact that paupers were simultaneously writing openly as individuals about the same issues is indicative of the complex rhetorical and strategic world of the poor. It also seems likely that the Plomesgate writers had been aware that the need to ensure opportunities for religious devotion by the workhouse poor was a live issue in public debate (see chapter 3) at about the time they were writing.[51]

In turn, those who were (or feared being) punished for complaining were particularly alive to, and willing to draw on, the power of public opinion. We see this keenly played out in an anonymous 1855 petition from Bradford

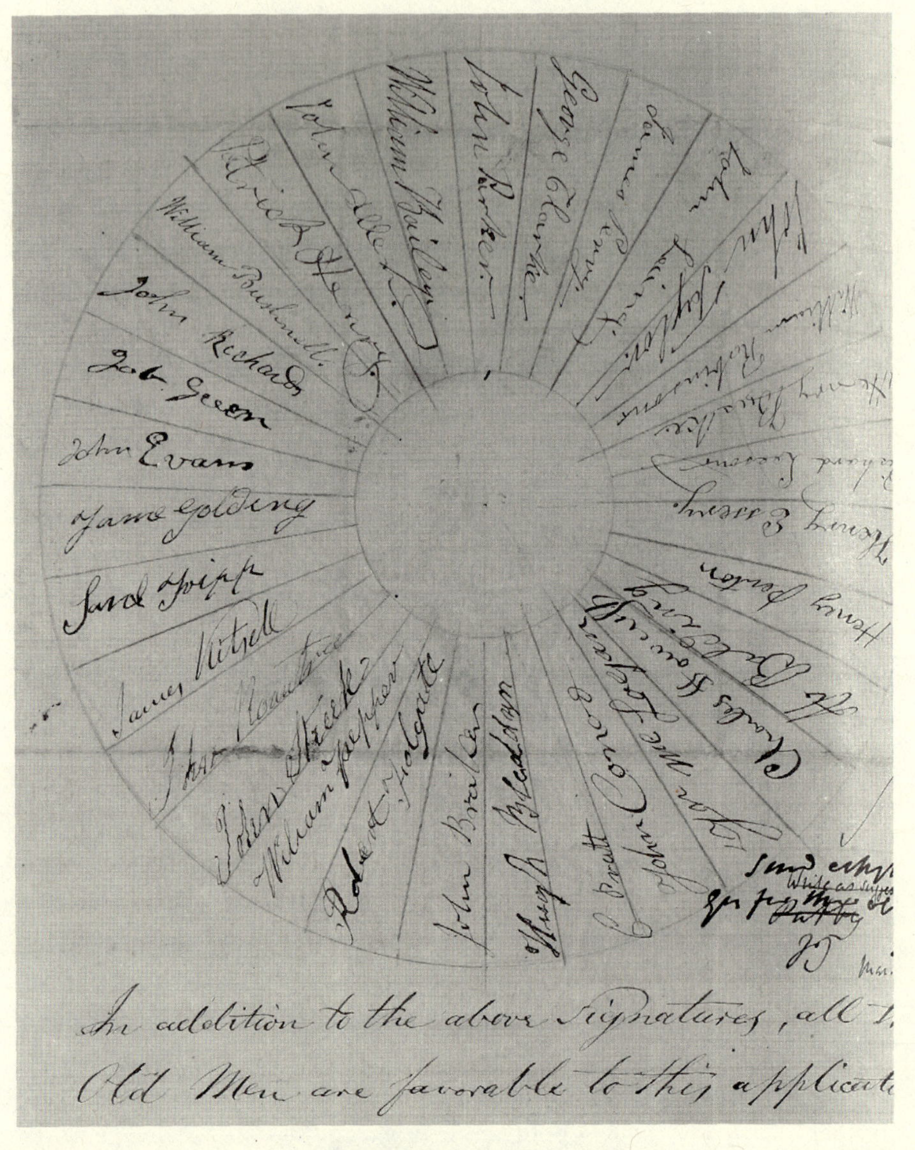

In addition to the above signatures, all t
Old Men are favorable to this applicati

10.1 Chelsea workhouse petition, 1871
Source: TNA: MH12/6996, 12662/1871.

which disputed reports carried in both the *Leeds Mercury* and the *Leeds Times and Intelligencer*. These reports had stated that "the [labour] test Men of Bradford Union had been Admonished and Stopped a Days Relief for insubordination." The anonymous writers protested that, contrary to the reports, they had not refused to work nor broken hammer shafts in consequence of being deducted a day's relief, but had "Earnestly appealed to the Gaffer to intercede with the Guardians to Allow us to Work inside," the weather being cold and the earth they were set to dig being frozen. The petition, as we saw in chapter 2, was signed under the wonderfully named collective, "the truth Loving test men of Bradford Union," a phrase that conveyed a clear rhetorical answer to accusations in the original newspaper articles that such men lacked moral probity and had scant regard for due process.[52] A further rhetorical feature of this sort of complaint was the accusation or inference of dishonesty on the part of those (guardians and officials) who were in charge of punishment regimes, often as a way of obtaining a central inquiry that might expose a wider range of grievances and abuses. By way of example, an anonymous petition, signed "From Inmates," was sent from the Aysgarth Poor Law Union (PLU) in Yorkshire to the LGB in October 1895. It accused local officials of using the workhouse as a site to lodge men who worked locally. The issue of food was raised and the writer(s) complained that, since a visit by a poor law inspector, the quality of their meals had deteriorated and that the master kept a number of chickens and ducks at the workhouse fed in part from the stewed meat that the paupers felt they should have had. Moreover: "The hens eggs are for making money on, not for the use of the house, i think it wants a stop putting on it." The text ended with the postscript that the master "deserves Removing altogether, he is what i call a Robber."[53] The fact that this letter was supposedly composed by a collective but written in the first person throughout, once again demonstrates the complex strategies used by the poor, both to emphasise their complaints and to protect themselves from being singled out as "troublemakers."

However, not all grievances were of a generalised nature and thus suitable to be expressed by a collective. A third strategy was thus to anticipate an angry response to correspondence with the Centre but seek to blunt its impact in terms of punishment by enjoining secrecy or highlighting practices so egregious that an inquiry would be necessary before the guardians had time to react, as we saw in the case of Thomas Swingler from Birmingham above. Similarly, William Waite from Bradford-on-Avon complained in 1848 that his relief was inadequate. His postscript read: "Please not mention my name if you write To our union Least they Should stop what Little I have from them."[54] Other individual writers simply wrote anonymous letters in the hope that their grievances would be investigated and that the local authority would not be able to trace the complaint back to them. An example of this was the Berwick pauper who in 1842 complained:

> I have a little Boy only eight years old has been Cruelly beate by the Master and is Still very bad and another sister was drove from the house and Struck by the Master and when I Complained to the guardians they only laughed at me I hope you will order the Case to be investigated as I have no other place to apply to not knowhing the assistant Commisioners name or address.[55]

The beating of children was a contentious topic at this date and there can be little doubt that the author, although anonymous, knew this and felt that it might spur the Centre to action.

A sense that officials were offending public decency and morals might also be a way of heading off punishment for writing. This is demonstrated in an anonymous 1846 letter signed "A Fellow Sympathizer" and sent from Abercarn (Monmouthshire) on behalf of Thomas Baun, who was described as a poor man:

> out of work, his wife is confined to her bed, & a little child, 3 weeks old, is now lying a corpse at her bed-side. He has no hope of getting employment here, he cannot seek it elsewhere, because there is no one to attend to his dying wife, & two little helpless children.

Three weeks earlier Baun's pregnant wife had been taken to Newport (ten miles away) to attend a guardians' meeting there. Having failed to get an order of admittance to the workhouse she was returned to Abercarn the following Saturday where her baby was delivered the next morning. The difficulty in securing relief was linked to their non-resident status – they lived in the Newport PLU but her settlement, derived from marriage, was that of her husband in Langtree (Torrington PLU, Devon). Nonetheless officials had clearly abrogated their moral and legal responsibilities. The writer claimed that:

> This is the saddest case of distress that ever existed in our little village … If therefore your honours would be pleased to attend to this distressing case in the best & earliest manner possible, you would be relieving a family which must otherwise die from starvation.[56]

As far as Baun was concerned, he had done everything required of a husband, and the fact that a child's corpse reportedly lay unburied demanded an official inquiry.

Occasionally we find that the Centre was so disturbed by allegations of cruelty or misbehaviour, and was so alive to the possibility of local retribution, that it tacitly approved of, and even imposed, a level of anonymity itself. Thus, in June 1878, a petition was sent in the name of eleven female paupers from Poplar workhouse to ask:

> wether it is right or decent for a male officer to drag or carry by Brutal force a female that female not one month out of her Accouchment while there are 5 or 6 female officers that could do that duty it states on the Regulations respecting disorderly & refractory paupers that no Woman pregnant or suckling a child shall be punished by alteration of diet or by confinement unless the Medical officer shall have previously certified in Writing that no injury to the Health of such Pauper is reasonably to be apprehended from the proposed punishment yet in the face of these regulations which are hung up in our Wards for the instruction of us for the dreadful offence of being found in possession of 2 loaves of bread 50zs each which was Kept for the purpose of feeding her infant this woman because she refused to continue her task of work the child was attempted to be taken from her by main force the male officers held the woman while the Matron dragged at the Child.

The writers alleged that the male officer, seeing that the woman was not going to let go of the child, grabbed her by the neck "carrying or rather dragg[ing] the Woman & Child until the Woman was black in the face." The petitioner(s) claimed the "system of Garot[ting]" was an oft-used tactic by this male officer and alleged that if this method was not stopped it would only be a matter of time before someone was killed. Although the woman in question was "carrying the marks of the ill usage she received at the hands of this Male Offi[cer]," a constable was summoned and the pauper was charged with an unspecified offence and taken before a magistrate. Despite the fact that the petition was apparently sent by a collective of paupers, the eleven names (along with the main body of the text) were all signed in the same hand and the writer lapsed into the first person, lamenting that "the Woman had undergone the most brutal treatment that it has been my lot to witness," and stating that what she was charged with "remains a mystery to me." Nonetheless, despite these anomalies the Centre considered the accusations to be so serious – alleging as they did that workhouse officers had breached law, regulation, order, the standards of manhood, and the expectations of just punishment and efficient administration – that they launched an inquiry after deciding that "the document be treated as anonymous."[57]

Finally, writers who were aware that they might be punished for the act of writing sought to rhetoricise a sense of urgency and threat as a means of stirring the Centre to pre-emptive action. Thus, an anonymous letter from the Cardiff PLU in October 1855 complained that the poor suffered in "extreme for the want of what is allowed them. They worst served than the Transports & poor Creatures, unless they are sworn they are afraid to speak." This implicit call for an inquiry, and the related referential mode of workhouse paupers being treated worse than criminal prisoners, is familiar from material elsewhere in our book. The writer, however, also reported collective non-literate resistance – panes of glass being broken only the week before – and now warned that, barring immediate action, the workhouse would be burned to the ground.[58] Another anonymous letter in September 1867 asked for an inspector to be sent to the Castle Ward workhouse (Northumberland) to check the quality of the food. The writer stated: "there is no one Can Eat it and there is no Remeday for it at the union. So I hope you will Come down and look after the interest of the poor human Beans that has to live opon such Rubbish," and noted the likelihood of riot if a remedy was not found.[59] These intriguing examples of how pressure could build within workhouses – how tipping points could be reached – reveal something of the fragility of workhouse governance and the dangers for union staff of punishing those who wrote to complain.

CONCLUSION

Pauper complainants who wrote to the Centre were routinely identified in their localities, as chapter 4 showed. Those who complained at guardians' meetings or provided statements during official investigations were, of course, known directly to local officials. This left individuals susceptible to retributive action and to pre-emptive attacks – their accounts might be denied and their characters besmirched in anticipation of any further enquiry. Here we have seen plenty of evidence of such retribution, including: having paupers disciplined through the criminal justice system or housed in less favourable parts of the workhouse; a variety of stopping, reducing, or otherwise changing an individual's relief; and charging the pauper with impossible work tasks which, when not achieved, could result in a variety of further officially sanctioned punishments. The complaints and issues raised in many of these texts, and the fear of persecution that they embody, paint a gloomy picture of workhouse conditions and the power of staff and guardians to impose tyranny.

Yet, it is clear that pauper writers knew, learned, and deployed a variety of strategies to avoid retributive action. They wrote directly, either providing their names in defiance of the threat or hiding their identity via anonymous texts. Such correspondence might be conveyed by an individual letter, a multi-signature document, or an ostensibly collective petition; or it might seek to convey accusations indirectly through advocate letters or witness statements. There was also considerable overlap in complainants' choice of writing method. Paupers who wrote individual letters in their own name also appeared on multi-signature petitions and at other times hid behind anonymous letters.[60] The anonymous, apparently collective, petition from the Plomesgate workhouse was sent unsigned, but in terms of the material document was seemingly written in the (several) handwritings of other previous letters.[61] Thomas Hartley, whom we met earlier in this chapter, was a long-term Kidderminster workhouse inmate who wrote five individual letters, and his name was included on two multi-named petitions between 1848 and 1863.[62] What runs clear throughout the corpus is the ingenuity of paupers and other poor people as they engaged with the Centre over immediate and long-running disputes with poor law administrators and staff, as well as occasionally with other inmates. Their written allegations are a testament to agency and willingness to engage in confrontation as they continually picked at and delegitimised the standing and power of local officials, whole local regimes, and in some cases the Central Authority. The evidence supplied by paupers themselves suggests that punishing complainants was a common and even routine process. Equally, we can be struck by the determined attempts of such writers to establish rights to fair treatment and to contest failings of process, humanity, and natural justice. We explore these matters further in chapter 11, using the lens of the experiences of perhaps the most iconic group of the deserving poor, the sick.

11

Limits to Agency? The Sick Poor

INTRODUCTION

In July 1836 Thomas Price wrote from Gwarclawdd near Aberystwyth claiming that, although in receipt of outdoor relief, it was "not half enough to maintain us & to have some Cloaths." He opened his appeal with "a true statement of my poor situation and the Cruelty of the parishioners[1] towards us poor family," as follows:

> as for myself I am very unable to subsist to myself I lost my sight in lead Meines [mines] now since 13 years and all my body was wounded at the same time I have one ~~Arm~~ harm I cannot do any thing with, My wife is ill now this 2 years ago and we expend a deal of money trying to cure her but we Cannot have any Cure for her, and One of my little Children is often fall in Fits Now this 4 years and I missto have any cure for him neither I have 5 Children all very young under Ten years of Age and we 2 are seven a large family to live upon 4s/6d week.[2]

Price's appeal was sent very early on in the new regime, and it is unsurprising that the language, rhetoric and motifs are so familiar from Old Poor Law pauper letters which systematically used sickness and disability as points of leverage.[3] Yet, the purpose of his letter was *not* to appeal for further or better medical treatment, either for himself or for his family. Rather the spectre of sickness and inability was deployed by Price as a way of establishing deservingness and entitlement to more financial assistance. He was disappointed; the Poor Law Commission (PLC) wrote back to note that they could not intervene in individual decisions, a familiar enough motif.

While much of the discussion in our book has emphasised the ways that paupers under the New Poor Law sought to influence, mitigate, moderate, or reinvent the welfare relationship through contact with the Centre, it is nonetheless self-evident that this was a relationship of unequals. To show that the English and Welsh poor had agency and that they exercised it is clearly not the same as suggesting that they were systematically in control of the nature or conditions of their welfare. This chapter therefore explores the *limits* of pauper agency under the New Poor Law. It does so by concentrating on the experiences of the largest and most vulnerable subgroup of those who came into contact with the poor law authorities in the nineteenth century (and, indeed, in any period in the history of welfare): the sick poor.[4] Illness was the single most important cause of pauperism under the English and Welsh poor laws, and by the mid-nineteenth century it was a contributory factor in the majority of relief claims.[5] For the Old Poor Law, our understanding of the experiences of the sick poor and the way that such people successfully employed rhetoric and strategies of sickness in their engagement with parochial authorities has become increasingly rich.[6] The same is not true of the New Poor Law, and this in itself would be sufficient justification for focusing on the sick here.[7] The more important reason, however, is that sick paupers and applicants are a totemic indicator of the essential sentiment of welfare after 1834 and its openness to the agency of poor people like Thomas Price.

In this context, and as chapter 1 showed, it is commonplace in the literature that at best little changed immediately after the passing of the Poor Law Amendment Act (PLAA) and at worst, the quality and quantity of medical care declined.[8] Jonathan Reinarz and Leonard Schwarz argued as recently as 2013 that, despite much variation in practice, "the New Poor Law marked a break with what had gone before, a caesura – even for medicine."[9] As we have already seen, neither the PLAA itself nor the voluminous report of the Royal Commission that preceded it, had much to say on the subject of medical relief. As Anne Crowther explained, they "paid remarkably little attention to the sick poor, since [they] were exclusively concerned with ways of discouraging the healthy poor from claiming relief." She went on to claim that the discussion of medical relief in the commissioners' report was "almost all concerned with finance – it was a matter of political economy, not public or personal health." Thus, in the early years of the New Poor Law, workhouses were neither envisaged as, nor equipped to become, receptacles of care for the sick poor, and it was even felt that the provision of good quality medical relief "might sabotage the natural and necessary responsibility of families to provide for their sick and elderly members."[10] While the PLC required each Board of Guardians to engage the services of district medical officers, initially at least there was very little concern about the calibre of those who were engaged. The normative conditions of employment strongly suggest that such men were unlikely to have been either willing or able to respond adequately to the needs of the sick poor under their charge.[11] This institutional ambivalence towards the quality of medical provision, alongside concerns about rationalising relief costs, deterring the undeserving poor, and standardising practice across the welfare landscape, adds weight to the orthodox view that gains made towards the end of the Old Poor Law in terms of the quality and availability of medical provision were quickly lost after 1834.[12]

On the other hand, chapter 1 traced a process by which the physical fabric of unions and the normative standards of medical care both rose noticeably, if unevenly, as the New Poor Law became more firmly established. Moreover, and as the example of Thomas Price illustrates, pauper (and advocate) appeals which sought to establish deservingness and entitlement on the basis of illness and disability continued to be sent to the Centre even as the new regime matured and settled into a familiar rhythm. The poor, as Peter Jones and Natalie Carter note, continued to seek out those "pockets of light in the … welfare architecture which allowed discretionary space for guardians and officials to interpret apparently rigid, centrally directed rules and regulations more favourably."[13] The question for this chapter, then, is how far the sick poor were, or could be, successful in seeking out those "pockets of light" in asserting meaningful agency. In this endeavour, it is important to make a tri-partite categorisation of the factors constraining or containing pauper agency. The first are those common to all poor and working-class people who were subject to the different hierarchies of "the State." Most notably, state power was held, exercised and defended by an administrative and elite collective, and it was well into the nineteenth century before associations, trade unions, or radical groups became systematically and continuously involved in challenging this collective power. We have, for instance, already seen in this book evidence of trade unions, trade associations, and unemployed worker collectives using individual relief cases to make wider points about the failings of New Poor Law processes from the 1860s. In this chapter we take these generic constraints as given. A second categorisation involves constraints that were common to all paupers, and might include punishment for complaining or the ability of guardians to question the character of both poor writers and advocates. We have focused on these issues in earlier chapters and revisit them lightly here. Finally, there were constraints particular to the sick poor as a group, which included, for instance, the many hierarchies of decision making about their relief which were not experienced by other groups of claimants or paupers. It is on these issues, and on pauper and advocate agency in relation to attempts at constraint and containment, that we focus here.

The chapter concentrates on two groups of writers. First, those who (like Thomas Price) contested inadequate or non-existent outdoor medical relief and/or resisted being ordered into the workhouse when sick.[14] Such appeals were numerically significant throughout the nineteenth century, but they declined in relative importance over time. By contrast, letters from our second group of writers – those who directly contested medical treatment or focused on the actions of specific officers – grew strongly in number, both absolutely and relatively. It is useful to subdivide the latter category of contestations still further into three groups: allegations of medical neglect by relieving officers, overseers, and other non-medical staff; complaints of neglect by a medical officer; and accusations of ill-treatment or neglect by nursing and auxiliary medical staff, usually within the workhouse. The last two subcategories are relatively self-explanatory. Letters alleging medical neglect on the part of non-medical staff require further elaboration, not least because the category covers two types of written contestation by sick paupers or their advocates.

The first type arose when evident, and sometimes medically certified, sickness, illness, and disability were ignored by local officials for relief purposes. This type of disregard affected both the outdoor and indoor poor. Samuel Curtis, for example, lay dangerously ill at his home in Lyme Regis (Dorset) in 1839 and his wife had obtained a certificate from a medical officer to that effect; yet when she approached the Axminster guardians for relief she "was turned off with a Gruff answer although she had come five miles of a cold rainy day and had not a dry Thread about her." John Champ, who wrote on the couple's behalf, was adamant that Curtis "now lays very ill and where it not for some charitable persons in this Town would in this have perishd for want."[15] David Bell, on the other hand, was resident in Tynemouth workhouse when he wrote in 1853 to complain of the actions of the workhouse master. Although by his own account a "young man," Bell suffered from heart disease and he included a copy of a medical certificate confirming that his condition "incapacitates him from following any laborious occupation." Yet, despite an order from the house surgeon stating that he should have meat with his evening meals, the master stopped it after only a fortnight's compliance, "for he said every body else would want it." Notwithstanding Bell's local appeals, the master continued to ignore the surgeon's order for a supplemented diet.[16] In both cases, the evidence and advice of the union's medical officer in relation to treatment for a specific medical condition was either ignored or discounted by non-medical poor law personnel.

The second type of complaint about the "medical" negligence of non-medical officers relates to the issue of work and labour. Work was acknowledged by paupers no less than by officials as being inextricably linked to payment of relief, and this relationship clearly strengthened over time.[17] However, many poor writers objected that, despite what they considered to be obvious and verifiable medical impediments to performing the work of able-bodied labourers, they were nonetheless still required to do so by local officials. We have seen the issue played out earlier in this book, but it is important to return to it here and set what the poor considered to be "abuses" into the wider context of medical relief. It is also important to emphasise the ubiquity of the complaint across our material. The letter of Joseph Beer of St Teath (Cornwall) is a good example. In 1851, he was required to do fieldwork for a local farmer in return for his outdoor relief even though "God have taken my sight from me," so that "I should perish in a open field not abel to do work sufficint to keep myself warm."[18] This category of complaint emphasises the peculiar vulnerabilities faced by sick and disabled writers after 1834, since it is clear that such circumstances would have disqualified them from certain activities or entitled them to special treatment under the Old Poor Law. That such people seem to have been thwarted by non-medical staff, or by officers who either usurped or ignored the evidence and advice of the doctors and surgeons employed to advise them, created potentially explosive situations. Moreover, the tensions between medical and non-medical staff after 1834 generated fault lines in relief administration that sometimes undermined the claims of the sick and disabled poor. As a group they retained a degree of legitimacy that others had lost, but even this was no guarantee of extended agency.

THE CORPUS

One third of our letters and petitions (pauper, poor writer, and advocate) and well over half of all witness statements had sickness, disability and/or medical welfare at their core. Much greater proportions than these contain at least a passing reference to sickness. It was the single most important reason for writing, just as it was under the Old Poor Law, and complaints, and allegations of medical negligence in particular, generate huge quantities of detailed evidence. The engagement of the sick poor with the Centre was not, however, uniform. Far more complaints and appeals (around 70 per cent) were written by men than women. More were received from urban, metropolitan, and industrial unions (around 65 per cent) than from rural or mixed unions, and this is broadly reflected in the regional spread of letters: far more were sent from London, the midlands and the north-west of England (47 per cent) than came from the rural south/south-west, sparsely populated northern counties, and Wales combined (29 per cent). Despite these variations, however, the most evident corpus-level observation is that the demographic, geographical, and typological trends reflected in letters from the sick poor match very closely those in letters received by the Centre overall. This resemblance further emphasises the practical and symbolic importance of sickness and disability in negotiations for relief.

The rhetorical and strategic construction of letters by or about the sick poor is complex at the corpus level, and this is most clearly marked in relation to our first category of appeals, those which deployed the impact of sickness and disability as a tool to establish deservingness, or directly to contest the relief decisions of local officers. Letters like that of Thomas Price find clear echoes in their Old Poor Law counterparts. Take, for example, James Wilson's, which was sent to his parish of settlement at Hulme (Lancashire) in 1831. Wilson wrote to the overseer that "my famely lies in the most desperate state," and that he had "buried my son, not 4 years old, last Tuesday." Wilson went on to explain that he had not been able to work because of ill-health, and asked the parishioners to "have a care and come to see our state with not the clothing we need," nor money to pay the rent. He concluded with a plea for the parish "not to dismiss our case … I beg your support for my famely once more" until he regained his health.[19] Both Price and Wilson's appeals are what we now understand as classic pauper letters in their strategic deployment of sickness and consequent family misfortune to leverage better treatment. In this context it is notable that the linguistic register was not obviously diluted over time even as literacy rates improved. In 1860, for example, James Caves wrote to complain that he had been denied outdoor relief by the Ampthill guardians and he opened with the familiar pre-1834 gambit that he was: "hoping you will stand my friend I have a wife and six children and I have had the rheumatics and lost the use of my limbs." Caves went on to explain that, as a result of his disability, he was "obliged to come into the Union [workhouse]," and asked "whether that is right for my wife and children to be out and I to be kept here as a prisoner against my will."[20] Although Caves received the familiar response that the Centre was by law hamstrung from intervening, that did not prevent him writing again in a similar vein two weeks later.[21] As Steven King has noted elsewhere, "poor relief in general *and medical welfare in particular* were negotiable" under the Old Poor Law, and it is clear from our corpus that the sick poor and their advocates felt that this was, and should be, the case under the New Poor Law as well.[22]

These are important observations but, as Jones and Carter have noted, paupers, poor applicants, and advocates could not ignore the fact that they were up against a body, the Central Authority, which was essentially unfavourable to such appeals in a way that parish officers often were not.[23] This was, as chapter 4 demonstrated, partly a reflection of legal reality: they *were*, to an extent, constrained by law from intervening in individual relief cases. Nonetheless, and as we have seen, the Centre usually sent details of each complaint back to the relevant Board of Guardians for their observations and comments, and it could well be that this in itself was enough to persuade sick and disabled letter writers that further attention might be taken of their case. As we have observed in other chapters, and as was the case under the Old Poor Law, perceptions of even the most minute "success" by poor writers and their advocates was enough to nourish further correspondence and could clearly have percolated through the widest possible community of paupers and the poor more generally.[24] Yet something *does* change over time in our corpus in terms of the presence of letters from the sick poor contesting individual relief decisions. Their number decreased from the 1840s onward, falling from 75 per cent of all letters dealing with sickness-related themes to just over 30 per cent in the period from 1870 to 1900. The most prominent decline occurred in the later period. This is not simply a function of the sampling regime for post-1871 unions, but it might reflect the beginning of the crusade against outdoor relief in the 1870s. As Elizabeth Hurren has demonstrated, even though the crusade was ostensibly aimed at restricting relief for the able-bodied poor, in practice it had a significant impact on the financing of medical aid and on the decisions made by officials in cases of sickness and disability.[25] Faced with a new harshness at both local and central level, the poor may simply have accepted that their agency had been fundamentally constrained in terms of writing to the Central Authority.

On the other hand, Hurren also shows that, while many unions took up some aspects of the crusading mentality, relatively few adopted it comprehensively, and so the decline in numbers of letters contesting individual relief decisions for the outdoor poor may also reflect other influences. Thus, it is possible to turn the argument on its head and to suggest that, post-1871, the expansion of the medical infrastructure in many areas (including hospitals, asylums, free doctoring, charities, and subscription schemes) took some of the sick poor beyond the ambit of the poor law. Similarly, the emergence of a new narrative of wider citizenship from the 1870s might be expected to have created a broadly accepted view that medical relief (inside and particularly outside the workhouse) was a necessity and thus that there was less to contest.[26] Certainly many of those who supported the poor in crusading areas believed this was and should be the case. Equally, and as Martin Gorsky and Sally Sheard have observed, the rapid expansion of the fabric and practice of poor law medical care in the later nineteenth century may have made the sick less resistant to entering the workhouse for that particular purpose.[27]

Whatever the reason for the decline of relief appeals with sickness and disability at their core, it is clear that they were overtaken in numerical and operational importance by complaints about medical negligence on the part of union officials. This is a phenomenon that forms the core of Kim Price's recent monograph; but our approach – and to an extent our findings – are quite different from his.[28] One major departure is that Price considers medical relief solely from the point of view of interactions between paupers and medical officers in and out of the workhouse. This is also the subject of the analysis below.[29] But in the following section we expand the boundaries of authority and influence to include interactions between sick and disabled paupers and non-medical personnel, demonstrating at length (and for the first time) that this was an area of medical relief that could – and did – have a profound impact on the care and welfare of many of the most vulnerable paupers in the nineteenth century.

CONTESTING THE CHAIN OF COMMAND

One result (intended or otherwise) of the piecemeal approach to the welfare of the sick under the New Poor Law was that overworked, underpaid, and (at the beginning, at least) underqualified medical staff were at times placed in direct opposition to the imperatives of Boards of Guardians and other non-medical officials. If the primary purpose of law and practice under the new regime was to cut costs and deter the undeserving, then it is easy to see how the exceptional needs of the sick and disabled could fall victim to the "rationalising" tendencies of local and national administrators.[30] As we have seen, relieving officers were responsible for day-to-day decisions about relief allocations (including for the sick and disabled), only referring cases to the guardians if problems or issues arose, including complaints about those decisions by paupers. Episodically across our corpus, however, paupers felt that they were obstructed by relieving officers from addressing the guardians even under these circumstances. In a very real sense, those officers acted as gatekeepers between sick paupers and medical relief, and made crucial decisions about access to medical welfare purely on the basis of their own, non-professional, judgement. This is not, of course, a new observation, but it does explain the many letters in our corpus where writers sought to contest medical neglect by non-medical union staff.[31]

The contestation (and the conflicts of interest that generated it) is clearly and colourfully visible in letters like that of Patrick McGarry, whom we initially encountered in chapter 4. He first wrote in December 1859, complaining about the actions of Alfred Boulton, one of the relieving officers for Wolstanton and Burslem poor law union (PLU). McGarry noted that his wages were "14 shillings a week when I work full time some weeks less and perhaps some weeks none according to the weather." Prior to his letter, the town had been "very much infected with scarlet fever, measels, hooping co and throat fever," and McGarry had "got my share of it all." Consequently, "this last nine months I cannot say that I was free from some one of my family sick." He applied several times to Boulton for a medical order, claiming that he was unable to pay the fee himself, but was refused each time. Later, with two of the children sick from scarlet fever, McGarry's wife pleaded for medical attendance, but again Boulton refused, telling her "to be of out to the office or else he would very soon put her out." A few days later, with three children now sick, she went back again, and this time Boulton "spoke roug[h]er than ever he would not let her Stand in the office [and] ordered her off."[32] In her desperation, McGarry's wife approached Dr Goddard, the medical officer, directly. Initially Goddard confirmed that he could not attend the family without a medical order. Finally, however, he relented and visited the family without the relieving officer's sanction and therefore was not eligible for payment. In his letter, McGarry contrasted the behaviour of Boulton with that of Dr Goddard, writing: "Mr. Gadard the parash doctor behave a kind gentleman to me he came to See [the children] and Sent some medison for them." Even though Goddard told them "it was not his duty to attend without a note [he] done me a great deal of Kindness I shall be forever thankful to him he is a kind Gentleman [and] I hope he shall have a reward for his Kindness to the poor." All the children recovered on this occasion but McGarry's letter consciously highlighted the gulf between the doctor's "Kindness" and what he describes elsewhere as Boulton's "unmerciful" behaviour towards him and his family.[33] This was not, however, the end of the McGarry family's troubles. Shortly after this first bout of sickness another of the children contracted scarlet fever, and this time it was accompanied by measles. Again Mrs McGarry went to Boulton for a medical order and yet again she was rebuffed. This time, however, the child died. Having insufficient funds for burial she approached Boulton one final time to ask for a coffin, only to be told that "if she was not able to berry her Child the Child should be left without berrying."[34]

The McGarry family's treatment at the hands of the relieving officer highlights fault lines in the administration of relief that both generated complaints of neglect and locate some of the boundaries of agency. In particular, Boulton made a number of qualitative decisions concerning McGarry's case without consulting the medical officer, and even despite the fact that Goddard's unpaid attendance showed the seriousness of the family's plight. It becomes clear in later correspondence to the Poor Law Board (PLB), and in evidence to a subsequent inquiry, that the reason for Boulton's treatment of the McGarrys was that he believed they should pay for medical attendance themselves. As we have seen, McGarry was intermittently employed during his family's illness; but he was adamant that his wages were insufficient to pay the doctor's fees, a familiar enough claim by the sick poor under the Old Poor Law as well. At one stage, Boulton tacitly admitted that he was fully aware of McGarry's situation, acknowledging that he had received a letter from McGarry's employer stating that work was slack and giving a good character reference.[35] Nonetheless, Boulton retained the complete confidence of the guardians, whose chairman heaped praise on his diligence and attention to duty.[36] More important, the Centre itself found little to criticise in this conduct, merely stating that Boulton should be careful in future to pass on such cases for the consideration of the guardians.[37] The fact that Boulton had not enquired fully into McGarry's circumstances before repeatedly making the decision to refuse medical relief – or, perhaps more strikingly, to assist with the burial of the dead child – was not considered sufficiently serious to warrant further action.[38]

What really stands out in McGarry's case is the *degree* to which the sick and disabled poor were subject to the decision-making (and potential discrimination) of non-medical personnel. On only one occasion was the family successful in obtaining a medical order for a sick child but the reason they succeeded on this occasion was that, unusually, Boulton was absent when McGarry went to see him. He made his request instead to George Clayton, another relieving officer, who immediately agreed to it.[39] Had Boulton been present it is likely McGarry would have been unsuccessful that time as well. The problem for the sick and disabled poor post-1834 was that the chain of command in medical matters devolved from guardians down to the paid (but unqualified) administrators and only then on to medical officers and workhouse surgeons. Hence, it was lay officers who controlled not only the purse strings but also the critical decisions about who was or was not in need of, or entitled to, medical relief. This line of command was often bitterly resented by doctors themselves and, although they gained a voice from the 1860s with the formation of the Poor Law Medical Officers' Association, it was relieving officers who "continued to have discretion over calling a doctor for the outdoor poor, and indoor medical officers controlled only those infirmaries which were completely separate from the workhouse."[40] Practitioner complaints about this appear in our corpus but they did not generally find their way to the Central Authority, quite possibly because of the invidious and subordinate position that practitioners occupied.[41] This contrasts sharply with the large number of letters from paupers and their advocates highlighting the tensions between medical and non-medical personnel and the impact these tensions had on their care. As we argued in chapter 1, individual personalities (poor applicant, pauper, staff, doctors, and guardian) mattered for how people navigated the poor law in any particular union and the cross-currents of power, information, and behaviour that they had to negotiate. In this context, as with the McGarry family, agency could be brutally curtailed. On the other hand, such limits could also be transient – dependent on the presence or absence of one man in this case – and situational, as we shall consider further below.

MEDICAL OFFICERS AND THE "EVERYDAY TRAGEDIES" OF THE NEW POOR LAW

Even though sick paupers, their advocates, witnesses, and poor writers in general often complained about the treatment they received from non-medical personnel, they were just as vehement in contesting the decisions and practices of medical officers themselves. Many commentators have observed that unions struggled to attract practitioners of the highest calibre, or those who were totally committed to their duties.[42] Indeed, it was not until 1842 that the Centre clarified minimum qualifications for the post. Even thereafter doctors may have been discouraged, given that they "had to reconcile the obligations of their profession with the Poor Law's intention of deterring paupers from seeking relief."[43] Conditions of employment were also problematic as we have already implied above; medical districts were often so large and populous that it was physically impossible for even the most conscientious officer to do his job properly.[44] The fact that they were expected to supply all medicines from notoriously low salaries meant that most could only afford to do the job in tandem with private practice, something which, according to contemporaries' no less than later historians, created an essential conflict of interest.[45] It thus comes as no surprise that the largest category of complaints from the sick and disabled poor in our sample relate to allegations of neglect by medical officers.

In her work on New Poor Law scandals, Samantha Shave has explored the mechanisms by which locally ignominious episodes involving medical officers and ill-treatment could escalate with the oxygen of publicity into events of national importance.[46] However, she also acknowledged that the "everyday tragedies" of neglect and mistreatment were more representative than the current emphasis on "scandals" would suggest.[47] Just how common they were is a question that has not been fully explored. In part, this is due to the fact that much of the literature has concentrated on the early years of the New Poor Law and the necessity of the anti–New Poor Law movement strategically foregrounding accounts of abuse and poor workhouse conditions through the sympathetic organs of the press.[48] The exception to this rule is Kim Price's work on medical negligence.[49] Price tackles the issue head-on; but in general he does so from the perspective of medical personnel themselves and the limitations placed upon them by the structural conditions mentioned above. While the voices of the poor and their advocates are audible in his study, they are not loud, and the main thrust of his work leads to the conclusion that pauper complaints were "seen but not heard"; that is, complaints tended to be used by the Centre to deflect attention away from systemic failings in medical relief and onto the failings of individual practitioners rather than being considered on their own merits.[50] There is much to applaud in Price's work, and we would certainly agree that poor writers often – and more vociferously than he allowed – contested local attitudes and practices. However, when we listen more attentively to the voices of the poor and their advocates, it becomes abundantly clear that there were marked variations in practice across the landscape of the New Poor Law and that, despite the failures of some aspects of central policy, the quality and attentiveness of some individual doctors and nurses could and did make a huge difference to the daily care of the sick poor within and between unions.

Similarly, although the evidence we present below does somewhat bear out Price's contention that the crusade against outdoor relief had a negative impact on the care of the sick poor, it also challenges his view that the crusade years constituted a defining moment. In our sample, the years after 1870 saw merely the extension of an upward curve of medical complaints which began in the 1840s and continued more or less consistently for the rest of the century. In recent work, Peter Jones and Steven King have also used the British Library online newspaper database to demonstrate that local instances of cruelty, neglect, and maladministration (only sometimes described in the press as "workhouse scandals") were more common in the final decades of the nineteenth century than they were in the 1830s and 1840s.[51] Up to now, the relative invisibility of pauper efforts to contest the attitudes and decisions of medical officers has reflected the nature of the records; it was all but impossible to measure the extent of these events across the whole landscape of the New Poor Law simply because of the scale of the archive. Yet the preponderance of "everyday tragedies" in our corpus is clear. Allegations of neglect and mistreatment by medical officers *and* their assistants pervade the material and there is hardly a union that was not subject to them. This was not simply a function of the early zealotry of guardians following the passing of the original legislation, or of the crack-down of the crusade years. Rather, it was consistent; although the upward curve in the relative abundance (and, therefore, the operational importance) of such complaints suggests that the sick poor became gradually more adept at negotiating the various structures which regulated their lives. Our findings thus add a layer of complexity that only a large-scale study such as this can identify.

Mostly, these allegations originated in specific cases where an individual's care was thought to have been inadequate. Sometimes they hinted at other similar cases and even of widespread neglect.[52] Thus, in February 1853 John Laurence of Elton (Northamptonshire) wrote to complain that a "poor woman in this place under the charge of the medical officer of the district Mr Webster," was then in a "very dangerous state" and "apparently suffering from neglect and improper treatment." Laurence was an overseer of the poor under the Old Poor Law and, having been alerted to the woman's case by the rector and another local dignitary, felt compelled to act: "I have no predilections in the matter," he wrote, "but where as in this case human life was perilled I feel bound to sink all other considerations and to come forward in the interests of the poor." Tellingly, Laurence concluded that local paupers were "very much at the mercy of their medical officer … in whom the Board of Guardians as well as the Poor ought to have perfect confidence."[53] He did not, however, elaborate on this veiled accusation.

If Laurence was rather coy in suggesting that the medical officer was negligent, others were much more direct. At Newport (Monmouthshire) local ratepayers and paupers consistently complained for almost fifteen years about the neglectful attitude of Jehoida Brewer, the medical officer for the Central District. The complaints began in 1851 with a letter from a Mr Jenkins, who signed himself "a friend to the poor" and warned the PLB that that Brewer "allows the poor to be attended by his apprentice a boy of about 19 years of age, much to the horror of the poor Creatures." He continued that the young assistant was sent to attend a woman in labour with her first child and was later heard to "[speak] openly in the town of what occurred." The boy, wrote Jenkins, was "not only young, but ignorant 3 years back he was surgery & errand boy."[54] As a result of his complaint, the PLB promised "consideration" of the allegations, and wrote to Brewer for his side of the story. However, the doctor cannot have been too severely dealt with, because he was the subject of a not dissimilar accusation a few years later. In October 1855 a local lawyer wrote on behalf of John Jones, a dockside labourer. Jones had been working on board ship when he fell into the hold injuring his shoulder. Having obtained a medical order from the relieving officer, he went to Brewer's surgery, but the doctor was not in attendance and Jones was treated by his assistant, Mr Popplewell. This assistant examined the injury and gave Jones medicine for what he later wrote on the medical certificate was a "badly bruised shoulder." The shoulder did not heal and Jones visited the surgery several times over the next month in great pain. Each time, he was attended by Popplewell as Brewer himself was always absent, and the writer of the letter stated that "Mr Brewer never once saw Jones." Unable to use his arm, and in considerable discomfort, Jones eventually went to the surgeon at the Nantyglo Iron Works where he had formerly worked, who "immediately discovered it to be a dislocation and reduced it ~~immediately~~ accordingly, but of course causing intense pain & fever."[55] The reduction process was graphically described by Jones and involved the surgeon at the ironworks and two burly assistants, a chair, a strap, two wooden blocks and a great deal of pulling and pushing. Unsurprisingly, Jones fell into a dead faint during the procedure, and even afterwards was unable to regain the full strength or movement of his arm.[56] The real issue for Jones, just as it had been for Jenkins four years earlier, was that the medical officer had neglected his duties through non-attendance and by delegating his care to an unqualified assistant. Yet despite this clear evidence, and the fact that Brewer was ordered to pay £15 in compensation and costs at a court hearing brought privately by Jones the following year, the guardians continued to back their medical officer.[57] More telling was the Centre's response to Jones's ongoing complaints. In an annotation to his second letter it was noted that "[t]he P.L.B. can have no more to do with the complaint against Mr. Brewer which they have already inquired into."[58]

Having retained the confidence of the guardians and the PLB, Brewer continued as medical officer long after Jones's case was completed. Nonetheless, complaints continued to be made about his negligent attitude. In 1860 Joseph Akeroyd, a Catholic priest, sent two letters containing further allegations to illustrate the fact that "Mr Jehoida Brewer does not attend paupers as he ought," noting: "He does not visit one in fifty himself. He leaves of late the whole of it nearly to his sons," neither of whom were qualified practitioners, "& one of them a boy under twenty." In his first letter, Akeroyd pointed out that "Brewer has several times been reported to the Guardians for the same thing." In his second, he suggested that "Mr Brewer wants to keep the situation for his Son – who if report speaks true has tried to pass his examination two or three times without success."[59] Despite almost a decade of allegations of neglect and the inappropriate delegation of his duties, Jehoida Brewer continued as a medical officer for at least another five years.[60] No specific reason was given as to why he was so eager to hand over his union duties to unqualified assistants, and of course he strenuously denied the accusations. As Price suggests, structural factors such as low wages, long hours, and excessive patient numbers may have been influential in this kind of conduct.[61] For example, in March 1856 Dr Davidson of the Basford PLU was said to have told the wife of a severely ill pauper that he would not attend, despite a medical order from the relieving officer because "he had so little for his services."[62] In January 1864 Dr Armstrong refused to attend a woman in Manchester during her confinement; he was far too busy to deal with midwifery cases, and besides his "appointment [with the Union] was a great disadvantage to his private practice."[63] On occasion, medical officers even used the character of sick paupers as a defence for their poor attendance. In 1860 Dr Ballenden of Upper Sedgley (Staffordshire) was said to have claimed, as a reason for not adequately attending a girl who was severely scalded, that "the [mother] was of immoral character, and therefore not to be believed." But, as happened with other, similar complaints, Ballenden also stated that he had not "been served with an order to attend upon the girl" at the time he was called, despite evidence that it was an emergency, and he "therefore was not legally bound." What seems to have been a deeply neglectful attitude towards the girl was compounded by the familiar accusation that: "it is notorious that since the appointment of Dr

Ballenden [as] Surgeon to this Parish, the sick Poor have been almost entirely consigned to the care of his Apprentices."[64]

Clearly, Jehoida Brewer of Newport was far from alone in his inadequate attendance on the poor. Yet, there are sufficient examples of letters from medical officers themselves complaining about specific instances of neglect – including complaints directed at fellow doctors – to suggest that, while failures of care were persistent and widespread, the overall picture was more complex than we might initially think, with instances of *both* neglect and care in the corpus. For example, when Henry Longstaff, a union surgeon at Ilkeston (Derbyshire), complained that a labourer's wife had been "found flooding" in labour without medical attendance, he not only stated, "never will I permit a case so shameful and disgraceful to be passed over in silence," but he expressed great surprise that the situation had arisen in the first place, because, "I have ever found the most prompt assistance from the Board of Guardians to cases requiring their Attention."[65] He clearly felt the fault lay with an individual officer rather than with the regime more generally. Moreover, it is also clear from our sample that complaints tended to cluster around particular unions at specific times, often in relation to the actions (or inaction) of one or more medical officers. Thus, at Bethnal Green a series of complaints alleging neglect by Dr Massingham were received by the PLB between 1863 and 1870, and these resulted in several letters to local newspapers and a number of internal inquiries.[66] But, on examining the full body of letters from Bethnal Green, it becomes clear that Massingham's neglect was only one aspect of a wider systematic problem with the management of the union and its workhouse. Over the same period, the workhouse master and matron (his daughter) were dismissed for misconduct, a porter was forced to resign, and two other medical officers – Drs Adams and Defriez – were also charged with neglect.[67] In fact, Bethnal Green PLU became something of a by-word for cruelty and mismanagement at this time, and the situation improved only after concerted intervention by the PLB.[68]

Overall, complaints by paupers, poor applicants, and their advocates of non-attendance on the part of medical officers, or of inappropriate delegation of duties to unqualified assistants, were overwhelmingly made in relation to the outdoor poor. This is not, however, to say that such contestation was absent within the walls of the workhouse. For instance, in 1868 the house surgeon of Tynemouth was accused of irregularity in his ward visits, and of non-attendance to newly admitted paupers which resulted in the spread of diseases that they brought in with them. He was also condemned for his imperious manner when he did attend: "[H]e would make us believe that he is something like Christ when he was on Earth," wrote an anonymous pauper: "The look of him should be sufficient to cure all diseases."[69] While colourful, however, there are only a handful of such cases and the concentration of narrative activity amongst the outdoor poor is perhaps best explained by the fact that non-attendance beyond the workhouse was far less easy to detect than it would have been within an institution. In turn, the letters and witness statements of the outdoor sick poor in this context strike at the heart of the issue of pauper agency and its limitations. The fact is that, regardless of the official line from the Centre and notwithstanding the lip service guardians paid to the treatment of the sick poor, the outdoor poor could find themselves at the mercy of hard-pressed, bad, or corner-cutting doctors. This situation was compounded by the desire of some ratepayers to keep costs low, but it was also a function of the original New Poor Law legislation. For all that the poor and their advocates attempted to take matters into their own hands by engaging with the commissioners through the proper channels, in the end they were up against a system which had not been established with the sick in mind. When George Jennings of Burford (Oxfordshire) accused a medical officer of failing to attend to the acute illness of John Pearn, he noted: "Mr Cheatle holds … sixteen parishes comprising an acreage of about 28,000 with a population of about 7,000," and he asked: "Is this legal?" Anticipating a stonewalling answer, he proceeded to observe: "it is utterly impossible under such circumstances for him … with his private practice to attend to pauper patients, to whom prompt attention is absolutely needed."[70] By 1860, when this letter was sent, it is very unlikely Jennings was telling the PLB anything it did not already know.

Melding such small-scale but recurrent accusations of medical neglect by professionals with larger scale and more well-known medical scandals under the New Poor Law, we can thus see many obvious constraints on agency. Our writers and their advocates generally complained retrospectively, itself evidence that, too regularly, medicine was (or was not) "done" to people inside and outside the workhouse. And surprisingly few of the medical officers implicated in these cases were disciplined or suffered sanction that kept them out of poor law business, either in the union where they were accused or somewhere else. The sick poor were, in other words, somewhat at the mercy both of non-medical staff and (even more so) of negligent medical men themselves. The fact that we see instances of neglect in almost every union can be read as suggesting that this situation was about more than just personality; that the sick poor were subject to much deeper failings. The contrast with the Old Poor Law is striking: pre-1834 most of those who wrote did so in order to shape their present or future engagement with the doctor rather than to complain retrospectively. Yet, if such instances show the limits of agency even for this totemic group, we also need to exercise caution. As we mention above (and as we have emphasised at times throughout this book) an increase in the numbers of complaints, inquiries, and medical "scandals" over time is not, in itself, necessarily an indication that things were getting worse, though they might have been. It could (and, as Jones and Carter have argued elsewhere, probably did) also indicate that, as the regime matured, the poor themselves came to understand that avenues were available for them to seek redress. Indeed, it is our contention that, in seeking out these "pockets of light" they were active in opening up those avenues themselves.[71] There is also no doubt, as the above discussion makes clear, that particular unions at particular times generated disproportionate numbers of complaints and inquiries, suggesting that medical "scandals," as well as the "everyday tragedies" of neglect, were not necessarily endemic, and were often the function of local mismanagement and maladministration. Moreover, the fact that the poor and their advocates *did* complain about this type of medical neglect is important in itself. Among other things, it suggests that such people knew what "decent" medical treatment should look like, that they tried to contest failings at the time, and (in a clear expression of agency) sought redress after the fact for what they could not control. Even during the experiences that they subsequently report, our writers elaborated and deployed small acts of resistance – turning up again and again, defying the rules and going directly to a doctor, seeking redress from other union officers – which have much in common with the way that James Scott thinks about the structuring, content, and deployment of everyday agency.[72] This is even truer for our third sub-category of medical neglect, that of workhouse nursing staff. Indeed, as we shall see, a few writers saved their most venomous commentaries for staff who had a more liminal place in the medical infrastructure of the New Poor Law.

THE LONG SHADOW OF SARAH GAMP: PAUPER NURSES AND CARERS IN THE WORKHOUSE

It is axiomatic that the bulk of the institutional care of the sick and disabled always fell on the shoulders of nursing and auxiliary staff. But for much of the period from 1834 until at least the early 1870s, the great majority of nursing and care work within the workhouse was done by untrained pauper inmates.[73] They were very often singled out for the job not because of any prior experience (though surprising numbers did have that) or because of their sensitivity to the needs of the sick, but because they were simply able or willing to take on what was a thankless, unremunerated role.[74] For some welfare historians this situation inevitably created "a general standard of care that was far below the level expected for the time," given wider and sustained attempts to professionalise institutional and domiciliary nursing.[75] Contemporaries also ensured that pauper nursing became and remained a subject of considerable controversy throughout the whole of the nineteenth century.[76] A large part of the efforts of reformers and campaigners for better treatment of the sick poor focused on the need for the professionalisation of nurse training and for the employment of paid staff in workhouses to combat the reign of pauper nurses who were, according to reformers, "too old, too weak, and too drunken" to do the job properly.[77] Indeed, being drunk on duty was one of the key complaints against pauper nurses, which is unsurprising given that they were in a position to appropriate the wine, beer, and spirits routinely prescribed by medical officers. For example, a letter from Bethnal Green accused the pauper nurses of watering down the beer and wine intended for the patients and drinking the rest themselves.[78] But despite concerted high-profile campaigns from the 1860s onwards, it took another thirty years for the Local Government Board to finally ban the use of unpaid nursing staff in workhouses, and even then a lack of suitably qualified candidates prevented the final demise of the much-maligned amateur nurse, made infamous by the character of Sarah Gamp in Dickens's *Martin Chuzzlewit*, until after the First World War.[79] This is not to say, of course, that there was no progress. Unions like Bolton (Lancashire), Whitechapel (Middlesex), Towcester (Northamptonshire), and especially Liverpool made early inroads into the balance of paid/trained versus pauper nurses, and certainly by the 1870s the majority of unions had begun to follow suit. External Workhouse Visiting Committees and (subsequently) female poor law guardians also did much to reform practice in this area.[80] And of course we should be cautious about assuming that all pauper nurses were of the low quality often assigned to them in the historiography. The boundaries between the workhouse infirmary and the healing women, female midwives, and domestic nurses who continued to play an important role in wider working-class communities were fluid, and many of the latter group ended up as inmates at one point or another.[81]

Nonetheless, our sample does contain complaints by or for the sick poor about *ad hoc* and untrained attendance. Stories of mistreatment by nurses and auxiliaries involved levels of cruelty that rivalled – and sometimes surpassed – any of those laid against medical men. These are only truly revealed in a systematic analysis of the poor law union correspondence because few of them resulted in formal inquiries. In 1857, for instance, Eliza France complained of the abuse and neglect of her youngest child at Kidderminster workhouse. Falling sick soon after admission, the child was put under the care of an unpaid nurse who, France alleged, beat her simply because she would not sit down when told to do so. France pleaded with the nurse not to beat the child again, and was grudgingly informed that this would be so. However (France implied), as a result of her intervention the girl later died from the nurse's malicious neglect. France alleged that her daughter was left in a "dirty filthy state" on the sick ward, and that later the nurse treated her with "powders" that the medical officer had expressly told her not to administer. Moreover, it was alleged that the nurse bathed the girl inappropriately, once again against medical advice. Finally, France claimed that the nurse vindictively took away the special allocation of wine that the doctor and matron had given her to moisten the child's lips during her final days, echoing the allegation from Bethnal Green that we have already encountered. Following the girl's death, France alleged, the nurse and another pauper assistant had treated her indifferently and even questioned whether it was worth washing the child's body in preparation for burial. On informing the master and matron of these circumstances, France was told that although it was "very bad," the nurse's behaviour could not be helped because "it seemed her Natural disposition to deal harshly in such Cases." During a subsequent altercation between the two women, France drew wider comparisons, telling the nurse: "You seem to treat me as you have treated my Children … and many more beside mine." However, in common with many allegations of medical negligence, the workhouse officials and guardians closed ranks against France and she was not permitted to go before the board to complain officially because she had not "taken her case down in writing."[82]

France's case reminds us that unpaid and unqualified paupers who were appointed to positions of privilege inevitably enjoyed a special – quite possibly protected – status within the workhouse, something that has obvious implications for those who sought to complain about their treatment or who were not part of a favoured group. There are many examples of this sort of situation in the underlying corpus, proof that the simple dichotomy (in power terms) between staff and inmates, so obvious in the literature that focuses on scandal, provides only the shallowest picture of the countercurrents of influence and animosity in workhouse life. Hence, Johanna Davis alleged that she had been systematically targeted by the nurses at Newport workhouse; they stole her food and mercilessly abused her both verbally and physically. When she was finally taken to the hospital for her injuries, the neglect continued: "[neither] the master nor mises [matron] did not come to see me [those] sixteen weeks."[83] Hence also the testimony of J.R. Onion, a campaigning guardian of Bethnal Green who gave evidence in the celebrated 1866 case against the workhouse master, Theobald Meyrick, and his daughter, that "Pauper Nurses & others [were] acting under their private & personal interest & control," and were "always ready to say & even swear falsely whatever is dictated to them by the Master, thro' fear of his Tyranny & Punishment, & for some pecuniary compensation."[84]

The potential for the complicit neglect and mistreatment of sick paupers on the part of nursing staff becomes even clearer when we remember that, for the greater part of the New Poor Law period, it was the matron of the workhouse who was in overall charge of the sick wards. This, too, was something that became clear at Bethnal Green in 1868 when the new matron was severely censured by the PLB for the lack of cleanliness in the sick and aged wards, and in particular for the filthy state of the linen and bed clothes. These had not been changed, it was reported, for three months, and were consequently (in the words of an anonymous inmate) "one mass of vermin."[85] The PLB inspector laid the blame firmly at the door of the matron, but also censured the nursing staff for their silence and for failing to alert either himself or the visiting committee to the situation. It is, perhaps, surprising that the inspector acted so quickly and decisively in this instance but, as we have seen, by this time the state of Bethnal Green workhouse – and particularly the behaviour of the master and matron – was under particular scrutiny and the state of the linen was very quickly taken up by the local press as further evidence of systematic neglect.[86] At Liverpool too, a series of complaints were made between 1884 and 1887 against nurses at the workhouse which episodically involved the complicity of more senior staff. In April 1884 an anonymous writer claimed that the nurses were "sporting … with the Doctors," or "lounging about and Drinking and eating what the Poor Patients should have," and "making certain Patients Do their work." Two years later, as we saw in chapter 10, another writer claimed that "the nurses in Brownlow Hill [workhouse] had me nearly killed as I can prove," while the doctors merely looked on. And the following year another pauper patient claimed that the head nurse in the male medical ward presided over a regime which involved "neglecting to keep [patients] in a cleanly condition … removing harshly & unnecessarily, patients in a dying state, from one Ward to another … refusing to respond to the calls of dying patients; & also with refusing to look after & see that complainant received the Dietary ordered by the Medical officer."[87] Unlike at Bethnal Green, however, these complaints came to nothing: no inquiry was initiated, and the writer complained bitterly that the visiting committee laughed at his allegations and refused to take them seriously.

Direct allegations of mistreatment and neglect against nursing staff and medical auxiliaries in the workhouse occur throughout our corpus, but they are nowhere near as common as those made by the sick and disabled poor against medical and relieving officers.[88] Paradoxically, this may reflect the fact that nurses and their assistants *were* very often unpaid and could not, therefore, be easily held to any professional standard. As we have argued here and elsewhere, the poor and their advocates under the New Poor Law quickly learned that this was a rule-based system and that officials and paid staff could – and, they believed, should – be held to account for their actions against the guidelines and standards established by the Centre.[89] Paupers themselves lived and worked beyond this system of formal rules and regulations. If they acted "cruelly" or inappropriately in the discharge of their duties within the workhouse, they could expect to be sanctioned, first, by the master and matron, and ultimately by the guardians, who might send them to a magistrate. It is very unlikely that the Centre would become involved. Such neglect would have been constructed as a matter of local workhouse discipline. Moreover, the fact that pauper nurses and auxiliaries were appointed by masters and matrons in the first place is itself likely to have compromised the chances of inmates who had a grievance against them gaining redress.

CONCLUSION

In earlier chapters we have argued that, despite the structural disadvantages that the poor inevitably faced, they and their advocates nonetheless found ways – and sometimes very effective ways – of mitigating and influencing the nature, extent, and quality of the welfare they received. Throughout the New Poor Law, but more particularly as overtly political advocates such as unemployed worker associations, trade unions, and the Independent Labour Party began to provide a collective platform to attack some of the generic constraints on agency, they were able to force open the cracks in welfare architecture and hold officials (and sometimes, whole regimes) to account. Indeed, we suggest that *en masse* pauper complaints to the Centre were influential in shaping official policy and practice, especially when taken together with calls for better treatment from advocates in a wider "reform movement."[90] These complaints were therefore a key expression of the continued agency of paupers and poor applicants all the way though from the end of the Old Poor Law to the start of the twentieth century.

This chapter has, however, added a necessary note of caution to the narrative by arguing that even the sick and disabled poor faced clear disadvantages in articulating, enforcing, and maintaining that agency under the new regime from the start. Moreover, many of the structural conditions which created that situation remained in place at least until the welfare reforms of the early twentieth century. Alongside the broad limits to agency traced for all poor writers in earlier chapters, the fact that sick and disabled poor were peripheral to the vision of the New Poor Law's architects, and that their presence created widespread problems for a system not established with their needs in mind, mattered for the attitudes of guardians and their staff. In particular, the sick were costly and problematic in care terms and required the attention of highly trained, specialist staff – conditions that ran contrary to the main thrust of the new law, particularly in its early years. This created a bottleneck, in terms of both the care available and the degree to which the sick and vulnerable were able to mobilise a long-standing sense of cultural and religious legitimacy to argue for improvements in that care – something that is consistently demonstrated in their complaints to the Centre.

There is no doubt that as the regime matured other narratives about the sick poor gained influence as well. The development of specialist workhouse infirmaries, the professionalisation of nursing and auxiliary staff, and the (slowly) growing influence of organisations such as the British Medical Association and the Poor Law Medical Officers' Association meant that medical care almost certainly improved. As Hurren and Price have both argued, the crusade against out-relief acted as a brake on these reforming tendencies in some unions during the 1870s and the 1880s. This and the great variation in levels of care and professionalism across the landscape of welfare means that narratives of abuse and neglect such as those which have unfolded in this chapter were a regular motif of the corpus throughout the nineteenth century.[91] Even so, our writers knew very well that the New Poor Law was from the very start "inhibited by its own history and tradition," and the absence of this group from the legislation gave a strong basis from which to deploy rhetoric of humanity, breach of process, natural rights, unnatural behaviours, protection, necessity, and urgency.[92] This rhetoric and the agency it embodied were inevitably shared with other groups of the life-cycle poor – after all the sick were only sick for part of their lives – and it is to this shared platform and its meaning that our final chapter is dedicated.

12

Experiencing the New Poor Law

INTRODUCTION

On 16 May 1857 Mr Thomas Johnson was called to give evidence for an inquiry into the case of Mary Irving, a woman in the Carlisle workhouse who claimed to have been beaten by the master, Mr Woodall. Johnson deposed that:

> On Saturday afternoon I was in our yard, smoking. I heard a noise and some person shouting "murder," and a great noise. I went into my own house and up stairs. My brother and wife also came up. Mr Woodall had a gutta percha tube in his hand and went into the bath-house and turned on the tap. Woodall said he would drown her. My wife saw this also: she was excited and wished to shout, but I would not allow her. I cannot say whether Woodhall pushed her [Irving] down the stairs or not; she fell, and lay there three or four minutes on her side; no one came to assist her. She then went down after. She then went down the yard, very wet, saying "I'm drowned; I'm drowned". Mr. Woodall <u>then struck her twice</u> in the washhouse, and closed the door for two minutes or so. Mrs Woodall came down after. I am quite sure I saw Woodall strike her. She was very wet. I could see them quite well. I heard the woman shout she was "drowned" and "murdered" after he struck her.

> She shouted once after he (Woodall) closed the door. After this, a suit of dry clothes was brought for her. I stayed in the window until they brought them.[1]

This version of events was confirmed by several other witnesses (including Johnson's own brother), mostly looking in on the proceedings from adjoining houses. The story is a reminder that many workhouses were located in the very heart of the communities they "served" but its lessons are far wider. In the week between the described assault and the inquiry, the witnesses would inevitably have done what ordinary people always do: reflect, fume, share, and gossip.[2] In this sense it is easy to see how the grim reputation of workhouses formed and was sustained across the period of the New Poor Law in the communities from which pauper cohorts were or would be drawn. This violent episode did not magnify into a high-profile scandal of the sort analysed by Samantha Shave;[3] the master was censured and the local press did not pick the story up, as was also the case with many other instances identified in this book. Nonetheless, it is inconceivable that the events left no local imprint.[4]

In one sense, and as we discussed in the Preface, our corpus privileges the determined writer and instances of abuse and tyranny. And we have certainly traced in this book many stories of cruelty across the spectrum from rape and sexual grooming, through starvation and to punishment for daring to complain. In turn, plenty of underlying drivers for the grim and gloomy reputation of the workhouse in particular emerge from our corpus, including, *inter alia*: that the New Poor Law and its processes and financing were never set up for most of the groups who came into its ambit; the slow professionalisation of staffing and the reluctance of many unions to adopt workable staff-to-pauper ratios; the particularities of regions or countries, especially Wales; the presence of bad people at all levels of poor law administration; uncertainty over what could and could not be done under the new central rules; the sheer contempt with which some newly elected guardians viewed the poor and their cost; and administrative incompetence or competing and contradictory administrative processes. The sense of a poor law finding its feet in the 1830s and 1840s is unambiguous, and the capacity for things to go wrong or not to have been thought out is reflected in the unbalanced number of witness statements versus other materials in our corpus for these decades as set out in chapter 2. Even by the later part of our period, however, collective working-class organisations, indoor and outdoor paupers, poor writers, and advocates found much to complain about, as did the women coming into poor law guardian roles from the mid-1890s.[5]

Of course, it is inevitable, given our data, that we find few examples of directly elaborated contentment with either outdoor relief or the experiences of the workhouse. The silence of the majority – most paupers did not engage in recorded or traceable literate or non-literate protest – can in this sense be read in many and contradictory ways across a spectrum from fear or limited literacy, through resigned acceptance, and to occasional contentment. For those who did write, as we have seen throughout the volume, it is sometimes possible to trace political, professional, personal, moral, and philosophical motives behind the writing, not least with working-class political organisations and the serial advocates and pauper writers who in effect conducted individual campaigns against the New Poor Law and its perceived failings. Yet, as we suggested in the preface, it is important *not* to be side-tracked by doubts about sources. There is likely to have been embellishment, omission, and untruth (both accidental and deliberate) in *all* of our sources, whoever authored them, and understanding all the material as to some degree fictive (as under the Old Poor Law)[6] frees us to address more fundamental issues. These include how we might make sense of the remarkable variability of experience for paupers, the poor, and their advocates (after all, some unions generated relatively few texts while others yielded many hundreds); whether the undoubted failings of the New Poor Law were commonplace and routine; and crucially, the nature and meaning of pauper agency in confronting, resisting, or disputing the conditions the poor encountered. The task for this chapter, then, is to understand how we can conceive of a New Poor Law history from below, starting with the question of how to understand the sheer variability of experience at local and personal level.

THE POOR LAW FROM BELOW?

It is important at the outset to acknowledge that, while we can find extended stories of abuse and abuse of power, there are some *partially* balancing stories of administrative competence and pragmatic responses to the needs of the poor. At their most sweeping, we see instances where officials and guardians (in their own letters to the Centre, through the writing of advocates who wished to contest changing relief patterns, or in witness statements) did *not* always seek to compel workhouse residence, because of cost, ideological resistance, or the simple practicality of people being cut off from alternative support networks.[7] When unions or their over-zealous clerks wrote to the Centre with thorny cases, to clarify the exact scope of regulations and orders, or because of queries by auditors, they were often told to lean towards the workhouse as per the rules. Yet we have also seen instances of the Centre offering pragmatic rather than simply dogmatic direction. Many unions did *not* even write in the first place, merely using the exemptions usually written into law and regulation in order to tailor policies to local circumstances.[8] Thus, we have seen the able-bodied and sick set to hard (sometimes undoable) labour both inside and outside the workhouse, while other unions simply ignored many of the established labour test rules, especially for the outdoor poor.[9] In a similar vein, most unions do not appear to have even tried to systematically enforce laws obliging children and other relatives to look after parents.

There are also some, albeit in smaller numbers, cases of real humanity and empathy within poor law officialdom to contrast with those of abuse and neglect. Thus, we saw in the last chapter Henry Longstaff's complaint, as the Ilkeston medical officer, about the neglect of a poor woman in labour without medical attendance. His letter from September 1844 rendered his feelings towards the assistant overseer who had refused the poor woman a medical order, with contempt metaphorically spitting from the page as he sought assurances that a similar refusal would never happen to a poor woman again: "From the great Loss of Blood I look with much Anxiety to the result, & I call upon the Board to prevent the recurrence of so cruel a procedure for the future, beyond doubt she should have been visited."[10]

Another example of such humanity can be found in Thomas Fletcher's letter of 1868. He was one of the medical officers for Bromsgrove and wrote to complain about a proposed change in the workhouse dietary. This internal piece of correspondence, later forwarded to the Centre, cited the example of "an Idiot eating gravel 'because he was hungry.'" Interestingly Fletcher referred to his experiment in 1837 of living a week on the workhouse diet for the able-bodied inmates. This experience gave him "cravings of hunger … more than I could possibly have imagined or can describe." He also referred to current workhouse inmates who had eaten "putrid horse flesh and Oil cake intended for the dogs," and others who had eaten their poultices. Fletcher complained that a new proposal to cut the quantity of meat per week that the able-bodied were allowed to only half a pound would be "a painful and dangerous standard." Such words and examples point to a genuine humanitarian concern for paupers as well as professional intervention on their behalf.[11] More widely, we have seen many examples in previous chapters of guardians criticising the inaction of their own visiting committees or neighbouring union officials; guardians disputing policy decisions in other places; and workhouse staff testifying against the unjust and inhumane actions of their fellow officers during inquiries. These instances do not negate the argument that the New Poor Law had an appreciable negative impact on the lives of the former parochial poor, or downplay the thousands of allegations of abuse and poor treatment to be found in our corpus.[12] Rather, they point to the diverse experiences of individual poor people and the organic and dynamic nature of local policy; they shift the lens from well-publicised scandal to the changing constellation of everyday practice.

In part, the varying experiences of "our" paupers, poor writers, and advocates – and some of the differences between local unions, or in the same union over time, in the form and intensity of writing – reflect this very observation about fluidity of practice. Great Yarmouth workhouse, for instance, was a byword for tyranny in the 1850s and 1860s, with riots, the censure of staff, and all manner of alleged abuses by the correspondent poor and their advocates, as we have often seen in prior chapters. Yet by the 1880s and 1890s a familial dynasty of masters had tightened administrative processes, stopped selling the dead bodies of paupers, and added more – and more professional – staff, thus providing fewer flashpoints for inmate contestation.[13] Much more of the variable yield in complaints and documents between different unions, even unions of the same "type," is explained by the presence of particular individuals, be they paupers, advocates, staff, or guardians. Thus, abusive workhouse masters, officers and nurses might percolate around the system, and their presence and actions – sometimes extending over decades as we have seen – could be a cause for fierce and sustained complaints. The serial advocate Joseph Rowntree called attention to such failings and extended them to guardians, identifying boards like Barnsley or Sheffield which (in his view) had fostered the ill-treatment of the poor year after year. We also find eloquent paupers – men and women such as Thomas Henshaw, David Bell, Harriet Cross, Samuel Templeton, John Hankeson, Mary Ann Taylor, and Henry Jones, all of whom we have met in the preceding pages – who stamped their personality on the surviving archive when they could alternatively have decided to remain silent, keep their collective heads down, known their place and accepted it. In acting on their perceptions of petty and major injustices, these poor people entered into a world of contestation, one where we also find "grumbling paupers"[14] such as John Rutherford or Mungo Paumier who waged sustained public and private campaigns against the New Poor Law and its institutions.

Examples like these bring us back to a core theme of our first chapter: the need to understand the New Poor Law as a network of individuals working within loose societal and legal frameworks, rather than as a single closely bound and unified system of law or practice. Put simply, people matter; and a variety of other reasons for the variability of experience and of writing within and between unions flow from this observation and a close reading of the corpus. Thus, some issues arose simply because there was a basic misunderstanding between individual officers and paupers about their respective rights and obligations, particularly in the early years of the New Poor Law when officers were unsure of how the law was meant to work. We see this in the diary of the Barnet workhouse master Benjamin Woodcock, who wrote in June 1837:

> Mrs Grimstone of Hadley sent some Tea & Sugar by her footman on Monday evening for Ann Annell, one of the inmates and during their

> Conversation in the hall I hird her say to the young man she was not well used and wished somebody would take her out of the Workhouse. We are not aware of ever giving her an Angry Word therefore it would be some satisfaction If the board wll be pleased to call upon her for an explanation.[15]

This entry highlights a striking mismatch of ideas on the treatment of pauper inmates. Neither may have uttered an untruth; Annell may have had greater expectations in regard to the treatment for paupers, while Woodcock had lesser ones. It is easy to see how these casual inmate words could magnify in the outside community and shape both the perception of the workhouse regime and the likelihood of advocacy, but equally easy to read a genuine mystification on the part of Woodcock. Moreover, close and extended reading of the material suggests that some of our cases simply *were* ambiguous. The remarkable ability of those who were in the same place, at the same time, and witnessing the same events to tell completely opposite stories when asked to be witnesses at inquiries is a striking feature of the corpus, and we have encountered it in prior chapters. There are of course many reasons why such testimony might differ – stretching across a spectrum from fear and intimidation through to personal enmities between the historical actors – but ultimately most of them come down to the particular constellations of the individuals involved.

Nor in this context should we forget the fictive nature of all our material. We see this in different parts of the corpus particularly where the archival backstory is sustained. Thus in chapter 4 we encountered briefly the case of Humphrey Hutchins who wrote from near Llandyssil in the Newcastle-in-Emlyn poor law union (PLU) begging to: "laybefore you my caus ei am in a very bad distres ei got no bread nor chees nor buter nor any sum of mony at my house this day because ei got no [Constant] Worke to feind a sufisiant livins."[16] He listed the names and ages of his eleven children. Some who were in service had returned ill, putting further claims on the household, and the family had suffered from an outbreak of smallpox. He claimed further that although relief had been forthcoming at an earlier date, it had now been withdrawn. Extending this story further illustrates well the fictive nature of some of our material. Thus, a second letter was written a few weeks later in which Hutchins restated and elaborated his case that his family was in "a very poor Estate of life." They were now starving and he asked:

> Ô fear felow christians ei hope you shall help me a poor chritian in hard distres of life and ei have no constant work to employ my famyly ei have been loock out about this nebourwood fore sum Job of labour of any kind with the famers and thay said thay canot pay fore worke

The eventual response to Hutchins's complaint by the Newcastle-in-Emlyn guardians painted a very different picture. They stated *inter alia* that Hutchins had eleven children with five still at home; that his two eldest co-resident boys had been clothed by the union; and that the previous year money was paid when his children contracted smallpox. Given that both parents were also able-bodied, the guardians labelled him an idle individual not deserving of relief. When informed of the guardians' response Hutchins was outraged that he had been "misrepresented" and claimed that the label of being idle would be disproved by "all my neighbours." In fact his rejoinder to the guardians' accusation of lying was to write a counterclaim that it was really the union telling an untruth. Hutchins likely understood that his word would be the one disbelieved over that of the guardians and so in his response he organised a pre-emptive set of references testifying that he was "a sober industrious and hard labouring man." This was confirmed by Enoch James, Llandyssil's vicar, the reverends John Davies and Daniel Davies, two local Baptist ministers, and John James, a local farmer and employer. The annotated answer to this counter-claim was, as we might now expect, that the Poor Law Commission (PLC) had no power to interfere in individual cases and entertained "no doubt that the Gns will discharge the trust placed in their hands in the most unexceptionable manner." How might we read this? Was Hutchins an "idle" fellow used to receiving relief, as claimed by the guardians, and then caught out in his own lies to the Central Authority? Was he wronged by the guardians (we see repeated and powerful phrases like "we have been misrepresented" and that lies about the family will be "unhesitatingly [be] disproved"), possibly frustrated at a large family headed by two able-bodied parents who had made demands on the union purse for clothing and medical assistance and now made further call for funds feigning unemployment? It is perfectly possible that Hutchins *was* the character that the guardians portrayed. On the other hand throughout this volume we have seen serial advocates such as Joseph Rowntree expressing grave doubts about the honesty and efficiency of officers and guardians. Against this backdrop, the most plausible reading is that there were fictive elements to all the statements made.

There is, then, a complex suite of reasons why some unions generate many more complaints than others, why the intensity of such complaints might vary over time within a union, and why we detect a wide spectrum of experiences for the poor in the resulting corpus. In the background of what we can see are those who just put up with things, found other ways, or actively navigated relief structures. Yet the repeated concerns of the poor in our material – the need for dignity in their dealings with poor law authorities; a sense that they should not be forced into workhouses; failings of process and failure to comply with orders and laws that resulted in the intense suffering of groups such as women, the aged, or the sick; harsh words and/or other ill-treatment by paid officials; and anger at being punished for raising those dissatisfactions in the first place – ring loud and clear across the corpus. They evidence widespread and sometimes systematic failings at union level, such that regardless of how else we might characterise the intent and experience of the New Poor Law it appears to us that the structural focus of the Central Authority created a framework that told against the poor and their advocates. Our corpus brings the consequences of this imbalance of power for the everyday lives of poor people to the fore, clearly signalling the importance of a history from below in understanding of role, character, and meaning of welfare post-1834.

As we have also argued, however, these same frameworks provided sustained opportunity for the agency of the poor and their advocates. Complaints to the Centre were atomised; the archive comprises individual documents from individual writers, occasionally punctuated by collective petitions or claims that the author spoke for a wider group or had systematically observed similar events. Yet it seems certain that the same Central Authority would have recognised patterns in the locus and nature of complaints and the linguistic, strategic, and rhetorical registers of the texts that were received. We can do the same in this national corpus. The results are striking. In chapters 4, 10, and 11 we encountered some of the structural and cultural limitations to the practical and literate agency of the poor and their advocates. The Centre routinely claimed that it could not act over individual local decisions even though it had numerous levers to do so: guardians sometimes ignored the Centre even if it did act; union staff (and sometimes guardians) sought to punish or otherwise make life uncomfortable for the poor who complained in their own right or got advocates involved on their behalf; and even the long-established claims to deservingness on the part of the sick poor could be trampled by inadequate processes, people, infrastructure, and penny-pinching. More widely, there can be little doubt that the workhouse and the various labour tests of the New Poor Law had a deterrent effect. Yet, we have also seen many instances of linguistic agency (across the spectrum from small or incremental and wrapped in rhetoric of apology, deference, and submission, through to bold and assertive) and resistance (across the spectrum from tiny acts of defiance and insubordination to violence and violent writing).[17]

Chapter 5 points to a complex rhetorical ecology. While some overlap in rhetorical terms between the Old Poor Law and the early stages of the New was inevitable and expected when the project started – after all advocates, the poor, and paupers were not suddenly reborn after 1834 – we trace some remarkable and remarkably powerful consistencies over the *whole* nineteenth century.[18] The aged in the 1880s asserted *de facto* rights both to favourable consideration and to outcomes based upon a combination of age and disability, just as they had done in the early 1800s. Women across the period employed core models of dependence (on male authority figures, the actions and inactions of others, and so forth), the need for protection, and compromised mothering roles. This notwithstanding their changing place in family, workplace, and family economies as the nineteenth century progressed.[19] The sick and their advocates understood ill-health and disability as the ultimate signals of deservingness, and it is no accident that cases of heavily protracted and detailed agency and confrontation in our corpus often centre on this group. Like their Old Poor Law counterparts, most of our writers constructed themselves as beyond family support and rooted in host communities (where they were outside their place of settlement), and almost all talked about the value of work and of renewed independence where age or ongoing sickness did not prevent it. While we detail and analyse spatial, chronological, and typological variations in this core rhetorical ecology, the remarkable thing is actually how little it varied in the face of changing conceptions of poverty causation, changing guidance from the Centre, or the development of wider linguistic registers in nineteenth-century society.[20] Even more strikingly, if we can trace greater distance between the linguistic registers and referential modes of advocates/officials and the poor than was the case under the Old Poor Law, it is still possible to observe a basic shared rhetorical matrix. The parties negotiating welfare all spoke the same language, especially as the poor and their advocates came to focus on rules, regulations, and expected behaviours and conditions.

We also, however, find significant change. Our poor and pauper writers became "on average" more literate, and this remains the case if we exclude writers of multiple letters, though even some of these demonstrate what Ivor Timmis labels "uncoached" writing skills.[21] In tandem there were some significant developments in the rhetorical construction of agency, which only become truly apparent in a corpus of this size and reach. We find little evidence of the rhetoric of masculine citizenship or honest poverty, but it is quite clear that writers did link rights to being heard and treated with respect to the citizenship derived from prior contribution.[22] That contribution might be twenty-one years of sustained work for the same employer by an immigrant Irishman or raising ten children without recourse to the poor law on the part of a woman from the Welsh valleys, but however constructed our writers grasped concepts of contributory citizenship. Nowhere is this clearer than in the collective petitions of the able-bodied who created a group identity not largely based upon masculinity or even exogeneity (though this was also a new strong rhetorical theme emerging in the nineteenth century) but upon their prior and future contributions as citizens. Much more than under the Old Poor Law, writers, advocates, and even witnesses saw themselves as temporary welfare citizens within a wider structure of lifelong belonging, contribution, and natural and legal rights.[23] This rhetorical matrix was largely shorn of direct political and radical language and reference points until trade unions and other class-based organisations became involved as advocates in the 1880s and 1890s, yielding a powerful "collective turn" rooted in justice, natural rights, logical action, and the tide of public sentiment.[24] A clear example of this can be seen in the letters from Charles Leonard, who wrote from Salford (Lancashire) on three occasions during 1886. In February he complained that he was unfit to undertake the stone-breaking work assigned to him and set out a series of critical observations on other local task work issues. In October he wrote that by the actions of the Manchester guardians, "the ratepayers of the city are 'humbugged' to the highest pitch and paupers suffer by the conduct of the guardians and men employed under them," and threatened to lay the case before his local MP. In November he wrote again complaining of the Manchester guardians' inaction in regard to his situation and asserting that since his last letter he had "been out, and am still – of employment – As a matter of necessity I must again apply for relief at the hands of the Board."[25] As we have seen elsewhere in this book, the Manchester guardians were often constructed as a problem by advocates and other paupers. Yet we can also observe from the wider corpus (partly explored in chapter 3) that Salford was a political hotbed in the mid-1880s and that only a couple of months later a meeting of the local unemployed established plans for the municipal elections whereby they would:

> do all in their power to wrest the seats from the retiring councillors and elect men of their own class – men who had some sympathy with the poor starving unemployed and who would devise means to find them work. The same "Plan of campaign" would be followed in the election of guardians of the poor, for only by that means could they ensure that relief would be administered to the deserving poor as it ought to have been.[26]

Through mechanisms such as large-scale open meetings, and also through newspaper reporting of inquiries, letters to editors, autobiographies, exposés, and case studies, the voices of our writers (paupers, the wider poor, advocates, and officials) seeped into popular and political discourse. Not only did this inherently politicise welfare long after the initial flurry of political argument about the formation of local unions to administer the New Poor Law had died down, but it provided a reference point for future poor writers. The number of people who threatened to make their concerns and complaints "public" compared to the number under the Old Poor Law is notable, and some of our writers understood very well that as former, prospective, or actual welfare citizens (or their advocates) they *were* the public. In turn, they shared with "the public" a core referential model which develops strongly post-1834: a rhetoricised sense that, while the welfare system was flawed, it should nonetheless be subject to basic logic and to the proper observance of its own regulations. When paupers and advocates complained that the rules of relief would either result in them losing their houses or prevent them from re-establishing their economic independence, they appealed to basic logic; when women noted that they simply could not survive as household heads without a little welfare support because they *were* women, they expected the basic logic of their position to weigh heavily. When any number of witnesses, writers, and advocates drew attention to systematic breaches of rules and orders at union level or to the particularly egregious actions of named officers, they sought to rhetoricise a corresponding duty for the Centre to enforce the poor law as it *should* have been. Almost all writers seem to have had a powerful grasp of the intent of rules, laws, and regulations and, more significantly, to be able to frame their writing with a sense of what decent treatment *should* look like. We find these things developed in most sustained fashion amongst our serial writers and advocates – "the grumbling poor" – and almost all unions had at least one of these characters over the period during which we engaged with them. This once again points to the importance of personality for an understanding of the New Poor Law, but the rhetorical matrix was one that we can see systematically employed by writers. They were anything but numbers and objects merely to be managed and counted.[27]

Our reading of the corpus, then, is that, notwithstanding the limits we trace in the latter part of our volume, the poor and their advocates had agency and they knew it. Attempts to crush that agency were played out in a system which legitimised and favoured the words of officialdom. However, such attempts often failed and the letter writers who fill the pages of this book are a testament to that failure. Consequently, in most places and at most times guardians, staff, potential advocates, and the poor reached enough of an accommodation in regard to enough of the poor to curtail potential scandal. That accommodation may have become easier in the later New Poor Law as some groups of paupers were largely removed from the workhouse context, but there is also perhaps a sense that the poor and advocates became more vigilant and even more confident in holding the system to account using its own rules and regulations. Nowhere is this clearer than when paupers redefined themselves as unemployed citizen workers rather than paupers. Across the period we cover, and notwithstanding the best efforts of the Centre on occasion, the poor and their advocates continued to write and provide testimony. The slightest of positive signals appears to have been enough to nourish further writing, and even where such signals were absent their very absence was enough to prompt sustained engagement and sometimes downright outrage.

The poor intended to confront and navigate the New Poor Law and to require its agents to act according to known principles on the one hand and their own (flawed) rules and regulations on the other. In the massive flurry of orders and regulations emerging from the Centre, it is difficult to see why the fabric of those regulations and expectations changed; or whether in fact nominal agency spilled over into practical agency. Yet the fact that the Centre kept registers of precedent is suggestive of a listening capacity, and we know very well that it was susceptible to the weight of public opinion, part of which at least was confected in the words of the poor and their direct experiences. It is even less easy to see how the rhetoric and practice of agency and resistance weighed on local administrations prior to their appearance at the Centre. Once again, though, we know from reactions to letter writers, and particularly to serial writers, that guardians were often stung by sustained criticism. Clearly, the rules of the New Poor Law were not as malleable as those of the Old but in the sense that the everyday New Poor Law operated on the basis of levels of ignorance – the Centre was often and sometimes deliberately ignorant of local policy; guardians were ignorant of the actions of their staff; and generally inadequate numbers of staff were often ignorant of what was going on in their own workhouses and districts – there was scope for small words and acts to make that New Poor Law navigable, intelligible, and liveable.[28] This is not to argue for a rehabilitation of the New Poor Law and its workhouses. It is to say that, in the wider traditions of history from below, rediscovering the words and ideas of the marginal and dependent poor in Victorian Britain changes our view both of them and of the New Poor Law that they contested. The scale and reach of this project shows that the poor not only speak from the archive; they are shouting at us.

OTHER DIRECTIONS

While our central focus in this volume has been the New Poor Law, the writers, witnesses, and advocates we have encountered provide evidence for a much wider range of debates. Sexual vulnerability in institutional settings was even more entrenched than often allowed, and we have also seen evidence of sexual predation on female paupers who were temporarily absent from workhouses in the wider community.[29] More widely, the corpus features homosexuality, cross-dressing, and all manner of sexual abuse and indecent exposure by one pauper on another. Children appear as uniquely vulnerable individuals in our data as one might expect from the historiography, but in common with the work of Alannah Tomkins, we also find some children in witness statements implying that their life indoors was content.[30] Moreover, there is some evidence of guardians actively using their influence to improve the life chances of young people even where that necessitated seeking exception from or bending rules and regulations. Thus, at Southwell in 1857 the guardians argued that William Crossley, a seventeen-year-old inmate who had lost a hand in an accident, was permanently disabled, and suffered from fits, should be allowed to receive instruction in the workhouse school with other boys. It was argued that although unable to do manual labour he could probably undertake work as a clerk if taught to read and write. It appears the guardians had already allowed Crossley to attend the school but felt it necessary to formalise the situation and secure the sanction from the Poor Law Board (PLB) to continue; which was agreed.[31] Notwithstanding sustained complaints about medical care across our corpus, we can see the extension and development of the medical infrastructure of unions, and certainly by the 1870s it was clearly the case that this extended infrastructure of place and people had raised expectations about the nature of indoor medical care[32] and the willingness of the poor and their advocates to complain when those raised expectations were not met.[33] For the aged we see that, long before the emergence of poverty lines, international discussion of old age pensions, or contributory models of welfare, a sense of the need for progressive retirement from the age of sixty was deeply entrenched across England and Wales. Subsequent discussion and legislation merely codified almost a century of working-class opinion.[34]

There is also much that we have observed in passing, fleetingly or latently, and which will require and deserve more sustained analysis when our data is released onto The National Archives website. The scope for an emotional history of the workhouse is immense.[35] Registers of precedent can be linked to MH12 in order to trace the exact lineage of decision making by the Centre. For those with interests in historical sociolinguistics, our use of corpus packages has been substantial but by no means exhaustive, and the corpus is ripe for studies of intertextuality, the presence and absence of dialect, and regional dimensions of the transition to Standard English. Our serial writers have a presence across different document types, and sometimes life-cycle stages, which would allow a sophisticated analysis of the changing positioning of language. While we have touched upon the punishment of poor writers for the act of writing, the data is replete with accounts of illicit and sanctioned punishments by workhouse staff and of violence amongst workhouse inmates themselves. The corpus also offers insight into people moving in and out of the workhouse, which will allow a much more nuanced understanding of how institutional sojourns were understood by and constructed in the community. There is scope for detailed regional studies of welfare – the use of the Welsh language as a weapon of resistance, for instance – work on advocacy, and for wider studies of privacy, citizenship, or the body. We have placed the agency of the poor and of their advocates front and centre of a New Poor Law history from below which we hope will shape future agendas for poor law research. However, our data takes us and historians of the future into much wider social and cultural territories.

APPENDIX

Sampling

As we have seen, MH12 is a vast and extraordinarily complex archive with minimal cataloguing of its 16,745 volumes, which encompass around 643 poor law unions. The main way into the records is still to investigate one volume at a time, scanning every piece of correspondence in turn, much of which will be irrelevant to the themes pursued by the reader. For the biggest unions this can involve somewhere between seventy and ninety large bound volumes for the period 1834–1900, running up to many thousands of pages. In this context, our data collection strategy had three dimensions. First, we developed a broad matrix of union typologies using conventional dichotomous yardsticks (urban/rural; south/north; ports/inland; England/ Wales; industrial/rural) and more complex signals such as a spectrum of socio-economic complexion, religious emphasis, and the cultural function of the central places in each union. We then applied this matrix to unions formed by the 1840s in order to generate a target list of 102 (90 from England and 12 from Wales) for detailed data collection and analysis. Our matrix could only provide a very broad indicator of the types of place we had chosen, not least because most unions combined urban and rural or industrial and agricultural parishes in various constellations. Nevertheless, judged on these indicators, the sample is both very substantial and broadly representative of English and Welsh unions as a whole. Adjustments and augmentations were made to ensure wide spatial coverage, and figure A.1 plots the distribution of the sample.

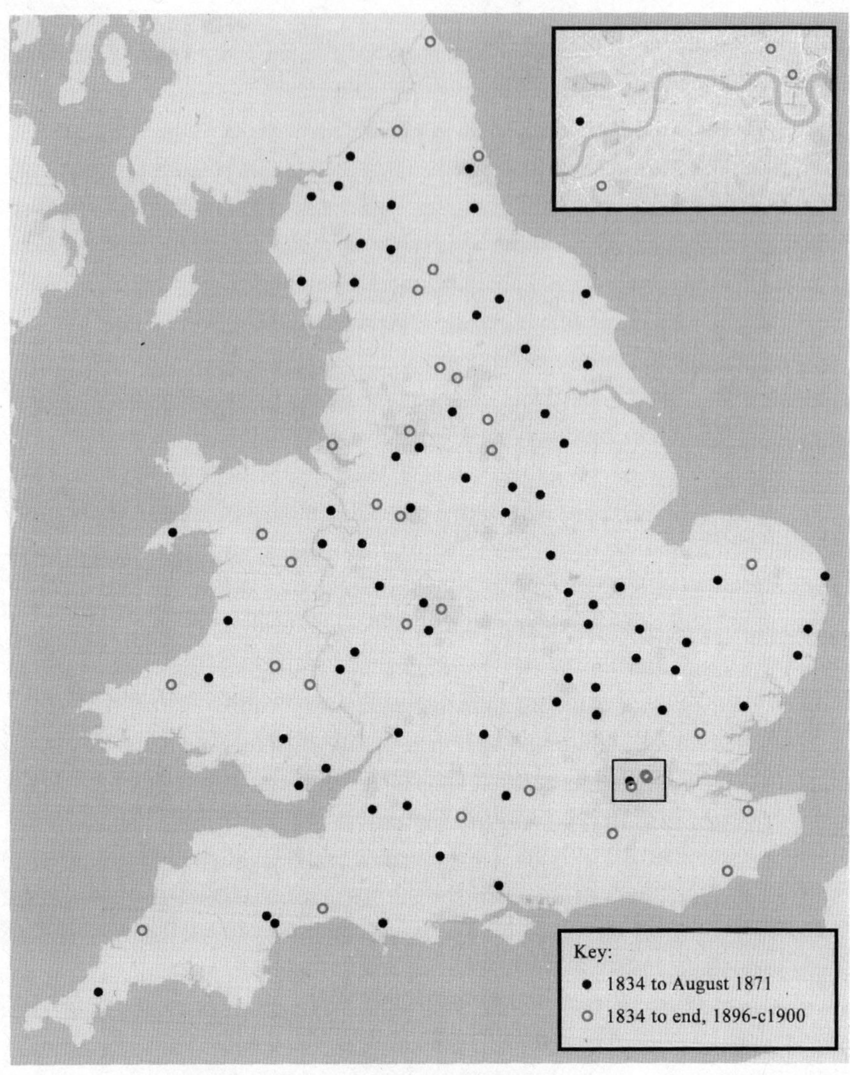

A.1 Map of the distribution of the MH12 sample
Source: MH12. Local Government Board and Predecessors: Correspondence with Poor Law Unions and Other Local Authorities, The National Archives.

The second stage of our data collection strategy involved surveying the volumes to identify core data (see chapter 2) from amongst myriad circulars, orders, letters, and other material with which it is interleaved. This long and complex task was undertaken by the team on our AHRC grant and a group of experienced volunteers at The National Archives (TNA). All identified material was imaged and summarised in a control spreadsheet. For the period from 1834 (or whenever the union was first created) until 1871, we identified and collected relevant material from every volume of correspondence for all of the 102 unions. In 1871 the formation of the Local Government Board meant that all the conventional correspondence and material continued to be received, but that the MH12 series began to include vast amounts of other paperwork, notably documentation associated with sanitation and public health. Consequently, the size of each MH12 volume increases radically, as do their number for each union. For this reason we surveyed and transcribed material in the post-1871 period for 32 of the 102 unions, as indicated in figure A.1. Some 68.6 per cent of our unions were considered from their inception to 1871, and the remaining 31.4 per cent were surveyed from their inception to their "end date." The latter differs for each union (roughly between 1896 and 1903) as the later volumes were destroyed by bombing in the Second World War. In total we surveyed 1,716 volumes of MH12 (10.25 per cent of the surviving material and 15.9 per cent of unions) equating to 2.4 million pages. Using our familiarity with the localities, the principles of the original sampling matrix, and a wider sense of how changes in the law (on welfare, education, and so forth) and evolution in sentiment about the causes and remedies of poverty might have affected the "meaning" of particular union types, we have avoided any obvious biasing in the sampled data.

The third task was the transcription process itself, which undertaken by the core team and the off-site project volunteer groups. Broadly, we transcribed text exactly as it appeared on the page, in common with Old Poor Law projects dealing with pauper letters. Adding replies from the Centre and other materials to the core document sets outlined in chapter 2, we have transcribed some four million plus words, generating a substantial national dataset for the study of the New Poor Law that will be released on TNA's website in 2023–24.

Notes

PREFACE

1 King, *Poverty and Welfare*, passim; Williams, *From Pauperism*, passim.

2 See Waddell, "Writing History" for a particular discussion of the approach in the early modern period.

3 Jones and King, *Pauper Voices*, chapter 2, make a similar point about the seam of public criticism of the workhouse.

4 Frankel, *States of Inquiry*, 36; Knights, "'The Lowest Degree of Freedom,'" 32–4.

5 Though for a rare example see TNA: MH12/6444, 12675/1842, Letter from the unemployed of Hinckley (Leicestershire) to the Board of Guardians, 18 July 1842, thanking them "for what you have done, you have acted wisely, honourably" and forwarded to the PLC; reproduced in Seaton and Seaton, *Letters*, 50–1, alongside a report from Inspector Robert Weale. He claimed to have talked to workhouse inmates who "expressed themselves satisfied with what the Guardians had done and were very thankful for the consideration shewn them."

6 Thompson, *The Making*, 267.

7 Roberts, "How Cruel," 107.

8 King and Beardmore, "Contesting the Workhouse."

9 King and Jones, "Fragments of Fury?"; Carter, James, and King, "Punishing Paupers?"

10 Reynolds, *A Poor Man's House*, 169.

CHAPTER ONE

1 The duties of relieving officers were detailed in the *First Annual Report of the Poor Law Commissioners for England and Wales*, 1835, 82–3.

2 BRO: D/P L32/L9/7, Letter.

3 For the parochial system see Hindle, *On the Parish?*; Hollen Lees, *The Solidarities of Strangers*; and King, *Writing the Lives.*

4 In the initial years of the New Poor Law, parishes paid contributions to union costs based upon the scale of parochial dependence. See Boyer, *The Winding Road*, 82–4.

5 One of which was medical emergency, the significance of which is explored in chapters 9 and 11. See Hurren, *Protesting about Pauperism.*

6 For at least the first three decades of the New Poor Law, the word "staff" must be understood loosely, since many of those involved in running the workhouse in particular were paupers. See Crowther, *The Workhouse System*, 113–34.

7 The crossover of personnel between Old and New Poor Laws and the inexperience and/or unsuitability of staff in the first decades after 1834 are referenced consistently in the early literature. See Ashforth, "The Poor Law in Bradford," 222; Newman, "The Place of the Pauper," 229; Crowther, *The Workhouse System*, 119–26.

8 Higgs, *The Information State*; MacDonagh, *Early Victorian Government*; Eastwood, *Government and Community.*

9 See Edsall, *The Anti-Poor Law Movement*; Knott, *Popular Opposition*; Driver, *Power and Pauperism*, 112–30; Randall and Newman, "Protest, Proletarians and Paternalists," 213–18; and Sen, "From Dispossession," 235–59.

10 For a timeline see Jones and King, *Pauper Voices*, 1–38, though note that they also argue that individual campaigns must be understood as part of a much longer-term public ambivalence to the principles and practices of deterrent workhouses.

11 Price, *Medical Negligence*; Hurren, *Protesting about Pauperism*; Shave, "'Immediate Death,'" 164–91; Gurney, *Wanting and Having*; Shave, "'Great Inhumanity,'" 339–63.

12 NRO: PL01/001, Brackley Union Minute Book 1835–7, September 1835.

13 King, "Rights, Duties and Practice," 263–91.

14 For a summary see King, "Thinking and Rethinking."

15 Harris, "Political Thought," 116–41; Hennock, *The Origin of the Welfare State*; Hennock, "The Measurement of Urban Poverty," 208–27; Finlayson, *Citizen, State and Social Welfare*; Levine-Clark, *Unemployment, Welfare*.

16 In this context see the important work of Levine-Clark, *Unemployment, Welfare*; MacKay, *Respectability and the London Poor*; Shave, *Pauper Policies*; Ryan, "Politics and Relief"; Green, *Pauper Capital*; and Brodie, *The Politics of the Poor*.

17 See Croll, "'Reconciled Gradually,'" 121–44; Evans and Jones, "'A Stubborn and Intractable Body,'" 101–21; Hooker, "Llandilofawr Poor Law Union," passim; Crowther, *The Workhouse System*, 47.

18 Bradley, "Welcoming the New Poor Law," 200–21.

19 *An Act for the Amendment and better Administration of the Laws relating to the Poor in England and Wales*, 1834, section 15, provides that: "from and after the passing of this Act the administration of relief to the poor throughout *England and Wales* according to the existing laws … shall be subject to the Direction and Control of the said [Poor Law] Commissioners … to make and Issue all such Rules, Orders, and Regulations, for the Management of the Poor, for the government of the Workhouses and the Education of the Children therein."

20 Hurren, *Protesting about Pauperism*.

21 Clark, "Welfare Reform, 1834," 241.

22 Williams, *From Pauperism to Poverty*.

23 Darwen, "Workhouse Populations," 33–53; Gritt and Park, "The Workhouse Populations," 37–65; Goose, "Workhouse Populations in the Mid-Nineteenth Century," 52–69; Jackson, "The Medway Union Workhouse," 11–32.

24 Hollen Lees, *The Solidarities of Strangers*; Finlayson, *Citizen, State and Social Welfare*; Harris, *The Origins of the British Welfare State*; and Kidd, *State, Society and the Poor*.

25 For an attempt to revise this approach in the context of the workhouse see Jones and King, *Pauper Voices*, passim.

26 Digby, *Making a Medical Living*, 224–54; Crowther, "Paupers or Patients?" 33–54; and Crowther, "Health Care and Poor Relief," 203–19.

27 King, *Sickness, Medical Welfare*, passim; Ritch, *Sickness in the Workhouse*.

28 King, "Rights, Duties and Practice," 268–73.

29 Mooney, "Diagnostic Spaces," 357–90.

30 Price, *Medical Negligence*, 23, 84–9.

31 "Report on the nursing and administration of provincial workhouses and infirmaries," *British Medical Journal* (1894–95).

32 Shave, *Pauper Policies.*

33 See, for instance, James, "Sophia Heathfield of Hawnes," 202–29.

34 Brown, "Pauperism and Profit"; Price, *Medical Negligence.*

35 Rothery, "Under New Management"; Hooker, "Llandilofawr Poor Law Union" See also Hollen Lees, *The Solidarities of Strangers*, 236; Crowther, *The Workhouse System*, 46, 76; and King, *Women, Welfare*, 116–21.

36 For a detailed discussion, see King and Jones, "Fragments of Fury?" 235–66.

37 One remarkable case is detailed in King and Beardmore, "Contesting the Workhouse," 65–94.

38 See King and Jones, "Fragments of Fury?"

39 Talbot, "North-South Divide"; Deane, "Late Nineteenth-Century Philanthropy," 126–54; and King, *Women, Welfare*, 78–84.

40 Jones and King, *Pauper Voices*, 39–72; Callanan Martin, *Hard and Unreal Advice*; and Gibson-Bryden, *The Moral Mapping of Victorian and Edwardian London.*

41 Crowther, *The Workhouse System.*

42 As well as studies referenced above, see Hinde and Turnbull, "The Population of Two Hampshire Workhouses," 38–53, and Boyer, "'Work for Their Prime,'" 3–32. We must, however, be precise as to what censuses show: they record those who through choice or *extremis* accepted the "offer of the house." Historians have yet to build a statistical account of applicants who refused indoor relief.

43 Some sense of this chronological flux can be found in contributions to Gorsky and Sheard, *Financing Medicine*. See also targeted local studies such as Ritch, *Sickness in the Workhouse*, and Smith, "Lunatic Asylum in the Workhouse," 225–45.

44 Driver, *Power and Pauperism*; Newman, "To Punish or Protect."

45 Gurney, *Wanting and Having*; Griffin, *The Politics of Hunger*, 160–6. Also Anstruther, *The Scandal of the Andover Workhouse*, and Brundage, *The Making of the New Poor Law.*

46 Rose, *Making, Selling and Wearing*, 33; Toplis, *The Clothing Trade*, 106; Richmond, *Clothing the Poor*, 274; Crowther, *The Workhouse System*, 195; and Humphries, *Childhood and Child Labour*, 295–305.

47 Jones, King, and Thompson, "Clothing."

48 For a quantitative discussion of punishments as recorded in such sources see Williams, "Paupers Behaving Badly," 772–81.

49 Shave, "'Immediate Death,'" 164–91; Williams, "Paupers Behaving Badly," 791–2.

50 Carter, James, and King, "Punishing Paupers?" 161–80.

51 Talbot, "North-South Divide."

52 Though see as a model James, "Sophia Heathfield of Hawnes."

53 Though see the thoughtful discussions in Green, "Pauper Protests," 137–59, and Hollen Lees, *The Solidarities of Strangers*, 149–50.

54 Higginbotham, *Voices from the Workhouse.*

55 Humphries, *Childhood and Child Labour*; Humphries, "Memories of Pauperism," 102–6; Tomkins, "Poor Law Institutions," passim. See also Chaplin, *My Autobiography*. On press reporting, Jones and King, *Pauper Voices*, chapter 2.

56 Robin, "The Relief of Poverty," 193–218. For recent research on the place of the Old Poor Law as a "public good" in early modern makeshift economies see Healey, "Coping with Risk," 100–17. See also Tomkins, "Poor Law Institutions," passim.

57 King, *Writing the Lives.*

58 Newman, "To Punish or Protect," 122–45. For an excellent recent article on gossip amongst workhouse inmates see Walton, "Taking Control," 23–41.

59 Frankel, *States of Inquiry*.

60 Green, "Pauper Protests," 137–59. This group was also problematic for Old Poor Law administrators. See Levene, *Children, Childhood and the Workhouse*, 56.

61 Jones and King, *Pauper Voices*; Koven, *Slumming*, 25–87.

62 Brodie, "Artisans and Dossers," 34–50.

63 Althammer, "Controlling Vagrancy," 187–211; Beier, "'Takin' It to the Streets,'" 88–116; Freeman, "'Journeys into Poverty Kingdom,'" 99–121.

64 Scott, *Domination and the Arts of Resistance.*

65 Hurren, *Protesting about Pauperism*; Sen, "From Dispossession"; Price, *Medical Negligence.*

66 Humphries, "Memories of Pauperism."

67 Englander, "From the Abyss," 71–83.

68 On the particular question of literacy see King, *Writing the Lives*, 78–83; Burnett, *Useful Toil*; and Crone, "Educating the Labouring Poor," 247–71.

69 Webber, "Troubling Agency," 116–36.

CHAPTER TWO

1 YE(A): PLU/3/2/1/13, York PLU Outdoor relief lists, March 1841, 11.

2 YE(A): PLU/3/1/1/22, York PLU Application and report book, City District, December 1845 and March 1846, 76; YE(A): PLU/3/1/1/24, York PLU Application and report book, City District, March and June 1847, 8.

3 For worklessness in female relief applications see Levine-Clark, "Gendered Roles," 57–60.

4 She almost certainly refers to an *Act to Amend the Laws Relating to the Removal of the Poor*, 9 & 10 Vict. c. 66, 1847; and *An Act to Amend the Procedure in Respect of Orders for the Removal of the Poor*, 11 & 12 Vict. c. 31, 1847. On the complex and fluid settlement laws of this period, see Snell, *Parish and Belonging*, 78–112.

5 TNA: MH12/14400, 625/1848, Mary Herbert, York, to the PLB, 5 January 1848.

6 TNA: MH12/14400, 625/1848, PLB to Mary Herbert, 10 January 1848; and 625/1848, PLB to Henry Brearey, Clerk, York PLU, 10 January 1848. Herbert was writing in the transition from the PLC to the PLB.

7 TNA: MH12/14400, 1913/1848, Henry Brearey, Clerk, York PLU, to the PLB, 17 January 1848.

8 TNA: MH12/14400, 1913/1848, PLB to Henry Brearey, Clerk, York PLU, 27 January 1848.

9 YE(A): PLU/3/1/1/28, York PLU Application and report book, City District, September 1848, 133.

10 YE(A): PLU/3/1/1/31, York PLU Application and report book, City District, June–December 1851, 76. TNA: Census, HO 107/2355, f.111v, 1851.

11 Carter, *Bradford Poor Law Union.*

12 Carter and Whistance, *Living the Poor Life*; Carter and Whistance, "The Poor Law Commission," 29–48; Carter and King, "Keeping Track," 31–52.

13 For example, the Kettering vestry minutes refer to detailed examples of setting the poor to work in textile trades. The Wimbledon vestry had similarly set paupers to work but provided no detail at all: Peyton, *Kettering Vestry Minutes*, 16–17, 23, and 62–3; Cowe, *Wimbledon Vestry Minutes*, 104, 175, and 419.

14 King, "'In These You May Trust.'" Also Tadmor, "The Settlement," 43–97.

15 Tate, *The Parish Chest*, 202.

16 *An Act for the Better Relief of the Poor of this Kingdom*, 14 Chas II, c. 4.

17 From 1697 certificate holders were not to be removed until they were chargeable. Such certificates were surrendered to the host parish and so survive in overseers' papers.

18 See HALS: DP12/12/2, Overseers' Accounts, c. 1720–1772. At the beginning of the volume is an alphabetical list of "certificate men" and their legal settlements for the period 1699 to 1772.

19 On the trigger points for examination, see Snell, "Pauper Settlement," 375–415.

20 Hollen Lees, *The Solidarities of Strangers*, 28–30.

21 Sokoll, *Essex Pauper Letters*, 14; King, "'It Is Impossible,'" passim.

22 Sokoll, *Essex Pauper Letters*, 16; King, *Writing the Lives*, 36–58.

23 King and Jones, "Testifying for the Poor," 789.

24 Contrast Tate, *The Parish Chest*, 236–9 and Durrant, *Berkshire Overseers' Papers*, xix, who both thought such letters rare, and the more optimistic view of Taylor, "A Different Kind of Speenhamland" or Taylor, *Poverty, Migration and Settlement.*

25 Sokoll, *Essex Pauper Letters*, 21. See also Jones and King, *Navigating the Old English Poor Law*, 1–18.

26 Sokoll, *Essex Pauper Letters*, 18–19.

27 King, *Writing the Lives*, 23–4.

28 Cocks, "The Poor Law," 473–506.

29 Brundage, *The English Poor Laws*, 9; Tanner, "The City of London," 16.

30 *Annual Reports of the PLC* (volumes 1–4) and *Annual Reports of the PLB* (volumes 4–5 and 13). See also Englander, *Poverty and Poor Law Reform*, 13–14.

31 Eastwood, *Government and Community*; Harling, *The Modern British State*; Higgs, *The Information State.*

32 Thus, the headings we find in the admission and discharge registers, punishment books, out-relief books etc. were standardised for publication. This was not coincidence, but planned, organised and enforced.

33 Higgs, *The Information State*, 66–7.

34 Not all pre-1834 documentation ended in 1834, because New Poor Law administration was rolled out over several years. The first union officially declared was that for Abingdon (Berkshire) on 1 January 1835, but some unions took much longer to organise, as Jones and King, *Pauper Voices*, 26–30, suggest. Moreover, much of the local legal apparatus was left intact: unions were based on collections of parishes which still nominated the overseers, and claimants were still

examined on settlement status, and so "familiar" Old Poor Law source types are still part of the New Poor Law archive.

35 There is no directory of the surviving English and Welsh records apart from the four-pamphlet guide by Gibson, Rogers and Webb, *Poor Law Union Records.*

36 Brown, "Supplying London's Workhouses," 36–59. On printing contracts, see Alford, "Government Expenditure," 96–112, and Frankel, *States of Inquiry*, 29–33.

37 C D Purnell and Sons, of Paulton and Radstock were sometimes used by the Clutton PLU (Somerset), for instance. See SHC: D/G/cl/23a/1, Clutton PLU, Weekly Returns of Numbers Chargeable Form B, 1881–1887.

38 If the formats were wrong or forms were wrongly completed then unions would be asked to complete them again. See, for example, TNA: MH12/9534/57, 26205/1867, f. 83, Samuel Lee, Assistant Overseer for Edwinstowe (Nottinghamshire) to the PLB, 24 June 1867, explaining that he had not kept a copy of the monthly statements recently because "Mr Sissons, his usual stationer" had sent the wrong books.

39 For example, *First Annual Report of the Poor Law Commissioners*, 1835, 68–70, 76–8.

40 *First Annual Report of the Poor Law Commissioners*, 1835, 76–8. Forms A to D.

41 Brown, "Supplying London's Workhouses," and King, "'In These You May Trust.'"

42 TNA: MH32/31, 153/A/1847, John T Graves to the PLC, 1 January 1847. The offending text (p. 124 in the original) was omitted from later editions. See *Shaw's Union Officers' Manual*, 62.

43 TNA: MH32/31, 1372/A/1847, John T Graves to the PLC, 23 January 1846.

44 *First Annual Report of the Poor Law Commissioners*, 1835, 106, Form 10: Estimate of Receipt and Expenditure for the Maintenance and Relief of the Poor and the Support of the Establishment in the Union for the Quarter Ending ___ day of ___, 83.

45 Ibid, 119–21. For broader context see Crowther, *The Workhouse System*, 54–87, and Williams, *From Pauperism to Poverty*, passim.

46 *Seventh Annual Report of the Poor Law Commissioners*, 1841, 22. On the sensitivity of the Centre to local punishment policy see: Shave, "'Great Inhumanity,'" 339–63, and Shave, "'Immediate Death,'" 164–91.

47 *Seventh Annual Report of the Poor Law Commissioners*, 118.

48 Parliament ordered data on workhouse punishments to be collected in 1835–42, 1842–43, 1852–53, and 1874. For contrasting use of punishment books and views

on their reliability see Carter, James and King, "Punishing Paupers?" 161–80, and Williams, "Paupers Behaving badly," 764–92.

49 *Seventh Annual Report of the Poor Law Commissioners*, 1841, 75.

50 King, "Rights, Duties and Practice," 267. Good examples encountered during this project are Leicester, Towcester, Bolton, and Haverford West.

51 NYRCO: BG/RI/2/1/1, General Letter Book (Out), 10, Helsop to Carling, 14 January 1853. Carling was presumably residing at Carlton and his settlement was with Ripon. King, *Writing the Lives*, passim, uses similar outgoing copy letter books for the Old Poor Law.

52 See for example the early guardians' minute books for the Axminster and Okehampton unions in Devon: DRO: PLU/Axminster/1, Guardians' Minute Book, 1836–1838; DRO: PLU/Okehampton/1, Guardians' Minute Book, 1836–1837. Both have detailed indexes even though this was not a requirement of the Central Authority.

53 See TNA: T 1/4101, long papers, bundle 591 PLC.

54 TNA: MH12 Local Government Board and Predecessors: Correspondence with Poor Law Unions and Other Local Authorities, 1834–c. 1900.

55 See Carter and King, "Keeping Track."

56 Jones and Carter, "Writing for Redress," 1–25. Under the Old Poor Law decisions may have been challenged through local magistrates, but their powers were constrained after 1834 and it is no surprise that we see an explosion of letters asking the Central Authority to act as arbiters in such matters. See P. King, "The Summary Courts," 125–72.

57 *Second Annual Report of the Poor Law Commissioners*, 1836, 340.

58 See Carter and King, "Keeping Track."

59 TNA: MH12/13076/75, 1443/C/1836, f. 200–210, Charles Pinson, Liverpool, to the PLC, 1 June 1836; MH12/5966/22, 264/A/1836, Charles Pinson, Liverpool, to PLC, 12 November 1836.

60 TNA: MH12/9230/160, 8079/B/1840, PLC to Edward Senior, 8 July 1840.

61 This deliberate preservation is one of the biggest differences to the Old Poor Law. See Sokoll, *Essex Pauper Letters*, 21, and King, *Writing the Lives*, 29.

62 The MH12 archive as a whole does suffer losses, with some unions missing the odd volume or volumes covering a run of years. The Andover PLU, for example, is missing crucial volumes for the years 1842–82.

63 Paper numbers started at 1 in January each year. If a letter was numbered 1/53

this would identify it as the first to be received in 1853. Each union was given a unique identifier as the Centre organised the unions first into Country (England then Wales), and then alphabetically by county and then union.

64 As chapter 4 notes, few of the letters from the Centre to individual writers survive. Looking at annotations, however, we can see that there is no systematic relationship between the broadly understood "outcome" of a complaint and the tendency for an individual to stop or continue writing. The issue of whether success fed into public knowledge and encouraged correspondence from others is considered in chapter 4.

65 King, *Writing the Lives*, 92

66 Driver, *Power and Pauperism*, 28–31; Brundage, *The Making of the New Poor Law*, 88. Famously Robert Weale, one of the early assistant commissioners, was reported to have travelled some 99,607 miles on official duties between 1835 and 1846, 8,300 miles per year. See "Statement of the Number of Miles Travelled by Robert Weale Esq., Assistant Poor Law Commissioner, from the 3rd of August, 1835, to the 31st of December, 1846," *Journal of the Royal Statistical Society*, 12, 1849, 78.

67 TNA: MH12/9252/175, 34335/1867, William Clarke, Bullwell, to the PLB, 2 September 1867.

68 Backing sheets also made binding easier.

69 TNA: MH12/14676, 38306/1854, anonymous, paupers "above 60 years of age," Barnsley, to H.B. Farnall, 2 November 1854.

70 Carter and King, "Keeping Track," 31–52.

71 TNA: MH9: PLC and successors: Paid Officers Department and Metropolitan Department: Registers of Paid Officers.

72 See MH9/15, 10331/98, Register of paid officers and staff appointed by the Board of Guardians, etc.

73 Many of these are included in Carter, "Joseph Bramley," 36–46.

74 TNA: MH32: LGB and predecessors: Assistant Poor Law Commissioners and Inspectors, Correspondence, 1834–1904; and MH33: Poor Law Commission: Assistant Poor Law Commissioners, Registers of Correspondence, 1834–1846. The assistant commissioners' correspondence and registers are complex; they survive for the period of the PLC (apart from 1847) and are organised alphabetically by the name of the assistant commissioner with each volume covering two or more of them. The registers give the address from which the commissioner

was writing followed by the paper number, date of letter and receipt, then coverage of the general subject matter followed by a more detailed precis of the particular subject. The second half of the page has columns for the "Minute Answer" (essentially a precis of the response) and the date of despatch and deposit. By using the name of the commissioner and the year, the registers reference the relevant correspondence volumes.

75 TNA: MH15: LGB and predecessors: Subject Indexes of Correspondence, 1836–1920. We do not include in this discussion internal indexes such as MH4: PLC and successors: Extracts from Minutes and Abstracts of Correspondence, 1839–1879. Nor do we include the indexes in MH10: Ministry of Health and predecessors: Circular Letters, 1834–1962, as these refer only to the internal orders and circulars in that record series.

76 Thus it is not an index to the whole of MH12, but rather an index to selected subjects and noted precedents.

77 From 1856 onward the registers covered more than one year per volume and the unique identifying reference number incorporated the year of the correspondence as well as the paper and union number.

78 TNA: MH15/22 LGB and predecessors: Subject Indexes of Correspondence. Part 2. O to W. 1856–1859.

79 TNA: MH12/9160, 28893/1856, PLB to S J Tibbs, Clerk, Tynemouth, 11 July 1856. On child punishment see King and Beardmore, "Contesting the Workhouse."

80 Crowther, *The Workhouse System*, 2.

81 TNA: MH12/9239/216, 2772/1850, Thomas Oscroft, Arnold, to the PLB, 16 January 1850.

82 TNA: MH12/3025, 21218/1870, Margaret Wallace, Durham, to the PLB, 7 May 1870. Our italics.

83 TNA: MH12/6057, 562/1865, Ann McKaan, Manchester, to the PLB, 9 December 1864.

84 TNA: MH12/13675, 36284/1866, James Butterworth, Bradford-on-Avon, to the PLB, 7 September 1866. The husband may have been part of a pauper emigration scheme; hence the language about hope and intent. See Howells, "'On Account,'" 587–608, and Howells, "Emigration and the New Poor Law," 145–64.

85 The precise way in which a specific set of local circumstances resulted in some form of complaint which a) generated a local inquiry, or b) reached the central authority and resulted in an official inquiry, is difficult to set out in any general

way. Some complaints would have been verbal, informal and settled locally. Such complaints would have left little archival footprint, though the self-referential nature of pauper letters often affords us some access to this informal world. Pauper inmate complaints may have been raised through the union visiting committees and recorded in their minute books along with any outcomes. Local complaints were also raised at the guardians' weekly meetings, usually from the visiting committee processes but not invariably so. Complaints may have been written directly to the central authority following dissatisfaction with the outcome of local processes. There were no published criteria determining which complaints or issues would warrant an official investigation.

86 Some of the reports were substantial, with manifold sets of statements. In 1862, for instance, Thomas Harvey Shacklock, guardian of the Mansfield PLU (Nottinghamshire), wrote to the Centre enclosing a copy of the evidence heard by a committee on 27 November 1862 into the case of Elizabeth Nicholson, the late matron. The case runs to almost a hundred pages: TNA: MH12/9367/158–161, 46127/1862, Thomas Shacklock to the PLB, 22 December 1862.

87 TNA: MH12/14017/116, 10586/B/1840, Thomas Saunders, Clerk, Kidderminster PLU, to PLC (with statements), 12 September 1840. See also Humphries, "Care and Cruelty," 115–34.

88 On this issue see Jones and King, *Pauper Voices*, passim; Seaber, *Incognito*; Gillie, "The Origin," 715–30; and Frankel, *States of Inquiry*, 28–70.

89 TNA: MH12/12691, 5247/A/1844, Mary White, Wandsworth and Clapham workhouse, to the PLC, 20 April 1844. Our italics.

90 TNA: MH12/10326, 25874/1867, Timothy Peirce, Clutton workhouse, to the PLB, 22 June 1867.

91 TNA: MH12/8095, 18628/1861, J. Moses, Newport workhouse, to the PLB, 22 May 1861.

92 TNA: MH12/15352, 8207/1851, "Memorial of the Kirkby Malzeard ratepayers to the PLB," February 1851.

93 TNA: MH12/14023/221, 49842/1864, Thomas Hartley, William Thornhill, James Hardiman and Samuel Smith, Kidderminster workhouse, to the PLB, 27 December 1864.

94 Hurren, *Dying for Victorian Medicine*.

95 TNA: MH12/7689, 35646/1869, "The Voice of the Inmates of Poplar Union Workhouse," to the PLB, 1 July 1869. Research on diets in the workhouse is now exten-

sive: Gurney, *Wanting and Having*; Griffin, *The Politics of Hunger*; and Miller, "Feeding in the Workhouse." On the cultural politics of workhouse food see Durbach, "Roast Beef."

96 See Huzzey and Miller, "Petitions, Parliament," 123–64; Lyons, "Ordinary Writings," 13–32; McGrath, "British Lobbying," 226–49; and Tilly, *Popular Contention*.

97 Newspaper cutting from the *Cardiff and Merthyr Guardian* enclosed in TNA: MH12/16248/43 and 44, 12614/B/1847, Richard Lewis Reece, Coroner, to the PLC, 12 June 1847.

98 Jones and King, *Pauper Voices*. Lyons, "Ordinary Writings," 15, styles this "borrowed writing."

99 Lyons, *The Writing Culture*. On public opinion see Jones and King, *Pauper Voices*, passim; Hilliard, "Popular Reading," 247–71; Frankel, *States of Inquiry*, 56–70.

100 Similar imbalances can be seen in Old Poor Law letters and in regionally focused studies of the New Poor Law. See Levine-Clark, "Gendered roles," 53–73.

101 King, *Writing the Lives*, 123.

102 Hollen-Lees, *The Solidarities*, 179–85; Snell, *Parish and Belonging*, 140–63; Williams, *From Pauperism*, passim.

103 Williams, *From Pauperism*, 156–7, notes that this procedure provided only a snapshot of pauperism, as opposed to turnover.

104 Williams, *From Pauperism*, 158–63 and 169.

105 King, *Writing the Lives*, 22.

106 Jones and King, *Pauper Voices*, passim.

107 This may reflect the fact the some crises were short-lived or that local poor law officials simply abandoned the logic of the New Poor Law at these times, leaving the poor and their advocates with little to write about.

108 Sokoll, *Essex Pauper Letters*, 19–23.

109 TNA: MH12/6845, 12420/1850, George Humm, Bethnal Green, to the PLB, 25 March 1850. His letter ran to 138 words, including the date, salutation, closing, and response address.

110 TNA: MH12/5985, 71517/1874, Jane Maylor, Liverpool workhouse, to the LGB, November 1874. John Rutherford of Poplar wrote at even greater length, with his five letters supplemented by a 45,000-word book in January 1886: Anon, *Indoor Paupers*. For more on Rutherford see Jones and King, *Pauper Voices*, 90–4.

111 TNA: MH12/16063, 20527/1868, Henry Jones, Pwllheli, to the PLB, 18 May 1868. Even categorising this as a pauper letter is problematic. At the end he noted being dismissed from the workhouse for interfering on behalf of other inmates, thus rendering himself not in receipt of relief.

112 TNA: MH12/3416, 90601/1884, Charles Linnet, Little Wattham, to the LGB, 1884.

113 TNA: MH12/14732, 5007/1855, "The Truth Loving Test Men of Bradford Union," to the PLB, 10 February 1855.

114 TNA: MH12/6843, 6762/1841, Thomas Claisse, Spitalfields, to the PLB, 5 July 1841. As Langhamer, "Who the Hell are Ordinary People?," 189, notes, the very ordinariness of people like Claisse allowed them to assert rights and make demands.

115 TNA: MH12/12737, 50304/1894, Mr Champion, Battersea, to the LGB, 15 May 1894.

116 TNA: MH12/12690, 2797/A/1841, Fred Holmes, Nine Elms, to the PLC, 15 March 1841.

117 TNA: MH12/11935, 6993/B/1842, H Muller, Aldeburgh, to the PLC, 23 May 1842.

118 TNA: MH12/6867, 77119/1874, Edward Coke, Bethnal Green, to the LGB, 3 December 1874.

119 TNA: MH12/165, 10110/B/1845, "A Parishioner," Hardwick, to the PLC, 18 June 1845.

120 TNA: MH12/165, 10110/B/1845, Henry Philip Powys, Hardwick, to the PLC, 9 July 1845 (printed in *The Times*, 11 July 1845). He was part of the wealthy Powys family of Hardwick House, Oxfordshire.

121 TNA: MH12/14762, 76752/1895, Mark Noble, Bradford workhouse, to the LGB, 12 June 1895. The implication that the mad poor could also contest workhouse care is developed in King and Jones, "Fragments of Fury?," 235–65.

122 TNA: MH12/5986, 19348/1876, Anonymous, Liverpool, to the LGB, 18 February 1876.

123 The circulation of the *Leeds Mercury* reached 10,274 in 1841. See Thornton, "Edward Baines," 281.

124 TNA: MH12/14680, 3179/E/1863, Thomas Smith, Barnsley, to the PLB, 26 January 1863.

125 The capacity for articles and letters like this to stoke intense debate is clear, given that provincial outlets (including local market town or borough weeklies, city morning papers, and weekend regional miscellany papers) constituted the majority of the newspaper press. Hobbs, "When the Provincial Press," 16–43.

126 TNA: MH12/14692, 37285/1883, Arthur Firth, Barnsley, to the LGB, 14 April 1883.

127 TNA: MH12/14692, 37285/1883, Arthur Firth, Barnsley, to Mr Marsden, Barnsley PLU guardian, 17 April 1883 (printed in the *Barnsley Chronicle*, 28 April 1883).

128 TNA: MH12/9163, 17393/1868, Alexander Leslie, Tynemouth workhouse, to the PLB, 25 April 1868.

129 TNA: MH12/6012, no paper number, John Joseph Macdonald, Liverpool workhouse, to the LGB, 22 February 1895.

130 TNA: MH12/8098, 4296/E/1866, T.F. Parsons, Maindee, to the PLB, 29 January 1866.

CHAPTER THREE

1 TNA: MH12/16330, 2604/1857, John Griffith, Aberdare, to the PLB, 13 July 1857. The deep knowledge of the pauper suggests some co-construction of the text. On this process see Walker and Grund, "Speaking Base," 5.

2 King and Jones, "Testifying for the Poor," 790.

3 Frankel, *States of Inquiry*, 1–71; Hennock, "The Measurement," 209–14; and Callanan Martin, *Hard and Unreal Advice.* Naturally, the line between advocacy for paupers and the "social action" of a committed individual is often blurred.

4 King and Jones, "Testifying for the Poor," passim.

5 King, "Friendship, Kinship"; Snell, "Belonging and Community"; and Tadmor, *Family and Friends.*

6 King and Jones, "Testifying for the Poor," 792.

7 Ibid., 794.

8 On Rowntree see Jones and King, *Pauper Voices*, chapter 2.

9 For instance, Rowntree persuaded the Manchester pauper Thomas Burke to take legal action against Francis Dalton, supervisor of the vagrant ward. The account of this action fills large parts of TNA: MH12/6058, Manchester PLU correspondence, January–May 1866.

10 On workhouse reform, see Jones and King, *Pauper Voices*, chapters 1 and 2.

11 Sometimes paupers whose cases he championed denied having sanctioned Rowntree's intervention, and even complained that they would rather he had never taken their part.

12 The letters from Reverend H. Binney, first to the PLC and then the PLB, are: TNA: MH12/255, 7992/E/1844, 21 May 1844; 16010/B/1844, 18 September 1844; 16283/B/1844, 26 September 1844; 16717/B/1844, 10 October 1844; 17475/B/1844,

30 October 1844; 18043/B/1844, 13 November 1844; 18069/B/1844, 13 November 1844; 18413/B/1844, 22 November 1844; 18414/B/1844, 22 November 1844; 19055/B/1844, 10 December 1844; MH12/256, 17931/1848, 19 June 1848; 31930/1848, 22 November 1848; 33499/1848, 8 December 1848; MH12/257, 36349/1852, 25 September 1852; MH12/258, 14588/1854, 29 April 1854; and MH12/259, 45796/1858, 29 November 1858. On the politics of the boardroom see Fraser, "The Poor Law," passim.

13 TNA: MH12/14692, 37285/1883, Arthur Firth, Barnsley, to the LGB, 14 April 1883. The LGB attached a cutting from the *Barnsley Chronicle* (Saturday, 28 May 1883), which noted that Firth was secretary of the Salvation Army in Barnsley.

14 TNA: MH12/2095/143, 3798/B/1837, Miss Philpot, Lyme Regis, to the PLC, 27 May 1837; 276, 778/B/1838, 29 January 1838; 356, 8735/B/1838, 15 December 1838.

15 Something we might have expected, given Samantha Shave's work on policy process. See Shave, *Pauper Policies*, passim.

16 Clergymen themselves were also the focus of direct complaints *by* the poor.

17 TNA: MH12/8483, 36932/1869, Wingfield Homfray, Bintree, to the PLB, 21 July 1869.

18 TNA: MH12/14614, 35970/1864, Thomas Jackson, Scarborough, to the PLB, 24 September 1864.

19 TNA: MH12/7, 38812/1863, J. Matthews, Ampthill PLU, to the PLB, 23 October 1863.

20 King and Jones, "Testifying for the Poor," 796.

21 TNA: MH12/14678, 39915/1858, E.W. Tinsdill, Halton, to the PLB, 22 October 1858.

22 Ibid.

23 TNA: MH12/10320/4, P.E. Coates, Pensford, to the PLC, 27 October 1834.

24 On widespread misunderstandings of the changing role of magistrates post-1834, see Snell, *Parish and Belonging*, 270–96.

25 TNA: MH12/10320/4, P.E. Coates, Stanton Drew, to the PLC, 27 October 1834.

26 Crowther, *The Workhouse System*, 129; Cunningham Glen, *The Consolidated*, 83.

27 Crowther, *The Workhouse System*, 129–30. For a detailed dissection of attempts by Catholic clergy to obtain a foothold in the Wolstanton and Stoke-on-Trent unions (Staffordshire) see Talbot, "North-South Divide," chapter 6.

28 Russell, *The Catholic in the Workhouse*, 1.

29 TNA: MH12/15487, 77136/1881, Father L Burke, St Catherine's, Sheffield, to the LGB, 25 July 1881.

30 TNA: MH12/15487, 77136/1882, Father L Burke, St Catherine's, Sheffield, to the LGB, 9 August 1882.

31 TNA: MH12/15490, 370008/1884, Father L Burke, St Catherine's, Sheffield, to the LGB, 9 April 1884. For context see Tenbus, *English Catholics*, passim.

32 TNA: MH12/15491, 35968/1885, Father L Burke, St Catherine's, Sheffield, to the LGB, 3 April 1885. The quotation is taken from the letter annotations.

33 The 104,000 words of correspondence by Rowntree in our corpus likely represent only the tip of his iceberg within MH12 overall. Add to this his extensive correspondence with Boards of Guardians (to which he alludes repeatedly in his letters to the Centre) alongside the long and detailed letters he published in the press (we have discovered more than 150 so far) and it becomes clear that he was an extraordinary advocate. For wider context on social investigation and policy see Whyte, "'The Too Clever by Half,'" 128–32.

34 TNA: MH12/9759, 11624/1857, R.H.S. Carpenter, Witney, to the PLB, 14 April 1857; contains the cases of both Green and Neale.

35 TNA: MH12/3023, 16566/1865, R.H.S. Carpenter, Durham, to the PLB, 5 August 1865.

36 TNA: MH12/3023, 42923/1866, R.H.S. Carpenter, Durham, to the PLB, 2 November 1866.

37 TNA: MH12/3023, 43661/1866, R.H.S. Carpenter, Durham, to the PLB, 5 November 1866. Rowntree received similar threats.

38 TNA: MH12/3023, 16566/1865, R.H.S. Carpenter, Durham, to the PLB, 5 August 1865.

39 TNA: MH12/3023, 28133/1865, R.H.S. Carpenter, Durham, to the PLB, 11 July 1865.

40 Jones and King, *Pauper Voices*, 15–23.

41 TNA: MH12/15801, 1607/1869, W.J. Davies, Aberystwyth, to the PLB, 5 January 1869.

42 As is consistent with investigative social work more widely from this period: Frankel, "Scenes of Commission," 20–41; Freeman, "'Journeys into Poverty Kingdom'"; Gibson-Bryden, *The Moral Mapping*; Wilcox, *The Church and the Slums*, passim; and Humphreys, *Poor Relief*, 23–95.

43 Jones and King, *Pauper Voices*, 55–8.

44 *Western Daily Mail*, 30 July 1869.

45 *The Aberystwyth Observer*, 27 February 1869.

46 Advocacy of this sort would likely have been conducted locally and thus passes largely unseen.

47 We rarely see for this group terms such as "begging leave" to write or "taking the liberty" to write, linguistic registers which highlight the writer's awareness of the threat posed to authority by the act of questioning or requesting a certain action. This implies that officials writing to the Centre as advocates did not see this as overstepping their status, role, or authority. See Del Lungo Camicotti, "An Atypical," 108–9, and Dossena, "Doing Business," 248.

48 On the internal politics of the New Poor Law see Ryan, "Politics and Relief"; Finlayson, *Citizen, State*; and Brodie, *The Politics*.

49 See Deane, "The Professionalisation of Philanthropy."

50 TNA: MH12/16253, 41999/1858, J. Willett, Cardiff, to PLB, 6 November 1858. Geoff Hooker, "Llandilofawr," shows that in-fighting was ubiquitous in Wales.

51 TNA: MH12/16114, 40325/1864, anonymous to the PLB, 31 October 1864.

52 TNA: MH12/16114, 40325/1864, anonymous to the PLB, 31 October 1864. Enclosed was the lengthy report by Rowntree in the *Wrexham Advertiser*.

53 TNA: MH12/16326, 4299/B/1842, J.W. Edwards, Merthyr Tydfil PLU, to the PLC, 14 April 1842.

54 TNA: MH12/6057, 10393/1865, Anon, Manchester PLU, to the PLB, 26 March 1865.

55 TNA: MH12/3431, 5048/A/1845, W.G. Dennis, St Michael Colchester, to the PLC, 26 April 1845.

56 Walsham references section 52 of the PLAA, which allowed for a departure from the regulations, but only with the Centre's express permission.

57 TNA: MH12/3431, 5048/A/1845, W.G. Dennis, St Michael Colchester, to the PLC, 26 April 1845. On the wider issue of charity and welfare see Humphreys, *Poor Relief*, passim.

58 In general the Centre resisted allowing dependents to enter or remain in the workhouse without parents or guardians as this might encourage abandonment.

59 Carter, "Joseph Bramley," 36–46.

60 Jones and King, *Navigating the Old English Poor Law*.

61 TNA: MH12/6847, 25188/1856, Anon ["A Poor Man"], Bethnal Green, to the PLB, 20 June 1856.

62 TNA: MH12/173, 16255/1876, Thomas Simmonds, Whitchurch, to the LGB, 9 March 1876.

63 TNA: MH12/6708, 5330/B/1843, Richard Willden, Bradford, to the PLC, 25 April 1843.

64 TNA: MH12/6708, 12154/B/1843, William Chadwick, Little Horton, to the PLC, 24 August 1843; MH12/6708, 14210/B/1843, William Chadwick, Bradford, to the PLC, 17 October 1843.

65 On the circulation of mentally ill paupers between workhouses and other institutions, see Dobbing, "The Circulation of Pauper Lunatics"; Smith, "Parsimony, Power"; and Smith, "Lunatic Asylum," 230–45.

66 TNA: MH12/7696, 104795/80, Emma Cost, Bow, to the LGB, 24 November 1880.

67 TNA: MH12/11199/136, 14127/1854, Anon, Burslem, to the PLB, 25 April 1854.

68 TNA: MH12/11199/14, 10095/1852, John Walker, Burslem, to the PLB, 29 March 1852.

69 TNA: MH12/2242, 24565/1865, William Worden, Dartmouth, to the PLB, 14 June 1865. For context see Hurren and King, "Begging for a Burial."

70 The Poor Man's Guardian Society was established for the overtly political purpose of "aiding the destitute in their approach for parochial relief, and for securing them the legal and humane dispensation of the Poor-law."

71 TNA: MH12/7681, 3688/A/1846, John Jones, Poor Man's Guardian Society, to the PLC, 12 May 1846.

72 TNA: MH12/8966, 8526/1849, Daniel Liddell to the PLB, 19 March 1849; 8966 [no original ref.], 4 April 1849; 8966, 20206, 3 July 1849; 8966, 23755, 6 August 1849; 8966, 25131, 25 August 1849; 8966, 25618, 29 August 1849; 8966, 26169, 4 September 1849; 8966, 20206, 3 July 1849; 8966, 28518, 2 October 1849. All subsequent quotes are drawn from this correspondence. See also MacSwaine, "Daniel Liddell."

73 Our italics. For Ironside see Salt, "Isaac Ironside," 183–92; Downing, "The 'Sheffield Outrages,'" 164–71; Weinstein, "'Local Self-Government,'" 1199–203; Sigsworth and Warboys, "The Public's View," 248. For context to the comment on Malthus see Wrigley and Smith, "Malthus."

74 TNA: MH12/14674, 8960/1850, Isaac Ironside, Sheffield, to the PLB, 1 March 1850; MH12/14674, 22171/1850, Isaac Ironside, Sheffield, to the PLB, 6 May 1850.

75 In the Lancashire Cotton Famine (1861–65) the proportion of the population receiving poor relief in textile areas increased sharply. Between September 1861 and November 1862, Blackburn, Preston, and Stockport saw a rise of 300 per cent, while in Ashton-under-Lyne it increased by 160 per cent. See Boyer, "Poor Relief," 58–63.

76 This resembles the rhetoric of masculine citizenship traced for the West Midlands by Levine-Clark, *Unemployment, Welfare*. However, we also see distinct class dimensions and resentments (the act of stooping) and a backward-looking rhetoric of Lancashire self-help. See King, "The Economy of Makeshifts."

77 TNA: MH12/6054, 8826/1863, Representatives of the Unemployed Lancashire Operatives, Manchester, to the PLB, 14 March 1863.

78 J. Derbyshire, Secretary to the Unemployed in Salford and Manchester, to the *Manchester Guardian*, 5 January 1887. Bound in immediately after his letter are newspaper cuttings which include the cited *Manchester Guardian* article.

79 TNA: MH12/6009, 54303/1892, J. Goodman, Liverpool and Vicinity United Trades & Labour Council, to the LGB, 30 May 1892.

80 TNA: MH12/6010, 124293/1893, C.E. Squire, Liverpool Association of the Unemployed, to the LGB, 14 December 1893.

81 TNA: MH12/13368, 33292/1896, William John Davis, National Society of Amalgamated Brassworkers, to the LGB, 3 March 1896.

82 TNA: MH12/13368, 23268/1896, Hugh Thomas Leonard, Birmingham Incorporation, 18 February 1896.

83 TNA: MH12/13368, 38510/1896, Thomas Paddock, Birmingham Branch of the Amalgamated Society of Carpenters and Joiners, to the PLB, 14 March 1896.

84 TNA: MH12/2106, 36247/1865, C. Woodcock, Chardstock, to the PLB, 6 October 1865. On the particularly contested area of female sickness see Levine-Clark, "Gendered Roles."

CHAPTER FOUR

1 TNA: MH12/9248/125, 23894/1862, Mary Chester, Arnold, to the PLB, 23 November 1862.

2 Jones and Carter, "Writing for Redress," passim.

3 TNA: MH12/6847, 4345/1858, Edward Lepley, Bethnal Green, to the PLB, 3 February 1858.

4 TNA: MH12/14019/1, 108/B/1847, William Bennett, Kidderminster, to the PLC, 1 January 1847.

5 TNA: MH12/9248/53, 9624/1862, George Ellis, Basford, to the PLB, 24 March 1862.

6 TNA: MH12/9248/12, 9624/1862, PLB to Mary Chester, Arnold, 6 June 1862.

7 King, "Rights, Duties and Practice," 274–90.

8 *First Annual Report of the Poor Law Commissioners*, 1–2. Driver, *Power and Pauperism*, 3 characterises this as an "administrative discourse of massive proportions."

9 We focus here primarily on the relationships between the Centre and PLUS, while acknowledging that the continuation of pre-existing forms of collective organisation under private acts or Gilbert Acts after 1834 posed acute problems of oversight for the Centre. See Walsh, "Poor Law Administration," passim.

10 Eastwood, "Amplifying the Province," 278; Higgs, *The Information State*, 68.

11 See for instance TNA: MH12/15949, 1738/A/1838, PLC to Humphrey Hutchins, near Llandyssil, Newcastle-in-Emlyn, 24 February 1838.

12 The sample unions are: Axminster, Basford, Berwick, Bromsgrove, Kidderminster, Liverpool, Llanfyllin, Manchester, Mansfield, Mitford and Launditch, Newcastle-in-Emlyn, Newcastle-under-Lyme, Uppingham, and Wolstanton and Burslem. The selection gives us a wide geographical and socioeconomic foundation.

13 We use the nomenclature "letters" and "petitions" interchangeably in our writing unless referring to individual cases.

14 For four letters from advocates and two from paupers, the location of the letter writer, either in or out of the workhouse, could not be determined. It is important to clarify the distributions. Most poor advocates wrote from outside the workhouse, even when they were writing for the indoor poor, and so while their inclusion here is important, the effect in this sample is to dampen the measured proportions of paupers writing from the workhouse.

15 TNA: MH12/9235/139, 6680/B/1845, John Lees, Gedling, to the PLC, 13 May 1845.

16 TNA: MH12/11200/215, 45822/1859, Patrick McGarry, Burslem, to the PLB, 29 November 1859. The backward-looking linguistic form "ye" is intriguing here and points to continuing tenuous literacy. An extended discussion of the McGarry correspondence can be found in chapter 11.

17 TNA: MH12/9248/456, 25014/B/1863, Edwin Mills, Carlton, to the PLB, 22 June 1863.

18 TNA: MH12/9808, 9841/B/1847, Harriet Staples, Gretton, to the PLC, May 1847.

19 These statistics are based only on letters which could be positively identified as being written either in or out of the house. Where the location of the writer could not be determined we have not included that letter within the underlying sample. Of the 181 outdoor letters, 127 (70.2%) were from paupers and the wider

poor and 54 (29.8%) from advocates. Of the total 184 letters concerning individual relief, 134 (72.8 %) were from men and 43 (23.4 %) from women. There were also four from both (couples) and three for which gender could not be determined.

20 By "initial response" we mean the response from the Centre to our core writers, *usually* sent on receipt of their originating letter, and before or at the same time as any further or additional correspondence.

21 This accords with King's conclusion that women had special claims – and correspondingly different rhetorical strategies – under the Old Poor Law, and Earner-Byrne's finding that Catholic Irish pauper petitions in the twentieth century were dominated by women writers. King, *Writing the Lives*, 291–2; Earner-Byrne, *Letters of the Catholic Poor*, 6, 253.

22 Carter and King, "'I Think We Ought Not,'" 117–44.

23 On the rise of the form in the context of the Old Poor Law, see Tadmor, "The Settlement," passim.

24 Hume, "Jeremy Bentham," 365. See also Driver, *Power and Pauperism*, 21.

25 Driver, *Power and Pauperism*, 34.

26 TNA: MH12/9237/293, 21638/B/1847, John Fisher, Arnold, to the PLC, 20 November 1847; and MH12/9237/294, 21638/B/1847, PLC to John Fisher, Arnold, 24 November 1847.

27 TNA: MH12/9237/311, 22603/B/1847, Richard Birch Spencer, Clerk, Basford PLU, to the PLC, 8 December 1847.

28 TNA: MH12/2096/278, 5079/A/1842, Elizabeth Gatch, Lisson Grove, to the PLC, 26 April 1842.

29 TNA: MH12/2096/285, 6304/A/1842, Charles Bond, Clerk, Axminster PLU, to the PLC, 21 May 1842; and TNA: MH12/2096/288, 6766/A/1842, Charles Bond, Clerk, Axminster PLU, to the PLC, 1 June 1842. A woman writing for her mother may have had particular claims on local sentiment. See Levine-Clark, "Gendered Roles," 58–61.

30 For example TNA: MH12/2096, 7504/A/1842, George Henry Scott, Colyton, to the PLC, 14 June 1842. An annotation directed Edward Tufnel, assistant commissioner, that: "It would be well that you should take an opportunity of investigating these charges."

31 Jones and Carter, "Writing for Redress," 390, n.65.

32 Neither of these two changes was used consistently enough to allow us to determine what administrative rules were introduced that required a yellow sticker.

33 As this later period is characterised by dwindling surviving draft responses, we have analysed annotations to indicate what response was given. Most commonly, we see "Acknowledge" or "Acknowledge and promise attention," as we have already noted.

34 TNA: MH12/5992, 59649/1881, John Bernard Gunn, Brownlow Hill workhouse, Liverpool, to the LGB, June 1881.

35 TNA: MH12/5992, 59649/1881, LGB to Henry J Hagger, Clerk, Liverpool Select Vestry, 29 June 1881.

36 TNA: MH12/5992, 62211/1881, Henry J Hagger, Clerk, Liverpool Select Vestry, to the LGB, 30 June 1881.

37 TNA MH12/8978/89, 1295/A/1843, Jonathan Middleton, Berwick-upon-Tweed workhouse, to the PLC, 29 October 1843.

38 TNA: MH12/8978/105 13911/A/1843, W&E Willoby, Clerks, Berwick PLU, to the PLC, 27 November 1843.

39 Such cases are difficult to find by their very nature. See MH12/5968/1/89, 25696/1851, Mary Roberts, Liverpool, to J Williams, 6 June 1851. She asked him to write a letter to the Liverpool Select Vestry as this would "be of much weight in my favour with them." Instead he forwarded her letter to the PLB: MH12/5968/1/89, 25596/1851, J. Williams, Chester, to the PLB, 9 June 1851.

40 TNA: MH12/2106, 36247/1865, Charles Woodcock, Chardstock, to the PLB, 6 October 1865.

41 TNA: MH12/2106, 41575/1865, C W Bond, Clerk, Axminster PLU, to the PLB, 13 October 1865 [misdated – should be 13 November 1865].

42 TNA: MH12/2106, 1603/1866, C W Bond, Clerk, Axminster PLU, to the PLB, 10 January 1866.

43 TNA: MH12/2106, 1603/1866, Internal note to Mr Gulson, 20 January 1866.

44 Her husband was seventy years old and had been receiving two loaves of bread per week.

45 TNA: MH12/2106, 1603/1866, Report from Edward Gulson, Poor Law Inspector, to the PLB, 2 February 1866.

46 TNA: MH12/2106, 1603/A/1866, PLB to Charles Woodcock, Chardstock, 16 February 1866.

47 These statistics are based only on those letters and cases which could be appropriately identified as indoor or outdoor writers, female or male writers. Six which we could not identify are excluded from the discussion.

48 TNA: MH12/6001, 107017/1887, Adam Hall, Blackrod, 30 November 1887. On forced emigration see Taylor, "Poverty, Emigration" and Taylor, "Insanity, Philanthropy."

49 TNA: MH12/9368, 8262/1864, William Goodacre, Mansfield PLU, to the PLB, 5 March 1864.

50 Driver, *Power and Pauperism*, 34.

51 Shave, *Pauper Policies*, 41.

52 TNA: MH12/9242/287, 34314/1853, William Saxton, Hucknall Torkard, to the PLB, 20 September 1853.

53 TNA: MH12/9242/299, 36097/1853, Richard Birch Spencer, Clerk, Basford PLU, to the PLB, 11 October 1853.

54 TNA: MH12/9242/300, 36097/1853, PLB to Richard Birch Spencer, Clerk, Basford PLU, 18 October 1853.

55 TNA: MH12/14017/252, 2775/B/1842, PLC to Henry Saunders, Clerk, Kidderminster PLU, 14 March 1842.

56 TNA: MH12/7695, 42769/1877, Mary Ann August, Poplar, to the LGB, 11 June 1877.

57 TNA: MH12/6886, 130308/1895, Joseph Fleming, Bethnal Green, to the LGB, 19 October 1895.

58 TNA: MH12/6884, 122611/1894, Joseph Fleming, Bethnal Green, to the LGB, 4 November 1894; TNA: MH12/6886, 111198/1895, Richard Wyatt, Bethnal Green, to the LGB, n.d. [September 1895].

59 TNA: MH12/6886, 130308/1895, Joseph Fleming, Bethnal Green, to the LGB, 19 October 1895; TNA: MH12/6886, 143820/1895, Pro-forma interview memorandum regarding the conduct of Dr Knox and others at Bethnal Green workhouse, 23 November 1895.

60 TNA: MH12/15949, 10455/A/1837, Humphrey Hutchins, Troedrhiwyriben near Llandyssil, to the PLB, 4 December 1837. For context on this union see Jones, *Newcastle-in-Emlyn*, passim.

61 TNA: MH12/15949, 12/A/1838, Thomas Jones, Clerk, Newcastle-in-Emlyn PLU, to the PLC, 30 December 1837.

62 TNA: MH12/15949, 1027/A/1838, Humphrey Hutchins, Troedrhiwyriben near Llandyssil, to the PLB, 29 January 1838.

63 TNA: MH12/14408, 31055/1867, Jane Mullarkey, York, to the PLB, 31 July 1867.

64 TNA: MH12/14408, 31459/1867, Jane Mullarkey, York, to the PLB, August 1867.

65 TNA: MH12/14408, 31459/1867, Jane Mullarkey, York, to the PLB, August 1867.

66 TNA: MH12/7698, 112036/1885, John Rutherford, Millwall, to the LGB, 4 December 1885.

67 TNA: MH12/7698, 114593/1885, John Rutherford, Millwall, to the LGB, 11 December 1885.

68 TNA: MH12/7698, 117415/1885, John Rutherford, Millwall, to the LGB, 21 December 1885. The sense of what was "adequate" time is striking and points to a real sense of heightened expectation about the professionalism to be expected of an expanded and expanding Centre.

69 TNA: MH12/7698, 117415/B/1885, LGB to John Rutherford, Millwall, 22 December 1885.

70 TNA: MH12/7698, 118037/1885, John Rutherford, Millwall, to the LGB, 23 December 1885. For a further discussion of Rutherford's "jousting" with the Centre and its inspectorate, see Jones and King, *Pauper Voices*, 90–101.

71 TNA: MH12/16104, 4077/C/1835, Hugh Matthie, Worthenbury, to the PLC, 30 January 1835.

72 TNA: MH12/16104, 4077/C/1835, PLC to Hugh Matthie, Worthenbury, 5 February 1835 (the draft is written on the back of his letter).

73 TNA: MH12/16104, 4244/1835, Hugh Matthie, Worthenbury, to the PLC, 9 February 1835.

74 TNA: MH12/9162, 19441/1865, James Oliver, Tynemouth workhouse, to the PLB, 20 May 1865. Our italics.

75 TNA: MH12/9162, 22312/1865, James Oliver, Tynemouth workhouse, to the PLB, 4 June 1865. Quotes are from the enclosed newspaper clipping.

76 TNA: MH12/9162, 22312/A/1865, PLB to S J Tibbs, Clerk, Tynemouth PLU, 12 June 1865.

77 TNA: MH12/9162, 24134/1865, S J Tibbs, Clerk, Tynemouth PLU, to the PLB, 16 June 1865.

78 TNA: MH12/9162, 29762/1865, N. Edward Hurst, Poor Law Inspector, to the PLB, 26 July 1865.

79 TNA: MH12/9162, 29762/A/1865, PLB to S J Tibbs, Clerk, Tynemouth P.LB, 15 August 1865.

80 MH12/9162, 34471/1865, S J Tibbs, Clerk, Tynemouth PLU, to the PLB, 16 September 1865.

81 On this concept see Langhamer, "Who the Hell."

CHAPTER FIVE

1 TNA: MH12/1594, 26407/1855, Samuel Templeton, Carlisle, to the PLB, n.d. [June 1855].

2 On Irish eligibility see Snell, *Parish and Belonging*, 146–71.

3 The classic view of the framework knitter as the "immiserated" victim of industrialisation can be found in Thompson, *The Making*, 579–90, Timmins, *The Last Shift*, and Ashforth, "The Urban Poor Law," 137. On the other hand, Treble, *Urban Poverty*, 27, argues that subtrades such as quilt weaving continued to do well, and Sharpe, "The Shiners," 105–20, suggests that decline may have been halted by 1845.

4 Gillie, "The Origin," 715–30; Hennock, "The Measurement of Urban Poverty"; MacKay, *Respectability and the London Poor.*

5 See Bailey, "Think Wot a Mother Must Feel," 15.

6 On these issues see King, *Writing the Lives*, passim.

7 On the "tribunal of the public" see Jones and King, *Pauper Voices*, 13–23.

8 See also Hurren, *Protesting about Pauperism*, passim, and Hurren, "World without Welfare," 292–320.

9 This approach is more suitable to structured narratives such as inquiry documents, but even then most of our witness depositions lack any clear question-response structure.

10 Moreton, "'I Never Could Forget,'" 323–7. Moreton coded thirty-five of her available ninety-nine letters, each with an average length of 329 words.

11 The unions are: Bala (Merionethshire); Carlisle (Cumberland); Dorchester (Dorset); Faversham (Kent); Gainsborough (Lincolnshire); Luton (Bedfordshire); Merthyr Tydfil (Glamorgan); Wandsworth and Clapham (Surrey); and Wilton (Wiltshire).

12 Levine-Clark, *Unemployment, Welfare.*

13 On citizenship and welfare see Harris, "Political Thought," 116–41; Harris, "Nationality, Rights and Virtue," 73–91; and Harris, "Gender and Social Citizenship," 29–60.

14 It is difficult to assign political backgrounds to some writers from their own writing, but the letter set is sometimes self-referential and provides supplementary evidence. Thus, when John Cartwright complained to the PLB in late 1848, he alleged he was threatened with violence by William Stubbs, the Wolstanton and Burslem PLU workhouse baker: TNA: MH12/11198/83, 147/1849, John Cartwright, Wolstanton and Burslem workhouse, to the PLB, 30 December 1848. There is no indication of Cartwright's Chartist affiliations until we see in the union's later report on the case that he was "constantly abusing those in authority and of thorough Chartist principles and a dangerous man." TNA: MH12/11198/92, 1267/1849 Joseph Lowndes, Clerk, Wolstanton and Burslem PLU, 12 January 1849

15 TNA: MH12/14727, 3800/1849, Robert Harrison, Bradford, to the PLB, 30 January 1849. We do, as chapter 3 shows, see the emergence of more class-based registers from advocate correspondence by working-class organisations from the 1880s.

16 As distinct from the visiting committees which were a sub-committee of the Board of Guardians and were supposed to be established from the day each union came into effect. On external visiting committees see King, *Women, Welfare*, 1–43.

17 Vorspan, "Vagrancy and the New Poor Law," 59–81; Althammer, "Controlling Vagrancy," 187–211.

18 Price, *Medical Negligence*, passim.

19 For context see Jucker and Taavitsainen, "Apologies in the History of English," 229–46. Such registers invite the generosity of the recipient.

20 Fitzmaurice, *The Familiar Letter* and contributions to Dossena and Del Lungo Camiciotti, *Letter Writing*. This rhetoric was also shared with *some* officials and advocates, pointing to the existence of a common linguistic register.

21 TNA: MH12/1013, 2467/C/1839, anonymous to the PLC [c.March 1839].

22 TNA: MH12/6053, 33983/1862, Elizabeth Burke, Manchester, to the PLB, 24 September 1862.

23 TNA: MH12/8499, 88776/1899, Emma Dorse, Derham, to the LGB, 4 July 1889.

24 We do detect (chapter 3) a change in this pattern for advocates, who became more direct in their opening and closing statements as the period progressed.

25 Bailey, "Think Wot a Mother Must Feel," 11, 16.

26 Levine-Clark, "Gendered Roles, Gendered Welfare"; Doolittle, "Fatherhood and

Family Shame," 84–108; Doolittle, "The Duty to Provide," passim; and Griffin, "The Emotions of Motherhood," 60–85.

27 TNA: MH12/14677, 6054/1856, Mary Powderley, Barnsley, to the PLB, 20 February 1856.

28 Boyer and Schmidle, "Poverty among the Elderly," 249–78. Heritage, "The Elderly Population," 151–203.

29 Thane, *Old Age in English History*; Thomson, "Workhouse to Nursing Home," 43–69, and Thomson, "The Decline of Social Welfare," 451–82.

30 TNA: MH12/15797, 2029/B/1847, David Jenkins to the PLC, 25 January 1847. Reference to the Old Poor Law nomenclature of the poor house is striking at this date.

31 Hennock, "Poverty and Social Theory," 67–91; Henriques, *Before the Welfare State*, 59; Gazeley, *Poverty in Britain*, 22–31; Rose, *The English Poor Law*, 236; Gillie, "Identifying the Poor"; Evans, *Social Policy*, 161–73.

32 King, *Sickness, Medical Welfare*, 68–114; Turner and Blackie, *Disability in the Industrial Revolution*, passim.

33 Snow, *Operations Without Pain.*

34 Hulonce, "'These Valuable Institutions,'" 310–37; Phillips, *The Blind in British Society*; Gooday and Sayer, "Purchase, Use and Adaptation," 27–47; and Smith, "Lunatic Asylum in the Workhouse."

35 Heritage, Hinde, and Clifford, "Household Living Arrangements."

36 Kirby, *Child Workers*; McIvor and Johnston, *Miners' Lung.*

37 TNA: MH12/8634, 14017/1851, Juliana Cox, Great Yarmouth, to the PLB, 27 December 1851. Note the consistent undertone of religion as a reference point and rhetorical vehicle post-1834 and notably post-1860. King, *Writing the Lives*, 278–310.

38 TNA: MH12/604, 62527/1868, "The Able Bodied Inmates of Caxton & Arrington Union," to the PLB, 22 December 1868. The sense that the rituals of Christmas had themselves become an important and symbolic point of leverage for the workhouse poor after 1834 is strong in the literature. See, for example, Durbach, "Roast Beef," 963–89, and Foster, "Christmas in the Workhouse," 553–78.

39 TNA: MH12/6854, 14583/1867, Mungo Paumier to the PLB, 25 April 1867.

40 TNA: MH12/6996, 32240/1871, James Kitsell, Chelsea workhouse, to the PLB, 17 July 1871. The knowledge of other workhouse practice is striking.

41 This number remains compelling even after we remove 426 instances where

those opposed to the New Poor Law claimed its very imposition was "un-Christian."

42 Snell and Ell, *Rival Jerusalems*, passim; Koven, *Slumming*; Gibson–Bryden, *The Moral Mapping*; and Ginn, *Culture, Philanthropy and the Poor.*

43 Jones and King, *Pauper Voices*, chapter 2.

44 TNA: MH12/1013, 2467/C/1839, Anon, Nantwich, to the PLC, n.d. [March 1839?].

45 Jarrett, *Those They Called Idiots.*

46 Smith, "Lunatic Asylum in the Workhouse," 225–45.

47 See for instance Maynard, "The Campaign."

48 King, *Women, Welfare*, 126–45.

49 Tomkins, "Poor Law Institutions."

50 Walton, "Taking Control," 23–41.

51 TNA: MH12/2096, 5079/A/1842, Elizabeth Gatch, Nantwich, to the PLB, 26 April 1842.

52 Burnett, *Useful Toil*; Griffin, "The Making of the Chartists," 578–605; Vincent, *Bread, Knowledge and Freedom*; Vincent, "Working-Class Autobiography," 165–78.

53 Jones and King, *Pauper Voices*, passim.

54 TNA: MH12/3404, 2358/1860, George Last, Chelmsford, to the PLB [January 1860].

55 Hulonce, *Pauper Children*, passim.

56 King and Beardmore, "Contesting the Workhouse," 65–94. This conclusion stands even when we allow for the fact that children were increasingly the focus for workhouse scandals and thus appear more frequently as subjects and in inquiry evidence.

57 TNA: MH12/604, 12340/B/1844, Richard Moore, Manchester, to the PLC, 14 July 1844.

58 TNA: MH12/14241, 7387/E/1867, Witness statement of Elizabeth White, Beverley workhouse, February 1867.

59 Jones and Carter, "Writing for Redress," passim.

60 Jones and King, "From Petition to Pauper Letter," passim.

61 Huzzey and Miller, "Petitions, Parliament and Political Culture," 123–64; Leys, "Petitioning," 58–62; Miller, "Introduction," 409–29.

62 TNA: MH12/9236/266, 11970/B/1846, James Holmes, Calverton, to the PLC, 29 August 1846.

63 Williams, *From Pauperism*, passim.

64 Callanan Martin, *Hard and Unreal Advice*, passim.

65 TNA: MH12/2096, 7504/B/1842, George Henry Scott, Colyton, to the PLC, 14 June 1842.

66 TNA: MH12/9231/161, 4940/B/1841, H. Bruce Campbell, Nottingham, to the PLC, 24 April 1841.

67 Sometimes associated with contribution either in terms of taxpaying for the "shamefaced" poor or a lifetime of contribution and struggle that should elicit better treatment.

68 TNA: MH12/775, 29432/1858, John Hankinson, Timperley, to the PLB, 10 July 1858.

69 TNA: MH12/598, 9849/B/1840, Hannah Ingrey, Chesterton, to the PLC, 24 August 1840.

70 Timmis, *The Discourse*, 156–76; Jones, "Looking through a Different Lens," 321.

71 For wider context see Crowther, *The Workhouse*, 113–55 and 193–221.

72 TNA: MH12/8636, 32341/1855, Thomas Lorick, Great Yarmouth workhouse, to the PLB, 14 August 1855.

73 Jones and King, *Pauper Voices*, chapter 3.

74 See Price, *Medical Negligence*; Hurren, *Protesting about Pauperism*; Shave, "'Immediate Death,'" 164–91; and Gurney, *Wanting and Having*.

75 Witnesses also employed these mechanisms as a way of establishing their credibility and trustworthiness.

76 Jones, "Looking through a Different Lens," 333.

77 TNA: MH12/14696, 81412/1886, George Lawton, Barnsley, to the LGB, 6 September 1886.

78 An alternative calculation, based on the cost to ratepayers of enforced dependence in the workhouse rather than semi–independence on outdoor relief, was also made by paupers. Sometimes this was explicitly a balancing rhetoric to the responsibility of unions to ensure that paupers continued to be able to contribute even when they required the assistance of the local state. See Jones, "Looking through a Different Lens," 330.

79 Goose, "Workhouse Populations," 52–69; Gritt and Park, "The Workhouse Populations," 37–65; Hinde and Turnbull, "The Populations," 38–53; Jackson, "Kent Workhouse Populations," 51–66; Purser, "The Workhouse Population," 60–80; Seal, "Workhouse Populations," 83–100.

80 King, *Poverty and Welfare*, passim.

81 Croll, "'Reconciled Gradually,'" 121–44; Hooker, "Llandilofawr"; Evans and Jones, "'A Stubborn and Intractable Body.'"

82 TNA: MH12/15951, 26804/1854, Mary Jones, Ysgoldy-bach Llannon, to the PLB, 14 July 1854.

83 As for instance did the Llandyssil Parish guardian and ratepayers from the Newcastle-in-Emlyn Union on 26 April 1842 when they wrote to the Centre asking for permission to use potatoes and clothing as a form of outdoor relief, given that the poor spring weather had prevented sowing and work for children: TNA: MH12/15949, 5604/B/1842, petition from guardians, overseers, and ratepayers of Llandyssil, to the PLC, 26 April 1842.

84 King, "Welfare Regimes," passim.

85 Turner and Blackie, *Disability in the Industrial Revolution.*

86 TNA: MH12/1015, 11757/B/1843, John Barker, Nantwich, to the PLC, 19 August 1843. Something worse in this case meant prostitution. See Pearson and Rayner, *Prostitution*, passim, and Jones and King, *Pauper Voices*, 51–2.

87 Carter, James, and King, "Punishing Paupers."

88 Ibid.

89 Jones and King, *Pauper Voices*, 76.

90 King, *Writing the Lives*, 151, 161.

91 The Frances Land letters are: TNA: MH12/8644, 9485/1851, 10 February 1851; MH12/8634, 47526/1851, 26 November 1851; MH12/8634, 31922/1852, 15 August 1852; MH12/8634, [no original reference], 14 July 1852; MH12/8634, 36988/1852, 1 October 1852; MH12/8641, 7131/1869, 30 January 1869.

92 Jones and King, *Pauper Voices*, chapter 3.

93 Scott, *Domination.*

94 Timmis, *The Discourse*, 1.

95 TNA: MH12/255, 2545/B/1846, James Franklin, Newbury, to the PLC, 19 February 1846.

CHAPTER SIX

1 TNA: MH12/9232/46, 1356/B/1842, Thomas Henshaw, Ilkeston, to the PLC, 5 February 1842. On the complex meaning of letter opening and closing see: King,

Writing the Lives, 231–5; Elspaβ, "Between Linguistic Creativity," 45–64; and Sairio, "Cordials and Sharp Satyrs," 183–200.

2 Section 54 states: "it shall not be lawful for any Overseer of the Poor to give any further or other Relief or Allowance from the Poor Rate than such as shall be ordered by such Guardians or Select Vestry, *except in Cases of sudden and urgent Necessity*" (our emphasis). *An Act for the Amendment and better Administration of the Laws relating to the Poor in England and Wales* (4 & 5 Will. 4 c 76).

3 TNA: MH12/9232/74, 1882/B/1842, Thomas Henshaw, Ilkeston, to the PLC, 17 February 1842.

4 TNA: MH12/9232/318, 11829/B/1842, Richard Birch Spencer, Clerk, Basford PLU, enclosing lists of able-bodied paupers for the week ended 30 August 1842, to the PLC, 2 September 1842.

5 King, "Negotiating the Law."

6 As well as "law" relating directly to poor relief, many extensions of legal provision indirectly affected the poor and their household economies, life chances, and health. Among them were: factory acts; laws around begging and theft; adoption law; education; public health and housing; and weights and measures. We might expect the poor and their advocates to have knowledge of these and to be able to revert to a wider narrative of "the law" when they wrote.

7 *An Act for the Relief of the Poor* (43 Eliz. 1 c 2, s 1).

8 King, *Crime and Law*, passim; King, "The Rights of the Poor," 235–62; and King, "Social Inequality," 60–87. See Costello, "More Equitable," 3–26, for the argument that the King's Bench was also important in clarifying central points of law.

9 Section 54 of the PLAA. The medical relief clause was subsequently the point of intense conflict between the poor and guardians during the crusade against outdoor relief. See Hurren, *Protesting about Pauperism*, passim. Its vagaries led one scholar to suggest that 1834 may have represented a significant organisational or administrative change, but not a substantial legal one. Martin, "From Parish to Union," 45.

10 For an overview see Ashforth, "Settlement and Removal," 78–81; Thomson, "'I Am Not My Father's Keeper,'" 265–86; and Thomson, "The Welfare of the Elderly," 194–221.

11 Even so, it was also specified that "nothing in this Act contained shall be

construed as enabling the said Commissioners or any of them to interfere in any individual Case for the Purpose of ordering Relief."

12 Additional examples would include: Bauke, *The Poor Law Guardian*; Walsh, *The Governor's Guide*; and Lumley, *Manuals of the Duties*.

13 The most complete set of such orders can be found at TNA in series MH10: Ministry of Health and predecessors: Circular Letters, 1834–1962. A decade's worth of such circulars has been reprinted in *Official Circulars of Public Documents*.

14 Levine-Clark, *Unemployment, Welfare*, passim; Rose, *The English Poor Law*, 236; Jones and King, *Pauper Voices*, 23–36.

15 Hindle, *On the Parish?*, 446.

16 King, *Writing the Lives*, 4.

17 Hollen Lees, *The Solidarities of Strangers*, 31. Richard Burn also declared in *The Justice of the Peace and the Parish Officer* that parochial officers were "by law empowered to refuse payment of such weekly allowance."

18 For instance, Thane, "Government and Society," 17; Green, *Pauper Capital*, 2–3; and Henriques, "How Cruel," 370.

19 Charlesworth, *Welfare's Forgotten Past*, 35–6. For a critique of this idea that historians have forgotten the importance of law, see Szreter's review of *Welfare's Forgotten Past* in *Economic History Review*, 64 (2011), 1384–5.

20 Charlesworth, *Welfare's Forgotten Past*, 5.

21 Englander, *Poverty and Poor Law Reform*, 47.

22 Snell, "Pauper Settlement," 400, and Rose, *The English Poor Law*, 191.

23 Snell, *Parish and Belonging*, 103, no. 61. Compare this with Paley, *Principles of Moral*, 80, who asserts: "A poor man has a right to relief from the rich; but the mode, season, and quantum of that relief, who shall contribute to it, or how much, are not ascertained."

24 Feldman, "Migrants, Immigrants," 91.

25 Kidd, *State, Society*, 32, offers a similar reading.

26 See Fraser, *The Evolution*; Cooper, *The British Welfare Revolution*; and Boyer, *The Winding Road*, 169–216.

27 Green, *Pauper Capital*, 18.

28 Waddington, "Paying for the Sick Poor," 99–102; Jones and King, *Pauper Voices*, chapter 1.

29 Vincent, *Literacy and Popular Culture*, 78–92.

30 Thus, Wood, *Poverty and the Workhouse*, 70–3, notes that paupers had the right to see their rations weighed out in public.

31 Digby, "The Rural Poor Law," 154–6.

32 King, *Women, Welfare*, passim.

33 Evans and Jones, "'A Stubborn and Intractable Body,'" 101–21.

34 King, "Negotiating the Law," 418.

35 Jones and King, *Pauper Voices*, chapter 2.

36 See Moreton, "'I Never Could Forget.'" For this exercise we coded the following unions in addition to those underpinning chapter 5: Reeth, Axminster, Bethnal Green, and Great Yarmouth.

37 TNA: MH12/163, 10774/1838, Mary Smith, Reading, to the PLC, 29 November 1838.

38 TNA: MH12/15800, 11543/1865 John Jones, Trefechan, to the PLB, 6 April 1865.

39 TNA: MH12/8488, 31716/1877, Jonas Bush, Mitford and Launditch PLU, to the LGB, 30 April 1877.

40 Thomson, "The Welfare of the Elderly," passim, argues that legal familial responsibility was often enforced and was certainly enforceable. Others such as, for instance, Hunt, "Paupers and Pensioners," 412–15, are more sceptical. Hurren, *Protesting About Pauperism*, passim, argues that during the crusade against outdoor relief familial responsibility was oppressively enforced.

41 Levine-Clark, *Unemployment, Welfare*; Jones and Carter, "Writing for Redress," 380–6.

42 TNA: MH12/9245/185, 4188/1857, John Hartson, Woodborough, to the PLB, 2 February 1857. The fact that the opinion was sought not about underemployment but about age is significant and replicated across our sample.

43 TNA: MH12/14400, 4931/1848, Jane Harton, York, to the PLB, 12 February 1848. On the construction of old age as a tally of years in the Victorian period, see Thane, *Old Age*, passim.

44 TNA: MH12/259, 45796/1858, Robert Alderidge, Newbury, to the PLB, 27 November 1858. Use of the word "case" here signifies a legal subtext, as the corpus analysis also suggests.

45 Jones and King, *Pauper Voices*, chapter 3.

46 TNA: MH12/6845, 17745/1850, William Walker, Bethnal Green workhouse, to the PLB, 21 April 1850.

47 TNA: MH12/3401, 31659/1852, anonymous, to the PLB, n.d. [1852].

48 TNA: MH12/14405, 2512/1859, Joseph Fletcher, York, to the PLB, 18 January 1859. For context see Midwinter, "State Intervention," 110; Roberts, *Victorian Origins*, 35–45; Midwinter, *Social Administration*, 45.

49 Doolittle, "The Duty to Provide"; Doolittle, "Fatherhood and Family Shame"; Frost, "Under the Guardians' Supervision."

50 TNA: MH12/16249/212, 18153/1852, William Morgan, Pontypridd, to the PLB, 19 May 1852. The fact that he aspired to read them and would if they were available is an important observation.

51 This is the other major driver (alongside soft language such as "case") of increasing incidence and density of legal rhetoric across the nineteenth century. See also Jones and Carter, "Writing for Redress," 386–90.

52 TNA: MH12/8973, 59671/1892, John Brydon, Bellingham, to the LGB, 22 June 1892. The question of whether the walls of the workhouse were, and were legally meant to be, permeable was a central one throughout the New Poor Law period.

53 TNA: MH12/6010, 98866/1893, John MacDonald, Liverpool workhouse, to the LGB, 30 September 1893. The letter was heavily annotated with references to precedent. Attached was a copy letter from the PLB to an unnamed union dated 13 April 1869, wherein it was stated that the Central Authority "do not think that the Statute 12 and 13 Vict. c.103 s 16 affords a legal justification for the appropriation by the Boards of Guardians of postage stamps sent to a pauper inmate of the Workhouse."

54 *Official Circulars of Public Documents*, vol. 3, 160. The PLC stated that there was nothing to prohibit the transmission of letters to paupers "under ordinary circumstances" although they were silent on what might constitute extraordinary circumstances. The union name was redacted.

55 TNA: MH12/9756, 9858/1849, Henry Jemmett, Witney workhouse, to the PLC, 26 March 1849.

56 TNA: MH12/7683, 22686/1873, George Lester Puttock, Poplar workhouse, to the LGB, 5 April 1873.

57 This is an excellent example of a pauper *almost* remembering the technical reference to the law. He is referring not to an act but to article 56 of the General Order – Workhouse Rules, which states that each board of guardians should appoint a visiting committee that would examine the workhouse weekly, inspect reports from the chaplain and medical officers, examine the workhouse stores, and ascertain the truth and circumstances of any complaints made to them.

See *Eighth Annual Report of the Poor Law Commissioners*, 100–1. Also Deane, "Late Nineteenth-Century Philanthropy," 122–42.

58 TNA: MH12/2542, 13333/1845, John Fin (sometimes Finn), Tavistock workhouse, to the PLC, 19 November 1845.

59 TNA: MH12/2542, 13333/1845, Draft letter from the PLC to John Fin, 26 November 1845.

60 TNA: MH12/2542, 13333/1845, Draft letter from the PLC to the Tavistock PLU, 26 November 1845; and MH12/2542, 13818/1845, Letter from John Physick, Clerk, Tavistock PLU, to the PLC, 2 December 1845. This accusation is logical, but Gurney, *Wanting and Having*, 95, suggests that want of food in workhouses was a leitmotif of the whole New Poor Law.

61 TNA: MH12/2542, 13869/1845, John Fin, Tavistock workhouse, to the PLC, 7 December 1845.

62 On pauper emigration schemes see Howells, "'For I Was Tired of England Sir,'" 181–94.

63 TNA: MH12/11198/64, 2987/1848, John Cartwrght, Wolstanton and Burslem PLU, to the PLB, 30 October 1848. The letter was annotated: "The Gns. Have come to a right conclusion–send copy of the ~~oct~~ Statute."

64 There are also extant three advocate letters and a multi-signature petition on Cox's behalf, all of them suffused with languages of law and process.

65 TNA: MH12/8634, 28816/1851, Thomas Cox, Great Yarmouth, to the PLB, 1 July 1851; TNA: MH12/8634, 32327/1851, Thomas Cox, Great Yarmouth, to Sir George Grey, Home Office (subsequently sent to the PLB), 24 July 1851; and TNA: MH12/8634, 14017/1851, Juliana Cox, Great Yarmouth, to the PLB, 27 December 1851.

66 TNA: MH12/8635, 9391/1851, Thomas Cox, Great Yarmouth, to the PLB, 21 March 1853.

67 Jones and Carter, "Writing for Redress," n.28.

68 TNA: MH12/2243, 9760/1868, Thomas Snelgrove, Exeter Incorporation workhouse, to the PLB, 20 March 1868. Snelgrove refers to the *Consolidated General Order*, 1847, articles 127 through to 147, Punishments for Misbehaviours of the Paupers.

69 Rogers refers to the same sections of the *Consolidated General Order*, 1847, as Snelgrove.

70 Thus, his complaint was not only that the wrong articles from the *General Order* were used in punishment but that this wrong article was extended in his case.

71 TNA: MH12/7691, 17166/1872, Frederick Rogers, Poplar workhouse, to the LGB, 22 March 1872.

72 TNA: MH12/14402, 30006/1851, Robert Cooper, York PLU, to the PLB, 5 July 1851.

73 TNA: MH12/14401, 28222/1849, William Petty, York PLU, to the PLB, 27 September 1849.

74 TNA: MH12/14402, 30006/1851, Robert Cooper, York PLU, to the PLB, 5 July 1851.

75 This elision of criminality and poverty is a consistent feature of our material. It adds weight to Gurney's claim that the New Poor Law encoded a "new criminalisation of the poor" (Gurney, *Wanting and Having*, 75) but is contradicted by mid- and late nineteenth-century doubts about how far individuals could be held responsible for their poverty. See Harris, *Unemployment and Politics*, passim, and Hennock, "Poverty and Social Theory," 67–91.

76 TNA: MH12/14406, 579/1860, Robert Cooper, Hungate, to the PLB, 5 January 1860. This reference to his settlement allowed the York PLU to dismiss legal claims to outdoor relief under the PLAA, Sec 27. On the other hand Cooper may have been referencing the 23rd section of the *Poor Law Board Act*, 1847, which stated: "when any Two Persons, being Husband and Wife, both of whom shall be above the Age of Sixty Years, shall be received into any Workhouse, in pursuance of the Provisions of the said recited Act or of this Act, or of any Rule, Order, or Regulation of the Commissioners appointed by Authority of this Act, such Two Persons shall not be compelled to live separate and apart from each other in such Workhouse." *An Act for the Administration of the Laws for Relief of the Poor in England*, 1847, 10 & 11 Vict.) c.109, section 23.

77 TNA: MH12/15489, 719/1883, Joseph Smith, Sheffield, to the LGB, 31 December 1883.

78 Ausubel, *In Hard Times*, 86–103; Koven, "Borderlands"; and Callanan Martin, *Hard and Unreal Advice*, 20–39.

79 Jones and King, *Pauper Voices*, chapter 3.

80 For an important example of this process, see Shave, "'Great Inhumanity,'" 339–63.

81 Frankel, *States of Inquiry*, 36.

82 Ibid., 30. Also Jones and King, *Pauper Voices*, chapter 1.

83 *Consolidated General Order*, 1847. Article 147. This insistence on open display was a staple of commercial guides such as Lumley, *Manuals of the Duties*, 90.

84 TNA: MH12/14406, 579/1860, Robert Cooper, Hungate, to the PLB, 5 January 1860.

85 Knott, *Popular Opposition*, and Navickas and Crymble, "From Chartist Newspaper," 232–47.

86 TNA: MH12/11196/303, 10408/B/1842, Robert Weale, assistant poor law commissioner, to the PLC, 7 August 1842. As Pickering, "'And Your Petitioner,'" 379, reminds us, however, such meetings and the petitioning that went with them implied "an acceptance of the authority of parliament," here in the guise of the PLC, PLB, or LGB. See also Tilly, "The Rise of the Public Meeting," 291–9; Knights, "'The Lowest Degree of Freedom,'" 18–34; and Benoît, "A Chartist Singularity?" 51–66.

87 Webb and Webb, *English Poor Law History*, 1.

88 Goldman, "Social Reform," 73.

CHAPTER SEVEN

1 TNA: MH12/4388, 40182/1853, Harriet Cross, Bodenham, to the PLB, 9 November 1853. On the particular problems faced by women paying rent see Sutcliffe, "The Growth of Public Intervention," 118. The tenuous literacy here is striking.

2 Zedner, *Women, Crime, and Custody*, 304–19, suggests that women generally comprised only 20 per cent of those convicted and occasionally much less. Men therefore loomed statistically larger in the senior courts where family-breaking sentences were handed down. See also Feeley and Little, "The Vanishing Female," 719–57, and van der Heijden and Pluskota, "Introduction," 661–71.

3 Though see Williams, *Unmarried Motherhood*.

4 *Report of the Poor Law Commissioners*, 1834, 262. The text of this recommendation in the report was emphasised in capital letters.

5 Webb and Webb, *English Poor Law*, 6–7.

6 See Williams, *Unmarried Motherhood*, 1–43, for a broad survey of the literature linking Old and New Poor Law.

7 Hollen Lees, *The Solidarities of Strangers*, 135–45. See also Kidd, *State, Society and the Poor*, 37, and French, "An Irrevocable Shift."

8 Clark, "The New Poor Law," 261–82.

9 Levine-Clark, "The Gendered Economy of Family Liability," 72–89. Horrell and Humphries, "The Origins and Expansion," 38, argue that "female domesticity and a male breadwinner became not only an accepted image but also a symbol of working-class respectability."

10 Wall, "Some implications," 312–35.

11 Thane, "Women and the Poor Law," 30–51. Mandler, "Poverty and Charity," 10, suggests that the public-facing roles of women were also vital for family economies.

12 King, *Writing the Lives*, 282–308.

13 Long, *Conversations in Cold Rooms*, 10–11.

14 Englander, *Poverty and Poor Law Reform*, 18. See also Levine-Clark, *Unemployment*, 21, and Crowther, "Family Responsibility," 141.

15 The corpus contains material by or about a very diverse set of women including vagrants, indoor and outdoor paupers, the aged, neighbours, friends, idiots and imbeciles, the insane, widows, mothers of illegitimate children, and advocates. Groups not picked up in this chapter nonetheless appear throughout the book.

16 This also translates to other epistolary relationships. See, for instance, Palk, *Prisoner's Letters*, xv.

17 These continuities lessen after 1896 as changes to concepts of citizenship, the shape of local electorates, and the rise of collectivism provided new registers and modes of contestation. See Hall and Schwarz, "State and Society," 7–10; Evans, *Social Policy*, 211; and Henriques, *Before the Welfare State*, 59.

18 TNA: HO 107/6, ff 13 and 14, 21–2. Flitwick, Bedfordshire, Census 1841.

19 TNA: MH12/3, 14858/A/1844, newspaper cutting/extract from *The Times*, "The New Poor Law Again = Death from Starvation and Neglect," 18 October 1844; and MH12/3, no paper number, newspaper cutting/extract from unidentified newspaper, "Ampthill Board of Guardians, Important Investigation, The Alleged Starvation Case at Flitwick," undated (1844). All the material that follows is drawn from this extensive record. For context on newspapers, see Jones and King, *Pauper Voices*, and Roberts, "How Cruel," 98.

20 The "woman called Deacon" mentioned in the newspaper is probably Susan Deacon, aged fifty, who also lived at Horns End with her two daughters Elizabeth (fourteen) and Dinah (twelve).

21 The surname of Pedder's sister is alternatively given as Spendelow or Spenlow.

22 On the Anatomy Act see Hurren, *Dying for Victorian Medicine*.

23 For the differences between indirect, direct, and represented speech acts in second-hand testimony of this sort see Walker and Grund, "'Speaking Base Approbious words,'" 5–10.

24 King, *Writing the Lives*, 270–91.

25 TNA: MH12/9248/480, 28452/B/1863, Mary Ann Taylor, Nottingham, to the PLB, July 1863.

26 On the complex history of how children came to be defined as orphans see Murdoch, *Imagined Orphans*, Taylor, "'Poverty, Emigration,'" 89–103, and Marks, "'The luckless waifs and strays,'" 113–37.

27 Bailey, "'Think Wot a Mother Must Feel,'" 5–19. Vincent, *Poor Citizens*, 3, 5, and 6, argues that such circumstances solidified the experience of poverty because people "could no longer keep their stories private" (quote at p. 3).

28 TNA: MH12/8488, 55219/1878, Maria Butterfield, Dereham, to the LGB, 29 July 1878.

29 For context see Levine-Clark, "From Relief to Justice," 302–21.

30 George Wallace was part of a group of four men convicted at the Durham Assizes in February 1870. Wallace received twelve months. TNA: HO 27/155, p. 159. For context see Osborne and Winstanley, "Rural and Urban Poaching," 187–212.

31 As Lyons, "Writing Upwards," 324, notes, the rhetoric of prior physical presence here was likely a deliberate strategy for validating the circumstances described.

32 For broad context to these words see Coombs, "'Concealing Him,'" 217–39.

33 TNA: MH12/13910/368, 2059/1854, Elizabeth Lester and Ann Merryman, Alvenchurch, to the PLB, 13 January 1854.

34 TNA: MH12/3025, 21218/1870, Margaret Wallace, Durham, to the PLB, 7 May 1870.

35 TNA: MH 12/9357/71, 4444/C/1838, Jane Hewitt, London, to Mansfield PLU, 9 April 1838. This letter was enclosed with a covering text from the clerk at Mansfield asking what they should do in such circumstances.

36 On non-resident letter styles see Sokoll, *Essex Pauper Letters*, 10–17. The letter here shows little gratitude and deference and this can perhaps be explained by its being akin to an Old Poor Law "renewing letter" under King's conceptual hierarchies of letter types, where the instigator letter had already contained the various signifiers of submissiveness. See King, *Writing the Lives*, 50.

37 TNA: MH12/9357/72, 4444/C/1838, PLC to W E Goodacre junior, Clerk to the

Mansfield PLU, 15 May 1838. Our italics. On the way that officials sought to rhetorically construct the poor, see Joyce, "The People's English," 169.

38 TNA: MH12/15798, 27647/1854, Hannah Roberts, Aberystwyth, to the PLB, 19 July 1854.

39 On the "fluidity of authority" in poor households, see Doolittle, "Fatherhood and Family Shame," 88.

40 For context see Crone, "Educating the Labouring Poor."

41 On "Club" benefits see Cordery, *British Friendly Societies.*

42 TNA: MH12/10325, 48301/1865, Harriet Robbins, Stowey, to the PLB, 19 December 1865. Our italics.

43 TNA: MH12/15774, 46395/1869, Emma Farr, Glasbury, to the PLB, 6 October 1869. On family tensions of this sort see Thomson, "The Elderly," 59.

44 Levine-Clark, "The Gendered Economy," 72–3.

45 Grantley was made a part of the Ripon PLU when it was declared in October 1852.

46 TNA: MH12/15323, 8210/1851, Inhabitants of the Township of Grantley, to the PLB, February 1851. On the wider context for this petitioning see Leys, "Petitioning," 45–64.

47 TNA: MH12/5055, 734/A/1842, James and Mary Cox, Barton, to the PLC, 24 January 1842.

48 TNA: MH12/4387, 9482/1852, Edward and Sarah Linning, Stoke Prior, 30 March 1852.

49 TNA: MH12/8487, 42218/1876, William and Mary Ann Ward, East Dereham, to the PLC, 29 June 1876.

50 TNA: MH12/5988, 51294/1877, Joanna Maddon, Liverpool workhouse, to the Home Office, 11 July 1877

51 Doolittle, "Fatherhood and Family Shame," 95, argues that workhouses were deliberately established as "celibate institutions."

52 Crowther, *The Workhouse System*, 42–3.

53 TNA: MH12/689, 5075/1852, James Danby Affleck, Dalham, to the PLB, 11 February 1852.

54 The itch, or scabies, is a contagious skin infestation by the mite *Sarcoptes scabiei*, which burrows under the skin causing intense itching. In workhouses the infection was passed primarily through bed sharing. Some workhouses had

"itch wards" where those infected were separated and treated away from other inmates.

55 TNA: MH12/6847, 5399/1857, "a Mother," Bethnal Green workhouse, to the PLB, 13 February 1857.

56 TNA: MH12/5, 34194/1856, Report of Robert Weale, poor law inspector, to the PLB, includes the witness statement of Sophia Heathfield, 28 August 1856. Jeff James has argued persuasively that her actions were those of "an individual not consumed by out of control emotions but level-headed, calm and able to think strategically." James, "Sophia Heathfield," 221.

57 TNA: MH12/5985, 71517/1874, Jane Maylor, Liverpool workhouse, to the LGB, November 1874.

58 TNA: MH12/6989, 15607/1849; 7466/1848; 4107/1849; 15091/1849; 23564/1849, Jane Rosier, Chelsea workhouse, to the PLB, 24 December 1847–August 1849.

59 TNA: MH12/12231, 75749/1886, Hannah Berry Pearson, Dorking workhouse, to the Superintendent of Police, Dorking, 22 June 1886.

60 TNA: MH12/12231, 75749/1886, Hannah [Berry] Pearson, Dorking workhouse, to the LGB, 24 June 1886.

61 Hurren, "Poor Law versus Public Health," 399–418, and Richardson, "The Uppingham Typhoid Outbreaks," 281–96.

62 TNA: MH12/12232, 52297/1891, Hannah Berry Pearson, Dorking workhouse, to the LGB, 8 June 1891.

63 For context see Hall and Schwarz, "State and Society," 7–32, and Levine-Clark, "From Relief to Justice," 302–21.

64 TNA: MH12/12232, 107649/1892, Hannah Berry Pearson, Dorking workhouse, to the Lord Mayor of London, 20 November 1892.

65 Rosier was unsuccessful in securing any intervention. Maylor's letter appears to have prompted a visit by Uvedale Corbett, LGB inspector, who raised several legitimate concerns and found that two of the people Maylor had complained of had left or were in the process of leaving; TNA: MH12/5985, 71517/1875, minute by Uvedale Corbett, to the LGB, 6 January 1876. Pearson was also successful with Herbert Jenner-Fust, LGB inspector, visiting the Dorking workhouse "on the day I received the complaint." Jenner-Fust refers to Pearson as an imbecile "suffering from 'dementia'" but considered her complaint referring to another inmate named Capon as "well founded." TNA: MH12/12231, 75749/1886, minute by Herbert Jenner–Fust, to the LGB, 31 July 1886.

66 See Price, *Medical Negligence*, 84. Focusing on witness statements does of course prioritise certain themes and rhetorical modes.

67 For a recent summary of the thematic writing, see Bourke, "'Animal Instincts,'" 1201–17.

68 Newman, "To Punish or Protect," 134.

69 TNA: MH12/14589/110, 29529/1855, statement of Ann Birkbeck, Reeth workhouse, 13 July 1855.

70 TNA: MH12/8639, 1079/1863, Report of John Walsham, poor law inspector, with statement of Mary Ann Chamberlin, to the PLB, 9 December 1862.

71 TNA: MH12/8483, 2353/1868, Charles Wright, Clerk of the Rye PLU, to John Walsham, poor law inspector, 16 January 1868. Includes statement of Elizabeth Rudd.

72 TNA: MH12/1018, 897/1851, James Broadhurst, Clerk, Nantwich PLU, to the PLB, 4 January 1851. Includes statement of Ann Hodgkinson, 4 January 1851.

73 TNA: MH12/8633, 54993/1850, Report of John Walsham, poor law inspector, to the PLB, 5 November 1850. Includes Statement of Mary Ann Wilson 21 October 1850. On the toxic atmosphere in the Great Yarmouth workhouse at this date, see King and Jones, "Fragments of Fury?"

74 TNA: MH12/1014, 13919/B/1842, Report of Charles Mott, to the PLC, 1 November 1842.

75 TNA: MH12/8483, 2353/1868, Charles Wright, Clerk of the Rye PLU, to John Walsham, poor law inspector, 16 January 1868. Includes statement of Elizabeth Rudd. See also Frost, "Under the Guardians' Supervision," 122–39, and Frost, *Illegitimacy*.

76 For example, in the Truro workhouse (Cornwall) in 1854 an enquiry was conducted into the behaviour of Thomas Treloar the workhouse master, who it was alleged had sex on a number of occasions with Elizabeth Kernick, a seventeen-year-old inmate. Kernick eventually confessed that it was false and that another inmate named Jane Burrows had put her up to it. Kernick stated that Burrows had said "she would lay a trap for Master … that she wished to get the Master out of his situation." TNA: MH12/1531/785, 36406/1854, Witness statement Elizabeth Kernick, to the PLB, 24 September 1854.

77 TNA: MH12/8633, 54993/1850, report of John Walsham, poor law inspector, to the PLB, 5 November 1850. Includes Statement of Mary Ann Wilson, 21 October 1850.

CHAPTER EIGHT

1 TNA: MH12/1148, 2938/1861, John Hankeson, Stockport, to the PLB, 14 January 1861. This was not the only letter sent by or on behalf of John Hankeson. In fact, it was not even the first; ten letters were sent in his name between July 1858 and February 1865 and collectively they provide an excellent extended record of the concerns and strategies of the aged poor in negotiations with the central authorities. Third-person writing by paupers is not unusual in the corpus, as we have seen, but the authorship of this particular letter is unclear. Other letters from Hankeson were written in a different hand to this one and constructed in the first person, but all were signed in his name. For a more detailed discussion of "co-authorship," or authorship by proxy, see Jones and King, *Navigating the Old English Poor Law*, 1–38.

2 Through later material we know that he would have been sixty-eight when this letter was written, and his wife sixty-six.

3 On the particular earning capacities of aged handloom weavers see Timmins, *The Last Shift*, 107–27.

4 Boulton and Schwarz, "'The Comforts of a Private Fireside,'" 221. On the deep chronological roots of this rhetorical trope for the aged see Botelho, "'The Old Woman's Wish,'" 59–78.

5 Lyons, "Writing Upwards," 318, suggests that this sort of approach was normative for those addressing the powerful, as was the rhetorical performance of gratitude.

6 Thomson, "Workhouse," 64; Thomson, "Welfare and the Historians," 370; Thomson, "The Welfare of the Elderly," 202–4.

7 Thomson, "Workhouse," 49–50.

8 Hunt, "Paupers," 408. Thus, Snell suggests that the weekly pension in the early–New Poor Law period was more likely to be between one and two shillings. Snell, *Annals of the Labouring Poor*, 132.

9 Thane, *Old Age*, 167, 171.

10 Goose, "Workhouse Populations," 57, 59, 67.

11 Ritch, "English Poor Law," 77. Andy Gritt and Peter Park found similarly large numbers of elderly residents in the workhouses of urban Lancashire in 1881 (albeit with a considerable degree of variation), as did Peter Jackson in Kent, Hampshire, Hertfordshire and Leicester for the same year: Gritt and Park, "The

Workhouse Populations," 37–65 and Jackson, "Kent Workhouse Populations," 51–66.

12 Crowther, "The Workhouse," 190.

13 King, *Poverty and Welfare*, passim.

14 Goose, "Poverty, Old Age," 351–68; Johnson, "The Employment," 106–28; Leivers, "Housing the Elderly," 56–65; and Thane, "The History of Provisions," 191–9.

15 Boyer and Schmidle, "Poverty," 255. Seebohm Rowntree suggested in 1899 that the amounts were 7s for a single person and 11s 8d for a couple. See Hennock, "The Measurement," 220.

16 See especially Boyer, "Work for Their Prime," 3–32, and Rose, "The Varying Household Arrangements," 113.

17 See, for example, the letters of Mungo Paumier of Bethnal Green and George William Stocks of Rye, both of whom complained of being refused admission to the workhouse when they believed their needs required it. Paumier, in particular, also resisted being turned out of the workhouse on several occasions, despite the promise of a regular pension. TNA: MH12/6863/49914/1866, Mungo Paumier to the PLB, 12 December 1866; TNA: MH12/6863/25310/1872, Mungo Paumier to the LGB, 3 May 1872; TNA: MH12/13092/108349/1882, G.W. Stocks to the LGB, November 1882.

18 For a review see Jones and King, *Pauper Voices*, 1–14.

19 Snell, *Annals of the Labouring Poor*, 135.

20 Crowther, *The Workhouse System*, 240–1.

21 Hall and Schwarz, "State and Society," 19.

22 Sokoll, "Old Age in Poverty."

23 Botelho, *Old Age*, 104.

24 Ottaway, *The Decline of Life*, 173.

25 Botelho, *Old Age*, 98–100; Ottaway, *Decline*, 174–5; and King, *Writing the Lives*, 178–200.

26 Charlesworth, "How Poor Law Rights Were Lost," 292; Feldman, "Migrants, Immigrants," 93.

27 King, "Rights, Duties and Practice"; Hollen Lees, *Poverty and Pauperism*, 4; Kidd, *State, Society and the Poor*, 4; and Goose, "Poverty, Old Age," 352.

28 TNA: MH12/10320, P.E. Coates, Clutton, to the PLC, 27 October 1834. For similar confusion over the role of magistrates see Green, "Pauper Protests," 153.

29 TNA: MH12/2095, 3798/B/1837, Mr Philpot, Lyme Regis, to the PLC, 27 May 1837.

This sort of rhetorical approach has similarities with the way that people advocated for immigrant neighbours. See Tabili, "'Having Lived Close,'" 369–87.

30 TNA: MH12/2102, 3746/1852, Clifford Shirreff, Colyton, to the PLB, 29 January 1852. On the importance of the difference between an age of sixty and that of seventy, see Hunt, "Paupers and Pensioners," 414.

31 TNA: MH12/8497/81157/E/1895, James Clitheroe, East Dereham, to the LGB, 25 June 1895.

32 Lyons, *A History of Reading*, 6, argues that the poor had a "shared imaginary library."

33 TNA: MH12/16058, 48530/1853, John Mark, Llanengan, to the PLB, 23 December 1853. Prochaska, "Philanthropy," 363, argues that running out of relatives was a "short-cut to the workhouse."

34 TNA: MH12/14026, 46034/1876, Charles Burchill, Kidderminster, to the LGB, 2 July 1876.

35 TNA: MH12/9239/292, 26413/1852, William Sturton, Arnold, to the PLB, May 1852. Vincent, *Poor Citizens*, 20–1, argues that such top-ups were collectively more important than relief to the household economies of the aged.

36 TNA: MH12/9248/53, 9624/1862, George Ellis, Arnold, to the PLB, 24 March 1862. King, *Writing the Lives*, 213, 286. See also Robin, "The Relief of Poverty," 201, 207.

37 King, *Writing the Lives*, 284. Also Thane, "'An Untiring Zest,'" 235.

38 Ritch, "English Poor Law," 66; Thane, *Old Age*, 167.

39 This was common under both the Old and New Poor Law; see King, "Nursing."

40 TNA: MH12/1300, 6224/A/1843, Catherine Baker, Trevie, to the PLC, 26 May 1843.

41 TNA: MH12/2097, 10898/A/1844, James Hoare, Collington (Colyton), to the PLC, 20 July 1844.

42 TNA: MH12/256, 12126/1849, George Caffin, Brimpton, to the PLB, 20 April 1849.

43 TNA: MH12/16059, 4104/1855, Evan Williams, Penrhos, to the PLB, 2 February 1855.

44 Joyce, "The People's English," 169.

45 TNA: MH12/9760, 12544/1859, John Phipps, Witney workhouse, to the PLB, 28 March 1859.

46 TNA: MH12/1150, 20357/1864, John Hankeson, Stockport, to the PLB, 1 June 1864.

47 TNA: MH12/2095, 3798/B/1837, Mr Philpot, Lyme Regis, to the PLC, 27 May 1837; TNA: MH12/14409, 29754/1871, Ann Willson, York, to the LGB, 3 July 1871.

48 *Second Annual Report of the* PLC, 1836, 8.

49 *Second Annual Report of the* PLC, 1835, 6. As with women the aged were sometimes constructed as equivalent to children, requiring protection from an interventionist Centre.

50 *Second Annual Report of the* PLC, 1836, 8.

51 Thus Goose, "Poverty, Old Age," 357–61, traces a male bias in workhouse populations, whereas Robin, "Family Care," 505–16, traces exactly the opposite.

52 Equally, however, both in the corpus and in wider record collection we find unions going out of their way to protect the interests of the aged poor, as for instance did the Billesdon union (Leicestershire) whose minutes 1836–39 reveal concerted attempts to place the aged in boarding or other care arrangements. Only when this failed – as for instance in May 1837 in the case of an eighty-four-year-old pauper with "no person consenting to take care of her at any price" – was the workhouse used. Leicestershire Record Office G/4/8a/1, Billesdon Union Minutes 1836–39.

53 TNA: MH12/9231/161, 4940/B/1841, H. Bruce Campbell, Nottingham, to the PLC, 24 April 1841. Our italics.

54 TNA: MH12/13892, 14914/A/1842, John Tarby, Wilton, to the PLC, 24 December 1842.

55 TNA: MH12/6846, 35021/1851, Daniel Rush, Bethnal Green, to the PLB, 22 August 1851.

56 TNA: MH12/1148, 26321/1861, John Hankeson, Stockport, to the PLB, 19 June 1861.

57 *Consolidated General Order*, article 99, no. 3, 1847.

58 TNA: MH12/1151, 28560/1866, James Ward, Stockport, to the PLB, 2 July 1866. This grounding of an appeal in the needs and weaknesses of a woman might well have been designed to make a positive decision easier. See Doolittle, "Fatherhood and Family Shame," 93. Male prisoners also constructed the suffering of their wives and families as a torment. See Marland, "Close Confinement," 277–90.

59 TNA: MH12/3401, 48398/1850, Charles Uggles, Chelmsford, to the PLB, 16 October 1850.

60 TNA: MH12/8479/243, 37286/1851, Harriet Johnson, Mitford and Launditch PLU, to the PLB, 13 September 1851.

61 TNA: MH12/14406, 8365/1861, William Ardington Cooper, York, to the PLB, 8 March 1861.

62 Even so, turnover of aged workhouse population could be high. Heritage, "The Elderly Populations," 157–200.

63 TNA: MH12/8978/15, 2363/A/1843, Anthony Perey, Berwick workhouse, to the PLC, 4 March 1843; TNA: MH12/8498, 156038/1898, George Batlock, Mitford and Launditch workhouse, to the LGB, 15 December 1898.

64 TNA: MH12/8636, 32341/1855, Thomas Lorick, Great Yarmouth workhouse, to the PLB, 14 August 1855.

65 TNA: MH12/6847, 45369/1857, anonymous to the PLB, 10 December 1857.

66 The phrase "rhetorical armoury" was used in relation to Old Poor Law pauper letters in Jones, "'I Cannot Keep My Place Without Being Deascent,'" 36, 46.

67 TNA: MH12/1147, 6069/1859, John Hankeson, Stockport, to the PLB, 6 February 1859. Blum and Krauss, "Age Heaping," 476, remind us that the migrant poor were the least likely of all population groups to accurately know age.

68 Snell, *Parish and Belonging*, 237–8. Non-resident relief was also discouraged post-1834 since it might blur the boundaries of responsibility between unions and their parish officials.

69 Quoted in Snell, *Parish and Belonging*, 238.

70 TNA: MH12/11363/112, 11346/C/1838, Peter Garnett, Otley, to the PLC, 18 December 1838.

71 TNA: MH12/11363/128, 3060/C/1839, John Ayshford Wise, Stoke, to the PLC, 16 April 1839.

72 Ibid. On proximate unions in Staffordshire see Talbot, "North-South Divide," passim. More widely Kidd, *State, Society*, 30–1.

73 TNA: MH12/11363/128, Commissioners' annotation on John Ayshford Wise, Stoke, to the PLC, 16 April 1839.

74 For an overview of removability clauses see Laybourn, *The Evolution*, 30. On the crusade see Hurren, *Protesting about Pauperism*.

75 TNA MH12/9363/32, 11448/1850, W.E. Goodacre, Mansfield PLU, to the PLB, 19 March 1850.

76 Ibid.

77 TNA: MH12/9369/109, 25359/1865, W. E. Goodacre, Mansfield PLU, to the PLB, 23 June 1865. On the enduring problem of "maiden settlement" see Sharpe, "Parish Women," passim.

78 Ibid.

79 The *General Order* relating to non-resident relief was published in 1845. In the preamble, the commissioners explicitly stated that this order "does not permit or forbid the allowance of non-resident relief in any case in which such relief is not now permitted, or is not now forbidden." See *The General Orders*, 27. It is clear from the commissioners' correspondence to guardians that they expected – or hoped – that they would be consulted in cases where non-resident relief was to be granted, but nowhere in the orders was this actually required. It seems very likely that non-resident relief continued to be routinely allowed. See Snell, *Parish and Belonging*, 238–9.

80 As Lyons, "Writing Upwards," 324, notes, an awareness of such opinion confirmed the utility of further writing.

81 *First Annual Report of the PLC*, 1835, 19–20.

82 *The General Orders*, 55.

CHAPTER NINE

1 TNA: MH12/252, Ratepayers of Newbury to the PLC, 2 April 1835. The similarity of this form of address to other sorts of petition from towns and ratepayer bodies is striking.

2 The phrase was widely, and disparagingly, used to describe the three unelected PLC commissioners. See Wythen Baxter, *The Book of the Bastiles*, 513.

3 For overviews see Neuman, "A Suggestion," 317–22; Neuman, *The Speenhamland County*, passim; and Sokoll, "Families, Wheat Prices," 83–9.

4 The historiography on the importance and impact of Speenhamland is considerable, and it started almost as soon as the Old Poor Law ended. See, for example, Anon, *Remarks on the Opposition*, 8; Nicholl, *A History*, 92–107; Blaug, "The Myth," passim; Blaug, "The Poor Law Report," 229–34; Jones, "Swing, Speenhamland," passim; and Griffin, *The Politics of Hunger*, chapter 3.

5 Neuman, "A Suggestion," passim. Still, we might note the conclusion of Williams, *From Pauperism*, 49, that the Old Poor Law in 1832 was "massively involved in relief to the able-bodied." For a contrasting argument on the importance of care for the sick as a spending category see King, *Sickness, Medical Welfare*, passim.

6 The phrase is George Nicholls's, reflecting on the Old Poor Law writings of

Jeremy Bentham. Nicholls, *A History*, 105. For a sophisticated re-statement of this argument see Block and Somers, "In the Shadow of Speenhamland," 274, and Wrigley and Smith, "Malthus."

7 TNA: MH12/252, Ratepayers of Newbury to the PLC, 2 April 1835. The rhetorical trope of the family was clearly a shared referential structure for officials, advocates and the poor.

8 Embodied in the quotation from George Nicholls, n.6, above. See also Williams, "Poor Relief, Labourers' Households," passim, and Williams, "Malthus, Marriage," 56–82.

9 Webb and Webb, *English Poor Law*. For a useful overview of the debate from the 1920s to the late twentieth century, see Mandler, "Tories and Paupers," 81–103.

10 Throughout the book thus far we have encountered men and women who were partially "able" in work terms. In this chapter we focus consciously on the fully able-bodied and on the classic group in this category, the un- or under-employed man.

11 Williams, *From Pauperism*, 158–63.

12 Brundage, "The English Poor Law," 410.

13 Williams, *From Pauperism*, 181–3 and 209.

14 For a good rendering, see Brundage, "The English Poor Law," 409–11.

15 Finlayson, *Citizen, State*, 148; Boyson, "The History," 163–78. This observation sits easily with Boyer and Schmidle, "Poverty among the Elderly," 260, who argue that outdoor relief was widely seen as a legitimate entitlement.

16 Though our material contains notes of rhetoric on masculinity or fatherhood, they were considerably less clear and intensive than the signature of motherhood. For wider context see Tosh, *Manliness*, 133–8 and 141.

17 As Pooley, "Travelling through the City," 605, notes, the question of travel distance and time became more prominent in all sorts of life-writing as the potential for rapid travel developed.

18 On the question of fragile minds see Suzuki, "Lunacy and Labouring Men," 122–5.

19 For moral citizenship see Sutton, "Liberalism, State Collectivism," 74–6.

20 Levine-Clark, *Unemployment, Welfare*.

21 On the systematic buying of tools for the able-bodied elsewhere see Boyson, "The History," 242.

22 TNA: MH12/6845, 9773/1848, James Archer, Shoreditch, to the PLB, 4 April 1868.

The phrase "perpetual pauperism" speaks to wider public debates about lifetime and inherited poverty. See Stapleton, "Inherited Poverty," 339–55.

23 TNA: MH12/7692, 51096/1872, George Dovey, Poplar PLU, to the LGB, 18 September 1872.

24 TNA: MH12/2241, 9280/1861, Thomas Smith, Exeter, to the PLB, 19 March 1861. Once again the ability to demonstrate current knowledge of public debate is striking, as is the sense that Smith had the power to not consent.

25 For background on the Durham union see Dunkley, "The Hungry Forties," passim.

26 TNA: MH12/3023, 37831/1866, John Gowland, Durham workhouse, to the PLB, 24 September 1866.

27 For a discussion of this group in a wider European context, see Wessel Hansen, "Grief, Sickness and Emotions," 35–41. It is of course more usual to think about the penalties accruing from child poverty; see Humphries, "Memories of Pauperism," 102–26.

28 TNA: MH12/16104, 8267/C/1837, Richard Lewis, Shocklach Oviatt, to the PLC, 2 October 1837. The dialect in this letter speaks to a particular type of literacy. See Mackie, "Talking Like a Native," 90–1.

29 Lewis's letter reflects a widespread antipathy in the region towards the incarceration of the poor in workhouses, as well as the reality that many ratepayers in rural Wales were barely above the level of paupers themselves. See Evans and Jones, "'A Stubborn, Intractable Body,'" 101–21.

30 TNA: MH12/8483, 37686/1868, Charles Wright, Dereham, to the PLB, 25 July 1868.

31 TNA: MH12/668, 5703/1839, W.H. Chapman, Rector of Balsham, to the PLC, 15 August 1839.

32 On able-bodied relief in Norfolk see Digby, *Pauper Palaces*, 143–60.

33 *An Act for Amending the Laws Relating to the Settlement*, Article IV.

34 Hitchcock, "The English Workhouse," 122.

35 Fissell, "Charity Universal," passim; Smithers, *Liverpool*, 295–7.

36 Jones and King, *Pauper Voices*, passim.

37 Thelwall, *The Rights of Nature*, 34.

38 Bernard, *An Account*, 8.

39 Anon, quoted in Clark, *Thoughts on the Management*, 36.

40 Mr Middleton, quoted in Anon, *The Complete Farmer*, under "Poor Laws" (NP).

41 Speech of S. Whitbread reported in Hansard, *The Parliamentary Debates*, 910.

42 Harris, *The Origins*, 44, table 4.1.

43 Fraser, *The Evolution*, 46, and Williams, *From Pauperism*, passim.

44 King, "Rights, Duties and Practice," 264–5.

45 TNA: MH12/6843, 2244/1841, Humphrey Moneypenny, Bethnal Green, to the PLC, 5 March 1841.

46 TNA: MH12/6843, 1412/1841, Humphrey Moneypenny, Bethnal Green, to the PLC, 10 February 1841.

47 This reference to being denied access to the public domain is a rhetorical refrain that we also find in Old Poor Law letters. See King, *Writing the Lives*, 276–85.

48 TNA: MH12/6843, 6762/1841, John Vickers, Bethnal Green workhouse, to the PLC, 5 July 1841.

49 For some excellent Lancashire examples of men being allowed "out" to work see Boyson, "The History," 325–28.

50 TNA: MH12/3398, 12004/1842, L. Chalke, Chelmsford PLU, to the PLC, 1 October 1842.

51 TNA: MH12/6846, 11640/1853, petition from inmates of the Bethnal Green workhouse to the PLB, 12 April 1853. Two of the signatories were disabled.

52 Jones, "Looking Through a Different Lens," passim.

53 TNA: MH12/7698, 91484/1884, Frank Burge, Poplar workhouse, to the LGB, 18 September 1884.

54 Copy Letter from Frank Burge to Mr J.R. Collins, originally dated 21 March 1884 and contained in TNA: MH12/7698, 91484/1884, Frank Burge, Poplar workhouse, to the LGB, 18 September 1884. The case for moral citizenship, rather than simply honest poverty, is clearly developed here.

55 Copy Calculation forwarded by Frank Burge to Mr J.R. Collins, 28 March 1884, previous to the meeting of the Board of Guardians on that day. Contained in TNA: MH12/7698, 91484/1884, Frank Burge, Poplar workhouse, to the LGB, 18 September 1884. The dripping sarcasm is notable in this letter, but it is also a regular feature of the rhetorical infrastructure for serial letter writers.

56 TNA: MH12/7700, 54238/1888, Printed copy of the ruling of the Court of Appeal in the case of Burge *v.* Power, 22 January 1887; *Hansard's Parliamentary Debates*, Vol. 326 (1888), 1525.

57 TNA: MH12/7698, 114278/1885, Frank Burge, Poplar workhouse, to the LGB, 10 December 1885.

58 For example, Ashforth, "The Urban Poor Law," 131–41; Brundage, "Reform of the Poor Law," 205; Midwinter, "State Intervention," 111; Rose, "The Allowance System," passim; Thane, "Women and the Poor Law," 30–1, 38–9.

59 Hurren, *Protesting about Pauperism*, 218–19.

60 TNA: MH12/9228/123, 2753/C/1837, Alfred Padley, Basford, to the PLC, 4 April 1837. See also Beckett, "Politics and the Implementation," 208–10.

61 Grover, *Social Security*, 38–9.

62 Hurren, *Protesting about Pauperism*, 19–20. See also Hurren, "Belonging, Settlement," 131–32. New systems of double entry bookkeeping made such interpretation easier to conceal. See Care, "The Significance," 125. The seasonality in our own sample is discussed in chapter 2.

63 Hurren, *Protesting about Pauperism*, 19.

64 Englander, *Poverty and Poor Law Reform*, 14, 29. However, see Boyson, "The History," 204, for a rendering of the remarkably patchy and superficial way the test was administered in Lancashire.

65 TNA: MH12/9246/1883, 13143/1858, Samuel Marriott, Bulwell, to the PLB, 15 April 1858.

66 TNA: MH12/9361/245, 3757/B/1846, Thomas Gresham, Mansfield, to the PLC, 19 March 1846.

67 TNA: MH12/9755, 16455/B/1844, Edward Cooper, Burford, to the PLC, 3 October 1844. Kidd, "Outcast Manchester," 57, argues that letters such as this, defending men "who according to official theory should have gone to the workhouse is suggestive of the manner in which the policy preferences of urban elites were undermined from within the middle class."

68 TNA: MH12/6078, 84686/1886, Charles Leonard, Salford, to the LGB, 17 February, 18 February 1886.

69 TNA: MH12/1145, 47787/1855, anonymous, Stockport PLU to the PLB, 15 December 1855.

70 TNA: MH12/1153, 4869/1870, the "working men" of Stockport, to the PLB, 26 January 1870.

71 Ibid.

72 Men were even disadvantaged compared to able-bodied women. See Levine-Clark, "Gendered Roles," 58–63.

73 Somers and Block, "From Poverty," 269, argue persuasively that in a system

underpinned by local discretion and definition, officials were particularly receptive to "signals" from the local population. On the scale of the problem see Treble, *Urban Poverty*, 13–90, and Gazeley, *Poverty*, 7–31.

CHAPTER TEN

1 TNA: MH12/237, 531/B/1845, Daniel Dixon, Clapham, to the PLC, 11 January 1845; King, *Writing the Lives*, 24–47, argues that writers under the Old Poor Law also feared punishment, often enjoining officials to forgive their persistent writing.

2 Crowther, *The Workhouse System*, 31; James, "Sophia Heathfield of Hawnes," 202–29; and Hurren, *Dying for Victorian Medicine*, passim.

3 Newman, "To Punish or Protect," 122–45.

4 Crowther, *The Workhouse System*, 209.

5 Green, "Pauper Protests," 137–59. Green's tabulated punishment offences are taken from 1873–74. Williams, "Paupers Behaving Badly," passim. See also Englander, *Poverty and Poor Law Reform*, 37–43.

6 Green, *Pauper Capital*, 157–87.

7 Carter, James, and King, "Punishing Paupers?" 161–80.

8 This distinction is an artificial one: in practice paupers punished for other reasons were also punished for writing.

9 *First Annual Report of the Poor Law Commissioners*, 1835, 100–1; *Consolidated General Order*, article 148, 1847. Visiting committees were to be organised by unions on their establishment. Their role as investigators of pauper complaints became more precisely defined over time. By 1847 the *Order* instructed guardians to: "appoint one or more Visiting Committees from their own body; and each of such committees shall carefully examine the Workhouse or, Workhouses of the Union, once in every week at the least, inspect the last reports of the Chaplain and Medical Officer, examine the stores, *afford, so far as is practicable, to the inmates an opportunity of making any complaints, and investigate any complaints that may be made to them.*" Our italics.

10 Paupers complained to third-party advocates about mistreatment in the hope, and sometimes knowledge, that these people would intervene. Advocate letters are dealt with in chapter 3 and thus not explored explicitly here. Even the pauper complainant who worked through advocates, however, still risked becoming known to local union officers and so similarly liable to punishment.

11 Much of the evidence for this is in text written on the back of, or annexed as notes to, the relevant pauper complainants' letters.

12 For such claims see Shave, "'Immediate Death,'" 168–73.

13 TNA: MH12/8634, 28816/1851, Thomas Cox, East Hill, to the PLB, 1 July 1851.

14 Great Yarmouth; Barnsley; Ampthill; Nantwich; Newbury; Bradford-on-Avon; Camelford; and Chelsea.

15 The case of John Cowles (sometimes John Coles) can be found across TNA: MH12/3964, 85/B/1843, William Mirehouse, Bristol, to the PLC, 2 January 1843; 368/B/1843, Etherbert Holborow, Clerk, Chipping Sodbury, to the PLC, 20 January 1845; 416/B/1843, William Mirehouse, Bristol, to the Rev Turner, 11 January 1843; 416/B/1843, William Mirehouse, Bristol, to the PLC, 11 January 1843; 1316/B/1843, William Mirehouse, Bristol, to the PLC, 2 February 1843; 2287/B/1843, William Mirehouse, Bristol, to the PLC, 22 February 1843; 2812/B/1843, Edward Carlton Tufnell (report with Cowles and union staff statements), to the PLC, 5 March 1843; 2812/B/1845, PLC to William Mirehouse, Bristol, 20 March 1843; 2812/B/1843, PLC to Charles Britten, workhouse master, Chipping Sodbury, 20 March 1843.

16 Absconding (including with workhouse clothing) accounted for 22.1 per cent of all summarily tried offences relating to English and Welsh workhouses between March 1835 and March 1841. Crowther, *The Workhouse System*, 209.

17 In a similar case, Sophia Heathfield and Elizabeth Spiers escaped the Ampthill workhouse in 1851 when the gruel there was alleged to be "unfit for human food." The women sought a local guardian who accompanied them to see one of the ex-officio guardians and local magistrates. He condemned it as "quite as bad as the women had represented." James, "Sophia Heathfield of Hawnes," 214.

18 A similar view can be found in the statement of Justice Ballantine from Limehouse in 1837, that: "the paupers had a perfect right to come before a magistrate if they had any just cause of complaint. Good God, if the poor creatures reduced to a workhouse were not to complain to the magistracy, who were they to complain to?" Green, *Pauper Capital*, 167.

19 "… places below the earth" is a reference to inmate accommodation in workhouse cellars.

20 TNA: MH12/14019/195, 11120/1848, Thomas Hartley, Kidderminster workhouse, to the PLB, 17 April 1848.

21 The reference to rationality has clear linkage to the way the able-bodied argued their cases.

22 TNA: MH12/14019/199, 12857/1848, Thomas Hartley, Kidderminster workhouse, to the PLB, 1 May 1848.

23 On workhouse gardens see Collinge, "'He Shall Have Care,'" 21–39.

24 TNA: MH12/14020/287, 1738/1853, W. Miles, Kidderminster workhouse, to the PLB, 10 January 1853.

25 See, for example, TNA: MH12/15468, 193/B/1845, Witness statement of Joseph Ledger, Sheffield workhouse, 7 January 1845; TNA: MH12/6991, 31506/1853, George Hancock, Chelsea workhouse, to the PLB, 22 August 1853; TNA: MH12/7698, 112036/1885, John Rutherford, Poplar, to the LGB, 4 December 1885.

26 TNA: MH12/5999, 41680, P.J. Cusack, Liverpool workhouse, to the LGB, 19 April 1886.

27 The letters are: TNA: MH12/16063, 41130/1868 (bound out of sequence), Henry Jones, Pwllheli, to the PLB, 13 May 1868; MH12/16063, 20527/1868, Henry Jones, Pwllheli, to the PLB, 18 May 1868; MH12/16063, 24689/1868, Henry Jones, Pwllheli, to the PLB, 5 June 1868; MH12/16063, 26621/1868, Henry Jones, Pwllheli, to the PLB, 12 June 1868; MH12/16063, 27126/1868, Henry Jones, Pwllheli, to the PLB, 13 June 1868, and MH12/16063, 28377/1868, Henry Jones, Pwllheli, to the PLB, 27 June 1868. See also Jones and King, *Pauper Voices*, 86–90.

28 See Foster, "Dirt, Dust and Devilment," passim, for a more detailed analysis of cleanliness and dirt in the workhouse.

29 The same James Hughes also wrote to the PLB under his own name, stating: "Since I have made my complaints Known to you Most Honble Gentlemen Amongst other complaints that Henry Jones Forwarded to your consideration. And since the board of Guardians Got an answer from you including a [copies] of the complaints. They have stopped payment of my weekly relief. Because I have made known to you Most Honble Gentlemen." TNA: MH12/16063, 32036/1868, James Hughes, Pwllheli, to the PLB, 3 July 1868.

30 On the groups of paupers who stood between inmates and paid staff see Walton, "Taking Control," 27–31.

31 This letter demonstrates a complex intertwining of biblical exegesis, the nature and meaning of motherhood and tyranny.

32 Such phrases usually signal hernia.

33 TNA: MH12/13311, 39441/1862, Thomas Swingler, Little Charles Street, Birmingham, to the PLB, 10 November 1862.

34 TNA: MH12/13311, 39824/1862, Thomas Swingler, Birmingham workhouse, to the PLB, November 1862.

35 The inversion of the term able-bodied here is pointed and meant to convey the inevitability of relief.

36 To "clem" a person to death is often used in place of "starve" someone to death. Its meaning can be broadened to include causing someone to suffer from hunger, thirst, or cold.

37 TNA: MH12/9250/177, 18949/1865, Joseph Brentnall, Carlton, to the PLB, 19 May 1865. TNA: RG 10/3524, f. 54, p. 30. The 1871 census shows Joseph Brentnall, a general labourer, partly blind, aged 35, and living alone in a lodging house at number 2, Knot Yard, Nottingham.

38 TNA: MH12/9250/178, Draft letter, PLB, to Joseph Brentnall, 25 May 1865 and draft letter, PLB, to R.B. Spencer, Clerk, Basford PLU, 25 May 1865.

39 TNA: MH12/9250/204, letter from R.B. Spencer, Clerk, Basford PLU, to the PLB, 23 June 1865.

40 TNA: MH12/9251/13, 6568/1866, Joseph Brentnall, Carlton, to the PLB, 14 February 1866.

41 TNA: MH12/9251/22, 8381/1866, Joseph Brentnall, Carlton, to the PLB, 27 February 1866. This short text concerning fraud was pasted into the volume next to the letter.

42 Carter, King, and James, "Punishing Paupers?" passim.

43 TNA: MH12/13362, 19460/1891, H. Minion, Birmingham workhouse, to the LGB, 25 February 1891.

44 TNA: MH12/11728/47, 3874/1834, petition from James Filnear, David Carver, William Reynolds, John Gould, John Witton, Robert Barnes, George Button, James Barton, Daniel Dunham, John Farington, George [Browning], William Baley, Joseph Fish, Robert Youngman, Robert Patrick, Thomas Curtis, Robert Aldred, George Manning, William Lusher, Simon Brown, William Moss, Samuel Carver, George Parsons, George Wagstaff, William Spall, John Howard and Daniel Mills, inmates of the Bulcamp/Blything workhouse, to the PLC, 27 March 1835. The Blything Incorporation was in the process of being dissolved at the time of writing and the Blything PLU was three months away from being declared.

45 TNA: MH12/13586, 22181/1849, petition from Samuel Jackson, Jonathan Stubbs, John Jones, Charles Richardson, Peter Callison, Jonathan Sawyer, John Downey, William Hardy, James Atkinson, John Bucks, Preston Redhead, John Blades, John Mills, Robin Gresdale, and John Wilkinson, Kendal workhouse, to the PLB, 22 July 1849.

46 TNA: MH12/5973, 18906/1860, petition from [Francis] Chambers, James [Ohal], Peter Byrnas, Edward Edwards, William Collins, Michael Naugton, John Hampson, Peter Hore, P Mcfarlon, John McNight, C Kelly, John Campbell, R. Murray, Arthur O'Hare, James Kerr and John McCarthy, Liverpool Poor Law Vestry workhouse, to the PLB, 21 May 1860.

47 TNA: MH12/1597, 9017/1862, petition from Charles Little, Robert Jack, Peter McLauchlan, Joseph Henderson, James Bill, Richard Clinton, Carlisle workhouse, to the PLB, 19 March 1862.

48 TNA: MH12/6996, 12662/1871, petition from James Perry, George Clarke, John Parker, William Bailey, John llen, Patrick Henry, William Bushnell, John Richards, Job Green, John Evans, James Goulding, Samuel Tripp, James Kitsell, John Rowntree, John Streek, William Pepper, Robert Holgate, John Braker, Hugh Bladdyn, C. Pratt, John Conor, John McLagan, Charles Howarth, A. Balding, Heney Penton, Henry Essery, Richard Leeson, Henry Buske, William Robinson, John Taylor, and John Laing, Chelsea workhouse, to the LGB, 20 March 1871. The round-robin petition would have been familiar to nineteenth-century writers, having been originated by eighteenth-century sailors to avoid individual punishment for collective complaints. Oxford English Dictionary Online, s.v. "round robin" (accessed 18 January 2022).

49 TNA: MH12/5058, 6775/1851, Anonymous, "the whole of the able bodied men," Faversham workhouse, to the PLB, 27 January 1851. Given the chronological proximity to Andover and other scandals, the writers might have hoped that this invitation to reveal the truth further would gain real traction. They were correct.

50 TNA: MH12/11939, 12003/1852, Anonymous, "the inmates of the union House," Plomesgate workhouse, to the PLB, 16 April 1852.

51 Outlined for instance in Maynard, "The Campaign for the Catholic," 528–31.

52 TNA: MH12/14732, 5007/1855, "the truth Loving test men of Bradford Union," to the PLB, 10 February 1855.

53 TNA: MH12/14435, 124529/1895, Anonymous, "From Inmates," Aysgarth workhouse, to the LGB, 11 October 1895.

54 TNA: MH12/13672, 25902/1848, William Waite, Bradford-on-Avon, to the PLB, September 1848.

55 TNA: MH12/8977/164, 6222/A/1842. "A Pauper," Berwick upon Tweed, to the PLC, 17 May 1842. On child punishment see Shave, "'Great Inhumanity,'" passim; King and Beardmore, "Contesting the Workhouse," passim, and Crompton, *Workhouse Children*, 120–45.

56 TNA: MH12/8089, 24096/1849, "A Fellow Sympathizer," Abercarn, to the PLB, 6 August 1849. The proximity of this accusation of starvation to the events at Andover is striking. See Gurney, *Wanting and Having*.

57 TNA: MH12/7695, 42746/1878, Petition from Catherine Devine, Margaret Leary, Catherine King, Caroline Sayers, Annie Pearson, Sarah Luke, Jessie Parks, Harriet Webb, Catherine Reynolds, Mary Cocklin, and Louisa Riley, Poplar workhouse, to the LGB, 4 June 1878.

58 TNA: MH12/16250, 48915/1855, Anonymous, Cardiff workhouse, to the Board of Guardians, Cardiff PLU, 27 October 1855. This is one of a series of threatening letters sent to the local guardians and subsequently passed to the PLB.

59 TNA: MH12/9008, 32376/1867, Anonymous, Castle Ward PLU, to the PLB, 24 September 1867.

60 This is certainly the case with Mungo Paumier, who wrote numerous forthright and assertive letters signed in his own name, yet also authored one letter anonymously. The anonymous letter (clearly Paumier's work, evident not only in the handwriting but also in the style and content) is TNA: MH12/6854, 3954/1867, "An Inmate" Bethnal Green workhouse, to the PLB, 30 January 1867.

61 TNA: MH12/11939, 12003/1852, "the inmates of the union House," Plomesgate workhouse, to the PLB, 16 April 1852. The letter was annotated: "Sir John Walsham 17 Apr 52 + I annex any former papers annexed. All the letters which the Board have so frequently [recd.] from the Inmates of this Workhouse appear to me to be written by the same party. Query however – send copies … to Wh. Gns. & invite their observations."

62 TNA: MH12/14023/221, 49842/1864, petition of Thomas Hartley, William Thornhill, James Hardiman and Samuel Smith, Kidderminster workhouse, to the PLB, 27 December 1864.

CHAPTER ELEVEN

1 The elision of the parish and union system here is important and points to the complexity of the initial transition period. See Midwinter, *Social Administration*, 31–6.

2 TNA: MH12/15796, 2737/A/1836, Thomas Price, Gwarclawdd, to the PLC, 27 July 1836.

3 King, *Sickness, Medical Welfare*, 24–7; King, '"Stop This Overwhelming Torment,"' 248–58; King, *Writing the Lives*, passim.

4 The chapter focuses on those with a physical illness/disability, though we acknowledge (as did contemporaries) the interlinkage with mental and learning disabilities. The requirements of the law regarding the mentally ill and incremental attempts to remove "lunatics" from workhouses mean that their experience of welfare presents particular historiographical challenges, and would require an extended discussion of its own. See King and Jones, "Fragments of Fury?," 244–7, and Smith, "Lunatic Asylum in the Workhouse," 225–45. In the case of the "infirm" poor, it is clear that infirmity under the New Poor Law was almost entirely identified with the afflictions of the elderly, just as it was under the Old, and the experiences of the elderly poor are discussed at length in chapter 8. See also Ritch, "English Poor Law," 69.

5 King, "Poverty, Medicine," 228; Ritch, *Sickness in the Workhouse*, 2–3; Tomkins, '"Labouring on a Bed of Sickness,"' 51–2.

6 King, "Regional Patterns," 61–75; Tomkins, "Workhouse Medical Care," 86–102; Boulton and Schwarz, "The Medicalization," 122–40; Crowther, "Health Care and Poor Relief," 203–19.

7 Though see Hurren, *Protesting About Pauperism*, and Negrine, "The Treatment," 34–44.

8 Digby, *Making a Medical Living*, 244–5; Hodgkinson, "Poor Law Medical Officers," 299; Marland, *Medicine and Society*, 52; Ritch, *Sickness in the Workhouse*, 9; Tomkins, '"The Excellent Example of the Working Class,"' 14.

9 Reinarz and Schwarz, "Introduction," 11. From 1846 to 1848 the costs of sickness and lunacy were shifted from the parish of origin/residence to the common fund. This may have generated some attitudinal change. See Laybourn, *The Evolution*, 28–32.

10 Crowther, "Health Care and Poor Relief," 212.

11 Price, *Medical Negligence*, 10–11; Hodgkinson notes that "during the first two years [of the Commission's existence] only two of the regulations issued for the direction of Guardians referred to the actual appointment of doctors." Hodgkinson, "Poor Law Medical Officers," 300.

12 This view has most recently been discussed by King in *Sickness, Medical Welfare*, 69–89. However, he also cautions that until we have a greater understanding of the realities of local relief practice it is difficult to make final judgements about the quality of medical relief across the early landscape of the New Poor Law.

13 Jones and Carter, "Writing for Redress," 385–6.

14 Appeals to the Centre against individual relief decisions provide the closest link with pauper letters sent under the Old Poor Law and are thus a useful yardstick of agency.

15 TNA: MH12/2096, 1098/B/1839, John Champ, Lyme Regis, to the PLC, 16 February 1839.

16 TNA: MH12/9159, 35345/1853, David Bell, Tynemouth, to the PLB, 23 September 1853.

17 On the particular importance of work narratives post-1871, see Levine-Clark, *Unemployment, Welfare*, 6–9.

18 TNA: MH12/1301, 50388/1851, Joseph Beer, St Teath, to the PLB, 15 December 1851.

19 King, *Sickness, Medical Welfare*, 84–5.

20 TNA: MH12/7, 32128/1860, James Caves, Ampthill, to the PLB, September 1860.

21 TNA: MH12/7, 33207/1860, James Caves, Ampthill, to the PLB, 26 September 1860.

22 King, *Sickness, Medical Welfare*, 70. Our italics. Hollen Lees, "The survival of the unfit," 83, argues that it was widely accepted that the sick had "special claims" on ratepayers in this period.

23 Jones and Carter, "Writing for Redress," 385–6.

24 King and Jones, *Pauper Voices*, 57, 86, also note this in relation to the workhouse reform movement.

25 Hurren, *Protesting About Pauperism*, 191–214.

26 Levine-Clarke, *Masculine Citizenship*, passim; Tosh, *Manliness*, 131–2; Henriques, *Before the Welfare State*, 59; MacKinnon, "Poor Law Policy," 229–36; and Sutton, "Liberalism, State Collectivism," 64.

27 Gorsky and Sheard, "Introduction," 5. Tanner, "The City of London," 276, suggests that the poor used union medical facilities *instead* of "the plethora of

hospital and dispensary services in the City." See also Doolittle, "Fatherhood and Family Shame," 100. For an alternative sense that the poor resisted being hedged into institutions, see Mandler, "Poverty and Charity," 18.

28 Price, *Medical Negligence*.

29 Such complaints in our corpus increase from 35 per cent of all letters from the sick poor immediately after the passing of the PLAA, to 65 per cent after 1895.

30 Kidd, *State, Society*, 38–43.

31 Lane, *A Social History of Medicine*, chapter 3; Wood, *Poverty and the Workhouse*, 108; Crowther, "Paupers or Patients?" 48.

32 TNA: MH12/11200, 45822/1859, Patrick McGarry, Stoke, to the PLB, 2 December 1859. Hollen Lees, "The Survival of the Unfit," 78, notes that women often took the lead in applications for welfare at times of familial sickness, given that they were more easily constructed as deserving.

33 Ibid.

34 Ibid. Under the Anatomy Act 1832, this would have meant the body's being sold for dissection. See Hurren, *Dying for Victorian Medicine*, passim, and Baker, *The Laws Relating to Burials*, 54–60.

35 TNA: MH12/11200, 233/1860, Report of Andrew Doyle, poor law inspector, into the conduct of Joseph Boulton, 28 January 1860.

36 Guardians often showed considerable attachment to officers, reflecting a complex mix of genuine support, a resistance to being told what to do by the press or Centre, and some recognition that many union jobs were done in very difficult circumstances. See James, "Sophia Heathfield of Hawnes," passim.

37 TNA: MH12/11200, 234/1860, Draft letter from Henry Fleming (Secretary to the PLB) to Joseph Lowndes, Clerk, Wolstanton and Burslem PLU, 16 February 1860.

38 The Centre was sometimes much more forthright in requiring the resignation of officers but as Crowther, "Paupers or Patients?" 40, notes there was a more general reluctance "to remove an officer if the Guardians defended him" given the ambiguous powers of the Centre to directly intervene in individual cases. Even so, in many other places refusal to bury the dead often resulted in misconduct charges.

39 TNA: MH12/11200, 229/1859, Patrick McGarry, Stoke, to the PLB, 30 December 1859; MH12/11200, 233/1860, Report of Andrew Doyle, poor law inspector, into the conduct of Joseph Boulton, 28 January 1860.

40 Crowther, "Paupers or Patients?" 37. Also, Price, *Medical Negligence*, 155–63.

41 See for example TNA: MH12/7, 38812/1863, J. Matthews, Ampthill, to the PLB, 23 October 1863.

42 For example, Digby, *Making a Medical Living*, 244; Loudon, *Medical Care*, 228–9; Ritch, *Sickness in the Workhouse*, 10–11; Shave, "'Immediate Death,'" 168–70; Tomkins, "The Excellent Example," 14.

43 Crowther, "Paupers or Patients?" 34–5.

44 Some unions created bigger districts served by fewer though better paid medical officers. While the Centre generally resisted such moves, they are nonetheless a persistent feature of our material.

45 Crowther, "Paupers or Patients?" 34–6; Hodgkinson, "Poor Law Medical Officers," 305–10; Price, *Medical Negligence*, 11–12; Shave, "'Immediate Death,'" 176–7.

46 Shave, "'Immediate Death,'" and Shave, *Pauper Policies*, 202–17.

47 Shave, "'Immediate Death,'" 165.

48 See, for example, Crowther, *The Workhouse System*, 192; Edsall, *The Anti-Poor Law Movement*, 17 and 120; Henriques, "How Cruel," 365–71; and Roberts, "How Cruel," 97–107.

49 Price, *Medical Negligence*.

50 Ibid., 175–6.

51 British Library Newspaper Archive Online: https://www.britishnewspaperarchive.co.uk/. Jones and King, *Pauper Voices*, 18–23.

52 It is important to remember as backdrop Kim Price's sense that local animosity between officials and between the poor and officials could drive significant embellishment (or even their fabrication) of failings to meet personal or political ends. Price, *Medical Negligence*, 190–201.

53 TNA: MH12/8813, 5600/1853, John Laurence, Elton, to the PLB, 12 February 1853.

54 TNA: MH12/8091, 30113/1852, Mr Jenkins, Newport, to the PLB, July 1852.

55 TNA: MH12/8092, 39607/1855, Augustus Champ, Newport, to the PLB, October 1855.

56 TNA: MH12/8092, 49538/1855, Witness statement of John Jones at an inquiry into the conduct of Jehoida Brewer, December 1855.

57 TNA: MH12/8093, 40150/1856, John Jones, Newport, to the PLB, 24 October 1856. Jones also alleged that the doctor and other union officials had interfered with witnesses at his trial. Price, *Medical Negligence*, passim, argues repeatedly that Boards backed medical officers until it suited them not to.

58 TNA: MH12/8093, 40150/1856, John Jones, to the PLB, 24 October 1856.

59 TNA: MH12/8095, 12903/1860, Joseph Akeroyd, Newport, to the PLB, 9 April 1860; MH12/8095, 16626/1860, Joseph Akeroyd, Newport, to the PLB, 9 May 1860.

60 TNA: MH12/8098, 4293/E/1866, Letter from T.F. Parsons, Chemist of Maindee, to the *Star of Gwent* newspaper, 6 February 1866. Parsons also wrote for other reasons, as we saw in chapter 2. In this final piece of correspondence referencing Brewer, there is a veiled implication that he had neglected to fully attend to a poor woman called Loverage, but the substance of the complaint was aimed at the guardians and relieving officers for reducing her to a "skeleton" by their refusal to allow her sufficient relief. For context see Gurney, *Wanting and Having*, chapter 3.

61 Those who defended medical officers in the press also drew attention to these structural problems. See for instance John White's letter to *The Times* defending the medical officer of the St Albans PLU on 22 October 1836.

62 TNA: MH12, 9245, 9731/1856, John Shaw, Nottingham, to the PLB, 26 March 1856.

63 TNA: MH12/6056, 5807/1864, Copy letter of John Lyall, relieving officer, 19 January 1864. Historians of welfare have often noted the ambivalence displayed towards midwifery cases which might otherwise be the province of midwives. See Digby, *Making a Medical Living*, 268–9; King, *Sickness, Medical Welfare*, 152–4 and 171; and Negrine, "Practitioners and Paupers," 203–4.

64 TNA: MH12/13965, 31352/1860, "A Ratepayer," Stafford, to the PLB, September 1860.

65 TNA: MH12/9233, 13465/B/1843, Henry Longstaff, Ilkeston, to the Basford Board of Guardians, 2 September 1843.

66 For example, TNA: MH12/6850, 25890/1863, Copy letter from George Stratford, Bethnal Green, to Sir George Gray, 25 June 1863; MH12/6851, 12138/1864, Witness statement of William White at an inquiry into the behaviour of Dr Massingham, 13 April 1864; MH12/6852, 10382/1866, John Adams, Bethnal Green, to the PLB, 20 March 1866; MH12/6854, 1127/1867, R. Furness, Victoria Park, to the Board of Guardians, Bethnal Green, 8 January 1867; MH12/6854 [no original reference], Cutting from an unnamed newspaper, 15 January 1867.

67 TNA: MH12/6855, 4122/1868, "Watchman" to the PLB, January 1868; MH12/6858, 49628/1866, Cutting from an unnamed newspaper, 1 October 1866; MH12/6860, 6635/1870, Cutting from the *Evening Standard* newspaper, 28 October 1870; MH12/6861, 9627/1871, Cutting from an unnamed newspaper, February 1871.

68 Jones and Carter, "Writing for Redress," 392–3.

69 TNA: MH12/9163, 13179/1868, anonymous to the President of the PLB, 12 April 1868. The irregular attendance of house surgeons to the needs of the indoor poor was a central concern of social investigators and unofficial workhouse visitors, such as Joseph Rowntree of Leeds. See Jones and King, *Pauper Voices*, 47, 50, and Price, *Medical Negligence*, 24.

70 TNA: MH12/9760, 13744/1860, George Jennings, Burford, to the PLB, 24 April 1860.

71 Jones and Carter, "Writing for Redress," 385.

72 Scott, *Domination and the Arts*, chapter 1.

73 *The Times*, commenting on a report from *The Lancet* in October 1867, condemned this practice: *The Times*, "Country Workhouse Infirmaries," 4 October 1867, 7. For the way in which unions either struggled to recruit paid staff or never tried, see Dunkley, "The Hungry Forties," 343.

74 This was particularly relevant for nursing pauper lunatics. See Murphy, "The New Poor Law Guardians," 45–74.

75 Wildman, "Changes in Hospital Nursing," 98–114; Maggs, "Profit and Loss," 176–89; Helmstadter and Godden, *Nursing before Nightingale*; Hawkins, *Nursing and Women's Labour*; and Hallett, "Nursing, 1830–1920."

76 Digby, *Making a Medical Living*, 246–7; Price, *Medical Negligence*, 127–8; Reynolds, *Infant Mortality*, chapter 3; Ritch, *Sickness in the Workhouse*, 189–90.

77 Reynolds, *Infant Mortality*, 104.

78 Ibid., 109–10; TNA: MH12/6852, 13453/1866, Sarah Brown, Bethnal Green, to the PLB, 17 April 1866.

79 Hallett, "Nursing, 1830–1920," 46–8 and 55–6; Price, *Medical Negligence*, 127–9; and Borsay and Hunter, "Nursing and Midwifery," 21.

80 King, *Women, Welfare*, and Waddington, "Paying for the Sick Poor," 95–111.

81 Davies, "Female Healers," 228–49.

82 TNA: MH12/14021/316, 45/1856, Eliza France, Kidderminster, to the PLB, 31 December 1856. This use of administrative process against a pauper's attempt to meld literate and oral cultures highlights the extent to which poor writers were still at this date "interlopers" in literary culture. See Lyons, *A History*, 86.

83 TNA: MH12/8091, 14915/1852, Johanna Davies, Newport, to the PLB, May 1852.

84 TNA: MH12/6853, 34276/1866, J.R. Onion, Bethnal Green, to Sir Gathorne Hardy, President of the PLB, 20 August 1866. For more on the case see Hepburn, *A Book of Scattered Leaves*, 181–9; Jones and Carter, "Writing for Redress," 392–3.

85 TNA: MH12/6855, 1157/1868, Anon, to the PLB, 9 January 1868.

86 TNA: MH12/6855, 1157/1868, Report in the *Clerkenwell News*, 21 January 1868.

87 TNA: MH12/5995, 36233/1884, "Patients of the Hospital," Liverpool, to the "Secretary of State," April 1884; MH12/5999, 41680/1886, P.J. Cusack, Royal Infirmary, Liverpool, to the LGB, 19 April 1886; MH12/6001, 66996/1887, Francis Baldwin, Brownlow Hill Hospital, Liverpool, to the LGB, 14 July 1887.

88 Though nurses do appear frequently in *wider* inquiries about medical care in workhouses, including at Mitford and Launditch in 1880, Newbury (1861), Sheffield (1859), and Tynemouth (1865). TNA: MH12/8489/82046, Deposition of Thomas Boyce, Mitford and Launditch workhouse to an inquiry into the behaviour of the workhouse nurse, 20 August 1880; MH12/262, 807/1869, Witness statements to an inquiry into the death of Ann Kempster at Newbury workhouse, 1 May 1869; MH12/15476, 17072/1859, Witness statement of Mary Watson to an inquiry into the conduct of a nurse at Sheffield workhouse, 4 April 1859.

89 Jones and Carter, "Writing for Redress," 385–95.

90 Jones and King, *Pauper Voices*, 94–101.

91 Finlayson, *Citizen, State*, 148.

92 Fraser, "The English Poor Law," 29.

CHAPTER TWELVE

1 TNA: MH12/1595, 18389/1857, Witness statement of Mr Johnson in the case of Mary Irving, 16 May 1857.

2 Walton, "Taking Control."

3 Shave, "'Immediate Death'"; Shave, *Pauper Policies*; Shave, "'Great Inhumanity,'" 340.

4 Gurney, *Wanting and Having*, 94–5, argues that every scandal helped to make the working classes fearful.

5 King, *Women, Welfare*.

6 King, *Writing the Lives*, passim; Lyons, "Writing Upwards," 318; Lyons, *The Writing Culture*, 56.

7 Digby, "The Rural Poor Law," 154–6.

8 Wood, *Poverty*, 82; Hurren, *Protesting about Pauperism*.

9 Finlayson, *Citizen, State*, 148, draws similar conclusions. See also Tanner, "The City of London,"153–87, and Ashforth, "The Urban Poor Law," 137.

10 TNA: MH12/9233, 13465/B/1843, Henry Longstaff, Ilkeston, to the Basford Board of Guardians, 2 September 1843.

11 TNA: MH12/13913/175, 46293/1868, Thomas S Fletcher, medical officer, Bromsgrove PLU, 22 September 1868.

12 Though forthcoming theses by Mary Rudling and Matthew Bayly on Sussex and Lincolnshire respectively both flag remarkably little change between the two systems.

13 King and Jones, "Fragments of Fury?"

14 Jones, "Looking through a Different Lens." See also Gurney, *Wanting and Having*, 76, who argues that local regimes were tempered because of "sustained pressure from below."

15 Gear, *The Diary of Benjamin Woodcock*, 78.

16 The full run of correspondence for this episode is: TNA: MH12/15949, 11177/A/1837, Humphrey Hutchins, Troedrhiwyriben near Llandyssil, to the PLB, 4 December 1837; MH12/15949, 10455/A/1837, Humphrey Hutchins, Troedrhiwyriben near Llandyssil, to the PLB, 26 December 1837; MH12/15949, 12/A/1838, Thomas Jones, Clerk, Newcastle-in-Emlyn PLU, to the PLC, 30 December 1837; TNA: MH12/15949, 1027/A/1838, Humphrey Hutchins, Troedrhiwyriben near Llandyssil, to the PLB, 29 January 1838.

17 Many of our letters also point, as we have already observed, to non-literate forms of agency, including criminal damage.

18 Perhaps unsurprisingly, if we accept Midwinter's claim in "State Intervention," 106, that "stripped of novel titles and terminology, the humdrum workings of both [the Old and New Poor Law] were fairly similar." See also Martin, "From Parish to Union,"45.

19 Thane, *Old Age*, 193; Levine-Clark, "Gendered Roles," 53–73; Long, *Conversations in Cold Rooms*, passim; and Vincent, *Poor Citizens*, 6.

20 Jucker and Taavitsainen, "Apologies in the History of English"; Lyons, *A History of Reading*, 75–9.

21 Timmis, *The Discourse of Desperation*, 1. On the poor law in general and the workhouse in particular as an arena for improving literacy see Digby, *Pauper Palaces*, 180–96.

22 See Levine-Clark, *Unemployment, Welfare*, 6–8.

23 For wider context see Hall and Schwarz, "State and Society," 19; Levine-Clark, *Unemployment, Welfare*, 4–9 and 46–72; Doolittle, "Fatherhood," 93; and

Englander, "From the Abyss," 79. Contrast this view with that of Vincent, *Poor Citizens*, 44–5, who argues that the citizenship claims of the poor were marginalised even in the early 1900s.

24 This point is also developed by Leys, "Petitioning," 62, and Gurney, *Wanting and Having*, 77, though we detect no evidence for the "discursive shift" consequent upon European revolutions in 1848 that Gurney found (105–14) in his study.

25 TNA: MH12/6078, 84686/1886, Charles Leonard, Salford, to the LGB, 17 February 1886; MH12/6078, 94286/1886, Charles Leonard, Salford, to the LGB, 16 October 1886; MH12/6078, 101327/1886, Charles Leonard, Salford, to the LGB, 13 November 1886.

26 MH12/6079, 4407/1887, Cutting "The Salford Unemployed Remarkable Proposals," 17 January 1887; pasted into volume following MH12/6079, 4407/1887, J Darbyshire, Secretary to the Salford Unemployed, 12 January 1887.

27 Green, *Pauper Capital*, 16.

28 The fact that it was liveable is also illustrated in some autobiographical accounts. See Tomkins, "Poor Law Institutions." There is little support in our corpus for the idea that the New Poor Law "gave a dogmatically uniform direction to English poor law policy," Webb and Webb, *English Poor Law*, 1.

29 For a particularly good discussion of the risks of sexual predation see Gurney, *Wanting and Having*, 85–6.

30 Tomkins, "Poor Law Institutions."

31 TNA: MH12/9531/239, John Kirkland, Clerk, Southwell PLU, to the PLB, 3 June 1857. Initially, male youths above thirteen (later revised to sixteen) were to be in the second classification of inmates with able-bodied males.

32 Waddington, "Paying for the Sick Poor," passim.

33 As Ritch, *Sickness in the Workhouse*, 220–6, also found for Birmingham.

34 Gillie, "Identifying the Poor," 321; Boyer and Schmidle, "Poverty among the Elderly," 253–60; Boyer, "Work for Their Prime," passim; Finlayson, *Citizen, State*, 150–61.

35 Though see Walton, "Taking Control," and her ongoing PhD dissertation on the emotional canvas in the workhouse.

Bibliography

ARCHIVE SOURCES

Berkshire Record Office (BRO).

D/P L32/L9/7. Tilehurst Miscellaneous Overseers' Correspondence, 1837–1844.

Devon Record Office (DRO).

PLU/Axminster/1. Axminster PLU Guardians' Minute Book, 1836–1838.

PLU/Okehampton/1. Okehampton PLU Guardians' Minute Book, 1836–1837.

Hertfordshire Archives and Local Studies (HALS).

DP/12/12/2. Baldock Parish Overseers' Accounts, c. 1720–1772.

Leicestershire Record Office (LRO).

G/4/8a/1. Billesdon PLU Minute Books 1836–1839.

The National Archives (TNA).

MH12. Local Government Board and Predecessors: Correspondence with Poor Law Unions and Other Local Authorities, 1834–1900.

Most volumes of union correspondence begin in 1834, often before the particular union was constituted (formally came into existence). This is because earlier correspondence of the future constituent parishes – with local parish officers, magistrates, for instance – was bound into the volumes of the newly formed unions. In the main, volumes for 1871 were bound to August of that year (when the Poor Law Board ended and the Local Government Board commenced). However, some bindings continued until December 1871. For unions which we carried on surveying after 1871, the end date of the volumes varies around 1900. These later (post-Victorian) union volumes were apparently stored separately from the earlier material and were destroyed during enemy action in the Second World War. These lacunae are reflected in the post-1871 list below.

Poor Law Unions (PLUS) Surveyed 1834 (unless otherwise stated) to August 1871.

Aberystwyth (Cardiganshire), 1836–1871: MH12/15796–15801.

Alston with Garrigill (Cumberland), 1836–1871: MH12/1557–1560.

Altrincham (Cheshire): MH12/770–781.

Ampthill (Bedfordshire): MH12/1–8.

Bakewell (Derbyshire): MH12/1799–1808.

Basford (Nottinghamshire): MH12/9228–9253.

Beverley (East Riding): MH12/14232–14241.

Bishops Stortford (Hertfordshire): MH12/4536–4545.

Blything (Suffolk): MH12/11728–11746.

Bootle (Cumberland), 1835–1871: MH12/1565–1570 (with gaps for 1863–70).

Bradford-on-Avon (Wiltshire): MH12/13668–13676. In TNA's Discovery Catalogue this is given as Bradford (Wilts).

Bromsgrove (Worcestershire): MH12/13903–13913.

Cardiff (Glamorgan): MH12/16246–16264.

Carlisle (Cumberland), 1850–1871: MH12/1593–1599. The first surviving volume dates from 1850.

Caxton & Arrington (Cambridgeshire): MH12/598–605.

Chelsea (Middlesex), 1844–1871: MH12/6988–6996 (with gaps for 1858–59). Chelsea was part of the Kensington PLU until 1841 when it became the Chelsea Parish Board.

Clutton (Somerset): MH12/10320–10327 (with gaps for 1841–42 and 1854–63).

Colchester (Essex): MH12/3428–3440.

Dorchester (Dorset): MH12/2777–2783 (with gaps for 1854–59).

Dudley (Worcestershire): MH12/13958–13968.

Durham (Durham): MH12/3018–3025 (with gaps for 1848–51).

Exeter (Devon): MH12/2238–2243.

Gainsborough (Lincolnshire), 1839–1871: MH12/6707–6712 (with gaps for 1851–54, 1862–66).

Great Yarmouth (Norfolk): MH12/8630–8642.

Huddersfield (Yorkshire): MH12/15063–15085.

Kendal (Westmorland): MH12/13581–13594.

Lampeter (Cardiganshire): MH12/15845–15850.

Leominster (Herefordshire): MH12/4385–4394.

Linton (Cambridgeshire): MH12/667–674.

Longtown (Cumberland): MH12/1675–1679.

Luton (Bedfordshire): MH12/96–105.

Madeley (Shropshire): MH12/9981–9987.

Mansfield (Nottinghamshire): MH12/9356–9371.

Melton Mowbray (Leicestershire): MH12/6609–6617.

Merthyr Tydfil (Glamorgan): MH12/16326–16334.

Newbury (Berkshire): MH12/252–262.

Newcastle on Tyne (Northumberland): MH12/9096–9106 (with gaps for 1846–50).

Newmarket (Cambridgeshire): MH12/684–695.

Newport (Monmouthshire): MH12/8086–8102.

Newport Pagnell (Buckinghamshire): MH12/487–494.

Oswestry (Shropshire): MH12/10019–10024.

Oundle (Northamptonshire): MH12/8809–8816.

Peterborough (Northamptonshire): MH12/8828–8838.

Plomesgate (Suffolk): MH12/11932–11944.

Pwllheli (Caernarvonshire): MH12/16052–16064.

Ripon (Yorkshire): MH12/15352–15356. Ripon PLU came into existence in 1852. Only a small number of letters date from the 1830s and 1840s.

Scarborough (Yorkshire): MH12/14610–14615.

Southampton (Hampshire): MH12/10997–11005. Southampton remained a Poor Law Incorporation.

Southwell (Nottinghamshire): MH12/9524–9534.

St Ives (Huntingdonshire): MH12/4742–4750.

St Thomas (Devon): MH12/2567–2582.

Stockport (Cheshire): MH12/1138–1153.

Swaffham (Norfolk): MH12/8539–8545 (with gaps for 1838–42).

Thirsk (Yorkshire): MH12/14639–14649.

Thorne (Yorkshire): MH12/15550–15557.

Thrapston (Northamptonshire): MH12/8861–8867.

Truro (Cornwall): MH12/1527–1537.

Uppingham (Rutland): MH12/9806–9813.

Wem (Shropshire), 1835–1871: MH12/10085–10092.

Weobley (Herefordshire): MH12/4428–4434.
East Ward (Westmorland): MH12/13560–13568.
West Ward (Westmorland): MH12/13625–13629.
Wheatenhurst (Gloucestershire), 1843–1871: MH12/4262–4265. The first surviving volume dates from 1843.
Wigton (Cumberland), 1837–1871: MH12/1748–1753.
Wilton (Wiltshire): MH12/13892–13896.
Winslow (Buckinghamshire): MH12/512–518.
Witney (Oxfordshire): MH12/9753–9763.
Wolstanton and Burslem (Staffordshire), 1835–1871: MH12/11196–11202.
Wrexham (Denbighshire): MH12/16104–16116 (with gaps for 1851–56).
York (Yorkshire), 1840–1871: MH12/14396–14409.

Poor Law Unions Surveyed from 1834 to 1896 or 1900 (unless otherwise stated).

Axminster (Devon): MH12/2095–2123.
Aysgarth (Yorkshire), 1869–1896: MH12/14428–14435. Aysgarth PLU came into existence in February 1869, previously part of the Bainbridge Gilbert Union.
Bala (Merionethshire), 1836–1896: MH12/16478–16485.
Barnsley (Yorkshire): MH12/14674–14705.
Bellingham (Northumberland), 1836–1900: MH12/8964–8975.
Berwick on Tweed (Northumberland): MH12/8976–9000.
Bethnal Green (Middlesex): MH12/6843–6899 (with gaps for 1865, 1893).
Birmingham (Warwickshire): MH12/13286–13376.
Bradfield (Berkshire): MH12/162–180 (with gaps for 1889–90, 1892).
Bradford (Yorkshire): MH12/14720–14767.
Builth (Breconshire), 1834–1892: MH12/15734–15745.
Camelford (Cornwall), 1835–1900: MH12/1299–1312.
Chelmsford (Essex): MH12/3396–3427.
Dorking (Surrey), 1836–1869: MH12/12219–12234.
Faversham (Kent), 1836–1900: MH12/5054–5074.
Hay (Breconshire), 1834–1892: MH12/15769–15781.
Keighley (Yorkshire): MH12/15158–15200.
Kidderminster (Worcestershire): MH12/14016–14038.
Liverpool (Lancashire): MH12/5966–6032 (with gaps for 1841–44, 1847–50, 1853–55, 1857, 1875). Liverpool was a Poor Law Vestry.

Llanfyllin (Montgomeryshire): MH12/16543–16563.

Manchester (Lancashire), 1837–1899: MH12/6039–6093 (with gaps for 1848–49, 1851–56, 1868, Sept. 1871–72, May–Aug. 1890, 1893–94).

Mitford and Launditch (Norfolk): MH12/8474–8501.

Nantwich (Cheshire): MH12/1013–1058.

Newcastle-under-Lyme (Staffordshire): MH12/11363–11388.

Newcastle–in–Emlyn (Carmarthenshire): MH12/15949–15963.

Pewsey (Wiltshire), 1835–1897: MH12/13830–13843.

Poplar (Middlesex), 1843–1900: MH12/7681–7717 (with gaps prior to 1843, and then 1868, 1883, and 1890).

Reeth (Yorkshire), 1835–1896: MH12/14587–14594.

Rye (Sussex): MH12/13076–13098.

Sheffield (Yorkshire): MH12/15465–15511.

Tynemouth (Northumberland): MH12/9156–9227.

Wandsworth and Clapham (Surrey): MH12/12689–12745.

Other Non-Sampled MH12 Volumes.

Castle Ward (Northumberland), 1867–18 Aug. 1871: MH12/9008.

Chipping Sodbury (Gloucestershire), 1843–1846: MH12/3964.

Hungerford (Berkshire), 1843–1846: MH12/237.

Tavistock (Devon), 1843–1846: MH12/2542.

Other TNA Collections.

HO 107/6. Census Return Flitwick, Bedfordshire, 1841.

HO 107/2355. Census Return York, 1851.

HO 27/155. Criminal Registers, Beds-Kent, 1870.

MH 1. Minutes of the PLC, 1834–1842.

MH 4. PLC and Successors: Extracts from Minutes and Abstracts of Correspondence, 1839–1879.

MH 9. PLC and Successors: Paid Officers Department and Metropolitan Department: Registers of Paid Officers, 1837–1921.

MH 10. Ministry of Health and Predecessors: Circular Letters, 1834–1962.

MH 15. LGB and Predecessors: Subject Indexes of Correspondence, 1836–1920.

MH 33. PLC: Assistant Poor Law Commissioners, Registers of Correspondence, 1834–1846.

T 1/4101. Long Papers, Bundle 591 PLC, 1790–1840.

Northamptonshire Record Office (NRO).
PL01/001. Brackley PLU Guardian Minute Book, 1835–1837.
North Yorkshire County Record Office (NYCRO).
BG/RI 2/1/1. Ripon Board of Guardians' General Letter Book (Out), 1852–1857.
Somerset Heritage Centre (SHC).
D/G/CL/23a/1, Clutton PLU Weekly Returns of Numbers Chargeable Form B, 1881–1887.
York Explore Archives (YE(A)).
PLU/3/2/1/13. Weekly Outdoor Relief List, City District, March 1841.
PLU/3/1/1/22, 24, 28, and 31. York PLU Application and Report Books, City District, 1845–1846, 1847, 1848, and 1851.

NEWSPAPERS

The Aberystwyth Observer
The Times
Western Daily Mail

PRINTED PRIMARY SOURCES (LEGISLATION AND PARLIAMENTARY PAPERS)

Legislation:
An Act for the Relief of the Poor, 1601, 43 Eliz. 1, c. 2.
An Act for the Better Relief of the Poor of this Kingdom, 1662, 14 Chas. 2, c. 12.
An Act for Amending the Laws Relating to the Settlement, Imployment, and Relief of the Poor, 1723, 9 Geo. 1, c. 7.
An Act for the Amendment and Better Administration of the Laws Relating to the Poor in England and Wales, 1834, 4 & 5 Will. 4, c. 76.
An Act to Amend the Laws Relating to the Removal of the Poor, 1847, 9 & 10 Vict. c. 74.
An Act for the Administration of the Laws for Relief of the Poor in England, 1847, 10 & 11 Vict. c. 109.
An Act to Amend the Procedure in Respect of Orders for the Removal of the Poor, 1847, 11 & 12 Vict. c. 31.

Parliamentary Papers:

Annual Reports of the PLC, 1835–1847.

Annual Reports of the PLB, 1848–1870.

Annual Reports of the LGB, 1871–1895.

Consolidated General Order, 1847.

Copies of Letters from the Poor-Law Commissioners to the Secretary of State, respecting the Transaction of the Business of the Commission, 1847.

Official Circulars of Public Documents and Information; Directed by the Poor Law Commissioners to be printed chiefly for the use of the boards of guardians and their officers, 1840–1851, vols. 1–10. New York: Augustus Kelly, 1970.

Return of the Number, Names, and Ages of all Persons Committed to any Prison in England and Wales for any Offence in a Union Workhouse established under the Provision of the Poor Law Amendment Act: 25 March 1835 to 25 March 1842.

Workhouses (commitments to prison). Return to an Order of the Honourable House of Commons, dated 28 July 1874. Return of the number of persons (inmates and casuals) committed to prison from each union workhouse (England and Wales) for the half-year ending 25 March 1874, stating their age, the offence alleged, and the period for which they were committed.

Workhouse Offences: Abstract or Returns to an Order of the Honourable House of Commons, dated 5 May 1842 and 21 February 1843.

Workhouses: Return to an Order of the Honourable House of Commons, dated 7 April 1853. Copies of [various]; and number of workhouse inmates in England and Wales committed to prison in 1852 for offences committed while they were such inmates.

PUBLISHED CONTEMPORARY SOURCES AND RECORD PUBLICATIONS

Anon [By One of Them; preface by Peter Higginbotham]. *Indoor Paupers: Life Inside a London Workhouse.* London: Workhouse Press, 2013.

Anon. *The Complete Farmer; or General Dictionary of Agriculture and Husbandry.* London: W. Flint, 1807.

Anon. *The General Orders and Instructional Letters of the Poor Law Commissioners, with an Extensive Index.* London: Charles Knight, 1845.

Anon [Nassau Senior]. *Remarks on the Opposition to the Poor Law Amendment Bill, by a Guardian*. London: W. Clowes and Sons, 1841.

Anon. "Statement of the Number of Miles Travelled by Robert Weale Esq., Assistant Poor Law Commissioner, from the 3rd of August, 1835, to the 31st of December, 1846." *Journal of the Royal Statistical Society* 12 (1849): 78.

Anon. "Report on the Nursing and Administration of Provincial Workhouses and Infirmaries." *British Medical Journal* (1894–95).

Baker, Thomas. *The Laws Relating to Burials, with Notes, Forms and Practical Instructions*. London: W. Maxwell and Son, 1873.

Bauke, Algernon. *The Poor Law Guardian: His Powers and Duties in the Right Execution of his Office*. London: Shaw and Sons, 1862.

Bernard, Thomas. *An Account of a Cottage and Garden near Tadcaster*. London: T. Becket, 1797.

Burn, Richard. *The Justice of the Peace and the Parish Officer*. London: A. Strahan, 1805.

Carter, Paul. *Bradford Poor Law Union: Papers and Correspondence with the Poor Law Commission October 1834–January 1839*. Woodbridge: Boydell, 2004.

Clark, William. *Thoughts on the Management and Relief of the Poor*. Bath: Andrew Thomas, 1815.

Cowe, Frederick. *Wimbledon Vestry Minutes, 1736, 1743–1788*. Shere: Surrey Record Society, 1964.

Cunningham Glen, William. *The Consolidated and Other Orders of the Poor Law Commissioners and the Poor and the Poor Law Board*. London: Butterworths, 1859.

Cunningham Glen, William. *Shaw's Union Officers' Manual*, 1847. London: Shaw and Sons, 1847.

Durrant, Peter, ed. *Berkshire Overseers' Papers, 1654–1834*. Newbury: Berkshire Record Society, vol. 3, 1997.

Gear, Gillian. *The Diary of Benjamin Woodcock, Master of the Barnet Union Workhouse, 1836–1838*. Hertford: Hertfordshire Record Society, 2010.

Gibson, Jeremy, Colin Rogers, and Cliff Webb. *Poor Law Union Records*, 3rd ed., 4 vols. Lancashire: The Family History Partnership Ltd., 2008.

Hansard, Thomas. *The Parliamentary Debates from the Year 1830 to the Present Time*, Vol. VIII: December 1806 to March 1807. London: T.C. Hansard, 1812.

Lumley, William. *Manuals of the Duties of Poor Law Officers*. London: Knight & Co., 1857.

Nicholl, George (with T. MacKay). *A History of the English Poor Law*, Vol. III. London: John Murray, 1899.

Oxley, Mary. *Thorne Guardians Minute Book: 4 October 1837 to 21 September 1842 Including Report on a Visit to Brigg Union Workhouse on 5 December 1838*. Doncaster: Doncaster and District Family History Society, 2006.

Paley, William. *Principles of Moral and Political Philosophy*. London: R. Faulder, 1785.

Palk, Deirdre. *Prisoners' Letters to the Bank of England, 1781–1827*. Loughborough: London Record Society, 2007.

Peyton, Sarah. *Kettering Vestry Minutes, A.D. 1797–1853*. Northampton: Northamptonshire Record Society, 1933.

Reynolds, Stephen. *A Poor Man's House*. Oxford: Oxford University Press, 1982. First published 1908.

Russell, Charles. *The Catholic in the Workhouse. Popular Statement of the Law As It Affects Him, The Religious Grievances It Occasions, With Practical Suggestions For Redress*. London: Nabu Press, 2012. First published in 1859 by Catholic Publishing and Bookselling Company.

Seaton, Paul, and Sarah Seaton. *Letters from the Workhouse: The Story of the Hinckley Union*. Bedminster: Private Publication, 2020.

Smithers, Henry. *Liverpool: Its Commerce, Statistics and Institutions*. Liverpool: T. Kaye, 1825.

Thelwall, John. *The Rights of Nature, against the Usurpation of Establishments*. Norwich: H.D. Symonds and J. March, 1796.

Walsh, Nugent. *The Governor's Guide: A Manual for Masters of Union Workhouses*. London: Nicholls Brothers, 1867.

Wythen Baxter, G. *The Book of the Bastiles; or, the History of the Working of the New Poor-Law*. London: G. Routledge, 1841.

SECONDARY SOURCES

Alford, Bernard. "Government Expenditure and the Growth of the Printing Industry in the Nineteenth Century." *Economic History Review* 17 (1964): 96–112.

Althammer, Beate. "Controlling Vagrancy: Germany, England and France, 1880–1914." In *Rescuing the Vulnerable: Poverty, Welfare and Social Ties in Modern Europe*, edited by B. Althammer, L. Raphael, and T. Stazic-Wendt, 187–211. Oxford: Berghahn, 2016.

Anstruther, Ian. *The Scandal of the Andover Workhouse: A Documentary Study of Events, 1834–1847*. London: Bles, 1973.

Ashforth, D. "The Poor Law in Bradford c. 1834–1871: A Study of the Relief of Poverty in Mid-Nineteenth Century Bradford." Unpublished PhD dissertation, University of Bradford, 1979.

Ashforth, David. "Settlement and Removal in Urban Areas: Bradford, 1834–71." In *The Poor and the City: The English Poor Law in its Urban Context, 1834–1914*, edited by M. Rose, 57–92. Leicester: Leicester University Press, 1985.

– "The Urban Poor Law." In *The New Poor Law in the Nineteenth Century*, edited by D. Fraser, 128–48. Basingstoke: Macmillan, 1976.

Ausubel, Hermann. *In Hard Times: Reformers among the Late Victorians*. New York: Columbia University Press, 1960.

Bailey, Joanne. "'Think Wot a Mother Must Feel': Parenting in English Pauper Letters c. 1760–1834." *Family and Community History* 13 (2010): 5–19.

Beckett, John. "Politics and the Implementation of the New Poor Law: The Nottingham Workhouse Controversy, 1834–43." *Midland History* 41 (2016): 208–30.

Beier, Lee. "'Takin' it to the streets': Henry Mayhew and the Language of the Underclass in Mid-Nineteenth-Century London." In *Cast Out: Vagrancy and Homelessness in Global and Historical Perspective*, edited by A. Beier and P. Ocobock, 88–116. Athens, OH: Ohio University Press, 2008.

Benoît, Agnes. "A Chartist Singularity? Mobilizing to Promote Democratic Petitions in Britain and France, 1838–1848." *Labour History Review* 78 (2013): 51–66.

Blaug, Mark. "The Myth of the Old Poor Law and the Making of the New." *Journal of Economic History* 23 (1963): 151–84.

– "The Poor Law Report Re-examined." *Journal of Economic History* 24 (1964): 229–45.

Block, Fred, and Margaret Somers. "In the Shadow of Speenhamland: Social Policy and the Old Poor Law." *Politics and Society* 31 (2003): 283–323.

Blum, Matthias, and Karl-Peter Krauss. "Age Heaping and Numeracy: Looking Behind the Curtain." *Economic History Review* 71 (2018): 464–79.

Borsay, Anne, and Billie Hunter, eds. *Nursing and Midwifery in Britain since 1700*. Basingstoke: Palgrave, 2012.

Botelho, Lynn. *Old Age and the English Poor Law, 1500–1700*. Woodbridge: Boydell and Brewer, 2004.

– "'The Old Woman's Wish': Widows by the Family Fire? Widows' Old Age Provision in Rural England." *Journal of Family History* 7 (2002): 59–78.

Boulton, Jeremy, and Leonard Schwarz. "'The Comforts of a Private Fireside'? The Workhouse, the Elderly and the Poor Law in Georgian Westminster: St. Martin-in-the-Fields, 1725–1824." In *Accommodating Poverty: The Housing and Living Arrangements of the English Poor, c. 1600–1850*, edited by S. Williams, J. McEwan, and P. Sharpe, 221–45. Basingstoke: Palgrave, 2011.

– "The Medicalization of a Parish Workhouse in Georgian Westminster: St. Martin in the Fields, 1725–1824." *Family and Community History* 17 (2014): 122–40.

Bourke, Joanna. "'Animal Instincts': the Sexual Abuse of Women with Learning Difficulties, 1830s–1910s." *Women's History Review* 29 (2020): 1201–17.

Boyer, George. "Poor Relief, Informal Assistance, and Short Time during the Lancashire Cotton Famine." *Explorations in Economic History* 34 (1997): 56–76.

– *The Winding Road to the Welfare State: Economic Insecurity & Social Welfare Policy in Britain*. Princeton: Princeton University Press, 2019.

– "'Work for Their Prime, the Workhouse for Their Age': Old Age Pauperism in Victorian England." *Social Science History* 40 (2016): 3–32.

Boyer, George, and Timothy Schmidle. "Poverty among the Elderly in Late-Victorian England." *Economic History Review* 62 (2009): 249–78.

Boyson, Rhodes. "The History of Poor Law Administration in North-East Lancashire 1834–1817." Unpublished master's thesis, University of Manchester, 1960.

Bradley, Sarah. "Welcoming the New Poor Law: The Bromsgrove Poor Law Union, 1836–1847." *Family and Community History* 22 (2019): 200–21.

Brodie, Marc. "Artisans and Dossers: The 1886 West End Riots and the East End Casual Poor." *London Journal* 24 (1999): 34–50.

– *The Politics of the Poor: The East End of London, 1885–1914*. Oxford: Oxford University Press, 2004.

Brown, Douglas. "Pauperism and Profit: Financial Management, Business Practices and the New Poor Law in England and Wales, 1834–c.1890." Unpublished PhD dissertation, King's College London, 2014.

– "Supplying London's Workhouses in the Mid-Nineteenth Century." *London Journal* 4 (2016): 36–59

Brundage, Anthony. "The English Poor Law of 1834 and the Cohesion of Agricultural Society." *Agricultural History Review* 48 (1974): 405–17.

– *The English Poor Laws, 1700–1930*. Basingstoke: Palgrave, 2002.

– *The Making of the New Poor Law: The Politics of Inquiry, Enactment and Implementation 1832–39*. London: Hutchinson, 1978.

– “Reform of the Poor Law Electoral System, 1834–94.” *Albion* 7 (1975): 201–15.

Burnett, John. *Useful Toil: Autobiographies of Working People from the 1820s to the 1920s*. London: Allen Lane, 1974.

Callanan Martin, Kathleen. *Hard and Unreal Advice: Mothers, Social Science and the Victorian Poverty Experts*. Basingstoke: Palgrave, 2008.

Care, Verna. “The Significance of a ‘Correct and Uniform System of Accounts’ to the Administration of the Poor Law Amendment Act, 1834.” *Accounting History Review* 21 (2011): 121–42.

Carter, Natalie, and Steven King. “‘I Think We Ought Not to Acknowledge Them [Paupers] as that Encourages Them to Write’: the Administrative State, Power and the Victorian Pauper.” *Social History* 46 (2021): 117–44.

Carter, Paul. “Joseph Bramley of East Stoke, Nottinghamshire: A Late Victim of the Crusade Against Outdoor Relief.” *Family and Community History* 17 (2014): 36–46.

Carter, Paul, and Steven King. “Keeping Track: Modern Methods, Administration and the Victorian Poor Law.” *Archives* 40 (2014): 31–52.

Carter, Paul, and Natalie Whistance. *Living the Poor Life: A Guide to the Poor Law Union Correspondence, c.1834 to 1871*. London: British Association for Local History, 2011.

– “The Poor Law Commission: A New Digital Resource for Nineteenth-Century Domestic Historians.” *History Workshop Journal* 71 (2011): 29–48.

Carter, Paul, Jeff James, and Steven King. “Punishing Paupers? Control, Discipline and Mental Health in the Southwell Workhouse, 1836–1871.” *Rural History* 30 (2019): 161–80.

Chaplin, Charles. *My Autobiography*. London: Penguin Classics ed., 2003.

Charlesworth, Lori. “How Poor Law Rights Were Lost but Victorian Values Survived: A Reconsideration of Some of the Hidden Values of Welfare Provision.” In *New Perspectives on Property Law, Human Rights and the Home*, edited by A. Hudson, 271–93. London: Cavendish Publishing, 2004.

– *Welfare’s Forgotten Past: A Socio-Legal History of the Poor Law*. London: Routledge, 2009.

Clark, Anna. “The New Poor Law and the Breadwinner Wage: Contrasting Assumptions.” *Journal of Social History* 34 (2000): 261–82.

Clark, Gregory. "Welfare Reform, 1834: Did the New Poor Law in England Produce Significant Economic Gains?" *Cliometrica* 13 (2019): 241–56.

Cocks, Richard. "The Poor Law." In *The Oxford History of the Laws of England: Volume 13*, edited by W. Cornish, J.S. Anderson, R. Cocks, M. Lobban, P. Polden, and K. Smith, 473–506. Oxford: Oxford University Press, 2010.

Collinge, Peter. "'He Shall Have Care of the Garden, its Cultivation and Produce': Workhouse Gardens and Gardening, c.1780–1835." *Journal for Eighteenth-Century Studies* 44 (2021): 21–39.

Combs, Mary Beth. "'Concealing Him From Creditors': How Couples Contributed to the Passage of the 1870 Married Women's Property Act." In *Married Women and the Law: Coverture in England and the Common Law World*, edited by T. Stretton and K. Kesselring, 217–39. London: McGill-Queen's University Press, 2013.

Cooper, John. *The British Welfare Revolution, 1906–14*. London: Bloomsbury, 2017.

Cordery, Simon. *British Friendly Societies, 1750–1914*. Basingstoke: Palgrave, 2003.

Costello, Kevin. "'More Equitable than the Judgment of the Justices of the Peace': The King's Bench and the Poor Law 1630–1800." *Journal of Legal History* 35 (2014): 3–26.

Croll, Andy. "'Reconciled Gradually to the System of Indoor Relief': The Poor Law in Wales during the 'Crusade Against Out-Relief', c.1870–c.1890." *Family and Community History* 20 (2017): 121–44.

Crompton, Frank. *Workhouse Children: Infant and Child Paupers Under the Worcestershire Poor Law, 1780–1871*. Stroud: Sutton Publishing, 1997.

Crone, Rosalind. "Educating the Labouring Poor in Nineteenth-Century Suffolk." *Social History* 43 (2018): 161–85.

Crowther, Anne. "Family Responsibility and State Responsibility in Britain before the Welfare State." *Historical Journal* 25 (1982): 131–45.

– "Health Care and Poor Relief in Provincial England." In *Health Care and Poor Relief in 18th and 19th Century Northern Europe*, edited by O. Grell, A. Cunningham, and R. Jütte, 203–19. London: Routledge, 2002.

– "Paupers or Patients? Obstacles to Professionalization in the Poor Law Medical Service Before 1914." *Journal of the History of Medicine and Allied Sciences* 39 (1984): 33–54.

– "The Workhouse." *Proceedings of the British Academy* 78 (1992): 183–94.

– *The Workhouse System 1834–1929: The History of an English Social Institution*. London: Batsford, 1981.

Darwen, Lewis. "Workhouse Populations of the Preston Union, 1841–61." *Local Population Studies* 93 (2014): 33–53.

Davies, Owen. "Female Healers in Nineteenth-Century England." In *Women's Work in Industrial England: Regional and Local Perspectives*, edited by N. Goose, 228–49. Hatfield: University of Hertfordshire Press, 2007.

Deane, Theresa. "Late Nineteenth-Century Philanthropy: The Case of Louisa Twining." In *Gender, Health and Welfare*, edited by A. Digby and J. Stewart, 122–42. London: Routledge, 1996.

– "The Professionalisation of Philanthropy: the Case of Louisa Twining, 1820–1912." Unpublished PhD dissertation, University of Sussex, 2005.

del Lungo Camiciotti, Gabriella. "An Atypical Commercial Correspondence: Negotiating Artefacts and Status." In *Letter Writing in Late Modern Europe*, edited by M. Dossena and G. del Lungo Camiciotti, 78–98. Amsterdam: John Benjamins, 2012.

Digby, Anne. *Making a Medical Living: Doctors and Patients in the English Market for Medicine*. Cambridge: Cambridge University Press, 1994.

– *Pauper Palaces*. London: Routledge and Kegan Paul, 1978.

– "The Rural Poor Law." In *The New Poor Law in the Nineteenth Century*, edited by D. Fraser, 149–70. Basingstoke: Macmillan, 1976.

Dobbing, Cara. "The Circulation of Pauper Lunatics and the Transitory Nature of Mental Health Provision in Late Nineteenth Century Cumberland and Westmoreland." *Local Population Studies* 99 (2017): 56–65.

Doolittle, Megan. "The Duty to Provide: Fathers, Families and the Workhouse in England, 1880–1914." In *The Welfare State and the 'Deviant' Poor in Europe, 1880–1914*, edited by B. Althammer, A. Gestrich, and J. Gründler, 58–77. Basingstoke: Palgrave, 2014.

– "Fatherhood and Family Shame: Masculinity, Welfare and the Workhouse in Late Nineteenth Century England." In *The Politics of Domestic Authority in Britain from 1800*, edited by L. Delap, B. Griffin, and A. Willis, 84–108. Basingstoke: Palgrave, 2009.

Dossena, Marina. "Doing Business in Nineteenth-Century Scotland: Expressing Authority, Conveying Stance." *IEEE Transactions on Professional Communication* 11 (2006): 23–39.

Dossena, Marina, and G. del Lungo Camiciotti, eds. *Letter Writing in Late Modern Europe*. Amsterdam: John Benjamin, 2012.

Downing, Arthur. "The 'Sheffield Outrages': Violence, Class and Trade Unionism, 1850–70." *Social History* 38 (2013): 162–82.

Driver, Felix. *Power and Pauperism: The Workhouse System 1834–1884*. Cambridge: Cambridge University Press, 1993.

Dunkley, Peter. "The Hungry Forties and the Poor Law: A Case Study." *The Historical Journal* 17 (1974): 329–46.

Durbach, Nadja. "Roast Beef, the New Poor Law, and the British Nation, 1834–63." *Journal of British Studies* 5 (2013): 963–89.

Earner–Byrne, Lyndsey. *Letters of the Catholic Poor: Poverty in an Independent Ireland, 1920–1940*. Cambridge: Cambridge University Press, 2017.

Eastwood, David. "'Amplifying the Province of the Legislature': The Flow of Information and the English State in the Early Nineteenth Century." *Historical Research* 62 (1989): 276–92.

– *Government and Community in the English Provinces 1700–1870*. Basingstoke: Macmillan, 1997.

Edsall, Nicholas. *The Anti-Poor Law Movement, 1834–44*. Manchester: Manchester University Press, 1971.

Elspaβ, Stefan. "Between Linguistic Creativity and Formulaic Restriction: Cross-Linguistic Perspectives on Nineteenth-Century Lower Class Writers' Private Letters." In *Letter Writing in Late Modern Europe*, edited by M. Dossena and G. del Lungho Camiciotti, 45–64. Amsterdam: John Benjamins, 2012.

Englander, David. "From the Abyss: Pauper Petitions and Correspondence in Victorian London." *London Journal* 25 (2000): 71–83.

– *Poverty and Poor Law Reform in 19th Century Britain, 1834–1914: From Chadwick to Booth*. London: Longman, 1998.

Evans, Eric. *Social Policy 1830–1914: Individualism, Collectivism and the Origins of the Welfare State*. London: Routledge and Kegan Paul, 1978.

Evans, Megan, and Peter Jones. "'A Stubborn and Intractable Body': Resistance to the Workhouse in Wales, 1834–1877." *Family and Community History* 17 (2014): 101–21.

Feeley, Malcolm, and Deborah Little. "The Vanishing Female: The Decline of Women in the Criminal Process." *Law and Society Review* 25 (1991): 719–57.

Feldman, David. "Migrants, Immigrants and Welfare from the Old Poor Law to the Welfare State." *Transactions of the Royal Historical Society* 13 (2003): 79–104.

Finlayson, Geoffrey. *Citizen, State and Social Welfare in Britain, 1830–1990*. Oxford: Oxford University Press, 1994.

Fitzmaurice, Susan. *The Familiar Letter in Early Modern English: A Pragmatic Approach*. Amsterdam: John Benjamin, 2002.

Fissell, Mary. "Charity Universal? Institutions and Moral Reform in Eighteenth-Century Bristol." In *Stilling the Grumbling Hive: The Responses to Social and Economic Problems in England 1689–1750*, edited by L. Davidson, T. Hitchcock, T. Keirn, and R. Shoemaker, 120–49. New York: St Martin's Press, 1992.

Foster, Laura. "Christmas in the Workhouse: Staging Philanthropy in the Nineteenth–Century Periodical." *Journal of Victorian Culture* 22 (2017): 553–78.

– "Dirt, Dust and Devilment: Uncovering Filth in the Workhouse and Casual Wards." *The Victorian Network* 6 (2015): 29–58.

Frankel, Oz. "Scenes of Commission: Royal Commissions of Inquiry and the Culture of Social Investigation in Early Victorian Britain." *The European Legacy* 4 (1999): 20–41.

– *States of Inquiry: Social Investigation and Print Culture in Nineteenth-Century Britain and the United States*. Baltimore: Johns Hopkins University Press, 2006.

Fraser, Derek. "The English Poor Law and the Origins of the British Welfare State." In *The Emergence of the Welfare State in Britain and Germany 1850–1950*, edited by W.J. Mommsen, 9–31. London: Croom Helm, 1981.

– *The Evolution of the British Welfare State: A History of Social Policy Since the Industrial Revolution*. Basingstoke: Palgrave, 2017.

– "The Poor Law as a Political Institution." In *The New Poor Law in the Nineteenth Century*, edited by D. Fraser, 111–27. Basingstoke: Macmillan, 1976.

Freeman, Mark. "'Journeys into Poverty Kingdom': Complete Participation and the British Vagrant, 1866–1914." *History Workshop Journal* 52 (2001): 99–121.

French, Henry. "An Irrevocable Shift: Detailing the Dynamics of Rural Poverty in Southern England, 1762–1834: A Case Study." *Economic History Review* 68 (2015): 769–805.

Frost, Ginger. *Illegitimacy in English Law and Society, 1860–1930*. Manchester: Manchester University Press, 2016.

– "Under the Guardians' Supervision: Illegitimacy, Family, and the English Poor Law, 1870–1930." *Journal of Family History* 38 (2013): 122–39.

Gazeley, Ian. *Poverty in Britain, 1900–1965*. Basingstoke: Palgrave, 2003.

Gibson-Brydon, Thomas. *The Moral Mapping of Victorian and Edwardian London: Charles Booth, Christian Charity, and the Poor-but-Respectable*. Montreal: McGill-Queen's University Press, 2016.

Gillie, Alan. "Identifying the Poor in the 1870s and 1880s." *Economic History Review* 61 (2008): 302–25.

– "The Origin of the Poverty Line." *Economic History Review* 49 (1996): 715–30.

Ginn, Geoffrey. *Culture, Philanthropy and the Poor in Late-Victorian Britain*. London: Routledge, 2017.

Goldman, Lawrence. "Social Reform and the Pressures of 'Progress' on Parliament, 1660–1914." *Parliamentary History* 37 (2018): 72–88.

Gooday, Graeme, and K. Sayer. "Purchase, Use and Adaptation: Interpreting 'Patented' Aids to the Deaf in Victorian Britain." In *Rethinking Modern Prostheses in Anglo-American Commodity Cultures, 1820–1939*, edited by C. Jones, 27–47. Manchester: Manchester University Press, 2017.

Goose, Nigel. "Poverty, Old Age and Gender in Nineteenth-Century England: The Case of Hertfordshire." *Continuity and Change* 20 (2005): 351–84.

– "Workhouse Populations in the Mid-Nineteenth Century: The Case of Hertfordshire." *Local Population Studies* 62 (1999): 52–69.

Gorsky, Martin, and Sally Sheard. "Introduction." In *Financing Medicine: The British Experience since 1750*, edited by M. Gorsky and S. Sheard, 1–16. Aldershot: Ashgate, 2006.

Green, David. *Pauper Capital: London and the Poor Law, 1790–1870*. Farnham: Ashgate, 2010.

– "Pauper Protests: Power and Resistance in Early Nineteenth-Century London Workhouses." *Social History* 31 (2006): 137–59.

Griffin, Carl. *The Politics of Hunger: Protest, Poverty and Policy in England, 1750–1840*. Manchester: Manchester University Press, 2020.

Griffin, Emma. "The Emotions of Motherhood: Love, Culture, and Poverty in Victorian Britain." *American Historical Review* 123 (2018): 60–85.

– "The Making of the Chartists: Popular Politics and Working-Class Autobiography in Early Victorian Britain." *English Historical Review* 129 (2014): 578–605.

Gritt, Andrew, and Peter Park. "The Workhouse Populations of Lancashire in 1881." *Local Population Studies* 86 (2011): 37–65.

Grover, Chris. *Social Security and Wage Poverty: Historical and Policy Aspects of Supplementing Wages in Britain and Beyond*. Basingstoke: Palgrave, 2016.

Gurney, Peter. *Wanting and Having: Popular Politics and Liberal Consumerism in England 1830–1870*. Manchester: Manchester University Press, 2015.

Hall, Stuart, and Bill Schwarz. "State and Society, 1880–1930." In *Crises in the British State 1880–1930*, edited by M. Langan and B. Schwarz, 7–32. London: Hutchinson, 1985.

Hallett, Christine. "Nursing, 1830–1920: Forging a Profession." In *Nursing and Midwifery in Britain Since 1700*, edited by A. Borsay and B. Hunter, 56–83. Basingstoke: Palgrave, 2012.

Harling, Philip. *The Modern British State*. Cambridge: Cambridge University Press, 2001.

Harris, Bernard. "Gender and Social Citizenship in Historical Perspective: the Development of Welfare Policy in England and Wales from the Poor Law to Beveridge." In *Gender and Wellbeing: The Role of Institutions*, edited by P. de Villota, J. Eriksen, and E. Addis, 29–60. London: Routledge, 2011.

– *The Origins of the British Welfare State: Social Welfare in England and Wales, 1800–1945*. Basingstoke: Macmillan, 2004.

Harris, Jose. "Nationality, Rights and Virtue: Some Approaches to Citizenship in Great Britain." In *Lineages of European Citizenship: Rights, Belonging and Participation in Eleven Nation-States*, edited by R. Bellamy, D. Castiglione, and E. Santoro, 73–91. Basingstoke: Palgrave, 2004.

– "Political Thought and the Welfare State 1870–1940: An Intellectual Framework for British Social Policy." *Past and Present* 135 (1992): 116–41.

– *Unemployment and Politics: A Study in English Social Policy 1880–1914*. Oxford: Clarendon, 1972.

Hawkins, Sue. *Nursing and Women's Labour in the Nineteenth Century: The Quest for Independence*. London: Routledge, 2010.

Healey, Jonathan. "Coping with Risk in the Seventeenth Century. The First Age of the English Old Poor Law: A Regional Study." In *Public Goods Provision in the Early Modern Economy: Comparative Perspectives from Japan, China, and Europe*, edited by M. Tanimoto and R. Wong, 100–17. Los Angeles: University of California Press, 2019.

Helmstadter, Carol, and J. Godden, *Nursing before Nightingale, 1815–1899*. Aldershot: Ashgate, 2011.

Hennock, Peter. "The Measurement of Urban Poverty: From the Metropolis to the Nation, 1880–1920." *Economic History Review* 40 (1987): 208–27.

– *The Origin of the Welfare State in England and Germany, 1850–1914: Social Policies Compared*. Cambridge: Cambridge University Press, 2007.

– "Poverty and Social Theory in England: The Experience of the 1880s." *Social History* 1 (1976): 67–91.

Henriques, Ursula. *Before the Welfare State: Social Administration in Early Industrial Britain*. London: Longman, 1979.

– "How Cruel Was the Victorian Poor Law?" *Historical Journal* 11 (1968): 365–71.

Hepburn, James. *A Book of Scattered Leaves: Poetry of Poverty in Broadside Ballads of the Nineteenth-Century England*. London: Bucknell University Press, 2000.

Heritage, Tom. "The Elderly Populations of England and Wales, 1851–1911: A Comparative Study of Selected Counties." Unpublished PhD dissertation, University of Southampton, 2019.

Heritage, Tom, Andrew Hinde, and David Clifford. "Household Living Arrangements and Old Age Pauperism in Late Victorian Britain." *Genealogy* 4 (2020). Online only; no pagination.

Higginbotham, Peter. *Voices from the Workhouse*. London: History Press, 2012.

Higgs, Edward. *The Information State in England: The Central Collection of Information on Citizens since 1500*. Basingstoke: Palgrave, 2003.

Hilliard, Christopher. "Popular Reading and Social Investigation in Britain, 1850s–1940s." *Historical Journal* 57 (2014): 247–71.

Hinde, Andrew, and Fiona Turnbull. "The Population of Two Hampshire Workhouses, 1851–1861." *Local Population Studies* 61 (1998): 38–53.

Hindle, Steve. *On the Parish? The Micro-Politics of Poor Relief in Rural England 1550–1750*. Oxford: Clarendon Press, 2004.

Hitchcock, Tim. "The English Workhouse: A Study in Institutional Poor Relief in Selected Counties, 1696–1750." Unpublished DPhil dissertation, University of Oxford, 1985.

Hobbs, Andrew. "When the Provincial Press was the National Press (c.1836–1900)." *International Journal of Regional and Local Studies* 5 (2009): 16–43.

Hodgkinson, Ruth. "Poor Law Medical Officers of England 1834–1871." *Journal of the History of Medicine and Allied Science* 11 (1956): 23–48.

Hollen Lees, Lynn. *Poverty and Pauperism in Nineteenth-Century London*. Leicester: Leicester University Press, 1988.

– *The Solidarities of Strangers: The English Poor Laws and the People 1700–1948*. Cambridge: Cambridge University Press, 1998.

– "The Survival of the Unfit: Welfare Policies and Family Maintenance in Nineteenth-Century London." In *The Uses of Charity: The Poor on Relief in the Nineteenth-Century Metropolis*, edited by Peter Mandler, 68–91. Pennsylvania: University of Pennsylvania Press, 1990.

Hooker, Geoff. "Llandilofawr Poor Law Union 1836–1886: 'The Most Difficult Union in Wales.'" Unpublished PhD dissertation, University of Leicester, 2013.

Horrell, Sara, and Jane Humphries. "The Origins and Expansion of the Male Breadwinner Family: The Case of Nineteenth-Century Britain." *International Review of Social History* 42 (1997): 25–64.

Howells, Gary. "Emigration and the New Poor Law: The Norfolk Emigration Fever of 1836." *Rural History* 11 (2000): 145–64.

– "'For I Was Tired of England Sir': English Pauper Emigrant Strategies, 1834–60." *Social History* 23 (1998): 181–94.

– "'On Account of their Disreputable Characters': Parish Assisted Emigration from Rural England, 1834–1860." *History* 88 (2003): 587–608.

Hume, John. "Jeremy Bentham and the Nineteenth–Century Revolution in Government." *Historical Journal* 1 (1967): 361–75.

Hulonce, Lesley. *Pauper Children and Poor Law Childhoods in England and Wales, 1834–1910*. Swansea: Rounded Globe, 2016.

– "'These Valuable Institutions': Educating Blind and Deaf Children in Victorian and Edwardian Swansea." *Welsh History Review* 27 (2014): 310–37.

Humphreys, Robert. *Poor Relief and Charity 1869–1945: The London Charity Organization Society*. Basingstoke: Palgrave, 2001.

Humphries, Jane. "Care and Cruelty in the Workhouse: Children's Experiences of Residential Poor Relief in Eighteenth- and Nineteenth-Century England." In *Childhood and Child Labour in Industrial England: Diversity and Agency 1750–1914*, edited by N. Goose and K. Honeyman, 115–34. Aldershot: Ashgate, 2013.

– *Childhood and Child Labour in the British Industrial Revolution*. Cambridge: Cambridge University Press, 2010.

– "Memories of Pauperism." In *Migration, Settlement and Belonging in Europe, 1500s–1930s*, edited by S. King and A. Winter, 102–26. Oxford: Berghahn, 2013.

Hunt, Edward. "Paupers and Pensioners, Past and Present." *Ageing and Society* 9 (1989): 408–22.

Hurren, Elizabeth. "Belonging, Settlement and the New Poor Law in England and Wales 1870s–1900s." In *Migration, Settlement and Belonging in Europe, 1500s–1930s: Comparative Perspectives*, edited by S. King and A. Winter, 187–201. Oxford: Berghahn, 2013.

– *Dying for Victorian Medicine: English Anatomy and Its Trade in the Dead Poor, c.1834–1929*. Basingstoke: Palgrave, 2011.

– "Poor Law Versus Public Health: Diphtheria, Sanitary Reform, and the 'Crusade' Against Outdoor Relief, 1870–1900." *Social History of Medicine* 18 (2005): 399–418.

– *Protesting About Pauperism: Poverty, Politics and Poor Relief in Late-Victorian England, 1870–1900.* Woodbridge: Boydell and Brewer, 2007.

– "World without Welfare? Pauper Perspectives on Medical Care under the Late-Victorian Poor Law 1870–1900." In *Obligation, Entitlement and Dispute under the English Poor Laws, 1600–1900*, edited by P. Jones and S. King, 292–320. Newcastle: Cambridge Scholars Press, 2015.

Hurren, Elizabeth, and Steven King. "Begging for a Burial: Death and the Poor Law in Eighteenth- and Nineteenth-Century England." *Social History* 30 (2005): 321–41.

Huzzey, Richard, and Henry Miller. "Petitions, Parliament and Political Culture: Petitioning the House of Commons, 1780–1918." *Past and Present* 248 (2020): 123–64.

Jackson, David. "The Medway Union Workhouse, 1876–1881: A Study Based on the Admission and Discharge Registers and the Census Enumerators Books." *Local Population Studies* 75 (2005): 11–32.

– "Kent Workhouse Populations in 1881: A Study Based on the Census Enumerators' Books," *Local Population Studies* 69 (2002): 51–66.

James, Jeff. "Sophia Heathfield of Hawnes, Bedfordshire: Punishment Victim or Victor?" *Family and Community History* 21 (2018): 202–29.

Jarrett, Simon. *Those They Called Idiots: The Idea of the Disabled Mind from 1700 to the Present Day*. London: Reaktion, 2020.

Johnson, Paul. "The Employment and Retirement of Older Men in England and Wales, 1881–1981." *Economic History Review* 47 (1994): 106–28.

Jones, Ken. *Newcastle-in-Emlyn Union & Workhouse.* Cardiff: Summerhill Publishing, 2011.

Jones, Peter. "'I Cannot Keep My Place without Being Deascent': Pauper Letters, Parish Clothing and Pragmatism in the South of England, 1750–1830." *Rural History* 20 (2009): 31–49.

– "Looking through a Different Lens: Microhistory and the Workhouse Experience in Late Nineteenth-Century London." *Journal of Social History* 55 (2022): 925–47.

– "Swing, Speenhamland and Rural Social Relations: The 'Moral Economy' of the English Crowd in the Nineteenth Century." *Social History* 32 (2007): 271–90.

Jones, Peter, and Natalie Carter. "Writing for Redress: Redrawing the Epistolary Relationship under the New Poor Law." *Continuity and Change* 34 (2019): 375–99.

Jones, Peter, and Steven King. "From Petition to Pauper Letter: The Development of an Epistolary Form." In *Obligation, Entitlement and Dispute under the English Poor Laws, 1600–1900*, edited by P. Jones and S. King, 53–77. Newcastle: Cambridge Scholars Press, 2015.

– *Navigating the Old English Poor Law: The Kirkby Lonsdale Letters, 1809–1836*. Oxford: Oxford University Press, 2020.

– *Pauper Voices, Public Opinion and Workhouse Reform in Mid-Victorian England: Bearing Witness*. Basingstoke: Palgrave, 2020.

Jones, Peter, Steven King, and Karen Thompson. "Clothing the New Poor Law Workhouse in the Nineteenth Century." *Rural History* 32 (2021): 127–48.

Joyce, Patrick. "The People's English: Language and Class in England 1840–1920." In *Language, Self and Society: A Social History of Language*, edited by P. Burke and R. Porter, 154–90. Cambridge: Polity Press, 1991.

Jucker, Andreas, and Irma Taavitsainen. "Apologies in the History of English: Routinized and Lexicalized Expressions of Responsibility and Regret." In *Speech Acts in the History of English*, edited by A. Jucker and I. Taavitsainen, 229–46. Amsterdam: John Benjamins, 2008.

Kidd, Alan. "Outcast Manchester: Voluntary Charity, Poor Relief and the Casual Poor 1860–1905." In *City, Class and Culture*, edited by A. Kidd and K. Roberts, 43–60. Manchester: Manchester University Press, 1985.

– *State, Society and the Poor in Nineteenth-Century England*. Basingstoke: Macmillan, 1999.

King, Peter. *Crime and Law in England 1750–1840: Remaking Justice from the Margins*. Cambridge: Cambridge University Press, 2006.

– "The Rights of the Poor and the Role of the Law: The Impact of Pauper Appeals to the Summary Courts 1750–1834." In *Obligation, Entitlement and Dispute under the English Poor Laws*, edited by P. Jones and S. King, 235–62. Newcastle: Cambridge Scholars Press, 2015.

– "Social Inequality, Identity and the Labouring Poor in Eighteenth-Century England." In *Identity and Agency in England, 1500–1800*, edited by H. French and J. Barry, 60–87. Basingstoke: Macmillan, 2004.

– "The Summary Courts and Social Relations in Eighteenth-Century England." *Past and Present* 183 (2004): 125–72.

King, Steven. "The Economy of Makeshifts in the Early Modern North of England." In *The Poor in England 1700–1850: An Economy of Makeshifts*, edited by S. King and A. Tomkins, 278–314. Manchester: Manchester University Press, 2003.

– “Friendship, Kinship and Belonging in the Letters of Urban Paupers 1800–1840.” *Historical Social Research* 33 (2008): 249–77.

– “‘In These You May Trust’. Numerical Information, Accounting Practices and the Poor Law, c.1790 to 1840.” In *Statistics and the Public Sphere: Numbers and the People in Modern Britain, c.1750–2000*, edited by T. Crook and G. O’Hara, 51–66. London: Routledge, 2011.

– “‘It Is Impossible for Our Vestry to Judge His Case into Perfection from Here’: Managing the Distance Dimensions of Poor Relief, 1800–40.” *Rural History* 16 (2005): 161–89.

– “Negotiating the Law of Poor Relief in England 1800–1840.” *History* 96 (2011): 410–35.

– “Nursing Under the Old Poor Law in Midland and Eastern England 1780–1834.” *Journal of the History of Medicine and Allied Sciences* 70 (2015): 588–622.

– *Poverty and Welfare in England 1700–1850: A Regional Perspective*. Manchester: Manchester University Press, 2000.

– “Poverty, Medicine and the Workhouse in the Eighteenth and Nineteenth Centuries.” In *Medicine and the Workhouse*, edited by J. Reinarz and L. Schwarz, 290–313. Rochester: Rochester University Press, 2013.

– “Regional Patterns in the Experience and Treatment of the Sick Poor, 1800–40: Rights, Obligations and Duties in the Rhetoric of Paupers.” *Family and Community History* 10 (2007): 61–75.

– “Rights, Duties and Practice in the Transition Between the Old and New Poor Laws 1820–1860s.” In *Obligation, Entitlement and Dispute under the English Poor Laws, 1600–1900*, edited by P. Jones and S.A. King, 263–91. Newcastle: Cambridge Scholars Press, 2015.

– *Sickness, Medical Welfare and the English Poor 1750–1834*. Manchester: Manchester University Press, 2018.

– “‘Stop this Overwhelming Torment of Destiny’: Negotiating Financial Aid at Times of Sickness under the English Old Poor Law, 1800–1840.” *Bulletin of the History of Medicine* 79 (2005): 228–60.

– “Thinking and Rethinking the New Poor Law.” *Local Population Studies* 99 (2017): 104–18.

– “Welfare Regimes and Welfare Regions in Britain and Europe, c.1750–1860.” *Journal of Modern European History* 9 (2011): 42–66.

– *"We Might be Trusted": Women, Welfare and Local Politics 1880–1920*. Brighton: Sussex Academic Press, 2005.

– *Writing the Lives of the English Poor, 1750s to 1830s*. London: McGill-Queen's University Press, 2019.

King, Steven, and Carol Beardmore. "Contesting the Workhouse: Life Writing, Children and the Later New Poor Law." In *Rebellious Writing: Contesting Marginalisation in Edwardian Britain*, edited by L. O'Hagan, 65–94. Bern: Peter Lang, 2020.

King, Steven, and Peter Jones. "Fragments of Fury? Lunacy, Agency and Contestation in the Great Yarmouth Workhouse, 1890s–1900s." *Journal of Interdisciplinary History* 51 (2020): 235–66.

– "Testifying for the Poor: Epistolary Advocates for the Poor in Nineteenth Century England and Wales." *Journal of Social History* 49 (2016): 784–807.

Kirby, Peter. *Child Workers and Industrial Health in Britain, 1780–1850*. Woodbridge: Boydell, 2013.

Knights, Mark. "'The Lowest Degree of Freedom': The Right to Petition Parliament, 1640–1800." *Parliamentary History* 37 (2018): 18–37.

Knott, John. *Popular Opposition to the 1834 Poor Law*. New York: Croom Helm, 1986.

Koven, Seth. "Borderlands: Women, Voluntary Action, and Child Welfare in Britain, 1840–1914." In *Mothers of a New World: Maternalist Politics and the Origins of Welfare States*, edited by S. Koven and S. Michel, 94–135. London: Routledge, 1993.

– *Slumming: Sexual and Social Politics in Victorian London*. Princeton: Princeton University Press, 2004.

Lane, Joan. *A Social History of Medicine: Health, Healing and Disease in England, 1750–1950*. London: Routledge, 2001.

Langhamer, Claire. "Who the Hell Are Ordinary People? Ordinariness as a Category of Historical Analysis." *Transactions of the Royal Historical Society* 28 (2018): 175–95.

Laybourn, Keith. *The Evolution of British Social Policy and the Welfare State, c.1800–1993*. Keele: Keele University Press, 1995.

Leivers, Clive. "Housing the Elderly in Nineteenth-Century Derbyshire: A Comparison of Almshouse and Workhouse Provision." *Local Population Studies* 83 (2009): 56–65.

Leys, Colin. "Petitioning in the 19th and 20th Centuries." *Political Studies* 3 (1955): 45–64.

Levene, Alysa. "Children, Childhood and the Workhouse: St Marylebone, 1769–1781." *London Journal* 33 (2008): 41–59.

Levine-Clark, Marjorie. "From Relief to Justice and Protection: The Maintenance of Deserted Wives, British Masculinity and Imperial Citizenship, 1870–1920." *Gender and History* 22 (2010): 302–21.

– "The Gendered Economy of Family Liability: Intergenerational Relationships and Poor Law Relief in England's Black Country, 1871–1911." *Journal of British Studies* 45 (2006): 72–89.

– "Gendered Roles, Gendered Welfare: Health and the English Poor Law, 1871–1911." In *Bodily Subjects: Essays on Gender and Health, 1800–2000*, edited by B. Brookes, T.P. Light, and W. Mitchinson, 53–73. Montreal: McGill-Queen's University Press, 2014.

– *Unemployment, Welfare and Masculine Citizenship: So Much Honest Poverty in Britain, 1870–1930*. Basingstoke: Palgrave, 2015.

Long, Jane. *Conversations in Cold Rooms: Women, Work and Poverty in Nineteenth-Century Northumberland*. Woodbridge: Boydell and Brewer, 1999.

Loudon, Irvine. *Medical Care and the General Practitioner 1750–1850*. Oxford: Clarendon Press, 1986.

Lyons, Martyn. *A History of Reading and Writing in the Western World*. Basingstoke: Palgrave, 2010.

– "Ordinary Writings or How the Illiterate Speak to Historians." In *Ordinary Writings, Personal Narratives: Writing Practices in 19th and Early 20th-century Europe*, edited by M. Lyons, 13–32. Bern: Peter Lang, 2007.

– *The Writing Culture of Ordinary People in Europe, c.1860–1920*. Cambridge: Cambridge University Press, 2013.

– "Writing Upwards: How the Weak Wrote to the Powerful." *Journal of Social History* 49 (2015): 317–30.

MacDonagh, Olive. *Early Victorian Government, 1830–1870*. London: Allen Lane, 1977.

MacKay, Lynn. *Respectability and the London Poor, 1780–1870: The Value of Virtue*. London: Pickering and Chatto, 2013.

Mackie, Clare. "Talking Like a Native." *Country Life* (9 May 2018): 90–1.

MacKinnon, Mary. "English Poor Law Policy and the Crusade against Outrelief." *Journal of Economic History* 47 (1987): 603–25.

MacSwaine, Judith. "Daniel Liddell." *North East History* 44 (2013): 81–5.

Maggs, C. "Profit and Loss and the New Hospital Nurse." *Society for the Social History of Medicine Bulletin* 41 (1987): 81–4.

Mandler, Peter. "Poverty and Charity in the Nineteenth-Century Metropolis: An

Introduction." In *The Uses of Charity: The Poor on Relief in the Nineteenth-Century Metropolis*, edited by P. Mandler, 1–37. Pennsylvania: University of Pennsylvania Press, 1990.

– "Tories and Paupers: Christian Political Economy and the Making of the New Poor Law." *The Historical Journal* 33 (1990): 81–103.

Marks, Lara. "'The Luckless Waifs and Strays of Humanity': Irish and Jewish Immigrant Unwed Mothers in London, 1870–1939." *Twentieth Century British History* 3 (1992): 113–37.

Marland, Hilary. "'Close Confinement Tells Very Much Upon a Man': Prison Memoirs, Insanity and the Late Nineteenth- and Early Twentieth-Century Prison." *Journal of the History of Medicine and Allied Sciences* 74 (2019): 267–91.

– *Medicine and Society in Wakefield and Huddersfield 1780–1870*. Cambridge: Cambridge University Press, 1987.

Martin, Edward. "From Parish to Union: Poor Law Administration, 1601–1865." In *Comparative Development in Social Welfare*, edited by E. Martin, 25–56. London: Allen and Unwin, 1972.

Maynard, Jean. "The Campaign for the Catholic Workhouse Children, 1834–68." *British Catholic History* 32 (2015): 526–56.

McGrath, Connor. "British Lobbying in Newspaper and Parliamentary Discourse, 1800–1950." *Parliamentary History* 37 (2018): 226–49.

McIvor, Arthur, and R. Johnston, *Miners' Lung: A History of Dust Disease in British Coal Mining*. Aldershot: Ashgate, 2007.

Midwinter, Eric. *Social Administration in Lancashire, 1830–60: Poor Law, Public Health and Police*. Manchester: Manchester University Press, 1969.

– "State Intervention at the Local Level: The New Poor Law in Lancashire." *Historical Journal* 10 (1967): 106–12.

Miller, Henry. "Introduction: the Transformation of Petitioning in the Long Nineteenth Century." *Social Science History* 43 (2019): 409–29.

Miller, Ian. "Feeding in the Workhouse: The Institutional and Ideological Functions of Food in Britain, c.1834–70." *Journal of British Studies* 52 (2013): 940–62.

Mooney, Graham. "Diagnostic Spaces: Workhouse, Hospital, and Home in Mid-Victorian London." *Social Science History* 33 (2009): 357–90.

Moreton, Emma. "'I Never Could Forget My Darling Mother': The Language of Recollection in a Corpus of Female Irish Emigrant Correspondence." *The History of the Family* 21 (2016): 315–36.

Murdoch, Lydia. *Imagined Orphans: Poor Families, Child Welfare, and Contested Citizenship in London*. New Brunswick (New Jersey): Rutgers University Press, 2006.

Murphy, Elaine. "The New Poor Law Guardians and the Administration of Insanity in East London, 1834–1844." *Bulletin of the History of Medicine* 77 (2003): 45–74.

Navickas, Katrina, and Adam Crymble, "From Chartist Newspaper to Digital Map of Grass-roots Meetings, 1841–44: Documenting Workflows." *Journal of Victorian Culture* 22 (2017): 232–47.

Negrine, Angela. "Practitioners and Paupers: Medicine at the Leicester Union Workhouse, 1867–1905." In *Medicine in the Workhouse*, edited by J. Reinarz and L. Schwarz, 121–42. Rochester: Rochester University Press, 2013.

– "The Treatment of Sick Children in the Workhouse by the Leicester Poor Law Union, 1867–1914." *Family and Community History* 13 (2010): 34–44.

Neuman, Mark. *The Speenhamland County: Poverty and the Poor Laws in Berkshire, 1782–1834*. New York: Garland, 1982.

– "A Suggestion Regarding the Origins of the Speenhamland Plan." *English Historical Review* 84 (1969): 317–22.

Newman, Charlotte. "The Place of the Pauper: A Historical Archaeology of West Yorkshire Workhouses 1834–1930." Unpublished PhD dissertation, University of York, 2010.

– "To Punish or Protect: The New Poor Law and the English Workhouse." *International Journal of Historical Archaeology* 18 (2014): 122–45.

Osborne, Harvey, and Michael Winstanley. "Rural and Urban Poaching in Victorian England." *Rural History* 17 (2006): 187–212.

Ottaway, Susannah. *The Decline of Life: Old Age in Eighteenth-Century England*. Cambridge: Cambridge University Press, 2004.

Pearson, Jane, and M. Rayner. *Prostitution in Victorian Colchester: Controlling the Uncontrollable*. Hatfield: University of Hertfordshire Press, 2018.

Phillips, Gordon. *The Blind in British Society: Charity, State and Community, c.1780–1930*. Aldershot: Ashgate, 2004.

Pickering, Paul. "'And Your Petitioner &c': Chartists Petitioning in Popular Politics 1838–48." *English Historical Review* 116 (2001): 368–88.

Pooley, Colin. "Travelling Through the City: Using Life Writing to Explore Individual Experiences of Urban Travel c.1840–1940." *Mobilities* 12 (2017): 598–609.

Price, Kim. *Medical Negligence in Victorian Britain: The Crisis of Care under the English Poor Law, c.1834–1900*. London: Bloomsbury, 2015.

Prochaska, Frank. "Philanthropy." In *The Cambridge Social History of Britain, 1750–1950. Vol. 3*, edited by F.M.L. Thompson, 357–93. Cambridge: Cambridge University Press, 1990.

Purser, Joanne. "The Workhouse Population of the Nottingham Union, 1881–1882." *Local Population Studies* 99 (2017): 60–80.

Randall, Adrian, and Edwina Newman. "Protest, Proletarians and Paternalists: Social Conflict in Rural Wiltshire, 1830–1850." *Rural History* 6 (1995): 213–18.

Reinarz, Jonathan, and Leonard Schwarz. "Introduction." In *Medicine and the Workhouse*, edited by J. Reinarz and L. Schwarz, 1–13. Rochester: Rochester University Press, 2013.

Reynolds, Melanie. *Infant Mortality and Working-Class Child Care, 1850–1899*. Basingstoke: Palgrave, 2016.

Richardson, Nigel. "The Uppingham Typhoid Outbreaks of 1875–1877: A Rural Case-Study in Public Health Reform." *Social History of Medicine* 20 (2007): 281–96.

Richmond, Vivienne. *Clothing the Poor in Nineteenth-Century England*. Cambridge: Cambridge University Press, 2013.

Ritch, Alastair. "English Poor Law Institutional Care for Older People: Identifying the 'Aged and Infirm' and the 'Sick' in Birmingham Workhouse, 1852–1912." *Social History of Medicine* 27 (2014): 64–85.

– *Sickness in the Workhouse: Poor Law Medical Care in England, 1834–1914*. Rochester: Rochester University Press, 2019.

Roberts, David. "How Cruel Was the Victorian Poor Law?" *Historical Journal* 6 (1963): 97–107.

– *Victorian Origins of the British Welfare State*. New Haven: Yale University Press, 1961.

Robin, Jean. "Family Care of the Elderly in a Nineteenth-Century Devonshire Parish." *Ageing and Society* 4 (1984): 505–16.

– "The Relief of Poverty in Mid Nineteenth-Century Colyton." *Rural History* 1 (1990): 193–218.

Rose, Clare. *Making, Selling and Wearing Boys' Clothes in Late-Victorian England*. Farnham: Ashgate, 2010.

Rose, Michael. "The Allowance System Under the New Poor Law." *Economic History Review* 19 (1966): 607–20.

– *The English Poor Law, 1780–1930*. Newton Abbot: David and Charles, 1971.

Rose, Sonya. "The Varying Household Arrangements of the Elderly in Three English Villages: Nottinghamshire 1851–1881." *Continuity and Change* 3 (1988): 101–22.

Rothery, Karen. "Under New Management: The Administration of the 1834 New Poor Law in Hertfordshire." Unpublished PhD disssertation, University of Hertfordshire, 2017.

Ryan, Paul. "Politics and Relief: East London Unions in the Late-Nineteenth and Early-Twentieth Centuries." In *The Poor and the City: The English Poor Law in Its Urban Context, 1834–1914*, edited by M. Rose, 133–72. Leicester: Leicester University Press, 1985.

Sairio, Anni. "Cordials and Sharp Satyrs: Stance and Self-Fashioning in Eighteenth-Century Letters." In *Touching the Past: Studies in the Historical Sociolinguistics of Ego Documents*, edited by M. van der Wal and G. Rutten, 183–200. Amsterdam: John Benjamins, 2013.

Salt, John. "Isaac Ironside, 1808–1870: The Motivation of a Radical Educationist." *British Journal of Educational Studies* 19 (1971): 183–201.

Scott, James. *Domination and the Arts of Resistance: Hidden Transcripts*. New Haven: Yale University Press, 1990.

Seaber, Luke. *Incognito Social Investigation in British Literature: Certainties in Degradation*. London: Palgrave, 2017.

Seal, Christine. "Workhouse Populations in the Cheltenham and Belper Unions: A Study Based on the Census Enumerators' Books, 1851–1911," *Family and Community History* 13 (2013): 83–100.

Sen, Sambhuda. "From Dispossession to Dissection: The Bare Life of the English Pauper in the Age of the Anatomy Act and the New Poor Law." *Victorian Studies* 59 (2017): 235–59.

Sharpe, Pamela. "Parish Women: Maternity and the Limitations of Maiden Settlement in England, 1662–1834." In *Obligation, Entitlement and Dispute under the English Poor Laws*, edited by P. Jones and S. King, 168–92. Newcastle: Cambridge Scholars Press, 2015.

– "The Shiners: Framework-Knitting Households in Nottinghamshire and Derbyshire, 1840–1890." *Family and Community History* 3 (2000): 105–20.

Shave, Samantha. "'Great Inhumanity': Scandal, Child Punishment and Policymaking in the Early Years of the New Poor Law Workhouse System." *Continuity and Change* 33 (2018): 339–63.

– "'Immediate Death or a Life of Torture Are the Consequences of the System': The Bridgwater Union Scandal and Policy Change." In *Medicine and the Workhouse*, edited by J. Reinarz and L. Schwarz, 164–91. Rochester: Rochester University Press, 2013.

– *Pauper Policies: Poor Law Practice in England, 1780–1850*. Manchester: Manchester University Press, 2017.

Sigsworth, Michael, and Michael Warboys. "The Public's View of Public Health in Mid-Victorian Britain." *Urban History* 21 (1994): 237–50.

Smith, Cathy. "Parsimony, Power and Prescriptive Legislation: the Politics of Pauper Lunacy in Northamptonshire 1845–1876." *Bulletin of the History of Medicine* 81 (2007): 359–385.

Smith, Leonard. "Lunatic Asylum in the Workhouse: St. Peter's Hospital Bristol 1698–1861." *Medical History* 61 (2017): 225–45.

Snell, Keith. *Annals of the Labouring Poor: Social Change and Agrarian England 1660–1900*. Cambridge: Cambridge University Press, 1985.

– "Belonging and Community: Understanding of 'Home' and 'Friends' among the English Poor, 1750–1850." *Economic History Review* 65 (2012): 1–25.

– *Parish and Belonging: Community, Identity and Welfare in England and Wales 1700–1950*. Cambridge: Cambridge University Press, 2006.

– "Pauper Settlement and the Right to Poor Relief in England and Wales." *Continuity and Change* 6 (1991): 375–415

Snell, Keith, and P. Ell. *Rival Jerusalems: The Geography of Victorian Religion*. Cambridge: Cambridge University Press, 2000.

Snow, Stephanie. *Operations Without Pain: The Practice and Science of Anaesthesia in Victorian Britain*. Basingstoke: Palgrave, 2006.

Sokoll, Thomas. *Essex Pauper Letters 1731–1837*. Oxford: Oxford University Press, 2001.

– "Families, Wheat Prices and the Allowance Cycle: Poverty and Poor Relief in the Agricultural Community of Ardleigh 1794–1801." In *Obligation, Entitlement and Dispute under the English Poor Laws*, edited by P. Jones and S. King, 73–101. Newcastle: Cambridge Scholars Press, 2015.

– "Old Age in Poverty: The Record of Essex Pauper Letters, 1780–1834." In *Chronicling Poverty*, edited by T. Hitchcock, P. King, and P. Sharpe, 127–154. London: Palgrave Macmillan, 1997.

Somers, Margaret, and Fred Block. "From Poverty to Perversity: Ideas, Markets and

Institutions over 200 Years of Welfare Debates." *American Sociological Review* 70 (2005): 260–87.

Stapleton, Barry. "Inherited Poverty and Life-Cycle Poverty: Odiham, Hampshire, 1650–1850." *Social History* 18 (1996): 339–55.

Sutcliffe, Anthony. "The Growth of Public Intervention in the British Urban Environment during the 19th Century: A Structural Approach." In *The Structure of 19th Century Cities*, edited by J. Johnson and C. Pooley, 107–25. London: Croom Helm, 1982.

Sutton, David. "Liberalism, State Collectivism and the Social Relations of Citizenship." In *Crises in the British State 1880–1930*, edited by M. Langan and B. Schwarz, 63–79. London: Hutchinson, 1985.

Suzuki, Akihito. "Lunacy and Labouring Men: Narratives of Male Vulnerability in Mid–Victorian London." In *Medicine, Madness and Social History: Essays in Honour of Roy Porter*, edited by R. Bivins and J. Pickstone, 118–28. Basingstoke: Palgrave 2007.

Simon Szreter. Review of *Welfare's Forgotten Past: A Socio-Legal History of the Poor Law* by Lorie Charlesworth. *Economic History Review*, 64 (Nov. 2011), 1384–85.

Tabili, Laura. "'Having Lived Close Beside Them All the Time': Negotiating National Identities through Personal Networks." *Journal of Social History* 40 (2005): 369–87.

Tadmor, Naomi. *Family and Friends in Eighteenth Century England: Household, Kinship and Patronage*. Cambridge: Cambridge University Press, 2000.

– "The Settlement of the Poor and the Rise of the Form in England, c.1662–1780." *Past and Present* 236 (2017): 43–97.

Talbot, Richard. "North–South Divide: The New Poor Law in Stoke-on-Trent 1871–1929." Unpublished PhD dissertation, University of Leicester, 2017.

Tanner, Andrea. "The City of London Poor Law Union 1837–1868." Unpublished PhD dissertation, University of London, 1995.

Tate, William. *The Parish Chest: A Study of the Records of Parochial Administration in England*. Cambridge: Cambridge University Press, 1946.

Taylor, James. "A Different Kind of Speenhamland: Non-Resident Relief in the Industrial Revolution." *Journal of British Studies* 30 (1991): 183–208.

– *Poverty, Migration and Settlement in the Industrial Revolution: Sojourners' Narratives*. Palo Alto: SPSS, 1989.

Taylor, Steven. "Insanity, Philanthropy and Emigration: Dealing with Insane Children in Late-Nineteenth-Century North-West England." *History of Psychiatry* 25 (2014): 224–36.

– "Poverty, Emigration and Family: Experiencing Childhood Poverty in Late Nineteenth-Century Manchester." *Family and Community History* 18 (2015): 89–103.

Tenbus, Eric. *English Catholics and the Education of the Poor, 1847–1902*. London: Routledge, 2015.

Thane, Pat. "Government and Society in England and Wales 1750–1914." In *The Cambridge Social History of Britain 1750–1950*, edited by F.M.L. Thompson, 1–62. Cambridge: Cambridge University Press, 1999.

– "The History of Provisions for the Elderly to 1929." In *Ageing in Modern Society*, edited by D. Jerome, 191–9. London: Croom Helm, 1983.

– *Old Age in English History: Past Experiences, Present Issues*. Oxford: Oxford University Press, 2000.

– "'An Untiring Zest for Life': Images and Self–Images of Old Women in England." *Journal of Family History* 25 (2000): 235–47.

– "Women and the Poor Law in Victorian and Edwardian England." *History Workshop* 6 (1978): 30–51.

Thomson, David. "The Decline of Social Welfare: Falling State Support for the Elderly since Early Victorian Times." *Ageing and Society* 4 (1984): 451–82.

– "The Elderly in an Urban-Industrial Society: England 1750 to the Present." In *An Aging World: Dilemmas and Challenges for Law and Social Policy*, edited by J. Eekelaar and D. Pearl, 55–60. Oxford: Clarendon Press, 1995.

– "'I Am Not My Father's Keeper': Families and the Elderly in Nineteenth Century England." *Law and History Review* 2 (1984): 265–86.

– "Welfare and the Historians." In *The World We Have Gained: Histories of Population and Social Structure*, edited by L. Bonfield, R. Smith, and K. Wrightson, 355–78. Oxford: Basil Blackwell, 1986.

– "The Welfare of the Elderly in the Past: A Family or Community Responsibility?" In *Life, Death and the Elderly: Historical Perspectives*, edited by M. Pelling and R. Smith, 194–221. London: Routledge, 1994.

– "Workhouse to Nursing Home: Residential Care of Elderly People in England since 1840." *Ageing and Society* 3 (1983): 43–69.

Thompson, Edward. *The Making of the English Working Class*. Harmondsworth: Penguin, 1963.

Thornton, David. "Edward Baines, Senior (1774–1848), Provincial Journalism and

Political Philosophy in Early Nineteenth-Century England." *Northern History* 40 (2003): 277–97.

Tilly, Charles. *Popular Contention in Great Britain 1758–1834*. Cambridge, MA: Harvard University Press, 1995.

– "The Rise of the Public Meeting in Great Britain, 1758–1834." *Social Science History* 34 (2010): 291–99.

Timmins, Geoffrey. *The Last Shift: Decline of Handloom Weaving in Nineteenth-Century Lancashire*. Manchester: Manchester University Press, 1993.

Timmis, Ivor. *The Discourse of Desperation: Late 18th and Early 19th Century Letters by Paupers, Prisoners, and Rogues*. London: Routledge, 2020.

Tomkins, Alannah. "'The Excellent Example of the Working Class': Medical Welfare, Contributory Funding and the North Staffordshire Infirmary from 1815." *Social History of Medicine* 21 (2008): 13–30.

– "'Labouring on a Bed of Sickness': The Material and Rhetorical Deployment of Ill–Health in Male Pauper Letters." In *Poverty and Sickness in Modern Europe: Narratives of the Sick Poor, 1780–1938*, edited by A. Gestrich, E. Hurren, and S. King, 51–68. London: Bloomsbury, 2012.

– "Poor Law Institutions through Working-Class Eyes: Autobiography, Emotion, and Family Context, 1834–1914." *Journal of British Studies* 60 (2021): 285–309.

– "Workhouse Medical Care from Working-Class Autobiographies, 1750–1834." In *Medicine and the Workhouse*, edited by J. Reinarz and L. Schwarz, 86–102. Rochester: Rochester University Press, 2013.

Toplis, Alison. *The Clothing Trade in Provincial England, 1800–1850*. Abingdon: Routledge, 2011.

Tosh, John. *Manliness and Masculinities in Nineteenth-Century Britain*. Harlow: Longman, 2005.

Treble, James. *Urban Poverty in Britain 1830–1914*. London: Routledge, 2020 reprint.

Turner, David, and Daniel Blackie. *Disability in the Industrial Revolution: Physical Impairment in British Coalmining, 1780–1880*. Manchester: Manchester University Press, 2018.

van der Heijden, Manon, and Marion Pluskota. "Introduction to Crime and Gender in History." *Journal of Social History* 51 (2018): 661–71.

Vincent, David. *Bread, Knowledge and Freedom: A Study of Nineteenth-Century Working Class Autobiography*. London: Methuen, 1979.

– *Literacy and Popular Culture: England 1750–1914*. Cambridge: Cambridge University Press, 1989.

– *Poor Citizens: The State and the Poor in Twentieth-Century Britain*. Harlow: Longman, 1991.

– "Working-Class Autobiography in the Nineteenth Century." In *A History of English Autobiography*, edited by A. Smyth, 165–78. Cambridge: Cambridge University Press, 2016.

Vorspan, Rachel. "Vagrancy and the New Poor Law in Late Victorian and Edwardian England." *English Historical Review* 92 (1977): 59–81.

Waddell, Brodie. "Writing History from Below: Chronicling and Record-Keeping in Early Modern England." *History Workshop Journal* 85 (2018): 239–64.

Waddington, Keir. "Paying for the Sick Poor: Financing a Poor Law Workhouse." In *Financing British Medicine: The British Experience since 1750*, edited by M. Gorsky and S. Sheard, 95–111. London: Routledge, 2006.

Walker, Terry, and Peter Grund. "'Speaking Base Approbious Words': Speech Representation in Early Modern English Witness Depositions." *Journal of Historical Pragmatics* 18 (2017): 1–29.

Wall, Richard. "Some Implications of the Earnings, Income and Expenditure Patterns of Married Women in Populations in the Past." In *Poor Women and Children in the European Past*, edited by J. Henderson and R. Wall, 312–35. London: Routledge, 1994.

Walsh, Victor. "Poor Law Administration in Shropshire 1820–1855." Unpublished PhD dissertation, University of Pennsylvania, 1970.

Walton, Caroline. "Taking Control: Gossip, Community and Conflict in Basford Union Workhouse 1836–1871." *Family and Community History* 23 (2020): 23–41.

Webb, Sydney, and Beatrice Webb. *English Poor Law History, Part II: The Last Hundred Years*, Vol. 1. London: Methuen, 1929.

– *English Poor Law Policy*. London: Frank Cass & Co., 1923 reprint.

Webber, Megan. "Troubling Agency: Agency and Charity in Early Nineteenth-Century London." *Historical Research* 91 (2018): 116–36.

Weinstein, Ben. "'Local Self–Government Is True Socialism': Joshua Toulmin Smith, the State and Character Formation." *English Historical Review* 123 (2008): 1193–228.

Wessel Hansen, Peter. "Grief, Sickness and Emotions in the Narratives of the Shamefaced Poor in Late Eighteenth-Century Copenhagen." In *Poverty and Sickness in Modern Europe: Narratives of the Sick Poor 1780–1938*, edited by A. Gestrich, E. Hurren, and S. King, 35–50. London: Bloomsbury, 2012.

Whyte, William. "'The Too Clever by Half People' and Parliament." *Parliamentary History* 37 (2018): 119–38.

Wilcox, Alastair. *The Church and the Slums: The Victorian Anglican Church and its Mission to Liverpool's Poor*. Newcastle: Cambridge Scholars Press, 2014.

Wildman, Stuart. "Changes in Hospital Nursing in the West Midlands, 1841–1901." In *Medicine and Society in the Midlands, 1750–1950*, edited by J. Reinarz, 98–114. Birmingham: Midland History, 2007.

Williams, Karel. *From Pauperism to Poverty*. Oxford: Routledge and Kegan Paul, 1981.

Williams, Samantha. "Malthus, Marriage and Poor Law Allowances Revisited: A Bedfordshire Case Study, 1770–1834." *Agricultural History Review* 52 (2004): 56–82.

– "Paupers Behaving Badly: Punishment in the Victorian Workhouse." *Journal of British Studies* 59 (2020): 772–81.

– "Poor Relief, Labourers' Households and Living Standards in Rural England c.1770–1834: A Bedfordshire Case Study." *Economic History Review* 58 (2005): 485–519.

– *Unmarried Motherhood in the Metropolis, 1700–1850: Pregnancy, the Poor Law and Provision*. Basingstoke: Palgrave, 2018.

Wood, Peter. *Poverty and the Workhouse in Victorian Britain*. Stroud: Sutton, 1991.

Wrigely, Edward, and Richard Smith. "Malthus and the Poor Law." *Historical Journal* 63 (2020): 33–62.

Zedner, Lucia. *Women, Crime, and Custody in Victorian England*. Oxford: Oxford University Press, 1991.

Index

Please note that page numbers in italics direct the reader to images. References to workhouses and the towns in which they were located are separated, with towns named under "England" or "Wales" as appropriate, and individual workhouses named under "workhouses." Professions (found under "employment") are separated from the forced labour undertaken by inmates of a workhouse (found under "workhouses, labour in").